The Genesis

◆ OF ◆

Chinese Communist
Foreign Policy

THE GENESIS

◆ OF ◆

CHINESE COMMUNIST
FOREIGN POLICY

MICHAEL H. HUNT

Columbia University Press

NEW YORK

Columbia University Press
New York   Chichester, West Sussex
Copyright © 1996 Columbia University Press
All rights reserved
Library of Congress Cataloging-in-Publication Data
Hunt, Michael H.
    The Genesis of Chinese Communist foreign policy / Michael H. Hunt
        p. cm
    Includes bibliographical references and index.
    ISBN 0-231-10310-7 (alk. paper). ISBN 0-231-10311-5 (pbk. :
alk. paper)
    1. China—Foreign relations—y1912-1949. 2. China—Foreign
relations—xHistory. 3. Chung-kuo hung ch` an tang—xHistory.
I. Title
DS775.8.H86 1995
327.51—dc   95-18885   CIP

Casebound editions of Columbia University Press books are printed on
permanent and durable acid-free paper.

Printed in the United States of America
c 10 9 8 7 6 5 4 3 2 1

To the memory of Dorothy Borg

Contents

Preface

This volume explores the origins of Chinese Communist foreign policy and seeks thereby to contribute to a rethinking of modern China's foreign relations. These goals have only slowly become clear in my mind. They were certainly not in my thoughts when more than a decade ago I first became interested in the problematic status of China's foreign-relations history. Had it not been for a set of unforeseen circumstances, my interest would not have matured into this book.

One of those circumstances was the dramatic improvement in Sino-American relations. The Sino-American opening in 1971–1972, and even more the establishment of full diplomatic relations in 1979, had a significant impact on students of China's foreign-relations past, altering angles of vision and inviting fundamental reappraisals of conventional wisdom on a variety of fronts. In the new political climate favorable to academic exchange each side gained an enhanced awareness of the scholarship and sources available on the other side. Indeed, no sooner had formal diplomatic ties been restored than Chinese historians received an authoritative green light to begin their own reevaluations of the history of Sino-American relations, while American scholars were already buzzing about the remarkable changes in China's external policy and beginning to reconsider China's earlier foreign relations in the light of rapprochement and the new "open-door policy." Contacts rapidly multiplied, as scholars traveled to investigate historical sources previously closed off, participated in international conferences, and sent manuscripts and publications back and forth across the Pacific.

In the United States political scientists with area studies training took the lead in this efflorescence of scholarly activity. Less interested in historical sources or historiographical issues than in international relations theory and even more the implications of the past for current policy, they nonetheless recognized the need for historical perspective and promoted cross-disciplinary collaboration. They thus sought in their various enterprises to include a participant who could serve as the repository of historical insight, standing guard against egregious interpretive violations of the past and suggesting plausible links between past and present. This commitment to what amounted to a disciplinary affirmative action program resulted in the presence of at least a token historian in the revival of foreign relations work in this country.

The invitations that I received to play this role were to a degree issued out of necessity, since to put matters bluntly there usually was not much choice. American historians of China on the whole regarded China's external relations as a passé topic, associated with an interpretive and research paradigm that no longer engaged them. Most American specialists on Sino-American relations were, on the other hand, too absorbed in the American archives to give serious thought to Chinese policy, and even had they wished to, they lacked the language skills to pursue original research and to follow publications in Chinese. I would thus have to do. This was the second circumstance propitious to this project.

My initial claims to expertise, though modest, were at least plausible. My first two books dealt with Sino-American relations, and featured enough treatment of the late Qing to inspire some confidence. For my part, I was curious enough about the work these China-watchers did and sufficiently sympathetic to their interest in historical generalization and in the relation of past to present to smother a few initial doubts. The more requests that came to join on panel discussions, prepare conference papers, and do public talks, and the more that I read, thought, and wrote about the history of Chinese foreign relations, the more I began to think of myself as a specialist.

A third circumstance of pivotal importance has been the appearance of historical sources on the Communist Party that have allowed me to translate an incipient interest into substantial research. Here too serendipity played a large role. Encouraged by Dorothy Borg, I had done some preliminary work on CCP policy in the late 1940s. Struck by the paucity of reliable sources, I directed my interest toward the more public and accessible issue of changing party views of the United States from the 1920s onward. A spring 1989 research stay in Beijing revealed to my astonishment and mounting excitement that a great outpouring of historical material relevant to party external relations had begun virtually unnoticed outside China. The more I explored new sources coming available in the People's Republic of China, the more I realized that a major rethinking was necessary. The old literature, written in days of documentary dearth, seemed badly dated.

Thanks to the circumstances noted above, I have gradually and certainly without design extended my reach. I began by seeing Chinese foreign relations through the window of the late Qing, and have since moved mostly forward, becoming, as I went on, increasingly intrigued with the guiding foreign policy ideas within the Chinese Communist Party and with continuities in diplomatic style between it and earlier makers of China's foreign policy. A year in Washington at the Woodrow Wilson International Center for Scholars and proximity to China specialists in the capital confirmed the decision to set aside my specialized research on Communist images of the United States and to move ahead instead with this more broadly cast project. Indeed, I vividly recall the moment at the Center in which an encouraging remark by Mary Brown Bullock provided the decisive push.

Three concerns framed my investigations and ultimately gave shape to this study. I felt, first of all, that greater historical perspective was needed on Communist Party external relations. How did the party's concerns, goals, and style fit within long-term patterns in China's dealings with the outside world? I also felt the time opportune to paint a broad-brush picture of CCP policy using the new party history material. I have long regarded John Gittings's *The World and China, 1922–1972* (1974) as a clear-headed approach to such key issues as ideology and personality worthy of emulation. No more than Gittings can I claim to offer the last word. To the contrary, the continuing appearance of materials, especially on Sino-Soviet relations, is bound to prompt revision of views offered here. But perhaps some of the interpretive themes and categories that I have laid out will help stimulate fresh inquiry and ultimately a better grounded and more nuanced picture of China's foreign relations as well as of the coming of the Cold War in Asia. Finally, I concluded that the time had come to examine some of the well-established tendencies in a field long starved for documentation and to highlight promising lines of investigation opened by the new materials.

Readers acquainted with my other work may notice a familiar thread running through this account—the effort to get inside the head of actors on the world stage and discover how they saw themselves and others and how those perceptions shaped their behavior. I hope prospective readers will find the treatment of party belief and behavior offered here at least half as engrossing as I have found putting the treatment together.

A brief overview of the resulting study may help readers to find their way. The first chapter makes the case for a more open and historically oriented understanding of Chinese foreign relations. It thus serves as a conceptual ground clearing and interpretive orientation for the substantive treatment to follow. The second chapter carries the reader back to the late Qing (1800–1912) and the interlocking crises—territorial, financial, institutional, and ideological—that served as prologue for much of China's subsequent politics and foreign policy.

With the stage thus set, the next section sketches in the intellectual response to these developments. Chapter 3 deals with the search by increasingly radicalized intellectuals from the 1890s to the 1910s for an understanding of their country's crisis and for means of restoring the state's potency and China's standing in foreign affairs. Their voices still echo in discussions by Chinese of their place in the world. The following chapter, the fourth, deals with one influential strain of thought that emerged out of that intellectual crisis. The focus is on the Chinese who embraced communist doctrine and in the process created the foreign affairs orthodoxy dominant within the Communist Party between 1920 and 1934.

The third part of the study traces the effort between 1935 and 1951 to transcend the old orthodoxy as the party shaped a foreign policy responsive to the needs of the revolution and the changing configurations of international politics. The two chapters making up this section feature the increasingly dominant personality and concerns of Mao Zedong, in effect delineating the origins of Mao's foreign policy.

The final part of the volume looks at the implications, both historical and methodological, that flow from a richer and broader conception of early CCP foreign relations. Chapter 7 makes the general argument that patterns that had taken form through the 1940s and early 1950s carried over into the subsequent period and even help us better understand recent Chinese outlook and behavior. The last chapter critically examines the prevailing approaches to the study of the party's foreign relations and makes the case for applying more historically informed questions and methods to the windfall of new research materials. A concluding essay offers a road map to those materials and to the relevant secondary literature.

Throughout this study I use the widely accepted abbreviation CCP for the Chinese Communist Party and PRC for the People's Republic of China. "Party center," a term that appears frequently here, refers to the highest formal decisionmaking bodies within the CCP: the Central Committee, the smaller Political Bureau, the smaller still Secretariat, or the Military Affairs Committee.

This preface is a good place to offer formal thanks to supportive colleagues and institutions. The various drafts of the pages that appear here have had the benefit of attention from a long line of acute critics. Steven I. Levine stands at the head of that line, having read the entire manuscript as well as parts in earlier incarnations. William Kirby and Sidney Rittenberg also read the entire manuscript. To all three special thanks for their critical evaluations and suggestions. Others who were good enough to comment on sections of this study include Mary Bullock, Sherman Cochran, Ralph Clough, Harry Harding, Burton I. Kaufman, Lyman Miller, Niu Jun, Ren Donglai, Tony Saich, Ronald Spector, William Stueck, Robert Sutter, Samuel F. Wells, Jr., Philip West, Odd Arne Westad, and Allen Whiting. I hope that all will recognize at some point or other in this work treatment of the topic sharpened by their criticisms and suggestions.

At the outset Harry Harding, Samuel S. Kim, Roderick MacFarquhar, and David Shambaugh, each guided by an interdisciplinary view of China's foreign relations, set before me a range of irresistible interpretive puzzles. The papers prepared in response to their invitations proved invaluable preparation for this study and ultimately formed the basis for the first four chapters that appear here. I got a chance to try out before colleagues some of the ideas developed in the balance of the chapters thanks to Don Higginbotham acting for the Triangle Universities Security Seminar, to James Reardon-Anderson acting for the Washington Area Modern China Research Seminar, to Peter Kuznick and Robert Beisner of the American University History Department, to Gar Alperovitz of the Working Group on the Cold War at the Institute for Policy Studies, to Mary Brown Bullock in her capacity as director of the Wilson Center's Asia Program, to Roderick MacFarquhar in his capacity as director of the Fairbank Center, to Melvyn Leffler and the University of Virgina History Department, and to Sherman Cochran and the East Asian studies program at Cornell University.

Personal contacts have played an unusually important role in clarifying a rapidly opening field. I have been lucky enough to have had Odd Arne Westad, Niu Jun, Ren Donglai, and Zhang Baijia settle for a time in Chapel Hill, where I learned from conversations with them just as I have learned from their scholarship. Conversations in China—with Chen Xiaolu, He Di, Jia Qingguo, Niu Jun, Rao Geping, Wang Jisi, Xiang Qing,

Xiong Zhiyong, Xu Yan, Yuan Ming, Zhang Zhuhong, and Zi Zhongyun—helped me better understand my topic.

Without the time to write and the intellectual stimulation provided by the Wilson Center during a fellowship year and by Harvard's Fairbank Center during a term spent as a visiting scholar, this study would never have come together. Much of part three was drafted at the Wilson Center, and part four had its start as a paper prepared for a conference on the CCP held at the Center. At the Fairbank Center Library, with its enviable holdings of party history materials, Nancy Hearst proved a most helpful presiding presence. I also received valuable financial and research support from the Committee for Scholarly Communications with China, from Yuan Ming and the Institute of International Relations at Beijing University, and from the Research Council as well as the Asian Studies curriculum at the University of North Carolina at Chapel Hill. Liao Xuanli at Beijing University, Chris Davies and Matthew Flynn at the Wilson Center, and Li Li and Chris Schulten at UNC provided much valued research assistance. Rachel M. Bowman at UNC prepared the Korean War map that appears in chapter 6. Kate Wittenberg proved a model of the supportive—and patient—editor as I searched for the best way to do this project. I thank her and her colleagues at Columbia University Press, especially Leslie Bialler, for their assistance.

None of those named here bears responsibility for what follows; that belongs to me.

M.H.H.
July 1995

THE GENESIS

◆ OF ◆

CHINESE COMMUNIST
FOREIGN POLICY

PART ONE

Setting the Stage

Chapter One

The Pertinence of the Past

History is essential and central, not optional and incidental, to an understanding of Chinese foreign policy. Yet all too often discussions of that policy have neglected history or drawn selectively from it, in either case denying the richness of the Chinese foreign relations experience. Any proper understanding of the genesis of the Chinese Communist foreign policy has as its logical starting point one basic proposition: China's approach to external relations has not been shaped by a single mold or imprisoned by a single tradition. We neglect its diversity and complexity at our own peril.

China's Multiple Traditions

First, let us clear away some of the underbrush that might obscure our perspective on the origins of contemporary Chinese foreign relations. One hardy weed, which flowered during the early Cold War from seeds sown in the 1920s, is an interpretation built almost exclusively around twentieth-century events. Concentrating on Communist China's leaders, it reduces their worldview to a function of an imported Marxist-Leninist ideology. As youths they had been captivated by the Bolshevik revolution; they had immersed themselves in leftist ideological currents in France and the

---

This chapter is a revised version of "Chinese Foreign Relations in Historical Perspective," in *China's Foreign Relations in the 1980s*, ed. Harry Harding (New Haven: Yale University Press, 1984), 1–42. I am grateful to Yale University Press and Harry Harding for permission to draw on that essay.

Soviet Union; later, they were tutored by Soviet advisers in China. During their years in the political wilderness from the late 1920s to the mid-1940s, when they were learning to make revolution, their contacts with the outside world were limited, so that their conception of international relations remained rigid and distorted. Once in power, this interpretation tells us, those leaders predictably followed their ideological predilections: they dutifully followed the lead of the USSR, predictably lashed out at "American imperialism," and freely gave their backing to like-minded Asian revolutionary movements.[1]

Beijing's apparent surrender to Moscow and its determined defiance of prevailing international practice made Chinese leaders seem—at least by liberal standards—inflexible and dangerous ideologues. Only over the last several decades has that image been charmed away by the apparent moderation and reason of a China ready first to set aside its quarrel with the United States, the better to hold the Soviet Union at bay, and then to pursue China's economic development. The more modest and tenable conclusion now to draw about the role of Marxist-Leninist ideology is that it has been but one source for policy and that, as a source, it can sustain not one policy but a wide variety of them.

A second hardy growth that has closed off our vista is also a species of ideological interpretation. It differs from the first by emphasizing the tyranny of an indigenous tradition. The Chinese elite had long nursed a conception of their land as a "middle kingdom," to which adjoining states owed tribute as political and cultural satellites. China thus laid claim to a position of dominance and centrality in the Asian state system. Arriving during the nineteenth century, Western observers and officials were appalled by the seemingly unshakable adherence of the Qing dynasty (1644–1912) to this anomalous hierarchical conception of interstate relations, and they seized on the apparent influence of the middle kingdom complex to explain China's tardy and ineffectual response to the West.

Even in the face of irresistible pressures to accommodate to a multistate system, China's short-sighted ruling elite (adherents of this view claim) rejected the new rules of the international game and tried instead to make contacts with the West fit into the institutions and practices associated with the "traditional," "sinocentric" "tribute system." The few modern-minded Chinese ("progressives" or "liberals") who recognized and were inclined to adjust to this new era in China's foreign relations found themselves blocked on every front—in military and economic affairs no less than diplomatic—by the single-minded defenders of tradition and by the persistence of time-honored but now outmoded practices. Though a socialist nation was to arise where a Confucian empire once stood, the old dreams of cultural glory and political dominance in Asia and the traditional hostility toward equal state relations and broad international contacts seemed to live on. Carried down to the mid-twentieth century, this interpretation served to account for the inability of the People's Republic of China to stomach Soviet direction, for its pretensions to a tutelary role in Asia, and for its calculated aloofness from, even contempt for, various forms of international exchange.[2]

Together, these two ideological interpretations provided a plausible explanation for the xenophobic and expansionist strains associated for a time with Chinese communism. Born and raised in the immediate afterglow of the imperial tradition, the first generation of Communist leaders imbibed, perhaps unconsciously, the old sinocentric assumptions associated with the tribute system and carried them into post-imperial China. To those assumptions they added the rigid, anti-Western rhetoric of Marxism-Leninism. Viewed in this way, the past became something of an embarrassment, a dead hand holding back China's accommodation to the contemporary international system.

It might be argued, however, that in seeing Chinese foreign relations in historical perspective we face not a single embarrassing tradition but rather an embarrassment of traditions. A moment of meditation on the Chinese past suggests that if we look back beyond the revolutions of the twentieth century, or even past the "middle kingdom" view of the nineteenth, we may find other, older styles of dealing with the world that have also persisted into the modern period.

It could be argued to begin with that the imperial style comes in two forms. The tribute system model described above, with its unshakable sinocentrism, would be one. But the other would be the decidedly more extroverted pattern of the Han (206 B.C.– 220 A.D.) and Tang (618–907 A.D.). Those two dynasties and the period between them saw extensive dealings with foreign peoples—Romans, Byzantines, Persians, and Arabs, to name some of the more distant. Foreign goods were widely accepted, indeed avidly sought, within China. A flourishing inland trade and a no less prosperous maritime trade reaching to Korea and Japan and across South and Southeast Asia to the Middle East fed new goods, aesthetic values, and ideas into China. At the same time the waxing and waning of Chinese strength along the inner-Asian frontier also contributed to the cosmopolitan nature of the age. At its peak China secured the inland trade routes and brought foreign peoples within its borders. At moments of Chinese weakness, these same people along the periphery would assert themselves, at times claiming political control over parts of China.[3]

The combined effect of long-distance commerce and frontier interaction was a "barbarization" of Chinese culture. It was reflected in clothing, furniture, food, music, dance, technology, mathematics, and, perhaps most strikingly of all, religion. Zoroastrianism, Manichaeism, Nestorian Christianity, and Islam had all penetrated through Central Asia by Tang times. But none left a deeper imprint than Buddhism. Arriving from India in the late Han, it was to grow in influence as China entered a period of political crisis, and in time to become an important part of both elite and popular culture.[4]

Cosmopolitan strains persisted beyond the Tang, even down to the supposedly inflexible and introverted Qing. At the outset of the dynasty the Kangxi emperor took great delight in the foreign learning and the command of technology displayed by the Jesuits resident at his court, while a noted scholar of that time, Gu Yanwu, warned against an ethnocentric outlook, noting that "there are some Chinese customs which are inferior to those of foreign countries."[5] The late Qing and Republican periods offer an even more striking example of foreign trade and frontier contacts bringing new material culture, new ideas, and new institutional patterns to a China in crisis. These took hold in urban centers along the coast and were absorbed into the cultural mainstream with sweeping consequences for all aspects of Chinese life.

From those periods of political division after the collapse of strong dynastic power comes yet another tradition for us to consider. Described in such classics of Chinese history as the *Chronicle of the Warring States* and in enormously popular historical tales such as the *Romance of the Three Kingdoms*, this tradition shows Chinese functioning in an amoral interstate system characterized by constant maneuver and ruthless competition.[6] Its leading figures are not burdened in their decisions by hoary tradition; rather, they repeatedly resort to the classic realist calculus, trying to achieve the desired end by the most economical means. Temporary accommodation, alliances made and abandoned, ambush and treachery, the careful cultivation of domestic resources and morale, psychological warfare, and of course raw military power all occupied an important place in the arsenal of the statesmen of these periods of disunity.[7]

The Warring States period (403–221 B.C.) is the original and most frequently consulted version of this model in Chinese history. That period began with seven major states contending for power; it ended with one of them, Qin, imposing centralized control over China for the first time, after having exploited divisions among the six and overcome them one by one. Though Confucian moralists later condemned the "opportunist and deceitful stratagems" that characterized that time, generations of Chinese have nonetheless looked back with admiration to the statesmen of that shadowy era who "knew how to manipulate the situation to their own advantage and inspire complete awe by their prestige."[8] Indeed, Qin has become a byword for hegemonic aspirations, and the man who realized them, the first emperor of the Qin, has long been regarded as the patron of a coercive, legalist style of government.[9]

The appeal of the Warring States model was particularly strong in the late nineteenth and early twentieth centuries. Leaders of the Qing were then caught up in a world startlingly similar to that mythic age, and not surprisingly engaged in their own effort to "manipulate the situation" and maintain "prestige" against the rebels within and the barbarians (always ready to exploit divisions among Chinese) without. While much of their public rhetoric was couched in terms of condescension toward the intruding foreigners, their private calculations by contrast often employed the vocabulary of strategic interest, balance of power, and diplomatic maneuver.

The period after the fall of the Qing, especially between 1916 and 1928, found Chinese divided against themselves and imperiled by outside powers—and constituted an even more direct parallel with the era of the Warring States. During this their heyday, warlords, each a power unto himself, made pacts only to betray them, marched their armies to and fro, and nursed their hegemonic ambitions, while the foreigners stood by ready to fish in troubled waters as the competing internal forces solicited their aid. The extended contest between the Nationalists and the Communists, with each group angling for foreign support, might be taken as the last act in a latter-day version of the Warring States drama that ended with the Communists in the role of the ruthlessly centralizing Qin. The similarities would be inescapable to an elite that took its history seriously and to a Mao Zedong who at times likened himself to the first emperor of the Qin.[10]

Finally, the Chinese foreign-relations tradition should make room for the unloved collaborator, called forth by foreign invasion and subjugation. When weakness rendered continued resistance imprudent, Chinese have made the best of it. The "barbarians" who established such major dynasties as the Jin (265–420 A.D.), the Yuan (1271–1368), and the Qing could conquer China but not transform it. To rule they needed Chinese assistance. While some members of the Chinese ruling elite would during these periods of subjugation withdraw into moral and intellectual self-cultivation in anticipation of a better day, others traded their services, indispensable to the handful of conquerors, for a share of power. Here, then, is another foreign relations model in which accommodation became the price for peace and administrative continuity.[11]

This tradition, too, has reemerged over the last century. Qing officials entered into a collaborative relationship with the British in the dynamic treaty-port sector. When they realized the foreigners were too powerful to resist, they helped collect the revenue, oppose "native" rebellion and anarchy, and restrain the hotheads in their own ranks. Qing power was thus prolonged and the British were spared the impossible burden of direct rule while maintaining access to the Chinese economy.[12] The fractured polity during the Republican era made so grand a collaboration impossible, yet in more modest forms it reappeared. The Japanese found disgruntled patriots, wistful monarchists, and thoroughgoing opportunists ready to serve in north and central China as well as the northeast provinces (Manchuria) and Inner Mongolia. Wang Jingwei, who headed the most infamous of these collaborator regimes, that at Nanjing between 1939 and 1944, articulated the predictable arguments. He wanted to stop the suffering brought on the Chinese people by Japan's 1937 invasion. A negotiated settlement with Tokyo would end the hopeless resistance and at the same time help eliminate the Chinese Communists (whom Wang had long opposed) and discomfit Chiang Kai-shek (who was Wang's long-time rival within the Nationalist Party).[13]

This resurgent collaborationist tradition in the modern era has created a fixation among Chinese patriots with the traitors within. The reaction was evident as early as the Opium War (1839–1842), when British victories sent Qing authorities looking for scapegoats.[14] The search for *han-jian*—Chinese traitors—among those associated with foreigners invariably intensified whenever the West threatened during the balance of the dynasty. This preoccupation with countrymen seduced by the foreigners carried over into the first half of the twentieth century, as Nationalists and Communists viewed each other as tools of American and Soviet interests respectively. And it remained alive even after 1949. Despite its striking success at reuniting China territorially and imposing central political control, the Communist regime betrayed that old streak of anxiety over foreign influence. Christian connections, Western training, or foreign employment could still at such a time of crisis as the Korean War or the Cultural Revolution evoke deep suspicion and even persecution.

The history of Chinese foreign relations thus consists of not just one or two traditions but a multiplicity traditions, some dating back several thousand years. These traditions constitute a rich source of instruction, inspiration, and political discourse. They show a Chinese people who have known the best as well as the worst: virtual political hegemony and cultural supremacy over much of Asia as well as repeated subjugation and internecine strife. They hold up many models of statecraft, from the lofty imperial style to shrewd Machiavellian cunning. They teach the use of brute force, of trade and cultural exchange, of secret diplomacy and alliances, of compromise and even collaboration with conquerors. We have, then, a tapestry of traditional foreign relations that is notable for its breadth and richness, not its narrowness and poverty.

Thinking in comparative terms can help make us still more sensitive to the richness of China's external relations. Like the people of other countries, the Chinese have had their enduring strategic concerns, though their ability to secure their borders and culture against challenge has varied over the millennia. During the last two hundred years, while the United States, for example, was moving away from colonial dependency and strategic inferiority and toward international ascendancy, the Chinese were going in the opposite direction. Territorial bounds defined in the eighteenth century, at a time of strong dynastic power, became ever more difficult to sustain, and encroaching powers shattered claims to imperial preeminence. This badly battered security line and an awareness of the urgency and at the same time the difficulty of restoring it have been a major legacy of the past to the PRC.

Chinese have, also like other peoples, often used the past to make sense of the present. In China's case, a territorial crisis forced the politically engaged to redefine their country's place in the world, drawing on their historical experience for guidance. One important product of that process has been the myth of China's humiliation at the hands of the West and Japan, a myth that gripped the imagination of three generations of Chinese and stung them into an ever more critical analysis of the international order and Chinese society. The result was an obsession, long sanctioned by official orthodoxy, with expunging the residue of a feudal-imperialist past.

Finally, the foreign relations of China, like that of other countries, can be made to yield its own persistent patterns, produced by the attempt to realize long-sanctioned strategic goals in a complex and sometimes threatening international environment. Perhaps the most striking of these patterns—and the pattern most worth developing—is the conflicting impulses toward autonomy and dependency that have governed China's external relations. Autonomy carried the risk of costly isolation—diplomatic, economic, and technological. On the other hand, dependency seemed to many modern Chinese too high and humiliating a price to pay for foreign assistance. Chinese leaders repeatedly have had to come back to the problem of striking a balance between the danger of either extreme.

China's foreign relations is clearly influenced not by one but by a variety of traditions. The resulting patterns do not alone explain all Chinese behavior. But they do provide a sense of the enduring pulse of China's interaction with the world. The elaboration of these patterns—the commitment to an inherited definition of security, the evolution of a historically conditioned worldview stressing China's humiliation by foreigners in the recent past, and the influence of a long-lived tension in dealing with the outside world—constitutes the burden of the balance of this chapter.

The Quest for Territorial Security

Let us begin with the historically derived definition of security that dominates contemporary Chinese foreign relations. Here we encounter an imperial legacy distinct from the sinocentric outlook associated with the tribute system. The last two dynasties—the Ming (1368–1644) and the Qing—formulated a territorial agenda that is still extant. They controlled a core cultural area that roughly corresponds to today's, and at the same time identified and, by the middle Qing, secured those peripheral areas important to the security of the core.

The core cultural area which the Ming and Qing consolidated and to which the PRC fell heir in 1949 was the product of an unbroken historical process going back roughly thirty-five hundred years. Beginning on the North China plain on the lower reaches of the Yellow River, Chinese culture spread outward. By the time of the first major dynastic period (Qin-Han) roughly two thousand years ago, it had reached the northern limit between lands favorable to intensive agriculture and the inhospitable steppe. A "great wall," begun under the Qin, roughly delineated this northern boundary, from Gansu in the west eastward to the sea. The southward march of Chinese culture was to carry it over a longer distance and to require a longer time before reaching geographical barriers—open sea to the east and unhealthy rain forests, towering mountains, and forbidding deserts to the south and west. In that march the lower Yangzi River valley was secured by the Han, and the great stretch of southern provinces brought fully under control by Mongol times. The population of this cultural core rose steadily—from almost 60 million under the Han, to at least twice that during the Ming, to 300 million by the late eighteenth century under the Qing. Conquerors might penetrate the geographic barriers that defined the core area, but they could not transform the deeply rooted culture shared by its dense and relatively homogeneous population.[15]

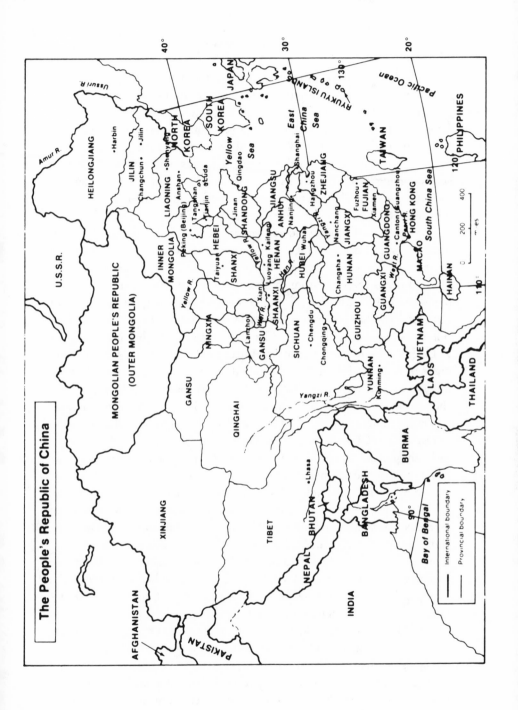

The People's Republic of China

U.S.S.R.

MONGOLIAN PEOPLE'S REPUBLIC
(OUTER MONGOLIA)

HEILONGJIANG
Amur R.
Ussuri R.
•Harbin

JILIN
Changchun•
•Jilin

INNER MONGOLIA

LIAONING •Shenyang
•Anshan
NORTH KOREA
SOUTH KOREA
JAPAN

Peking (Beijing)
HEBEI
•Tangshan
•Tianjin
Jinan•
SHANDONG
Qingdao
Yellow Sea
East China Sea
RYUKYU ISLANDS

Yellow R.
SHANXI
Taiyuan•
HENAN
Kaifeng
Luoyang•
JIANGSU
Nanjing•
Shanghai•
ZHEJIANG
Hangzhou•

Yellow R.
Xian•
SHAANXI
HUBEI
Wuhan•
ANHUI
China
TAIWAN

Yellow R.
GANSU
Lanzhou•
Wei R.
SICHUAN
Chengdu•
Chongqing•
HUNAN
Changsha•
JIANGXI
Nanchang•
FUJIAN
Fuzhou•
Xiamen•

QINGHAI

XINJIANG

TIBET
•Lhasa

NEPAL
BHUTAN

AFGHANISTAN

PAKISTAN

INDIA

BANGLADESH

BURMA

YUNNAN
Kunming•

GUIZHOU

GUANGXI

GUANGDONG
Canton (Guangzhou)•
Pearl R.
HONG KONG
MACAO
HAINAN

LAOS
VIETNAM
THAILAND

Bay of Bengal

Yangzi R.

Yangzi R.

South China Sea

PHILIPPINES

Pacific Ocean

International boundary
Provincial boundary

0   200   400
miles

40°
30°
20°

90°
110°
120°
130°

Beyond the solidly Chinese core lay a contested periphery. Parts of it, imperiled and even lost to outside political control in the nineteenth and twentieth centuries, were nonetheless substantially sinicized by the late Qing, thanks in the main to a belated yet nonetheless effective policy of colonization. Settlement and its usual concomitant, the penetration of Chinese and sometimes foreign commerce, was a disruptive force that stirred indigenous resentments and even armed resistance, stimulated a keener sense of local identity, and tempted regional power-holders to look outside China, particularly to Russia and Britain, for support. Yet once having gotten a demographic and economic foothold, central authorities found resistance easier to meet and master in these distant territories now more closely bound to the Chinese core.[16]

On Taiwan, migrants from southern coastal Fujian and eastern Guangdong established Chinese cultural dominance following the expulsion of the Dutch in 1662. Despite occasional Qing attempts to halt this population movement, Chinese on the island had come to number 1.9 million by 1811. In 1887, following an official decision to encourage settlement in order to head off Japanese ambitions, the population had climbed to 3.2 million and the island had assumed full provincial status. Though lost a short time later (1895) to Japanese control, the island remained fundamentally Chinese in culture, a fact that contributed to the Allied decision to restore it to China at the end of World War II.[17]

In the northeast, too, migration secured a peripheral territory. By the Ming dynasty the southernmost section had become predominantly Chinese, but beyond that stretched a great sweep of land thinly populated by tribal peoples, notably the Mongols and the Jürcheds. One group of Jürcheds had already conquered China once and ruled as the Jin dynasty, and a second, the Manchus, were to repeat the feat in the mid-seventeenth century. Once established as the Qing, this group quickly moved to define its territorial claims in the northern portion against Russia (through the Treaty of Nerchinsk of 1689) and at the same time to limit Chinese settlement in this, the Manchu homeland.[18]

The Manchus slowly and reluctantly retreated from their restrictive settlement policy. Increased Russian pressure, which had led to the cession of the lands north of the Amur and Ussuri rivers by the treaties of 1858 and 1860, had contributed to the policy reversal. Intense population pressures in north China completed the process of undercutting resistance to Chinese migration into this resource-rich but thinly settled region. A policy favorable to new settlement and the incorporation of the northeast into the regular system of provincial government took shape after the Russo-Japanese War, and the flow of population traveling northward on the recently built railroad along the narrow corridor that connected north China to the southern part of the northeast became a torrent, overwhelming tribal peoples and filling out the once remote northern regions. By 1911 the northeast had a population of 15 to 17 million, 90 percent of whom were Chinese—a sharp contrast to the estimated one million inhabitants of the entire area at the end of the eighteenth century. Against this continuing flood of peoples, both Russian and, after 1905, Japanese occupiers were unavailing. Like Taiwan, the northeast was to be returned to China after World War II on the basis of its unquestioned ethnic identity.

In Mongolia too the Qing was driven reluctantly to an active policy of direct rule and promotion of Chinese settlement. A long decline in Mongol power and Beijing's effective exploitation of the differences between the Oirat Mongols in the west from other tribes in the east had at first left the Qing satisfied with indirect control and opposed to Chinese settlement and trade. A buildup of Chinese settlers and penetration of commerce had nonetheless occurred, setting off sporadic protests throughout Mongolia in the late nineteenth and early twentieth centuries. This unrest, coupled with the lengthening shadow of Russia and Japan, precipitated a sharp reversal of Qing policy in favor of vigorous promotion of colonization, facilitated by railway building into the area. Contemporary Chinese feared any call for independence as an invitation for foreign intervention. The Mongols seeking to break from China were "like the young sparrow boasting that it can fly, or the young rabbit bragging that it can run. They will surely not escape the mouths of hungry vultures or ravenous tigers."[19]

A slow rate of migration and a sharp Mongolian reaction against the growing Chinese presence eventually led to the loss of Outer Mongolia and a running battle to secure Inner Mongolia (now one of the autonomous regions of China). The prolonged period of internal instability in China following the 1911 revolution gave the Mongols their chance to pursue independence and Outer Mongolia the chance to detach itself from China. In 1924 it declared itself a people's republic completely separated from China. That step enjoyed Soviet backing, while Mongols elsewhere attracted the attention of Japanese expansionists.[20] However, in Inner Mongolia the policy of colonization, carried forward from the Qing by Republican governments, brought an end to local resistance and foreign competition. By the late 1920s Han immigrants had come to outnumber Mongols, and by the mid-1950s Mongols accounted for only 15 percent of the total population (7.5 million) of that region.

To the west, in Xinjiang, Chinese governments, both Qing and Republican, made claim to political control but failed to establish a cultural dominance that would have legitimized and facilitated that control. As early as the Han period Chinese had begun to penetrate through the Gansu corridor into Xinjiang. By the nineteenth century, the Chinese buildup, leading to the incorporation of Xinjiang as a regular province in 1884, had been sufficient to stir Uighur and Kazakh resentment but not overwhelm it, and thus the Qing had repeatedly to put down rebellions. Subsequently, the Nationalist government struggled to maintain a grip on the semi-autonomous region against both local insurgents and Soviet penetration. Its efforts were finally rewarded when, following the weakening of Soviet authority during World War II, the Nationalists finally installed their own governor. Local resistance continued, but so too did colonization, inexorably tying Xinjiang more tightly in China's orbit.[21]

Tibet, yet another long-time focal point of competition among inner-Asian powers, came still closer to slipping away from Chinese control. The indirect control exercised by the Qing was challenged early in this century by the British operating out of India, but a 1906 agreement with Britain left China with its claim to suzerainty unimpaired. In its remaining years the Qing sought to consolidate its position in Tibet by implementing reforms favorable to Chinese influence and by strengthening its military presence. Before the collapse of imperial authority in 1911, a brutal military occupation had brought eastern (or "inner") Tibet under China's direct control, and that region remained subordinated during the Republican period. But western (or "outer") Tibet, closely supervised before 1911, thereafter slipped China's grasp and remained out of reach until 1951.[22]

Farther out on the contested periphery China was unable to protect its interests during the decline of the late Qing and the disarray of the Republican period. At the height of Ming-Qing power, Korea, the Ryukyu (Liuqiu) Islands, and much of Southeast Asia fit to one degree or other into the tribute system and were kept there by the promise of trade, the attractions of contact with the advanced Chinese culture, the legitimizing role the Chinese emperor played vis-à-vis lesser rulers, the careful cultivation of personal relations between members of the elite, Chinese patronage of Lamaism and Buddhism (influential in Tibet and Mongolia), and even diplomatic and military support against rebels or invaders. But these methods were to prove unavailing in the last half of the nineteenth century as the European maritime powers as well as Russia and Japan not only quickly sheared China of this outermost security zone but also began encroaching on China's peripheral territories, and even intruded on the core of China itself. By 1860 it had become clear to Beijing that it faced a crisis of a magnitude unknown since the Mongol conquest some six hundred years earlier.

Devising a response to this foreign threat on several widely separated fronts, an inherently difficult task, was rendered virtually impossible by the outbreak of several major rebellions, most notably the Taiping. By the time the Qing had restored internal order, Russia had seized territory north of the Amur River and would soon threaten Chinese influence on the entire inner-Asian frontier from Xinjiang to Korea. The European powers had simultaneously imposed their treaty system along the China coast and extinguished Chinese political influence in Southeast Asia, climaxing in the French takeover of Vietnam. China tried to extend its protection but failed in a war against France in 1884–1885 and had to renounce all claim to suzerainty.

Japan, responding to Qing decline and European intrusion, made good on its claim to the Ryukyus with the help of a simultaneous crisis between Russia and China over the Xinjiang frontier. Beijing tried to blunt Japanese ambitions in Korea from the 1860s onward but here too failed and had to abandon all hope of influence following defeat at the hands of the Japanese in 1894. As a result of that defeat, China also lost Taiwan to Japan. One reverse now followed another in quick succession as Russia, Germany, Britain, and France went to work defining their own separate spheres of influence within China proper through a combination of railway, mine, and other concessions. Despite a world war that thereafter distracted and weakened these European powers, Chinese governments were helpless to reassert Chinese interests along the periphery or even to hold back rising Japanese ambitions within China itself.

This decline of Chinese power also spelled the virtual abandonment of pockets of overseas Chinese scattered along the Southeast Asian periphery and beyond (chiefly in Japan and the Americas). Chinese had set off from the south China coast in large numbers beginning in the early nineteenth century in response to the push of economic and social crisis and the pull that overseas capital development exerted on unskilled labor. During the last quarter of the century alone, 4.85 million were counted emigrating, and the number continued to grow into the first decades of the twentieth century. Many returned home, but a substantial residue accumulated overseas. (A 1970 estimate of Chinese in Southeast Asia set the figure at 14.6 million, about 6 percent of the area's total population.)[23]

By the late nineteenth century these overseas Chinese began to encounter a rising tide of sinophobic nationalism. The resulting efforts to eliminate their economic dominance and integrate them into the indigenous culture or see them expelled served in turn to consolidate overseas Chinese communities, to orient the overseas Chinese more than ever toward China as protector and cultural fount, and to make them avid supporters of building a China strong and progressive enough to command respect for Chinese living abroad. Against this background the attitude of hostility or studied indifference displayed by Qing officials toward these emigrants gradually gave way to one of solicitude from the 1870s onward. By dispatching diplomatic missions and concluding a number of agreements with host countries, the Qing implemented a new policy of protecting contract laborers and established communities abroad against exploitation and abuse. In the end the Qing effort proved unavailing, and the Republic, despite the important contribution of overseas Chinese to its creation, was able to do no better. A China unable to defend itself was in no position to defend its even more vulnerable countrymen abroad.[24]

Even at the nadir of China's strength in the 1930s, its leaders insisted that Muslim peoples, Tibetans, and Mongols (in both Inner and Outer Mongolia) would in some way or other have to be attached to a revived China. They acted in line with the same compelling strategic logic that had long informed imperial policy. Loss of control on the periphery had repeatedly—both in the Qing and under other dynasties—rendered the cultural core vulnerable to penetration and attack. Most recently, Russian encroachment along the inner-Asian frontier had proven the prelude to meddling at China's expense in the northeast, Mongolia, and Xinjiang, and it had stimulated a brief flurry of British activity in Tibet. France had used Indochina as a base for securing influence in south China. Japan had moved from Korea into the northeast and Mongolia, and from Taiwan it pursued its ambitions in Fujian. Thus for reasons of realpolitik if no other, post-Qing rulers were quick to align themselves with the objectives of the Qing, exerting control directly along the periphery where possible, and cultivating influence in other ways in more remote areas where overt interference might prove costly and even counterproductive.

This policy toward the periphery, imperial in its genesis, is also clearly imperial in its fundamental impulse toward exercising control over neighboring peoples consonant with available Chinese power. Like all imperial policies, it thus has had its risks as well as its reasons. It has bred resentment and revolt, opened opportunities for meddling by outside powers, and even led to serious international confrontations. The clash of arms with the United States in Korea, maintenance of an occupation army in Tibet and Xinjiang, the border war with India, and the military tensions generated by a Vietnam occupied in the south by the United States and aligned in the north with the Soviet Union must be counted as but some of the costly byproducts of contemporary China's inherited strategic policy.

The Cosmopolitan Response to China's Humiliation

The lessons drawn by Chinese from their country's foreign-relations experience constitute the second form in which the past has left its mark on the present. That experience in the modern era, beginning with the Opium War against Britain and ending with the Yalta concessions to the USSR, has been essentially one of humiliation and one-sided struggle. The late Qing and the Republican era witnessed the collapse of China's forward position on the periphery, the imposition of unequal treaties, invasion by foreign forces (with the capital falling twice), a carving up of China proper into spheres of influence, and finally occupation by Japan. It should be no cause for wonder that this long string of setbacks made an ever deeper impression on Chinese observers of international affairs. Confronted by repeated reverses, these observers sought to diagnose the nature of the problem afflicting their country in order to prescribe a cure.

Scholars of "China's response to the West" have tended to emphasize the degree to which a creative response to the new foreign challenge was impeded by old outlooks, practices, and institutions. While it would be wrong to insist, in the spirit of contrariness, that the Chinese response was actually flexible, innovative, and sophisticated, it is nonetheless important to note that some Chinese observers were quicker than others to grasp the changed circumstances and act on them. At one extreme, to be sure, a conservative and at times even obscurantist outlook prevailed, reaffirming China's cultural superiority and advocating staunch adherence to basic Confucian values as the key to a successful foreign policy. This view had originally arisen in reaction against the Buddhist intrusion and the barbarian invasions that had brought down the Tang early in the tenth century, overwhelmed the Song in the thirteenth, and immediately thereafter resulted in a century of Mongol dominance. When the Ming restored Chinese political control in the fourteenth century, intellectuals turned introspective, looking for the moral and ethical flaws that might account for China's recent vulnerability to foreign intrusion. The replacement of the Ming by yet another barbarian dynasty, the Manchus, intensified this preoccupation with ideological orthodoxy and laid the basis for a stand-pat foreign policy position that tended to equate the nineteenth-century "barbarian" challenge with earlier ones. By the turn of the century this outlook, finally discredited by repeated failure, had lost its appeal.

But at the other extreme, there developed a more cosmopolitan line of analysis in the 1830s and 1840s along the south China coast among scholar-officials most intimately involved in dealing with those "sea-going barbarians." Cultivated by successive generations of intellectuals, this outward-looking view was to survive, even flourish. It was to lead to substantial cultural transformation. And, most to the point for our purposes here, it was to contribute significantly to the framework of post-1949 Chinese foreign relations. Thus it deserves attention for this reason as well as to offset the more familiar image of a sleepy China slow to awake to the dramatic changes going on about it.

The term "cosmopolitan" is used here advisedly, to suggest a recurrence of one of those earlier periods of responsiveness to foreign ideas and material culture. To some of the pioneering students of maritime affairs, not to mention a growing number of their intellectual successors, it became increasingly clear that the problem posed by the West required not just a simple mastery of new armaments but also a willingness to encompass new cultural worlds in order to draw instruction from them and to protect the Chinese state against their power.

But the resonances from Han and Tang should not keep us from hearing echoes of the Warring States model. Some of these early observers and makers of Chinese policy, no more wide-eyed naifs than hidebound dogmatists, quickly recognized that China had been thrust into a new world system where claims to cultural superiority would count for naught and where a diplomacy of delay and maneuver would be essential to win time to mobilize the power requisite to China's survival and safety. This insight, never far below the surface of the tribute relationship, became more pronounced in an international environment that became progressively more threatening. The parallels between a contemporary system described by some Chinese as early as the 1840s in terms of cutthroat competition and the intense struggle among the Warring States must have been striking. Indeed, the implicit conclusions to draw about an appropriate policy must have been unavoidable to leaders with a penchant for seeing current problems in terms of the past.

A search for paternity of the cosmopolitan line in modern times might take us to a number of figures. Wei Yuan, a pioneer in what was to be a long and dogged effort to devise a defense strategy for China, was the most remarkable.[25] An expert on inner Asia, Wei had turned his attention to the maritime frontier in the 1830s. The resulting prescriptions that he offered for imperial security were perceptive and comprehensive, and they would find a strong resonance among later policymakers.

Wei quickly realized that the penetration of Western and especially

British naval power into Southeast Asia posed a geopolitical threat to China and, combined with Muslim unrest in the deep interior, constituted an unprecedented peril. He advocated a long-term policy of Chinese settlement as the surest means of overwhelming restive Muslims, while recommending cooperation as an ancillary approach to be applied selectively on the maritime frontier. China needed to borrow from foreigners to help develop a navy, and he advocated making common cause both with China's southeast Asian dependencies and Britain's rivals to check the British advance.

Another, less prominent exemplar of this cosmopolitan strain is Xu Jiyu, an official from landlocked Shanxi. Xu, who served through the 1840s along the southern coast and ultimately became governor of Fujian, shared Wei's practical commitment to understanding the maritime threat. In 1848, then in his early fifties, he published a world geography that in penetration and balance compared favorably with contemporary foreign accounts of China. Xu built on a foundation of work prepared by other notable coastal officials and their aides, such as Wei Yuan as well as Ruan Yuan and Lin Zexu. Like them, he was troubled by the threatening foreign presence. Also like them, he believed that Chinese would have to learn about this threat in order to keep it at bay while China sought to return to the road of virtue from which it had already strayed, to judge from mounting peasant rebellion.

Xu's significance and his achievement owe much to his belief that other cultures deserved study and even emulation where they pointed China back to good practices that had fallen into decay. To be sure, Xu sought not to assault the sensibilities of his readers. He affirmed China's place as the "lord of Asia" and avoided any direct comparisons with the West unfavorable to China.[26] But at the same time he left no doubt that peoples usually referred to contemptuously as "barbarians" (a term nowhere to be found in his survey) might repay study. The European countries, for example, boasted ancient cultural roots, efficient domestic organization, great wealth, and remarkable technological development.

As Xu saw it, the growing peril of British hegemony gave China little time to act. Already Africa, India, and Southeast Asia had fallen victim to Britain and the other European powers. China was certainly, as the recent war made clear, the next target. Thus China had been engulfed by a new and dangerous world order which brought to mind—in a comparison Xu made explicit—the Warring States period. Salvation, Xu seemed to say to his readers, lay through careful study of foreign ways so that China could borrow their strengths and exploit their rivalries and weaknesses.

Xu fell from imperial favor, and his geography at first wielded little influence. But in the 1860s Xu returned to official life, and his book enjoyed wide circulation as an important, perhaps the single most important, survey of China's new international environment. Xu's cosmopolitan conception was incorporated into much late-nineteenth-century thinking on foreign affairs. It sanctioned a search for admirable qualities in foreign countries from which China might learn or draw inspiration: Petrine Russia and Meiji Japan offered a model of controlled reform; the Germans had quickly developed national prowess to which Chinese sought the secret; while the United States showed that it was possible to throw off outside oppressors and achieve rapid economic development. Xu also served as a point of intellectual departure for early-twentieth-century Chinese as diverse as Liang Qichao, Sun Yat-sen, and Mao Zedong, all of whom continued to search for a solution to China's crisis.

The Conflict between Dependency and Autonomy

The cosmopolitan impulse identified above stimulated a potent populist reaction, thus investing in Chinese foreign relations a pervasive tension. Those of a more cosmopolitan persuasion had preferred to transcend China's weak international position by playing the powers off against each other while borrowing foreign techniques that would make China less vulnerable. Those inspired by populism had responded that self-strengthening and unequal alliances were pernicious in their effect. China would have to draw on popular strength, contended this alternative view, as a substitute for inadequate conventional power and a debilitating dependence on foreign techniques.

This conflict between those disturbed by the high costs of autonomy and those anxious over the perils of dependency dominated China's foreign policy debates from the 1840s to the end of the dynasty. The xenophobic variety of populism that prevailed in this period was rooted ideologically in a Confucian view of the people as the sole source of the mandate to rule and the prime object of solicitude on the part of good officials. An 1858 memorial to the throne put the fundamental proposition: "The foundation of the state is wholly in the hearts of the people."[27] A close bond between ruler and ruled not only reflected and ensured harmony and virtue but also strengthened the state against external challenge. Preoccupied with winning the hearts of the people, early populism quite naturally worried about the ways the foreign presence might pervert or delude and thereby create social demoralization, economic disruption, and lawlessness.

Populists with their fear of dependency worked up and employed with considerable effect a long list of foreign-associated evils. Early trade had brought the opium curse and a deflationary outflow of silver as Chinese imports exceeded exports. The Taiping Rebellion, a Christian-influenced movement that engulfed central China at mid-century and nearly brought the dynasty down, highlighted the missionary menace. The treaty ports filled up with Chinese—merchants, translators, converts, and even officials—dependent on foreign protection and largesse and in awe of foreign power.[28]

To expel the foreigners and punish Chinese seduced by foreign money and deluded by foreign ideas, populists wanted to rely on the righteous wrath of the people. While patriotic provincial and metropolitan officials would sternly refuse further diplomatic concessions, the local elite would organize militia units to drive out the barbarian intruders and inspire grassroots efforts to put straying countrymen in their place.

Ye Mingchen, the governor-general who held the British at bay outside Canton in the 1850s, epitomized this early populist outlook. Ye preached to the court, with considerable effect, on the need to deal with foreigners only on Chinese terms. Inscrutable and unreasonable, barbarians could not be accommodated in safety. Those who rebelled against the imperial benevolence would have to be punished and expelled. If it came to a conventional test of strength, regular forces might fail, but not the inexhaustible strength of the common people. In a long war of attrition popular forces would wear down and eventually prevail over foreign troops. The emperor and his officials had, Ye advised, only to cultivate popular loyalty, avoid even a hint of appeasement, and snuff out heterodoxy in order to see tranquility restored.[29]

More than any other late Qing official, Li Hongzhang embodied that effort to shape an outward-looking foreign policy pronouncedly at odds with populism and its fear of foreign entanglements. Recent experience had convinced Li that China's weakness relative to other powers made immediate armed resistance self-defeating. Thus China would have to accept the status quo defined by the recently imposed treaties, use those treaties to bind the powers against further demands, and in the chief tribute states along the periphery try to preserve China's influence by playing the powers one against the other. But that was at best a short-run solution, as Li well knew. To achieve safety China needed an armed force and navy up to Western standards, needed its own system of modern communications (railroads, steamships, and telegraphs), needed modern arsenals to equip Chinese forces, and needed schools to train Chinese in Western science, law, and languages. As Li was quite free to admit, his was a vision profoundly legalist in its emphasis on power as the foundations of the Chinese state and informed to a degree by the example of the Warring States.[30]

Feng Guifen, an adviser to Li Hongzhang, offers insight into the premises on which Li and like-minded late Qing officials acted. Feng's overriding concern was to "restore our original strength, redeem ourselves from further humiliations, and maintain the integrity of our vast territory." But if China were to reach this goal and in time surpass the foreigners and become "the leading power in the world," then the emperor would have to "set us in the right direction" and the very foreigners who subjected China to humiliation would, for a time at least, have to be taken as teachers and models.[31]

But the cosmopolitan consensus in which Li and Feng operated was rent from the beginning by disputes over strategic priorities and the appropriate responses to specific foreign challenges. That consensus was, moreover, faced by the late 1890s with a sharp revival of populist sentiment within officialdom. Populists had kept up a steady sniping at Li's self-strengthening measures. They argued that foreign influences were undermining the foundations of the Confucian society and state without improving China's security. Restored to power in 1899, the populists convulsed China's foreign relations into still deeper crisis. Following the failed Boxer experiment in popular resistance in mid-1900, xenophobic populism fell into permanent eclipse as a policy alternative.[32]

Even so, populism and its fear of a fatal dependent relationship with the foreign powers was not dead; its concerns were absorbed by a patriotic movement that began to spread across China, overriding the centrifugal forces of class, linguistic, and regional differences.[33] This transition was clearly under way by the last decade of the Qing, when a series of urban protest movements developed against foreign mistreatment of overseas Chinese and foreign demands against China. Already these urban protests had acquired their defining characteristics, which were to persist into the Republican period. They were spearheaded by students, with officials, merchants, and journalists joining in. They encountered an ambivalent if not hostile government response, and after an initial outburst of fervor they died away with their specific goals usually unmet. They were slow to evoke—or even to seek—peasant support, a serious failing in a country overwhelmingly agrarian. Students fancied themselves successors to the gentry, the self-appointed spokesmen for China's interests and the natural leaders of the Chinese people. But when the students took to the street, the "people" were nowhere to be seen.

For a brief time in the mid-twenties—during the Northern Expedition led by the Nationalists allied with the Communists against the northern warlords—the promises of a populist patriotism were fulfilled. Peasants as well as workers were drawn into the cause. The result was a crescendo of anti-imperialist activity. The decade had begun with students denouncing mission work as a source of superstition and a form of cultural imperialism. Demonstrations, boycotts, and strikes paralyzed Shanghai and spread to other cities in 1925, and in 1927 Nationalist forces entering Nanjing turned on foreigners there, looting their property, killing six, and forcing the rest to seek safety on gunboats lying offshore. The Nationalist Party, itself in step with this popular anti-imperialism, demanded an end to the unequal treaties. No longer would foreign troops be stationed on Chinese soil, nor would foreign gunboats patrol Chinese waters; and foreign residents would be brought under the jurisdiction of China's legal and fiscal system.

The collapse in 1927 of the unstable Nationalist-Communist united front marked the beginning of a steady drift away from the popular mobilization and sweeping anti-imperialism on which Chiang Kai-shek as leader of the Nationalists had taken his party to power. Thereafter he clamped down on student-led anti-Japanese demonstrations, which he regarded with almost as much alarm as peasant unrest in the countryside. To deal with these domestic problems Chiang launched the "new life movement" in an attempt to create a citizenry responsive to state authority and resistant to the siren call of social revolution and political dissent. On the foreign policy front, Chiang struck a series of short-term compromises with the Japanese and then retreated to defensive positions in the interior, while flirting with their major nemeses, first the Soviet Union and then the United States. Chiang's strategy gained him enough time, materiel, and diplomatic support to carry him successfully through the Pacif c war, but left him facing the Communists with his regime's popular prestige impaired and his economic base in shambles.[34]

As noted above, the Communists followed from the mid-twenties a different path, one that combined populist and cosmopolitan strains. Their populism was reflected in their resort to mobilizing the peasantry and appeals to patriotic resistance to Japan. It was also reflected in their determination to turn back foreign cultural penetration and economic exploitation and to reintegrate into the nation those Chinese who had unwittingly served foreign interests. On the other hand, the Communists looked abroad—to the Soviet Union—for ideological inspiration. To be sure, imported Marxist-Leninist doctrine underwent a self-conscious process of sinicization. But this was precisely, as one of Mao's aides with a sense of perspective pointed out, what Chinese had always been good at doing—taking foreign ideologies "to embellish and develop . . . , thus rendering them particular creations of our nation."[35] Buddhism, not Marxism, was the topic used to illustrate the point, but the parallels between the cases were—and still are—hard to miss.

The populist and cosmopolitan strains (with their respective, contending fears of international subordination and isolation) remained in uneasy juxtaposition after 1949, creating in subsequent Communist policy an unresolved tension that accounts for some of the recurrent debates and major shifts in PRC foreign relations. Here again we have the familiar set of problems: How was a weak China to maintain true independence and security if it did not locate reliable outside diplomatic support and draw on appropriate developmental models and foreign technology to become strong? But might not such a course entangle China in a one-sided, neo-colonial relationship with militarily and economically stronger powers, dividing and demoralizing the nation? Was not dependence on the genius, industry, and patriotism of the Chinese people a surer path to independence and strength? These questions have echoed in the debates over whether to align with the United States, the USSR, or neither; over whether economic development should follow the Soviet model (as in the First Five-Year Plan), concentrate on tapping popular energies (as in the Great Leap Forward), or emphasize importation of capitalist technology and techniques (as under the Four Modernizations); over whether to rely on a mass, guerrilla-style military strategy or develop a conventionally equipped and trained army; and even over how many and what kinds of foreign transplants should be tolerated in the people's garden of art and literature.

This persistent tension between the temptations of dependency and the quest for autonomy is hardly unique to China. Indeed modern communications, transportation, and weaponry have made all national boundaries more tenuous. The particular experience of foreign domination has made many countries of Asia and Africa, not just China, peculiarly sensitive in this regard. Yet for the Chinese the tension has seemed unusually acute, perhaps because of the broad sweep of land that the Chinese have come to occupy. It confronts them with the massive difficulties of securing it and adjacent territory against unfriendly powers. That acute tension may also derive from the lively memory of an unusually long and powerful tradition of imperial greatness. That memory has goaded the Chinese, whose nation was by their own admission still poor, weak, and in many respects backward, to "stand up" so that their greatness will at last receive world recognition.

Finally, the conflict between dependency and autonomy has been accentuated by the events of the last two centuries, which serve as a constant reminder of the perils no less than the inescapability of involvement in international affairs. From the vantage point of the late twentieth century, a Chinese could not help but be impressed with the repeated problems created by borrowing technology and models of development burdened with unwanted cultural baggage. Nor could our observer brush away China's long and sorry experience with foreign allies, beginning with the Russian betrayal in the late 1890s, continuing through the sellouts at Paris and Yalta after coming out of the two world wars on the winning side, and culminating in the metamorphosis of the Soviet Union from chief friend to the primary enemy. But that same observer would also have to acknowledge that China's episodic attempts at self-isolation, from the Boxer uprising to the Cultural Revolution, have been costly and ultimately futile.

The Future of the Past

Viewed in historical perspective, the topic of China's foreign relations is perhaps most notable for its long cumulative record, its repertoire of traditions and models, and its enduring tension between populism and cosmopolitanism and between dependency and autonomy. In short, it should impress us with its complexity and the inadequacy of simple explanations.

Set in this context, the incorporation of Marxist-Leninist ideas into Chinese thinking (once made so much about) seems not so much a case of inappropriate or unfortunate borrowing as a demonstration of the staying power of cosmopolitan instincts, while the transformation of Marxism-Leninism into "Mao Zedong Thought" illustrates the countervailing influence of an indigenous populist tradition. Similarly, the middle kingdom world view (also once of broad interpretive appeal) may not satisfactorily account for China's obsession with some of its former tributaries and its ambivalence toward intimate cultural and political relations with other states. We might do better if we trace these same characteristics of Chinese foreign relations back to the persistence of the power-oriented approach to international policy handed down from the Warring States period, to a sound appreciation of the potent economic and cultural pull of the major capitalist powers, and to the hard lessons drawn from alliances that backfired.

We may by this point take it as a given that the study of China's complex past sheds important light on some of the central patterns and problems of China's contemporary foreign relations and serves as an antidote to simplistic conclusions. But is it safe to take the next step and assume that the past will remain a force to be reckoned with in Chinese foreign relations in the years ahead? Does the past, in other words, have a future as a source of insight into China's external relations? In broad terms the answer is an assured yes, though surely some aspects of that past will prove more influential than others and hence more deserving of our attention in the years ahead. Which ones? The very multiplicity of ways in which China's past influences its outlook and behavior and the depth and subtlety of that influence rules out a single simple or authoritative answer. Even so, a few informed guesses are possible.

History seems to have left its deepest mark by setting a demanding security agenda that will continue to guide Chinese leaders against challenges from intrusive outside powers, resentful and nationalistic neighbors, and restive ethnic groups. For Beijing to turn its back on that agenda would be not just to surrender the practical advantages of defense in depth but to repudiate a heritage in which all Chinese take considerable pride. The latter is far and away the weightier consideration.

A close second in the potency of its influence would seem to be that unresolved tension between the temptations of dependency and the impulse toward autonomy that affects development policy and security calculations. Chinese leaders in the years ahead are likely to draw on outside technology, models, and resources, and yet they will surely watch with concern the unintended and unwanted social and economic changes produced by the multiplication of foreign contacts. Much as their predecessors did, those leaders will nervously look for—and have difficulty finding—a straight and open road, avoiding on the one side the wasteland of self-reliance that leaves China poor and weak and on the other the swamp of international diplomatic and economic involvement that compromises the ideal of self-determination.

The third area of historical influence, the place of the past in the Chinese consciousness, poses the most formidable and intricate challenge to the powers of prediction. Which of the remembered pasts, we want to know, is likely to have the liveliest influence on policy? Chinese commentators with official standing long answered that the only past that was meaningful was the recent one, defined by them in terms of oppression and struggle over the last century and a half. Built into mythic proportions, this orthodoxy traces the rise of a revolutionary spirit, the triumph over Chinese collaborators who had shamefully capitulated to imperialism, the eradication of imperialist influence within China, and the emergence of a post-1949 foreign policy built on the principles of full and formal reciprocity and equality in dealing with others and of opposition to great power dominion, whether expressed in the form of hegemonism or imperialism. This officially sanctioned history retains an important place in the thinking of Chinese concerned with foreign policy, though its emotional power drains away as the years pass and the drama of the pre-1949 period gradually looms less large on the broad canvas of Chinese history.

There are good grounds for arguing—contrary to the claims of the exponents of historical orthodoxy in the PRC—that the century of humiliation and the lessons drawn from it have already forfeited their monopoly claim as the relevant past. Rather it seems fair to say that the century of humiliation, which constitutes the negative pole of Chinese experience, is inextricably joined to a positive pole defined by recollections of the imperial past, especially in the guise of its great dynasties of Han and Tang. It is also conceivable that as the negative pole loses strength, the appeal of the positive pole will concomitantly increase. This rise in appeal of the imperial past seems likely to happen in any case, for it offers the only indigenous benchmark for measuring progress toward a position of restored national power and pride. To the extent that this long and rich imperial past defines the future for which Chinese strive, it is not in the crude sense some would have it—as a system of middle kingdom arrogance to be revived—but rather as a standard (or perhaps more accurately a national myth) of cultural achievement and international power and influence to live up to. The distinction could end up as an excessively fine one, however, for a restoration of China to a position of greatness is likely to lead inexorably, though not by design, to increasing dominance over adjoining peoples and states and to sharpen still lively fears of the middle kingdom in the minds of neighbors.

Other aspects of the past are likely to be of lesser influence in the future. The romantic past identified with the Warring States and Three Kingdoms periods has served its purpose as a compass for China's coming to terms with the new Western-imposed international order. To the degree it remains important, it will be as a source of inspiration for Machiavellian stratagems and maneuvers particularly appropriate to a still developing country with great ambition. It will, in short, influence style. But it is doubtful that it has today or will have in the immediate future an impact on the basic goals of policymakers.

Perhaps the most problematic component of this set of historical influences to appraise is the Marxist-Leninist-Maoist one. A revolutionary ideology would clearly seem to play a role in the way policymakers see the world, and thus to a very sizable extent it should be expected to influence behavior. Yet the major strategic crises through which the PRC has passed—in Korea in 1950, in the Taiwan Strait in 1958, along the Indian border in 1962, in Vietnam in 1965, and along the Soviet border in 1969— would seem essentially to have less to do with Communist ideology and more to do with the maintenance of historical boundaries and influence along the periphery.

Praise of proletariat internationalism has passed out of Beijing's rhetoric, and condemnation of imperialism is now muted. Today more than ever, a weak China will hesitate to risk scarce resources on foreign adventures. And even when the time comes when growing strength will give Beijing the luxury of putting aside its cautious, low-risk foreign policy, action is far more likely to come in nearby areas of strategic concern than at distant points beyond China's established horizon. The tempting conclusion to reach is that Communist ideology has done little to transform in any fundamental sense China's inherited strategic calculations and concerns, nor is the rise of a more assertive China in the future likely to change dramatically that state of affairs.

There is an urgent need for sensitivity to the persistent and complex role the past plays in Chinese foreign relations. It would be convenient to think of Chinese leaders as mere mechanical gauges accurately registering the international forces impinging on them or as computers impersonally assessing their alternatives by the program of power politics. No doubt Chinese leaders, like those of any other country, perform both functions to some degree. But like their counterparts in other lands, they also act on inherited outlooks and goals and are subject either personally or politically to fixations and ambivalences rooted in the experience of their generation and culture. Their behavior may be perfectly explicable and in a sense rational in the Chinese context at the same time that it seems puzzling and even irrational from the perspective of an outsider attuned to power politics but not to the power of the past.

To understand how the past has wielded its power, we need to look back to the crisis that afflicted China in the nineteenth century. That crisis was the intellectual crucible for the founding fathers of the Chinese Communist Party as well as their political sons and heirs. Coming to political maturity in that crisis, all had to learn from and live with its pervasive and debilitating consequences.

Chapter Two

The Crisis of the Late Qing, 1800–1912

The late Qing, marked by the near collapse of the Chinese empire and the recurring rounds of foreign encroachment on China proper, presents a doleful picture that would seem at first glance to have relatively little to do with an ultimately triumphant Chinese Communist Party and its foreign policy. The decades preceding the fall of the Manchu dynasty in 1912 were witness to a string of bitter defeats—the steady erosion of sovereignty, the loss of territory, and the end of any semblance of military security. By the time the Qing gave way to the Republic, foreign policy was demonstrably bankrupt, and the future seemed to hold in store nothing but more defeats and humiliation. Facing disaster, Chinese engaged in foreign policy issues could not even then agree on a long-term strategy for survival.

How could the developments of this period possibly bear on a party not even organized until 1921 and bereft of anything like a foreign policy until the 1940s? How could early party leaders, most mere children when Beijing had last fallen to foreign forces, be significantly influenced by events beyond their direct experience and for the most part well before their day? In fact, the record of the last imperial dynasty's twilight period is essential to understanding CCP external relations in several basic ways. In considering that record this chapter will in effect further develop the claim

This chapter is a revised version of a conference paper entitled "Late Qing Foreign Relations and the Problem of Cooperation." I am grateful to Harry Harding, the conference organizer, for permission to make use of that paper here.

advanced in the previous chapter about the pertinence of the past by show-ing how the late Qing constituted the matrix out of which the CCP's approach to world affairs would in a variety of ways emerge.

Conventionally the late Qing is remembered for its shattering losses and repeated humiliations and the resulting burning sense of shame and dis-orientation felt by many Chinese, not least a younger generation coming into its political consciousness in the immediate wake of the imperial col-lapse. This point, so frequently reiterated that it has become cliché, is not wrong but it does obscure a more complex legacy that is positive as well as negative.

On the negative side of the ledger, the reverses that marked the late Qing and continued into the early Republic not only inspired outrage and confusion but also evoked almost at once among future party leaders, as well as many of their politically engaged contemporaries, a patriotic deter-mination to somehow restore the Chinese state and with it China's stand-ing in the world and the crumbling empire. But, as they soon discovered, the problem of state collapse that they confronted was not the result of some sudden accident or simple failing. Rather, state collapse had profound structural sources that served not only to make the crisis deeply disturbing and difficult to explain but also to render it acutely resistant to easy solu-tions. Calls to restore the state soon turned (as we will see in the next chap-ter) into a search for ways to remake China from top to bottom. State col-lapse, in other words, inspired revolutionary impulses that brought the CCP to life and informed its thinking on foreign relations.

On the positive side, the CCP, however revolutionary a party, did not effect a sweeping break with the past. To take the most obvious case in point, the late Qing defense of the empire was of critical, though largely unacknowledged, importance to the CCP. Qing policymakers had few resources to bring to their holding action, but their determination and ingenuity carried them a long way toward their overriding goal—the preservation of the empire that was the pride of Manchus and that Han Chinese took as their patrimony. Success at avoiding a serious fragmenta-tion of the Chinese empire, at promoting international acceptance of imperial borders, and at maintaining and even strengthening China's demographic leverage within some imperiled regions was an indispensable contribution to the ultimate salvage of the empire. As heirs of the Qing, the Communists would take up where Qing officials had left off and prove as jealous and determined in defense of the territorial expanse defined by the high-water mark of Qing conquest as their predecessors had been. Indeed in less than a hundred years after the first occupation of the Chinese capital by foreign invaders a revived Chinese state had the empire back on its feet, with the only major territorial losses Outer Mongolia and some distant and sparsely settled reaches of the inner-Asian frontier.

That so much of the empire was preserved with so few resources points to a more general and also easily overlooked positive legacy, a tradition of sophisticated statecraft that manifested itself in a foreign policy of maneuver and manipulation. This flexible, even opportunistic approach so characteristic of Qing policymaking would eventually emerge as a prime feature of CCP foreign policy. Whatever the intellectual gulf between the party and its Qing forebears, the limits on the CCP's resources, its fascination with stratagems, and its faith in suasion carried it to a strikingly similar style in dealing with the outside world. For this and all the other reasons the late Qing bears closer scrutiny, the better to set the CCP in context.

Statecraft and Imperial Defense

Qing policymakers over three successive generations faced a grave challenge, both on the maritime frontier as Britain and the other powers pushed their way up the coast and on the inner-Asian frontier as restive minorities and outside powers challenged Chinese control. Policymakers charged with responsibility for meeting this challenge would have understood Machiavelli's contention that a state had only two ways to get what it wanted—"o la forza or l'amore"—and they would have shared his preference for force over suasion and compromise.[1]

They knew from experience that military campaigns supplemented by frontier settlement programs were the most effective means to secure territory even if they were costly and took time. The cultivation of amity and goodwill was, by contrast, a last resort offering but a weak basis on which to build policy. Such cooperation could even be dangerous. As Zeng Guofan, a leader of the restoration of late Qing imperial power, observed in 1860, "From time immemorial barbarian assistance to China, when followed by barbarian success, has always involved unexpected demands."[2]

Whatever the attractions of a more muscular approach, Qing officials did nonetheless try cooperation (*l'amore*) as a cheaper and, for a weak power, a more prudent way of stabilizing or pacifying a turbulent frontier. Usually the reasoning was straightforward. Rather than have concessions wrung from China, why not use those concessions creatively to secure diplomatic support and even economic assistance? The key was to play on foreign greed and jealousy in a way that would block aggression while helping China acquire the skills essential to make it strong and ultimately break the cycle of foreign coercion.

Cooperative strategic and economic arrangements were an especially important means of managing the maritime frontier, where the Qing suffered from acute vulnerability. But even on the inner-Asian frontier, where Qing policymakers enjoyed a logistical advantage over other powers and a technological superiority over restive peoples of the region, the costs of exercising that power made cooperation an attractive option.

In the 1830s Qing policymakers began to confront the mounting danger on the maritime frontier. Opium imports had produced an alarming outflow of specie as well as widespread addiction that reached even into the bureaucracy and the army. The Chinese determination to halt this debilitating commerce was matched by a British determination not only to continue it but also to remove the more general commercial restrictions imposed at the chief trading center, Canton. Imperial commissioner Lin Zexu's effort to impose prohibitions finally precipitated war in 1839. In the resulting conflict China was overwhelmed by British naval power. The Qing had not developed its own navy and relied instead on a passive coastal defense strategy that proved ineffective against trouble-making foreigners.

Policy swung to conciliation in 1842 when Qiying made peace with the advancing British with the backing of the grand councillor, Muzhanga, and the sanction of the Daoguang emperor. Qiying concluded that the British—and for that matter the Americans and the French—wanted only trade, not Chinese territory, and could be appeased by the grant of commercial privileges that did not threaten the security of the Qing state. Britain got a mercantile base in Hong Kong while the new system of treaties that was concluded over the following decade opened ports up and down the coast for trade, imposed fixed tariffs, allowed foreigners to live under their own laws, and stipulated that all treaty powers would share in these concessions.

This conciliatory solution may well have drawn directly from models developed along the inner-Asian frontier that offered an alternative to the costly use of force or maintenance of large garrisons. There amicable relations were based on the grant of trade privileges along with collaboration with local authorities who would accept subordination to Chinese rule. The Chinese part of the bargain was to accommodate to indigenous religions (such as Lamaism and Islam), cultural practices, and language, while employing divide-and-rule tactics and gradual sinicization to reinforce this low-cost strategy of control. Qing officials assigned duties on the turbulent southern coast knew that political, economic, and cultural accommodation of inner-Asian neighbors and subjects had proven one effective way to end their discontents and create a local status quo favorable to Qing interests, and not surprisingly they put that insight into practice.[3]

Ye Mingchen profoundly disagreed with this policy of conciliation. From his position as governor of Guangdong and then as governor-general of Guangdong-Guangxi between 1848 and 1858, he argued instead for a policy of renewed resistance. The death of the Daoguang emperor in 1850 and the support Ye received from the newly installed Xianfeng emperor was crucial in this shift. Ye set about blunting previous treaty concessions and keeping the foreigners away from Beijing. Conflict recommenced in 1856 and ultimately brought another demonstration of the superiority of Western arms.

In 1860, with the capital occupied by Anglo-French forces and rebellions raging in the provinces, a policy of cooperation, now closely tied to a program of reform, got its first sustained trial. In Beijing during what is known as the Tongzhi restoration, the youthful Prince Gong (then only in his late twenties) and the elderly Wenxiang took the initiative, using the newly created proto-foreign office (*Zongli yamen*) as their institutional base.

The leading figures in the restoration shared a "statecraft" (*jingshi*) approach to government affairs. They gave the writings of Wei Yuan, an earlier advocate of self-strengthening and reform, a privileged place in their thinking. The events since Wei's observations of the 1830s had vindicated his fears and made more timely his call for urgent action to direct scholarship to the pressing, practical problem of arresting the decline of state power, preserving China's territory, and restoring China's glory. They sought to promote "men of talent" (meaning those with demonstrated ability in political affairs as well as moral cultivation), train specialists in Western techniques, launch military, economic, and diplomatic projects that would add muscle to the state, and experiment with institutional innovations.

The logic behind their policy resembled Qiying's of a decade earlier. They had purchased peace through a new round of treaty concessions. More ports were opened; ministers were allowed to reside in Beijing; toleration was extended to Christian missionaries; and more territory was ceded (Kowloon to Britain and to Russia vast lands north of the Amur River and a considerable area adjoining present-day Xinjiang). The powers, foremost Britain and France, now had no territorial ambitions in China. They "do not covet our land and our people," so Prince Gong and Wenxiang reported.[4] Sincere dealing by Qing officials within a treaty framework that satisfied foreign commercial interests would build diplomatic trust, while a firm enforcement of those treaties would enable China to rein in aggressive foreigners, especially the missionaries who created unrest in the interior. Strongly reinforcing this line of argument was the threat to the dynasty and the empire posed foremost by the Taiping and Nian rebels and by the wave of ethnic unrest in inner Asia but also by the territorial ambitions of the Russians along that same frontier. Prince Gong and his allies assigned first claim on imperial resources to the campaigns to defeat the rebels in the interior and on the frontier. In the meantime they would seek to hold the Russians at bay and maintain amicable relations with the maritime powers.

As the 1860s progressed, cooperation grew in significance and appeal thanks to the supportive attitude of Britain and the other maritime powers. Favoring an open and stable China, those powers as well as Russia worked with the Chinese foreign office in enforcing the terms of the treaties and even entered into negotiations for treaty revision along lines favorable to China. The efficient functioning of the British-dominated Imperial Maritime Customs added to the all-around attractiveness of cooperation. This customs service assured the Qing a steady revenue, while foreigners appreciated its honest and efficient handling of foreign trade.

Cooperation on the maritime frontier not only made it possible to use the treaties to calm the foreigners and limit their activities; it also created an attractive environment for drawing on foreign skills, technology, and money to save the dynasty from its domestic enemies and to strengthen China for the long haul. Officials in the 1840s had discussed ways of borrowing from foreigners to China's advantage, particularly to put China in possession of "strong ships and powerful cannon." But they had made virtually no headway. Now officials moved with greater determination and on a broader front.

They realized that a program of self-strengthening could contribute at once to suppressing rebellion. Private foreign loans, Western weapons, and to a minor degree foreign mercenaries gave the forces of Zeng Guofan and Li Hongzhang an important edge in putting down the Taiping and Nian. Private foreign loans also helped Zuo Zongtang in the mid-1870s to complete the pacification of Shaanxi and Gansu and then to move his forces into Xinjiang. There he defeated Muslim rebels, forced the withdrawal of Russian forces occupying the Ili territory, and thus restored Qing authority.

But self-strengthening also gave rise to a longer term program of technological and economic development. Qing officials both in the capital and in the provinces worked with foreign specialists to establish schools and arsenals dedicated to mastering the languages, legal systems, and technology of the foreigners. Those same officials introduced foreign weaponry and training techniques, established commercial enterprises such as mining, textile mills, and steamship companies, and dispatched Chinese representatives abroad, all so that China could master those secrets that made the West strong and prosperous.[5]

Into the 1880s cooperation, especially in the diplomatic realm, remained an important element in meeting the challenge to the maritime frontier. Qing policy toward Korea is the best case in point. The leaders of the foreign office, convinced of the strategic importance of this buffer state, had begun in the 1860s to lead it out from behind the screen of tribute relations, which foreign pressure was rapidly rendering untenable. Their ultimate goal was to transform the formal relationship without relinquishing China's predominance on the peninsula or allowing other powers, especially Japan, to gain undue influence there. In this scheme to make a tribute dependent over into a sphere of influence as in other cases, the foreign office perceptively recognized (as Mary C. Wright has argued) "that it was quite impossible to keep the frontier areas sealed off; that there were many worse things than foreign trade; that trade could in fact be turned to a certain limited advantage; that diplomatic negotiations, instead of an outrage, were a most useful weapon for a weak country; that if China was to survive, many new languages and skills must be quickly learned."[6]

The effort begun by Prince Gong to strengthen China's strategic position on the northeast frontier was carried forward after 1879 by Li Hongzhang.[7] His plan was to assist some of the more tractable, commercially minded powers in establishing treaty relations with Korea. He would give them a stake on the peninsula to defend against Japanese encroachment and thereby create an international equilibrium favorable to Korea's independence and China's interests. At the same time he would seek to strengthen the Chinese position through Sino-Korean commercial agreements, an aid program, and the dispatch of agents, advisers, and even troops.

The first step was to get the United States, a country (as Li saw it) lacking any territorial or political ambitions, to conclude a treaty under Chinese auspices. In 1882, after two years of effort, he had talked the Korean court into signing the American treaty, and Britain, France, and Germany soon signed their own, also with Li as sponsor. Li's policy did not, however, have the desired results. None of the powers would play the game Li had assigned them of blocking Japan or shoring up the Chinese position. The Korean court remained divided in the face of mounting Japanese encroachment and Chinese interference.

Elsewhere in the 1870s and 1880s China was also thrown on the defensive. The massacre of French citizens in Tianjin in 1870 revealed the explosive tensions generated by aggressive Christian missionaries. That event brought to an end a decade of relative calm in Sino-foreign relations. A Chinese mission of apology quieted French outrage, but control over foreign missionaries and their converts continued to slip. Foreign penetration of the interior was matched by fresh, direct threats to Qing control of coastal territories. Japan led the way, probing Taiwan's defenses with an armed expedition in 1874 (and winning an indemnity for its efforts), incorporating China's Ryukyu (Liuqiu) tributary in 1875, and chipping away at Chinese hegemony in Korea (a process that had begun in 1876 with a treaty imposed on the Korean court). France followed, occupying northern Vietnam. Qing resistance to the French resulted in a war in which the southern part of the fleet was lost, Taiwan was almost taken, and foreign assistance was proven worthless. Beijing secured a peace in 1885 at the price of conceding French control over Vietnam. Over the next two years China had also to concede to Britain a free hand in Burma and to Portugal sovereignty over Macao.[8]

These setbacks served as the first intimation that officially sponsored efforts at strategic and technical cooperation were not having the desired effect. Proponents of cooperation had tried to manipulate foreign interests or change foreign attitudes to China's advantage. But the powers continued probing for points of vulnerability, and even those who so sincerely expressed concern for China's well-being withheld all meaningful help at moments of crisis. At the same time self-strengthening fell far short of expectations. Those trained in foreign techniques proved hard to integrate into the bureaucracy. Officially sanctioned enterprises, four-fifths of which operated under Li Hongzhang's supervision, ran up against a multitude of difficulties—opposition from foreigners and vested native interests, widespread hostility within officialdom, waste and mismanagement, loans carrying cripplingly high interest rates, and tensions between merchant managers and their official patrons.[9] The overhaul of China's military and naval forces was no more successful. While they were effective against ill-armed and poorly disciplined rebels, combat against the foreigners quickly exposed their glaring inadequacies—from sand-filled shells to corrupt, incompetent, and cowardly commanders.

By the 1890s domestic unrest had combined, as it had in the 1850s, with the foreign threat to make the handling of foreign affairs fiendishly difficult. China faced a renewal of great-power rivalry for advantages in and around China. A rebellion in Korea had served as the spark. Li Hongzhang had dispatched Chinese troops to help the Korean court suppress it. He had not counted on the arrival of Japanese forces carrying their own demands for reform of the Korean government. Li sought without success to avert the looming collision by appealing first to Russia for support and then to Britain for mediation. War came in August 1894. The crushing defeat of Li's military and naval forces dealt a dramatic blow to the dreams of the self-strengtheners. Li himself was in disgrace with some calling for his execution. Thirty-five years of effort had come to naught.

With Beijing again lying open to invasion, the court capitulated and called Li Hongzhang back to center stage. He first served as envoy to Japan. To gain peace he had to surrender claims to influence in Korea, cede Taiwan and the Liaodong peninsula (the southern portion of China's northeast known as Manchuria), and grant a large indemnity. The court ratified the treaty containing those concessions in May 1895 despite sharp domestic opposition. Partition of the empire seemed only a matter of time. Over this same period one violent anti-Christian incident after another inflamed Sino-foreign relations and left Chinese policymakers in the impossible position first glimpsed after the Tianjin massacre. They could not control the missionaries who caused the difficulties, nor could they settle missionary incidents without unleashing a storm of criticism at home.

With policy in disarray and the strategic situation more desperate than ever, policymakers returned to the idea of cooperation in the mid-1890s. Li Hongzhang was predictably the boldest of its advocates. He turned to Russia to stop the Japanese. In 1895 he had gotten Russia along with France and Germany to intervene in the peace process, forcing Japan to return Liaodong. He had also gotten Russia to help China meet its now increased indemnity obligations to Japan. Li then traveled in 1896 to St. Petersburg to attend the coronation of Nicholas II but more substantively to conclude a defensive alliance already sanctioned by the Empress Dowager Cixi. The alliance rested on a bargain: the right to extend Russia's Trans-Siberian Railroad across China's northeast in return for a promise of Russian military support in case of a Japanese attack on either China or Korea.

This alliance promptly proved a failure. Having collected their price for the pact, the Russians proceeded to join in despoiling their nominal ally. The powers began to mark out spheres of influence and consolidate control within them. Russia and the two other countries, Germany and France, that had intervened to moderate Japan's peace terms were the first to ask for compensation. Russia took payment in the form of concessions all along the Chinese border—in Xinjiang, Mongolia, and the northeast. Germany took a leasehold on the Shandong peninsula, while the French got mining concessions in the three southern provinces adjoining Indochina.

China's acquiescence on these points precipitated another round of demands in 1897 and 1898. Russia quickly moved to strengthen its hold on the northeast by seizing the ports of Dalian (Dairen) and Lüshun (Port Arthur) and by gaining the right to extend Russian rail lines to those ports. Britain signaled its determination to dominate the Yangzi valley. And France directed its claims to the southern provinces.

Foreign policy was once more poised to swing through another cycle—from prudent accommodation to militant rejection of foreign demands and back to accommodation. The failure of Li's Russian alliance, the repeated concessions that brought no benefit to China, and finally in 1899 the successful rebuff dealt Italian demands—all these combined to give credibility to the call for a new, tougher policy. At the same time xenophobia in the provinces surrounding the capital strengthened the case for renewing the policy of resistance. The court could either enlist the popular spirit of opposition to the foreign presence or itself become a target for the wrath of the people. Thus the Boxer movement received the blessings of the empress dowager in early 1900. The consequences were the familiar ones: a sharp division among leading officials over the wisdom of this course; the decisive defeat of imperial forces (with the capital again falling to foreign occupation and the court put to flight); and a new round of demands (contritely accepted after prolonged negotiations).[10] The Qing got a new lease on life, but at the cost of having its ancestral homeland in the northeast occupied by Russian troops, its debts increased by an enormous indemnity, and its sovereignty still further hedged about.

The Boxer experiment had proven a form of shock therapy. Its leading supporters now fell silent, quieted in some cases by suicide, in others by the prospect of execution at the hands of foreign forces. The chastened court called Li Hongzhang, old and ailing, back for one last diplomatic salvage operation, and soon thereafter lent its support to officials contending that a moderate, cooperative foreign policy linked to internal reforms was the only way to save China (and not incidentally the dynasty). With the empress dowager's blessing the two senior officials most ready to take up where Li had left off, Yuan Shikai and Zhang Zhidong, launched a two-pronged campaign in 1902 that resurrected and broadened the cooperative and self-strengthening goals of the 1860s. They sought to restore rights lost through the unequal treaties, while emphasizing state-directed economic development and institutional innovation that included laying the basis for a constitutional monarchy inspired by foreign models.[11]

The new policy was marked by a search for foreign allies. With the Russian alliance discredited, voices within officialdom could be heard already in the late 1890s arguing for other eligible partners—Germany, Britain, Japan, and the United States. Neither then nor later could Germany or Britain give encouragement as they began their retreat from East Asia, the better to confront the other in Europe. Britain was additionally constrained by its alliance to Japan, initially concluded in 1902 to combat the Russian advance and thereafter valued for freeing the British fleet to concentrate close to home.

The possibility of a Japanese alliance or even a Sino-Japanese alignment seemed even less plausible. The Japanese, who enjoyed a free hand thanks to the retrenchment by the European powers, proved a growing menace. China watched helplessly as Japanese forces drove back the Russians in the war of 1904–1905 and made claim to mastery of northeast Asia. Japan took hold of the developed southern portion of China's northeast and annexed Korea, while also staking out the coastal area (Fujian) opposite Taiwan as a sphere of influence.[12]

Despite all this, the notion of close ties to Tokyo remained attractive to some Chinese policymakers. Already in the late 1890s, officials such as Zhang Zhidong had stressed the common interests China had with its neighbor in stemming the tide of Western aggression. Common culture added to the attractiveness of a program of Sino-Japanese cooperation. The growing muscle Japan displayed in its confrontation with Russia between 1900 and 1905 reinforced the hard-headed view that resistance to Japan would find China isolated and would stimulate a more aggressive Japanese policy. Quiescence and a modicum of cooperation would, on the other hand, win time for China and shore up the status quo.

After 1905 arguments for cooperation with Japan amounted in the eyes of most officials to a sellout. That left the United States as the only power on which China might rely.[13] Washington had made a strong verbal commitment to the open door, a policy formulated (to be sure) not to facilitate working with Qing policymakers but rather to restrain the other powers. But Chinese officials quickly perceived the possibility that those restraints on foreign aggression might be made even more effective if China and the United States acted jointly. Those intent on an American alliance linked it to a broad-gauge policy of using American capital to promote China's security and economic development.

China's U.S. policy unfolded in three stages. Its origins go back to the late 1890s when Zhang Zhidong sought American capital to underwrite Chinese-sponsored railroad construction in south China (between Hankou and Canton). Zhang had given a group of American investors a contract in 1898 because in his estimate Americans were the only foreigners with capital yet "no intention of taking advantage of our territory."[14] He counted on an American presence that would counteract the spheres of influence staked out by the other powers and give Washington an incentive to stand up against any attempt at partition. As it turned out, Washington used its diplomatic influence to protect American investors, not Chinese interests. After those investors secretly sold out to Europeans, Zhang moved to abrogate the contract.

After 1905 those entrusted with the defense of the northeast tried to enlist the United States, this time against Japan. Yuan Shikai, now a powerful presence in Beijing, and two local officials, Xu Shichang followed by Xiliang, recognized that a Sino-American partnership might bolster China's position in the region. American capitalists were to be given a role in railway development and financial affairs, and in order to protect this economic stake Washington would join with China in defense of the northeast—so at least these officials reasoned. When put to the test, Washington disappointed by simply backing away from a confrontation with Japan.

Finally, in its last troubled years following the death of the empress dowager and the fall of Yuan Shikai in 1908, the central government desperately turned to the United States for funds to carry out reforms. Once more loans were freighted with diplomatic expectations. And once more those expectations fell short. Rather than supporting China, Washington lined up with the other powers in creating an international banking consortium determined to control the flow of capital and exercise supervision over Chinese finances.

The ambitious program implemented during the last decade of the Qing led to some signal achievements, especially in limiting and even turning back the foreign presence. Plans for treaty revision were put under way to bring foreigners under greater Chinese control. Government officials promoted Chinese economic enterprise with an eye to blunting foreign penetration. They made headway in buying out or abrogating foreign-held mine, railroad, and other concessions. Perhaps most striking of all was the way that they exploited the retreat from Shandong of a Germany isolated from the other powers.[15] But at the same time China's finances, already hamstrung by past indemnities and loans, fell ever more deeply under foreign control. By 1911 the Qing had virtually lost its financial independence.

China's foreign policy problems intensified under the early Republic. The Western powers were soon locked in struggle on the battlefields of Europe, while China's ability to defend itself was further diminished by intensifying factionalism and the devolution of power from Beijing to the provinces. Quick to exploit this opportunity, Japan seized Germany's Shandong leasehold in 1914, advanced a set of twenty-one demands in 1915 designed to extend dramatically its special rights in China, and steadily strengthened its economic grip on the Republican government.[16] At the same time China's hold on its vast inner-Asian frontier further weakened. The new central government could not sustain the vigorous late Qing effort to control Tibet. In 1913 western Tibet declared its independence, and Britain endorsed autonomy though not a complete break with China. Outer Mongolia for its part moved out of China's orbit with Russian support. Here too Beijing clung to the fiction that the region was merely autonomous. But in fact China's claim to both areas was now in deep peril.[17]

Strains on the State

We have seen that Chinese policymakers during the nineteenth and early twentieth centuries put up a staunch defense of the empire. They exercised their considerable powers of calculation and initiative and struggled, usually tenaciously and often creatively, against foreign penetration and control. Yet their attempts to manage—to turn back, deflect, or coopt—the powers proved largely abortive. The most obvious explanation for this discrepancy between effort and achievement can be found in relative weakness. The repeated effort to maneuver out of danger was above all an expedient response to vulnerability on the maritime frontier. The weaker China became, the more effort policymakers invested in a variety of schemes to entice or manipulate foreigners into providing assistance. Born out of weakness, the impulse to cooperate also foundered on weakness and repeatedly produced its opposite, the effort to drive out the foreign presence in one mighty blow. The powers recognized the desperation that prompted Chinese initiatives. They exploited the weakness that they saw in cooperative enterprises and faced down resistance that threatened their position in China.

It is possible, however, to carry this analysis beyond obvious inequalities of power and to consider some of the structural features of the Qing state and the contemporary international system, which together made cooperation no less than resistance self-defeating.

The recurrent if ineffective resort to these two strategies can, first of all, be explained by the battered condition of the Chinese state. Beset simultaneously by external predators and internal conflict, that state suffered from an empty treasury, divided and weak leadership, inefficient institutions, ineffective personnel, and a crisis in its ideology. Not surprisingly, that state was eventually to fall into the hands of disaffected elites that had turned to revolution.[18] This state crisis was long in the making, with its roots going back not just to the mid-nineteenth century and the development of the maritime danger but to the eighteenth century and the rise of internal threats to imperial authority. Its severity first became apparent in the decade-long rebellions by the White Lotus Society and the Miao around the turn of the century, well before the Opium War.

Within the realm of the state nothing was more fundamental than mounting fiscal difficulties in driving policymakers toward low-cost but risky cooperative efforts. To some extent those difficulties can be traced back to China's own aggressively expansionist policy. By dint of considerable and costly effort the Qing had by 1792 doubled its territory, bringing under control the greatest expanse of land in Chinese history. The Qianlong emperor's ten campaigns, though not uniformly successful, had brought this process of conquest to its high-water mark. But these glorious conquests carried costs both immediate and long-term. The outlays on expeditionary forces themselves were followed by expenditures running through the nineteenth century required to underwrite new campaigns against restive subjects in areas remote from the centers of Chinese wealth and population and to subsidize the administration of these resource-poor and unstable frontier areas.

For example, Qianlong's campaigns cost at least 150 million taels. Zuo Zongtang's campaigns in the northwest between 1866 and 1874 required about 36 million taels. His follow-up effort in Xinjiang in 1875–1881 cost 52.5 million taels, and thereafter maintaining regional forces to assure Xinjiang's stability against Muslim warriors and security against Russian troops constituted an annual drain of as much as 7.9 million taels. The total expended in Xinjiang alone in just a quarter of a century was probably on the order of 185 million taels.[19]

To the funds laid out to gain and maintain the inner-Asian frontier must be added those expended to put down rebellions in the heart of China and meeting the maritime challenge. Each rebellion imposed a twofold cost: not only was pacification expensive but provinces in chaos supplied diminished revenue to hard-pressed central authorities. The suppression of the White Lotus alone cost 200 million taels. Putting down the rebellions that later erupted all across the late Qing empire would extract an even heavier cost, something on the order of 422 million teals (according to Peng Zeyi's estimate) with suppression of the Taiping accounting for forty percent of the total.[20] By then fiscal troubles forced the government to rely on foreign loans to finance the suppression of rebels.

On top of these foreign obligations, the Qing carried a growing burden of debt occasioned by wars, massive indemnities, and urgent projects of economic development and political reform. For example, the Opium War ended with a 21 million tael indemnity. The Sino-French struggle cost 100 million taels and left the central administration with a 20 million tael debt. The 1895 peace settlement added another 230 million taels to the debt (including 30 million taels for the return of Liaodong). The post-Boxer settlement in 1901 resulted in a crushing indemnity of 450 million taels. One estimate puts total Qing borrowing between 1894 and 1911 at 747 million taels, a figure that does not include an additional 331 million taels in self-servicing railway loans.[21]

To set these various figures in perspective, it should be kept in mind that total annual revenue for the central government in 1895 was 89 million taels, a little less than two-fifths of the total extracted by Japan in just that one year. Budgets in the early 1890s were already one-third devoted to frontier defense and international security. The addition of indemnities and loans in 1895 and after drained away more and more of the government's revenues and seriously limited its ability to pursue reforms, provide needed services, or augment defense.[22]

At the same time reserves in the imperial treasury dropped precipitously. In 1777 Beijing had as much as an 82 million tael cushion. By 1797 the figure had fallen to 28 million, and by 1843 had dropped below 10 million never to surpass that figure again. As the dynasty launched its restoration project in 1860–1861, reserves did not exceed 2 million taels. Rebel suppression, fighting along the coast, and foreign indemnities had by then stripped the Qing of its nestegg.[23]

This alarming fiscal trend made a reliable, indeed increasing flow of revenue critical not just to an effective defense policy but to the very survival of the state itself. Imperial revenues in the 1880s and 1890s were nearly double those of mid-century thanks chiefly to the growing returns from foreign and domestic commerce. But Beijing could not exploit these promising sources of income to the full. The provinces had established first claim on a substantial part of the internal transit tax during the suppression of the mid-century rebellions, and guarded their prerogatives jealously. In general, the provinces fended off Beijing's efforts from the 1880s onward to create a centralized and uniform fiscal system, one that put an end to gross underreporting of actual collections at the local level. Duties on a growing foreign trade, another promising source of revenue, were fixed by treaty at five percent. The powers not only avoided tariff revision but also in 1854 established foreigners as the exclusive collectors of those duties. These various fiscal restraints meant that the Qing during its last decade and a half, when its financial needs were greatest, could lay hold of less than forty percent of the *formally* reported revenues (equivalent to only about three percent of China's total output of goods and services).[24]

A state already whipsawed by diminished resources and mounting internal and foreign threats had the additional misfortune of encountering in its last, most troubled decades a string of weak rulers. At a time when a clearly defined policy and strict discipline over metropolitan and provincial officials were most needed, the emperor was least able to supply them. During the confrontation with the British the imperial hand in foreign affairs was not strong and steady. From the 1860s on the youthful Tongzhi, Guangxu, and Xuantong emperors fell under the shadow of their elders. The empress dowager exercised a powerful but seemingly intermittent influence over policymaking, intervening decisively at moments of extreme crisis. She appears in any case to have lacked any clearly defined vision of China's course in international affairs, and she would not give strong and consistent support to others such as Prince Gong and Li Hongzhang who did. Moreover, her legitimacy as a source of political authority was in question. The leaderless and divided Grand Council, which had earlier grown in power and autonomy at the expense of the emperor, did not function well as a forum for decisionmaking, and the creation of the foreign office merely added another administrative unit in need of policy guidance and support.[25]

This weakening of central authority began to cast a pall of demoralization and confusion over the state apparatus. The most obvious symptom of crisis was the fragmentation of the foreign policy bureaucracy into competing centers, each with its own needs and priorities. In the 1840s and 1850s imperial commissioners had been posted to Canton and Shanghai to manage the foreigners and block their way to the capital. Thereafter those two positions survived in new guise as the commissioners of northern and southern ports headquartered in Tianjin and Shanghai respectively. While the court vacillated, strong-minded incumbents such as Li Hongzhang gained a degree of autonomy in diplomacy as well as in economic and defense policy. Still other claimants to a role in the making of late-nineteenth-century policy were the heads of China's overseas missions and Robert Hart, the head of the foreign-run customs service. As the locus of authority and decisionmaking became diffuse, competition for power and patronage intensified, and factionalism flourished.

This disintegration of the state apparatus meant a carefully calculated policy, rapidly formulated and consistently pursued, tended to elude the grasp of the Qing state. The coastal crises of 1839–1842 and 1856–1860 are replete with instances of false reporting and unauthorized concessions made under foreign pressure. After 1860 paralyzing insubordination and rivalry became if anything worse. In 1879 Beijing's envoy to Russia signed an agreement ceding some twelve hundred square miles of Xinjiang (the Ili territory) in defiance of explicit foreign office orders to the contrary. The state's authority was further brought into question on this occasion when the foreign powers stepped in to save the envoy from capital punishment.

During the early stages of the Sino-French crisis, Li Hongzhang refused to assume responsibility because he wanted to concentrate his attention and resources on Korea. Once fighting began, he actually balked at moving his forces south into the combat zone. The empress dowager then placed policy in the hands of the militant Prince Chun, while purging Prince Gong and the members of the foreign office. Li reasserted himself in the search for a peace settlement, vying with Hart (and Hart's own agent in London) as well as with the Chinese minister in Paris in a free-for-all race to complete negotiations with France.

Decisionmaking during the Sino-Japanese War reveals the same rivalry and confusion. In that case, the initiative passed from Li (who had shaped Korean policy since the 1870s), to the court (where the Guangxu emperor advocated war and the empress dowager acquiesced), to the foreign office (assigned the task of opening peace talks), and thence back to Li (who was to handle the actual negotiations of peace terms). The only thing that can be said in favor of this decentralized and unstable system was that it made diplomatic intervention somewhat more difficult for foreigners, who could not be certain who was in charge and what they were doing! The Boxer crisis in 1900 brought more of the same, including a refusal by Yuan Shikai and other reform-minded provincial officials to come to the aid of the court until it abandoned its militant course.

These ominous trends within the Qing state were accompanied (as suggested in the previous chapter) by deepening ideological divisions among the elite from which policymakers issued. In particular, the linked strategy of reform and cooperation gave rise to heated and at times fratricidal conflict. Official advocates of reform and cooperation had to proceed warily and often anxiously. They knew that attempts at strategic cooperation would fuel the fires of political controversy and that militants, both inside the government and out, stood ready to pounce on any arrangements that even hinted of a sellout.

The reverses suffered by the reformers from the 1870s onward left them vulnerable to those long opposed to making any foreign policy concessions or adopting foreign models. These critics attacked the misplaced and ineffective attempts at self-strengthening. They denounced the meek accommodation to the disruptive missionary presence and the insatiable commercial and territorial demands of the Westerners. Invoking foreign assistance to redress China's weakness was risky, they warned, especially because it tempted all the powers to press their own pet projects. Policymakers needed to devote themselves instead to strengthening the popular and moral foundations of the state. The militants' program of ideological revitalization stressed strong links between the throne and the people. An enlightened and virtuous ruler, sensitive to the mood of his subjects and open to the views of his orthodox officials, could lead a united and aroused country to victory. Senior officials had to listen to the voice of the people and enlist this enormous popular force against the foreign danger. Beijing for its part would have to be prepared to sanction popular violence and where necessary embrace warlike measures.

Adding force to the militant argument and increasing the practical difficulties of the self-strengtheners was the social unrest that sporadically erupted across the empire. Popular challenges to local order threatened imperial control and prestige, sometimes imperiled foreign lives and interests (most often missionaries and their Chinese converts), and often resulted in new openings for foreign demands and the extension of influence. For militants, this social unrest was a force to be harnessed to the interests of the dynasty. Focusing on the foreign danger was one way of winning support from an apathetic if not disaffected public. For reformers on the other hand, social unrest was a distraction from their desperate race against time to set the Qing state on a new foundation and thus contain foreign penetration, and it endangered the short-term policy of cooperation. Repression was their favored response.

War with Japan in 1894–1895 sharpened the internal tensions between the two very different points of view, each with its own notion of how to integrate domestic and foreign policy. Official reformers, reinforced by those outside the government with even more radical views, called for sweeping institutional changes. Militants responded by reiterating that self-strengthening had proven bankrupt and that cultural revitalization was the key to a vigorous and ultimately successful policy.

The militant prescription gained powerful adherents through the late 1890s and finally was taken up by the court in 1900. Backed by such courtiers as Ronglu and Kangyi, the empress dowager decided to test the claim that a united and determined China could bring a halt to repeated and demeaning foreign demands and withstand even a strong invader. To official objections that the Boxers were a weak reed to lean on and that their claims to immunity from firearms were laughable, the Empress Dowager Cixi responded in the language of the militants. "Perhaps their magic is not to be relied upon; but can we not rely on the hearts and minds of the people? Today China is extremely weak. We have only the people's hearts and minds to depend on. If we cast them aside and lose the people's hearts, what can we use to sustain the country?"[26] The Boxer crisis marked the end of this debate as the powers intervened to purge officialdom and to silence the militants.

While developments within China are central to understanding the alternation between cooperation and resistance, the international system within which Qing policymakers operated also deserves mention for the constraints it imposed as well as the opportunities it sometimes opened for Chinese policymakers to explore. Fundamentally, that system was defined from the mid-nineteenth century to the early twentieth by keen competition among the powers that tended to make aggression against China self-perpetuating. China's ever more pronounced weakness reinforced this tendency. Thus, just as the militants had claimed, one demand led to another as each power scrambled to keep up with its competitors.

However, the very rivalry and anxiety that drove the powers also seemed to proponents of cooperation a condition that might be turned to China's advantage. Conflicting interests and mistrust among those powers offered a handle for Qing policymakers to grasp. By granting special favors to foreigners deemed less dangerous to China, those policymakers calculated that they could strengthen their own position and at the same time give pause to the more dangerous of the outsiders. What they did not count on was the strategic caution and contemptuous attitudes that set limits on how far the less dangerous powers would go in cooperating with China. In the end, it would prove inherently difficult for a weak power to manipulate the stronger.

During the late Qing the international system went through three distinct stages, each presenting different dangers as well as opportunities for Chinese policy. The first was the period between the 1830s and the 1860s of British dominance and relative passivity by other powers. Because international contradictions were not yet pronounced enough to exploit effectively, China had no diplomatic cards to play against the British-led united front in the 1840s and 1850s. The French, Russians, and Americans alternately took advantage of the British advance and stood on the sidelines.

Their occasional talk of friendship and sympathy for the Qing meant little. During the 1860s, with British demands satisfied and rivals soothed by
equality of commercial treatment, China enjoyed a period of calm during
which the cooperative policy briefly flourished.

A more complex and increasingly unstable international system prevailed from the 1870s to the 1890s. It was marked by intensifying rivalry
among a growing number of major powers. The presence of new powers—
Germany and Japan—alongside the previously established ones eroded
British dominance. When France's unsatisfied missionary ambitions provoked a confrontation with China in 1870, the stage was set for a new
round of demands. The powers picked off China's tribute states over the
following fifteen years. Then the Qing's crushing defeat in 1895 at the
hands of the Japanese set the imperialists on a feeding frenzy, with China's
finances, commerce and industry, and even territory itself as the main meal.
Desperate for outside support, Qing policymakers found that the rapidly
shifting relations among predatory powers made control extraordinarily
difficult, as Li Hongzhang's troubling experience with Russia indicates. A
concession made to enlist the assistance of one power would at once bring
the ministers of three others storming into the foreign office demanding
the same or equivalent concessions.

The Boxer crisis ushered in the third phase in the evolution of the international system that prevailed down to the fall of the dynasty and beyond.
This new phase was filled with new opportunities as well as new difficulties for advocates of cooperation.[27] The powers were in the main cautious.
All had been shaken by the Boxer uprising, which had highlighted the
costs and difficulties of managing an inflamed China. And most were to
become increasingly distracted by the rising tensions in Europe. Treaties
tying Britain, Japan, France, and Russia together between 1902 and 1909
registered this new concern with security close to home and the concomitant desire to minimize their East Asian commitments. Outflanked, Germany began a retreat from China that became a rout with the outbreak of
World War I. Finally, in the case of Russia the tendency toward caution
was reinforced after 1905 by defeat at the hands of Japan and by the
domestic revolutionary peril.

Japan and to a lesser degree the United States were the exceptions to this
tendency toward great-power caution and even disengagement. Japan continued the expansionist policy of the late nineteenth century. To its possession of Taiwan (gained in 1895), it added a sphere of influence in coastal
Fujian, and established itself firmly in the northeast at the expense of the
Russians. The United States was also becoming more active as it dis-

48

patched the open-door notes in 1899 and 1900, acquired the Philippines as a base to defend East Asian interests, participated in the Allied expedition against the Boxers, and opposed Russian occupation of the northeast. After 1905 Japanese claims in northeast China further aroused American policymakers and marked the onset of a trans-Pacific rivalry that would persist unresolved for forty years.

During the last decade of the Qing, policymakers revived the strategy of cooperation, directing it against the Russian threat before 1905 and the Japanese threat thereafter. Japan with British backing undercut Russian pretensions. But no such international combination appeared to deal with the advancing Japanese. Tokyo combined with London, Paris, and St. Petersburg in a power bloc that served as an effective barrier to Chinese challenges to the status quo. The United States had seemed the most promising alternative source of support, but the limits of American commitment in China soon became evident in 1910 when Washington blinked in a showdown with Tokyo over the northeast. Soon thereafter, the outbreak of World War I did almost as much to distract the Americans as it did the European powers. China had thus arrived at the worst of all situations—facing alone one dominant power intent on maintaining firm control despite growing nationalist opposition.[28]

Learning from the Past

The failures of the late Qing carried two powerful lessons for politically engaged Chinese in the twentieth century. First, they concluded that hopes for an advantageous and secure if not peaceful relationship with the powers depended on the vitality of the state. Cooperation had failed, above all, for want of such a vital state, and cooperation would become a possibility only after the state was rebuilt on a stronger basis. But political leaders disagreed on how to reach this goal. The militant-reform split of the late Qing was to give way to a disagreement between reformers and revolutionaries that was to prove every bit as deep-seated and bitter as the earlier conflict. But even if Chinese might now disagree on the desirability of political revolution or even more violently over social revolution, what none doubted was that only with the state back in command, its power and legitimacy restored, could China emerge as a purposeful and secure international actor, one that could inspire hope and pride in its people.

Second, politically engaged Chinese looking back at the late Qing record saw a compelling indictment of foreign behavior. When Qing officials sought strategic partners, particularly on the dynamic maritime frontier, foreign diplomats seldom responded as desired—with the result that sponsors of cooperation found themselves vulnerable to criticism and their policy displaced by other, more antagonist approaches. When those officials promoted various kinds of economic, educational, and technological partnerships, they encountered fewer risks, especially when they engaged individual foreigners whose service to the Qing could be divorced from the interests of their own governments. Central, provincial, and even local authorities found reasonably tractable those individual foreign merchants, bankers, educators, and mercenaries drawn to profits or personal influence.

By contrast, when the diplomats got involved in these partnerships, trouble soon followed. Seemingly friendly powers drawn to attractive self-strengthening projects almost invariably turned to exploit China's evident weakness, and then domestic critics pounced on the official sponsors of these arrangements as traitors to China's overall interests. Despite these risks, policymakers kept coming back to this high-yield, high-risk strategy of drawing on foreign technology and wealth, and the powers that they sought to implicate kept exploiting China's weakness to continue the cycle of concessions, humiliations, and retreats for which the late Qing was to prove infamous.

The disasters that had shaken the Chinese state, imperiled the empire, and divided officialdom thus raised fundamental questions—about China's heritage and its future, its political and social system, and its relationship to the outside world. These questions were to echo in Chinese politics long after the empire had been reconstituted and the structural crisis reversed. It is now time to turn to see how patriotic Chinese from the turn of the century, including the early leaders of the Chinese Communist Party, grappled with these questions.

PART TWO

Intellectual Ferment

Chapter Three

The Patriotic Impulse, 1890s-1910s

After suffering a series of blows through the nineteenth century at the hands of rebels and foreign invaders, the Qing state finally collapsed in 1911. Subsequent attempts to rebuild on new foundations would prove abortive. The republican government in Beijing quickly became a creature of regional powerholders and exercised but circumscribed power. The Nationalist regime in Nanjing sought to make a fresh start, but in the end domestic rivals and Japanese invaders diverted Chiang Kai-shek from state building to the more pressing issues of survival. It would fall to the Communist movement to finally begin to make headway in the battle to restore the Chinese state.

Responding to State Crisis

What bears closer examination is the turn-of-the-century response of politically informed and engaged Chinese—not least those who would found and lead the Chinese Communist Party—to this profound state crisis.[1] Policymakers and intellectuals saw the state as the center of a constellation of vital concerns. The state was indispensable to the maintenance of internal order and the preservation of China's long and vulnerable frontier.

This chapter is a revised and expanded version of "Chinese National Identity and the Strong State: The Late Qing-Republican Crisis," in *China's Quest for National Identity*, ed. Lowell Dittmer and Samuel S. Kim (Ithaca: Cornell University Press, 1993), 62–79. Cornell University Press was good enough to grant permission to borrow from that essay.

The state was expected to promote cultural orthodoxy, to patronize the arts and letters, and to ensure the proper functioning of key sectors of the economy. The state was, moreover, tied to the social order in a remarkable variety of ways; the proper functioning of one depended on the other. The state also stood as a cultural symbol with a place in a world of dreams and aspirations in which Chinese saw themselves as descendants of the great imperial regimes of the past and measured their own virtues and achievements against those of their worthy ancestors. The state was not only the mechanism for raising the prestige and dignity of China but also the mirror for reflecting restored glory. Only by resolving the crisis of state power would it be possible to achieve a modicum of security and stability along the frontiers, staunch the flow of resources being consumed by the indemnities and wars that a weak China's rear-guard defense of its interests gave rise to, stimulate economic development, turn back foreign economic and political penetration, and ultimately return China to a position of preeminence in Asia if not the world.

Politically engaged intellectuals displayed such a marked sensitivity to the health of the state and such a remarkable willingness to devote their lives to its recovery that they seem from an outside perspective obsessed. The contrast with a twentieth-century Filipino or a nineteenth-century American (to take but two possible examples) could not be greater. As Benjamin I. Schwartz has noted, there are good reasons for this Chinese obsession.[2] Chinese intellectuals knew the state intimately as the commanding feature of the historical, political, and cultural landscape, and as a structure of power whose fate was intimately tied to that of their own class.

"Patriotism" (aiguozhuyi), not "nationalism," is the term that best describes this set of concerns centering on the state. The latter term when applied to China is awkward in its paradoxes.[3] Chinese (or at least the politically dominant Han) have been both victims and perpetrators of imperialism. They have vigorously denounced the dominion of one state over another (especially when China was that other state!), but they have also been determined defenders of China's own multiethnic empire against foreign meddling and separatist movements. As a result, the Chinese elite has had difficulty seeing nationalism in a way that corresponds to any generally accepted definition. For them to emphasize the importance of shared language, myths, and cultural patterns as the basis of a nation was to sanction at least in principle the independent identity of other peoples—Mongol, Uighur, Tibetan, and Miao—and thereby to imperil the very multiethnic empire they were determined to defend. Those speaking for the Nationalist and Communist Party alike have responded that the "people" was not limited to the Han but also embraced the various "minority nationalities" (*shaoshu minzu*) living in China's far-flung territory, but their claim reminds us of the paradoxical quality of Chinese nationalism (a nationalism of multiple nations) and thus only heightens our doubts about the applicability of the term.

The term "patriotism" avoids these difficulties while boasting several advantages of its own. First, Chinese historians have recently begun to give greater attention to *aiguo* on the basis of compelling textual evidence that suggests the term enjoyed wide currency across political lines over the decades treated here.[4] Moreover, in the Chinese context *aiguo* has the additional advantage of suggesting links between the pre- and post-May Fourth intellectual world rather than allowing the Bolshevik revolution and the consequent impact of Marxism in China to slice modern Chinese history in two.[5]

Far from a fixed formula, patriotism embodied a set of concerns about the welfare of the state and China's greatness. Indeed, patriots advanced a striking and rapidly changing assortment of specific diagnoses and remedies for China's illness. The differences that developed among patriots turned largely on three issues, each essential to the proper functioning of the state and to any scheme to resuscitate it.

First, what ideology would shore up the state and give its operation legitimacy and direction? Could the state crisis be resolved within the framework of the existing imperial value system or some alternative indigenous system, or did it require the importing of some new, foreign-derived ideology?

Second, where were the cadres to come from that were to manage the bureaucracy and to occupy the leadership positions, and what rules were to govern their behavior? Here too the imperial system with its exams and elaborate rules of official behavior offered a foundation for reform. But as this system fell into disfavor, proponents of change would look elsewhere for ways to recruit and control political activists—to the secret societies, the Western parliamentary system, or the Leninist party model.

Third, who were the "people" and what was the proper basis for their relationship to the state? Though the people were always regarded as in some sense the foundation of the state, the precise identity of the people, the degree of popular involvement in saving the state, and the values that the "people" were to be mobilized on behalf of all gave rise to considerable disagreement.

Much of the impetus for wrestling with these questions through the late Qing and the early Republic would come from the repeated blows struck by foreign powers. Each new imposition or humiliation set off a wave of alarm among patriots by revealing afresh China's vulnerability and the inadequacy of previous efforts to reverse the crisis. Strategies for saving the state shifted rapidly as patriots of various persuasions experimented with different mixes of state ideology, political recruitment, and popular mobilization. They couched their appeals in ever more sweeping and radical terms. The self-strengtheners' modest hopes for institutional innovation would give way to calls for changing basic popular and political values, transforming society, and embracing a starkly internationalist foreign policy. What follows is a sketch of how several generations of the politically engaged beginning in the 1890s sought to think their way out of the downward spiral of defeat and weakness in which China had become caught.

The Last Years of the Qing

The patriotic response during the late nineteenth century has already been noted in the previous chapter. Both populists with their militant reaction to foreign intrusion and the cosmopolitans with their more measured, reformist program were deeply devoted to saving China, the dynasty included. Their divergent strategies had brought them into increasingly sharp political and ideological warfare throughout the nineteenth century. By the 1890s the repeated reverses both sides had suffered in their periods of political ascendancy gave rise to a tendency on both sides to transcend the conflict by borrowing from the program of the other. Thus winning the hearts of "the people" was important but so too were the initiatives intended to bring about significant changes in aspects of the Chinese polity, society, and economy. This syncretic tendency in effect took up and extended the self-strengthening program of institutional reform but supplemented it with an emphasis on the popular base of the state that echoed the views of the militants.[6]

A group of marginal intellectuals that included Wang Tao had helped to pull these two elements together. They articulated the familiar and fundamental concern with catching up with the power of the Western states so that China could compete effectively. But they also warned that the self-strengtheners had not gone far enough in winning popular support for government policy. "Of all the great evils in the world," Wang had written in 1893, "the greatest is when the people lack confidence in their rulers." China suffered from precisely that evil—"the failure of communication between ruler and ruled and the distance separating the sovereign and the people." To bring the two together would require institutional changes anathema to the militants but essential to opening avenues of expression for the bureaucracy and even broad sectors of the politically minded public.[7]

Writing against the backdrop of an almost feverish search for new policies, the reformer Kang Youwei skillfully drew these new ideas together. Take for example his 1898 memorials intended for the emperor himself: "Your official has heard that all the countries in the world today which have held to old ways have without exception been partitioned or put in great danger." With China helpless to stem the rush of foreign demands, it was evident that the state would have to undergo extensive renovation. China would have "to dismantle the building and build anew if we want something strong and dependable." The Meiji reforms in Japan offered one example of what vigorous action could achieve. Turkey and Poland, both helpless and exploited, were warnings of the disasters inaction would bring.[8]

Kang's proposals moved well beyond the more modest changes advocated by the earlier self-strengtheners to include a thorough shakeup of the bureaucracy, a top-to-bottom revision of economic and educational policy, higher taxes, a popular army equipped with the most advanced equipment, the removal of the capital to a more defensible position inland, and the development of an extensive railway system. Though all these proposals were intended to make the state stronger, Kang had not lost sight of the people. "If we cannot think how to foster those people, then we ourselves destroy our own foundation."[9]

Liang Qichao, a central figure in China's intellectual transformation at the turn of the century, carried forward Kang's analysis of China's crisis and prescription for integrating reform with populism. Like Kang, Liang had been deeply troubled by the relentless foreign penetration of China. Defeated in war, outmaneuvered in diplomacy, humiliated daily on their own soil, the Chinese were demoralized and uncertain how to fend off total subjugation. In the late 1890s Liang complained bitterly against the unending stream of contempt that Westerners directed against China in hopes of reducing the Chinese to passivity. "When they intend to conquer a country, . . . day after day they will criticize the corruption of that country's government, the disorder of its society, and the tyranny of its officials."[10] This foreign intrusion had greatly exacerbated what Liang saw as a long cultural decline from the diversity and vitality enjoyed before the Qin unification. The foreign presence also created worrisome divisions among the Chinese people, inducing shamelessly self-centered compradors and Christians to serve outsiders.

Also like Kang, Liang remained loyal to the Qing (to be sure after some vacillation) and pressed for an extensive, officially sponsored program of borrowing from abroad. He looked to Meiji Japan, where another Asian people had succeeded in turning back the foreign threat, as the best model for China to follow. Liang wanted Beijing now to emulate Japan and pursue a sustained, top-down effort at political integration, popular education, and economic development. A constitutional monarchy was one critical element. A parliamentary system would secure popular participation; it would bind the ruled to the rulers actively, not passively; and in the final analysis it would strengthen the state in its ability to deal with foreign affairs. Schooling was also important in inculcating new virtues that had served to make the West and Japan vital and dynamic. The new citizen in a new China would, unlike his forebears, be optimistic, active, future-oriented, productive, and, above all else, devoted to the nation. Finally, stimulating the capitalist ethic and industrialism in China would produce strength and prosperity. "If our people at this time could collect capital and use Western techniques to seek profit from our cheap labor, the national wealth would rush ahead, and after a decade no one in the world could withstand us."[11] Such a display of "practical statesmanship" would revitalize the state, create national "wealth and power," and shape a "new citizen" devoted to the interests of the nation.

Post-Boxer officialdom picked up the themes sounded by Kang and Liang (both ironically now exiles, having been branded traitors for their meddling in court politics). The disastrous Boxer crisis had silenced the last of the militant populists and cleared the way for official promotion of reform on a broad front. The result was a flurry of activity all intended to strengthen the state, restrict foreign privileges, and lay the basis for a constitutional monarchy.[12] Backing this ambitious program was a coalition that harnessed the heirs of Li Hongzhang such as Yuan Shikai, who were more interested in immediate gains in state power, together with former militants such as Zhang Zhidong and Xiliang, more preoccupied with popular mobilization.[13] These officials, resolutely loyal to the dynasty they served, hoped that a strengthened state backed by a public-spirited population would stem foreign encroachment.

A growing number outside official circles and some even within were, however, afflicted with growing doubts about the Qing commitment to either part of the patriotic platform, popular mobilization on the one hand and institutional change on the other. The result was a patriotism that took an increasingly anti-dynastic direction as the dynasty itself was cast as the major obstacle to China's salvation. A weak foreign policy did much to nurture if not create this sentiment. Even as foreigners continued to impose new humiliations and extract new rights and as patriots protested and sought to mobilize popular support and spur reforms deemed essential to saving China, Qing officials continued to acquiesce or temporize. If, as it seemed, the Qing could not reverse the country's declining fortunes, then China needed a political clean sweep, clearing the way for a republic that could save China.

These very calculations had made Sun Yat-sen an early, sharp critic of the Qing. The 1894 manifesto announcing the creation of his Revive China Society (*Xing Zhonghui*) contended that "our country can be invincible in the world if we are determined to make it strong. But incompetent courtiers who misruled our country and rode roughshod over the people have plunged it into an abyss of impotency." Reacting the next year to the disastrous defeat at the hands of the Japanese, Sun's society issued another manifesto passionately denouncing the dynasty for plunging the country into international peril. "The great Powers which surround China are like hungry tigers ready to jump upon their prey or like hovering eagles about to swoop down on their victim below. . . . They have grabbed pieces of Chinese territory one after another. The present danger is outright partition. Oh, what a fearful spectacle it is!"[14]

The Qing's cautious foreign policy after 1900 bred frustration and ultimately disaffection in a new generation. Protesters against Russian occupation of the northeast began in 1901 appealing to the court to save its ancestral land and to trust in support of the people. By 1903 protesters were sounding more militant in the face of the court's continuing failure to recover the occupied territory and its branding of criticism as sedition. More and more they identified the northeast as the land of the Chinese people and described the crisis as a test of popular vigor. With the court seemingly sunk in passivity, patriots were more ready to argue that nothing, including the Manchus, should stand in the way of saving China from partition by the powers. Chen Tianhua gave voice to this feeling in its fiercer form. "As the saying has it, a dog driven to the wall will turn and attack. Do you mean to tell me that four hundred million men are less than a dog at bay? . . . If the Manchus help the foreigners to kill us, then we will first exterminate the Manchus."[15]

The protest movement against ill-treatment of Chinese in the United States in 1904–1905 marked another step in this disaffection. Appeals to Beijing to take a firm stand reinforced by a boycott of American goods found the government at first cool and then hostile. Student activists along with merchants and women's groups had organized the boycott, and then when they failed to evoke the sympathy of Beijing, they began sharply to condemn Qing ineptitude and weakness. Finally, the central government, fearing domestic turmoil and trouble with the United States, turned on the protest, ordering officials in Canton and Shanghai to suppress it.[16]

By 1905 the anti-dynastic cause had won a considerable following, and Sun's new political vehicle, the United Alliance (*Tongmenghui*), emerged that year as the most visible force for the political revolution thought necessary to end China's crisis. Some patriots still could not accept revolution because they could not betray the dynasty that they had served. Others such as Liang Qichao feared that a political upheaval would open the way for foreign intervention and almost surely lead to popular excesses. But the Qing's constitutional reforms seemed to many a sham and its defense of China's international interests half-hearted. Thus Sun's diagnosis that China was "suffering from both the yoke of an alien race and the oppression of foreign powers" gained growing acceptance.[17]

Consistent with this political alienation, the alliance put growing stress on the Manchus as the root cause of China's crisis, and at times blamed virtually all China's ills on this "foreign" dynasty. Only a republic purged of all traces of those self-serving and inept Manchu rulers could make the state strong, win the support of the people, and realize long-standing patriotic goals—"to rescue the ancestral country" (as the woman revolutionary martyr, Qiu Jin, phrased it) or (in the more chauvinistic language of another prominent revolutionary, Song Jiaoren) to live up to "the mighty accomplishments of our ancestors over the past five thousand years—in conquest, administration, expansion of our national territory, and the elevation of our national prestige."[18]

The May Fourth Era

The 1911 revolution and the republican government that it gave rise to did not, to the dismay of patriots, resolve China's crisis. New political arrangements failed to bring unity and order, not to mention legitimacy. Representative government degenerated rapidly into an autocracy equally hostile to popular participation and impotent in foreign policy. Japanese encroachment intensified. The outbreak of World War I along with rampant political factionalism and the devolution of power under the Republic allowed Japan to tighten its grip on China. After taking Shandong in 1914, the Japanese government followed in 1915 with a collection of twenty-one demands designed to extend greater control over China's administration, economy, and territory. Finally, in 1917 and 1918 it granted political loans to the financially strapped government of Duan Qirui to ensure its dependency. These loans cleared the way for agreements strengthening Japan's claim to Shandong and extending broad rights for Japanese forces to operate in China (nominally in joint opposition to the Bolshevik threat). This aggressive Japanese policy and the supine attitude of the Beijing government had already provoked public demonstrations and boycotts between 1915 and 1918.

These developments revived the debate about how far changes in China would have to go. Was social as well as political renovation necessary, and, if so, how much of the old culture would have to be swept away? With the Manchus gone and China worse off than before, the question of "what next" confronted intellectuals and activists more starkly than ever before. They grappled with that question through the teens, a period of intellectual ferment and political chaos that would come to a climax with the May Fourth movement, so named for the date in 1919 when anti-government demonstrations exploded in Beijing.

Though China had joined in the war effort, there was no reward from the victorious Allies meeting in Paris. Quite the contrary, the settlement left in Japan's hands the German possessions in Shandong. That decision, reached on April 30, 1919, bitterly disappointed Chinese patriots, setting off demonstrations throughout China. They had hoped to see Japan surrender its Shandong concession in deference to a Chinese claim based on justice, strengthened by China's entry into the war on the Allied side in 1917, and seemingly sanctioned by Woodrow Wilson's call for respect for the principles of equality among all nations and respect for self-determination for each. But Britain, France, and Italy had stood by their secret 1917 agreements recognizing Japan's Shandong claims. Wilson had failed to hold his ground. The arguments of the Chinese delegation (representing a country divided politically into the Canton government as well as one in Beijing) had proven unavailing. News that the Allies had left Japan in control was, one Beijing University graduate later recalled, a great shock. "We at once awoke to the fact that foreign nations were still selfish and militaristic and they were all great liars."[19]

This shock ignited organized protests. Early in the afternoon of May 4, three thousand students from thirteen colleges and universities in Beijing gathered in front of Tiananmen, denouncing the Shandong decision. Their manifesto, drafted for the occasion by Luo Jialun, warned that the loss of this territory carried China an important step toward annihilation. It called on all citizens "to strive to secure our sovereignty in foreign affairs and to get rid of the traitors at home."[20] Those traitors were Cao Rulin, Zhang Congxiang, and Lu Congyu, all high-ranking pro-Japanese officials. The protesters marched through the central city to Cao's house, which they set on fire, and then beat Zhang when they found him there. Police finally abandoned their benevolent neutrality and arrested thirty-two students.

Their comrades continued to organize and agitate, while demonstrations spread to more than two hundred other cities. Another round of arrests in early June only served to broaden the base of support for the protest. So great did the popular pressure become that the Beijing government was forced on June 10 to announce the resignation of the three "traitors." On June 28 the Chinese delegation refused to sign the treaty sanctioning the giveaway of Shandong, and the Beijing government reluctantly endorsed their position.

Like earlier "foreign shocks," the Allied position forced on patriots a painful reappraisal. They could look back on eighty years of defeats and the steady decline of their country's standing in the world. The Opium War and the imposition of the first of the unequal treaties was followed by the loss of dependent states along the periphery, the deep incursion of foreign economic and cultural influence, and the repeated use of force and threats of force to guarantee foreigners their new-won dominance. Chinese policymakers had alternately responded with a stubborn policy of military resistance and diplomatic delay; bold initiatives in education, technology, commerce, and finance to make China stronger; desperate reliance on popular support; and expedient attempts to align with sympathetic foreign powers. All these strategies had failed, leaving patriots in ever deeper despair.

The string of setbacks encountered following the overthrow of the dynasty began to drive deep divisions among the ranks of patriots. Sun held the Nationalist Party to the task of restoring the state through a political revolution, and his successor, Chiang Kai-shek, kept on that course. As a patriot, he wanted a state strong enough to restore unity and order, end foreign humiliation, abolish unequal treaties, regain lost territory, and ultimately restore China's grandeur. But the chief means Chiang would rely on was military might; moral homilies and half-hearted efforts at popular mobilization were decidedly secondary to the main military effort.

For some among the students who took to the streets in mid-May 1919 and for their intellectual mentors, political revolution seemed less and less adequate to encompass China's salvation. The continued decline of the state and widespread popular apathy over China's future convinced them that only a China thoroughly made over could be expected to function effectively in international affairs, perhaps even survive at all. The idea of a revolution that would (in Liang Qichao's phrase) "make the people new" by effecting fundamental social and economic changes gradually gained converts.

This deepening concern with popular mobilization and transformation was reflected in the efforts of May Fourth demonstrators to reach beyond people like themselves—the well placed and the well educated. For the first time they sought to translate into action the long-standing concern with awakening the nation—above all, the overwhelming majority of the population that was not so well educated and hence cut off from the demonstrators' more abstruse statements, petitions, and appeals. In this innovative educational effort, patriotic and international topics figured prominently. For example, student teams that fanned out from Beijing University throughout the city on May 18 and 25, 1919 included prominently in their repertoire of topics the relation of the Allied settlement in Paris to world peace, the Shandong issue (dealt with from a variety of perspectives), the role of the citizenry in an awakened China, and China's defense against economic aggression.[21]

The conviction that the rebuilding of China would have to start from scratch and involved recasting basic political and cultural values predated May Fourth. In the years just before the revolution a small band of anarchists and socialists had rejected a simple anti-Manchu program as inadequate. They had already put social revolution on the agenda. Sensitive to contending class interests, they attacked inequalities of wealth, the bureaucratic abuse of power, the disabling illiteracy and ignorance pervasive in the countryside, and the oppression of women. Constitutional reform would not resolve these problems. Indeed, the elites promoting it would only strengthen their positions and their power over the disadvantaged. What China needed was fundamental change—the dismantling of elite power, land reform, universal education, and rights for women.[22] The New Culture movement initiated in the mid-teens extended and popularized this critical outlook, and added to the urge of intellectuals to explore iconoclastic foreign "isms."

The result was to push patriots into positions that seem paradoxical. To save China meant destroying important parts of it. The state would have to be torn down, and a society filled with pernicious practices and feudal attitudes would have to be uprooted. Only on a firm political and a fresh social foundation was it possible to build a new China. To save China also required patriots to put their faith in Russia, a country that only recently had been one of China's most dangerous tormentors. But the Bolshevik revolution seemed to offer the only successful model of social revolution and state building, and the USSR was the only power that appeared sympathetic to the aspirations of radical Chinese patriots. Finally, to save China required breaking down what little political order and unity was left in the name of anarchism, federalism, or revolutionary base-building.

While the resulting division and disruption might facilitate foreign meddling and impose domestic hardship, destruction of the old political and social system was the painful but unavoidable path to unity and order and ultimate renewal.

The Founders of the Chinese Communist Party

Out of the May Fourth generation came the founding members of the CCP. Some would survive the grim winnowing of the 1920s and 1930s. And out of those that were not lost to execution, assassination, exhaustion, or disillusionment would emerge the leaders who would in 1949 found a new state meant to realize long-nurtured patriotic aspirations. An examination of their road to social revolution and the resulting rough consensus about China's course in world affairs helps us to see from yet another angle the importance of patriotic concerns and the way that foreign crisis sharpened and radicalized those concerns.[23]

For the two leaders instrumental in the party's creation, Li Dazhao and Chen Duxiu, patriotic concerns gave urgency to their thinking about China's future. Wrestling with the problem of how to shake the elite out of its pessimism and the people out of their passivity ultimately carried both Li and Chen from their early studies in the classical curriculum to Marxism and a faith in the power of social revolution and an alliance with the Soviet Union to restore greatness to China.

Patriotism was particularly stark in Chen's thinking. Born in 1879 in Anhui province, Chen had been shaken in his youth by the foreign assault on China. In a pamphlet written in 1897 on the defense of the Yangzi from attack, he called for the government to act "to avoid the ruin of our nation" and for the people to awaken and "care about the fate of the country." Later, as a student in Japan, he reacted angrily to the Qing failure in the northeast, and helped organize a band of student volunteers determined to fight the Russians and stiffen the backbone of Qing officialdom. On his return to China he visited an uncle serving in the northeast, and there saw at first hand the Russian occupation. Once back in his native province, Chen joined the 1903 anti-Russian protests and helped draft an emphatically populist charter for a local patriotic society whose goals were to pressure the Qing and instill the people with a spirit of patriotism. "Because the foreign calamity is daily getting worse, the society seeks to unite the masses into an organization that will develop patriotic thought and stir up a martial spirit, so people will grab their weapons to protect their country and restore our basic national sovereignty." His own public comment at the time hinted at Manchu betrayal.[24]

Chen was also driven by a realization that China's society was rotten. The imperial examination was bankrupt, and to prepare for it, he recalled, was a torture. The exam itself, he remembered from his own experience in Nanjing in 1897, was "just like an animal exhibition of monkeys and bears performing every few years; and then I pondered whether this system was not as defective as every other system in the nation."[25] To pass the exam and become an official was, he concluded, to launch oneself on a career of swindling and aggrandizement that might honor ancestors and benefit family but not save the nation. By 1903 Chen had extended his critique to the Chinese people, who passively watched their country's humiliation and accepted its backwardness. He would never forgive the popular indifference to the patriotic imperatives that exercised such a strong hold on him and other politicized youths. As late as 1921 he was still harshly describing his countrymen as "a partly scattered, partly stupid people possessed of narrow-minded individualism with no public spirit."[26]

Chen's search for a way out carried him through several intellectual stages in a short time. He first fell under the spell of the moderate reformers Kang Youwei and Liang Qichao. He assigned responsibility for China's ills to flaws in the society created by China's rulers. Once those rulers and the social problems for which they were to blame were eliminated, China would move ahead rapidly toward wealth and power. When the 1911 revolution failed to bring the hoped-for era of rapid reform, Chen called for a more thoroughgoing reconstruction of China. Rethinking the meaning of patriotism in 1914, Chen rejected the traditional notion wherein the people were thought subordinate to and in the service of the prince. In its place he advocated taking up the kind of patriotism practiced in Europe and Japan. There, he had learned, the state served the people by safeguarding their security, welfare, and rights. The first and most important step toward such a refashioning of the political system in China was to alter the popular outlook. Writing two years later, he observed, "Our ultimate salvation must be sought through reform of the conduct and character of our people."[27]

In this phase of his intellectual journey, Chen was to establish himself as a leader of the New Culture movement taking form in 1915 and as editor of its most influential journal, *New Youth*. In 1916 he was appointed professor at Beijing University, and from that post advocated Western constitutional models, popular education, and basic reform of social values as the keys to China's salvation. He had already fastened on dedicated youth as the prime agent of this transformation, breaking with a bankrupt past and confronting the future in a confident, practical, and cosmopolitan frame of mind.[28]

By 1918–1919 Chen was poised on the edge of another major shift in his thinking. The disillusionment inflicted by the Paris peace helped move him forward. The Allied powers, whose cause he had earlier thought just, had proven to be the exact opposite. Their victory did not bring, as he had hoped, an end to militarism and inequality among peoples. "At the peace conference in Paris everyone of the countries emphasized our own country's [China's] rights. All fairness, all permanent peace, all President Wilson's fourteen-point declaration have turned into hollow words not worth a cent."[29] Chen was also moved by the Bolshevik revolution. Here was a case that seemed to fit his analysis of China's needs. A small, determined, and far-seeing group had seized power and set about transforming the old society.

Chen's support for the May Fourth demonstrations led to his arrest and two and a half months in jail. Once out, he began to look at China's problems in more explicitly Marxist terms. By December 1919 Chen had turned against the Anglo-American model of progress and democracy, stressing instead the danger that capitalism and imperialism posed. Now repelled by the materialism and exploitation that international trade and finance had brought to China's major cities, Chen wanted his country somehow to jump over the capitalist stage of development. Capitalism also fell under indictment as the source of China's international problems. Overproduction forced on the capitalist countries a frenzied search for foreign markets, leading to domination of other peoples and wars among themselves. As China had been brought under their sway, a Chinese bourgeoisie with interests tightly bound to that of their foreign patrons had emerged.

Chen saw China's hopes coming from two directions. One was the proletariat, the class most alive to the harm being done China and the core of any resistance to outside control.[30] The other was the Marxist program coming out of the Soviet Union. He accepted its promise of moving China toward a more just social order and toward a higher level of political and economic development than could be found in Europe, the United States, or Japan. In 1920 Chen (then age forty-one and living in Shanghai) turned to creating China's own Communist Party with the assistance of the Moscow-based Communist International (Comintern).

Chen's partner in that effort, Li Dazhao, is known for his internationalist loyalties, but even he demonstrates how a broader vista could evolve out of and continue to rest on a concern with China's regeneration. Born in Hebei in 1889, Li was raised in the house of his grandfather, a landlord. He began classical studies at age four, and left home at sixteen to attend a middle school that included Western subjects in the curriculum.

Like Chen, Li followed a tortuous path as he sought a solution to China's crisis. By the time he graduated from college in Tianjin in 1913, his views were a mix of Confucian and Western constitutional ideas. Underlying both was a desire to have a state strong enough to make China secure and a political system enlightened enough to protect the people's welfare against predatory politicians, bureaucrats, and warlords. In 1913 Li left to study in Japan, embracing there Sun Yat-sen's revolutionary goals. Li returned to China a confirmed constitutionalist, a strong admirer of European and American democracy, and an active opponent of Yuan Shikai's monarchical schemes. In early 1917 Li stepped up his attack on China's traditions, which (he contended) were responsible for choking off sprouts of democracy in China. He moved steadily toward the belief the old China would have to die and in its place "a new and glorious China should be born."[31] It fell to youth to create that new China. The next year he joined Chen at the journal *New Youth* and assumed the post of chief librarian at Beijing University.

In 1919 and 1920 following the May Fourth upheaval, Li turned to the close study of Marxism. Through his office passed such disciples as Zhang Guotao, Qu Qiubai, Deng Zhongxia, and Mao Zedong, all later prominent in the CCP, and through their hands passed the library's collection of literature coming out of the Soviet Union. Though not present at the formation of the CCP in 1921, Li did assume the direction of its Beijing area activities.

Two menacing international developments gave considerable impetus to the evolution of Li's thinking between 1915 and 1921, ultimately converting him to social revolution and a strong internationalism. One was the growing Japanese threat to China that so unsettled many of his peers. Japan's steady wartime encroachment caused Li to suffer great shame over China's decline from past eminence and to fear the prospect of his country's extinction (*wangguo*). Li was particularly disturbed by Japan's pan-Asian pretensions, which he regarded as a mask behind which that country's militarists and imperialists hid their ugly intentions.[32]

The other development was World War I and the Paris peace settlement. For Li, as for other Chinese observers, the behavior of the victorious Allies provided a fresh lesson in the ruthless nature of international politics. As the war came to an end, Li assigned its origins to economic imperialism that generated competition among the capitalist powers for foreign markets. He was thus prepared for the Allies' acquiescence in Japan's aggression. Their decision highlighted the treachery of a system run by the rules of "a robbers' world," one in which China could expect no justice.

Even China's professed friends were hypocrites. The American president talked of self-determination and then betrayed that principle and China's hopes. Li found in the West the same set of villains he identified in Japan—militarism and imperialism.[33]

In the face of these grim developments, Li found hope in China's people. Unlike Chen Duxiu, Li had an unshakable faith in the people as the prime source of the country's salvation. Responding in 1915 to Chen's sharp attack on China's bankrupt culture and backward people, Li pleaded, "We ought not to stop thinking about our country and refuse to love it because the country has deficiencies." He urged patriots to have confidence that the Chinese, like any other people, could transform their condition and restore "the springtime of our nation." Reliance on outsiders and such techniques as "barbarian management" to secure China would fail. "Those incapable of self-help cannot receive assistance from others," Li warned. The Chinese (including national minorities) had to save themselves by achieving popular unity and a sense of common purpose. Li pointed to a tradition of ever more vigorous popular resistance to foreign aggression going back to the Opium War as a hopeful sign of a rising patriotism and as the basis for a more self-reliant foreign policy.[34]

Li also hoped that the popular forces so strong in China also existed abroad and might ultimately create a new international order of peace and equality. Li saw elsewhere in Asia the most immediate counterpart and ally for the popular unity growing up in China. The weak and oppressed throughout the region had a common enemy in a Japan bent on domination. He expected that even the Japanese people would join in toppling their own rulers and creating this new regional order. China's struggle would thus not proceed in isolation, but neither was it simply one part of the broader process. Rather, in Li's view, "the rebuilding of the Chinese state and the revival of the Chinese nation was absolutely the key" to a regional revival that would itself in time merge into what he hoped would become a reorganization of the global system. As colonies and weak and small nations as well as peasants, workers, women, and children gained liberation, they would erase old boundaries and unify humankind into a new "great harmony" (*tatong*). "The contemporary era is an era of liberation," Li declared optimistically in February 1919; "the contemporary culture is a culture of liberation."[35]

Finally, Li found hope for China in the Bolshevik revolution, and increasingly thought of China's future as well as that of other peoples struggling for liberation in terms of the triumph of socialism. The failure of the experiment in republican government and the resulting rise of warlord governments led Li in 1918 and 1919 to follow closely news filtering into China about that revolution and to consider its relevance to China's future. In July he detected in the revolution with all its faults "the birth pangs of a new creation" not just for Russia but for the world. While the European countries had reached their peak and all would soon be on the decline, Russia was entering a period of vitality and ascendancy and bringing "the dawn of a new world civilization." That "revolution of the twentieth-century type," he wrote in December 1918, would sweep aside the "things that are the vestiges of history—all the emperors, warlords, aristocrats, bureaucrats, militarists, and capitalists."[36]

For someone impatient with China's seeming immobility and backwardness, he saw in the revolutionary upsurge in Russia a demonstration of how much could be accomplished in a short time. At the same time the spread of the revolutionary spirit out of Russia into war-ravaged Europe, so striking to Li early in 1919, gave assurance that a China struggling for rebirth would find a growing number of countries going through the same process and hence sympathetic to China's effort. He drew additional cheer from the decision by the new Soviet government to restore rights to China extracted by the Czarist regime, and praised this expression by the Soviets of a "humanistic and universal spirit" so exceptional among the powers of the day.[37]

Li's gravitation to the Soviet model reveals some of the same concerns that moved Chen Duxiu. Li viewed with antipathy the treaty port culture created by foreign penetration and did not want to see China's salvation held back by the painfully slow unfolding of capitalist development. Betraying a voluntarist bent that made human will more important than economic forces, Li thought a chosen few constituting a vanguard party could lead China rapidly ahead to socialism, even though peasants overshadowed the minuscule number of industrial workers. Rapid progress was in Li's view possible for a country that was in spirit if not in sociological fact a proletariat nation because he saw the country as a whole suffering, much like the proletariat in advanced countries, from domination and exploitation by the foreign capitalists. Thus backward China might with proper leadership quickly become one of the most advanced countries in a world turning to socialism. Here was a dream to entrance any patriot!

Political Heirs

The generation of intellectuals who were still students at the time of May Fourth were to play an unusually influential role in the shaping of modern China. "They defined parameters of thought and action in a decisive, innovative fashion," as one suggestive survey puts it.[38] Drawn into the nascent CCP by their mentors, most prominently Li and Chen, some of these young intellectuals began to take up the reins of power in the 1920s and 1930s, and a few would dominate the upper reaches of the party well into the 1970s.

Zhang Guotao, one to gain early prominence, nicely illustrates once again the way foreign aggression continued to spur patriots on. Zhang was born in Jiangxi province in 1897 into a well-to-do Hakka family whose recent degree holders commanded local prestige. He had begun his schooling in his county of birth, continued in the provincial capital, and finally enrolled in Beijing University in 1916. Fascinated as a youth by the rebel traditions of his birthplace and increasingly disturbed by China's ills, he had welcomed the 1911 revolution and admired Sun and his Nationalist Party.

Zhang himself has testified to his own early standing as "a passionate patriot," preoccupied with "China's becoming rich and powerful." The burgeoning Japanese ambitions in China between 1914 and 1919 and especially the twenty-one demands in 1915 inflamed his patriotism, and he "began to pore over the modern history of China and accounts of how India and Korea had lost their sovereignty. Many were the discussions I had with teachers and friends about how to save our country."[39] As a result, he joined in student efforts to boycott Japanese goods. In 1918 he participated in demonstrations against Japanese loans to the Beijing warlord government. When it became clear that the student voice was weak and ineffectual, he debated with his classmates whether new, more radical measures were needed to save the country.

May Fourth raised Zhang's concerns to a new pitch and drove him deeper into political activism. Disillusioned by Wilson and the injustices of the Allied settlement, Zhang reacted bitterly. As a leader of the student-initiated protest, he sought to reach out to his countrymen beyond the narrow circle of his Beijing University friends. In the immediate wake of May Fourth Zhang kept up his political activities, traveling to Shanghai where he met repeatedly with Chen Duxiu. There too he had the seemingly inevitable and embittering encounter with a foreign policeman that reminded him that Japan was not the only country holding China down.

Zhang returned to Beijing University in 1920 depressed by China's dim prospects. He had given up on Sun Yat-sen's narrow political vision and short-term goals, his inadequate resistance to foreign aggression, and his aloofness from the masses. Zhang began his study of Marxism and the Bolshevik revolution under the direction of Li Dazhao. Grasping eagerly at the possibilities for national salvation that he saw in this new ideology and foreign model, he joined the Beijing communist group in 1920 and the next year participated in the formal founding of the CCP in Shanghai.

Zhou Enlai, only twenty-one years old when the May Fourth movement began, brought to his politics the same strong patriotic concern seen in the other cases treated here. Born in 1898 in Jiangsu into a large and well-established gentry family, Zhou experienced an unsettled childhood.[40] His economically hard-pressed father entrusted him to Zhou's uncle. By the time he was ten, Zhou had lost first the uncle and then his wife. In 1910 he moved to the home of another uncle, a Qing official serving in Shenyang. Classically educated to this point, Zhou enrolled in 1913 in a mission-sponsored middle school in Tianjin, where he flourished. He was active in student theater, led student organizations, and won academic prizes. Already Zhou was displaying the traits associated with the future leader: a polished, engaging, and controlled personal style and a well-schooled and absorptive intelligence.

Restless to know more about the world beyond China, he left for Japan in 1917. He came back to Tianjin in 1919, and stayed long enough to enroll in Nankai University and take part in student demonstrations, for which he was briefly jailed. Almost hyperactive politically, he launched into a ceaseless round of meetings, protests, marches, publishing, popular education, and lecturing. He even used the time in prison to teach Marxism to cell mates. In mid-1920 he left for an extended stay in Europe, spent mostly in France. There he was active in the Chinese student community, helping to establish the European wing of the CCP in 1921–1922, editing a party journal, and working for the Comintern. Zhou returned to China in September 1924 to continue in Canton the collaborative work with the Nationalists that he had begun in Europe.

Zhou's early political views had been formed to some degree by the tales of rebels that he had been raised on as a child and by the personal exposure to Japan and Russia preying on the northeast. In middle school in the midteens Zhou had fallen under the sway of Liang Qichao, and his own school essays stressed patriotic themes, especially the importance to China's salvation of popular unity and popular welfare. A prize-winning student essay, written in November 1916 while Zhou was still in middle school, divided the world in two. Britain, Germany, the United States, and Japan were powerful and culturally advanced countries from whom Chinese should extract the secrets of wealth and power. The other group included such weak and backward countries on the verge of extinction as Korea, Egypt, and India. These latter countries also had lessons to teach—albeit distinctly negative ones.[41]

The late teens, coinciding with the World War and the disillusioning peace terms, marked an important new stage in Zhou's intellectual development. During his sojourn in Japan, he turned his attention to the socialist literature readily available there. By the time of the May Fourth protests he, like other agitated patriots, had begun to acquire an internationalist faith. For example, in August 1919 he appealed to Japanese students to overthrow their own warlords, bring an end to their country's aggressive spirit directed against China, and then unite China and Japan in one "national social movement."[42]

The ship to France onto which Zhou stepped in 1920 carried him toward an even more international and comparative perspective on China's future. From his observation post in France Zhou carefully watched great-power politics and the European scene. His extensive writings from those years reveal a strongly descriptive style, an easy command of detail, and a determination to grasp the chief contours of this new landscape. As an observer and reporter, Zhou would almost seem to be serving an apprenticeship for the foreign service.[43]

That ship also carried Zhou to a commitment to Marxism. As early as January 1921, at the very beginning of his residence abroad, Zhou wrote admiringly from London of the Russian revolution as an event of world historical significance. He announced that just as the Renaissance, the Reformation, and the French Revolution had propelled the West to the front ranks of civilization, so the explosion in Russia heralded an age of social revolution in which China would advance. The Bolsheviks had demonstrated how a swift, insurrectionary assault could be "effective in thoroughly cleaning out old abuses. If as in the case of China where long-standing abuses are so deep the French and Russian type of revolution is not followed, then it will not be easy to make effective changes." An article the following April on a British miners' strike introduced the idea of struggle between capitalists and workers and between bourgeois countries and proletarian countries.[44]

These early hints of a drift to the left became more pronounced in writings between February and August 1922. It was then that the telltale categories and topics—the references to "class conflict" and "imperialism," the Bolshevik revolution, the imperialists' global rivalries, and imperialist pressure on China—became a prominent part of Zhou's reportage. By the time of his return to China in 1924 Zhou had thoroughly assimilated his new Marxist outlook, and he had made imperialism one of the interpretive keys for understanding China. He made sense of a political scene where a complex network of warlord power almost defied analysis or prediction by pointing to the imperialists' backstage management. Each of the powers kept on retainer its own Chinese warlord and then used him to fend off international rivals and maintain its exploitative grip on China.[45]

But even after Zhou's pronounced intellectual turn to the left, something of the stylistic restraint and the preoccupation with the concrete remained in his approach to the broader world. In his later observations are no enthusiastic predictions of the global revolution in the making, no utopian hopes for liberation from the trammels of authoritarian systems of power, and no denunciation of evil exploiters. To the contrary, Zhou continued to reveal a marked capacity for empathy and an often striking reluctance to judge or impose outside categories of analysis. In his writings he would often assume the voice of the foreign leader or take the point of view of the country under examination. While interested in the implications for China of the international developments abroad he reported on, he often came to those implications almost incidentally, as though they were secondary to understanding the developments and the leading international actors themselves. The general impression left by Zhou's commentary, then, even after his shift to the left, is of someone with a gift for the descriptive, not the analytical, for the concrete, not the abstract, for the practical and immediate, not the soaring vision. Once again we see in the young Zhou a prefiguring of the style of the future leader.

The early years of Nie Rongzhen offers additional evidence of the link between patriotic frustrations and growing radicalism.[46] Born in Sichuan in 1899, Nie entered a modern school in a county seat in the immediate aftermath of the 1911 revolution. He himself became caught up in political protests while a middle school student in 1915. His involvement in the anti-Japanese boycott of that year was followed by another round of activism in 1919. Students then, Nie would later recall, threw themselves into the patriotic cause heedless of consequences, and they were caught up in a swirl of "isms," including socialism but even more prominently anarchism.

Determined above all else to see China made wealthy and strong, Nie resolved in 1919 to go to France to learn the requisite science and technology. His trip down the Yangzi River to catch his ship in Shanghai evoked (at least as Nie remembered it) raptures about the beauty of China's rivers and land but also resentment at foreign concessions in the treaty ports along the way and a heightened resolve to work to save China. Memories of a run-in with British authorities in Yichang during that trip would still trouble Nie decades later: "That a Chinese moving around on his own territory can unexpectedly come under foreign jurisdiction is really outrageous."[47]

While studying in France and Belgium, Nie's hopes and resentments carried him to the readily available communist classics. (He recalled initiating his education with Karl Marx's *Communist Manifesto*, V. I. Lenin's *"Left-wing" Communism, an Infantile Disorder* and *State and Revolution*, and Nikolai Bukharin and Evgeny A. Preobrazhensky's *The ABC of Communism* along with the CCP's newly inaugurated *Guide Weekly*.) "From the Marxist-Leninist theory I began to recognize that if one wanted to rescue the state and people from peril and to ensure clothing and food for all four hundred million countrymen, then there was nothing but to establish a workers' dictatorship and implement socialism."[48]

The discovery of an alternative road to saving China and feeding and clothing the Chinese people led him to join the European branch of the CCP in August 1922 and the CCP itself on his return to China in 1923. That commitment in turn led to formal political schooling first in Moscow where he was sent by the party in 1924, and then in the Whampoa Military Academy in Canton in 1925. Nie had begun his revolutionary odyssey along what was to be a long and twisting road guided from the start by patriotism.

The Young Mao

Mao Zedong, who was to emerge as the most prominent of the May Fourth generation, was also shaped by the patriotic spirit of desperate searching. Writing in 1952, Mao located the origins of the Chinese revolution in the popular resistance to the British invaders during the Opium War and flatly stated that "China's modern revolutionary struggle has for its goal, first and foremost, the opposition against the invasion of imperialism."[49] Mao's own early years reflect this symbiotic relationship between patriotic concerns and the turn toward radical social and political programs.

The young Mao Zedong embarked on what was to be an extraordinary personal journey from peasant origins to mastery over all China. Born in 1893 in Shaoshan, Hunan, Mao attended a primary school between 1901 and 1911 with three years off to work on his father's land. He moved to Changsha for further studies. But no sooner had he gotten there than he was caught up in the anti-dynastic cause and served briefly in the republican army. In 1912 he returned to Changsha, and in 1913 enrolled in a teacher training school in Changsha, from which he graduated in 1918.

In the years between 1917 and 1921, spent primarily in Changsha, Mao made the transition from student to teacher and finally to full-time politico. He engaged in student political activities, published his first essays, helped organize discussion groups, and promoted programs of popular education and study abroad. By 1918 he was teaching an evening class for workers. His gravitation to collective action and his fascination with the latent power of the people reveal an incipient populism evident in the figures sketched earlier in this chapter.

At this point Mao began to extend his horizons beyond the borders of Hunan, making the acquaintance of intellectuals in the more cosmopolitan Beijing and Shanghai. In September 1918 he moved to the capital, where he worked as an assistant in Li Dazhao's library at Beijing University. In 1919 he visited Shanghai to see friends off to study in France before returning himself to Changsha to begin teaching in the primary school and to edit two short-lived local journals, *The Xiang River Review* and *New Hunan*. After another prolonged visit to Beijing, Mao returned to Changsha in July 1920 to become director of the primary school section of a teacher training school. All the while he kept up his political activities and discussions.

Mao's politics were powerfully conditioned by an anxiety over the peril facing China. Mao entertained an ever more imposing picture of foreign power and an ever more alarming vision of China's vulnerability in an international order governed by amoral struggle. His earliest years had coincided with the loss of Korea and Taiwan, the occupation of Beijing, the repeated payment of indemnities to foreign powers, and the informal partition of the northeast, so all these events were fresh in mind. Sometime around 1910–1911, while at the Dongshan upper-primary school in Xiangxiang, Mao (then in his late teens) picked up an 1896 pamphlet on China's imminent dismemberment. It so impressed him that years later he could still recall its opening line—"Alas, China will be subjugated"—and his own feeling of depression "about the future of my country" and the dawning realization "that it was the duty of all people to help save it."[50]

In his quest to understand China's crisis Mao was, like his contemporaries, prompted by strongly patriotic feelings. Like them, he was concerned with the revival of state power and all that implied, above all the restoration of China's prestige and power in the world. Also like those contemporaries, Mao drew on a rich heritage—a robust and complex Chinese intellectual tradition—into which he sought to assimilate foreign ideas and foreign models. That quest sent Mao's early political views through an almost kaleidoscopic set of changes with all the dramatic twists and turns familiar from his contemporaries.

His thinking on international affairs appears initially to have drawn on the statecraft school with which both Wei Yuan and Xu Jiyu had been associated. Mao shared with them a longing for China's revival and security.

Mao also toyed with the balance-of-power expedient that had been a mainstay of late-Qing policy discussions. In a letter written in the midst of his studies in Changsha, Mao reflected on how Japanese aggression against China had gone unchecked, leaving the fate of Mongolia and the northeast in deep doubt and north China the next potential victim. Looking abroad, Mao suggested China enlist a major maritime power, the United States, in a joint effort to roll back the Japanese advance on the Asian continent.[51]

More influential still for Mao were the early-twentieth-century reformers, including Yan Fu, a translator of Western writings, and Kang Youwei and Liang Qichao. Liang's influence was especially marked. For a period in his middle teens (while still at Dongshan) Mao had been a devoted reader of Liang's journal, *New People's Miscellany*, and he had (in his own words) "worshipped" Liang. When he wanted to mobilize opinion in 1915 against Yuan Shikai's plan to reestablish the monarchy, he turned to the writings of Liang, including them in a pamphlet intended to rally the opposition. Even after Hu Shi, Chen Duxiu, and their journal *New Youth* had displaced Liang in the pantheon of his heroes, Mao continued for a time to cling to Liang's expressive writing style, a simple and clear classical language mixed with foreign words and slang.[52]

In the midst of the intense activities of 1917–1921 and intimately linked to them came a rapid, general development of Mao's political philosophy. He avidly followed domestic and international affairs and engaged in a fervent and self-conscious search for guiding principles. The resulting intellectual turn, strikingly evident by mid-1919, would create a complex and unstable amalgam of anarchism, populism, voluntarism, internationalism, and anti-imperialism that incorporated his once dominant patriotic concerns.

In 1917–1918, after much worry "over the coming destruction of our country," Mao had become convinced it could be averted, but "what I am not yet clear on are the ways in which changes can be successfully brought about."[53] Mao's outlook was strongly populist. "[I]f all the hearts in the realm are moved, is there anything which cannot be achieved? And . . . how, then, can the state fail to be rich, powerful, and happy?"[54] At the same time he supported a sweeping political and social overhaul of China and regarded a process of destruction as the precondition for reconstruction. Mao also expressed a strong ultimate faith in concentrated state power, firmly if not ruthlessly exercised, as the key to the livelihood of the people and China's survival. "The first and foremost need," Mao is supposed to have asserted at that time, "is for a strong and powerful government! Once that is established, the people could be organized!"[55]

Mao later recalled that his views following his arrival in Beijing in September 1918 were still jumbled—"a curious mixture of liberalism, democratic reformism, and Utopian Socialism. I had somewhat vague passions about 'nineteenth century democracy,' Utopianism and old fashioned liberalism." He conceded that even anarchism (a bugaboo within the early CCP) had had a place in this accumulation of ideas through which he was then sorting.[56]

The critical point in the evolution of Mao's view seems to have come in the middle of 1919. Mao had followed closely in the press the war in Europe and then the conference of the victorious allies meeting in Paris. He had been drawn into the May Fourth protest movement when it reached Changsha. Now after stepping back for reflection, he indulged one of those bouts of concentrated and focused activity that would characterize his later career. Composing rapid-fire, Mao filled *The Xiang River Review* with his observations influenced to an important degree by Li Dazhao. Mao's views began appearing in mid-July and continued into early August, when the local warlord would shut the troublesome journal down. Readers will search these early writings in vain for a system of thought, but they do reveal the further unfolding of what had begun as a patriotic preoccupation.

The most striking general feature of this commentary was Mao's now passionate preoccupation with political and social justice. In the very first issue Mao fused an enmity for the existing structures of authority with an emphatic expression of faith in the people to control their own destiny.[57] His "Great Union of the Popular Masses," serialized in the last three issues of the journal, again brought together the new elements in his thinking. Mao praised the Chinese people for their "great inherent capacities," and foresaw the overthrow of bureaucrats, militarists, and capitalists and the rescue of a Chinese people sunk deep in darkness and oppression. "The more profound the oppression, the greater its resistance . . . . [O]ne day, the reform of the Chinese people will be more profound than that of any other people, and the society of the Chinese people will be more radiant than that of any other people. . . . We must all exert ourselves! We must all advance with the utmost strength! Our golden age, our age of glory and splendour, lies before us."[58]

While Mao's concerns were largely with China, he was, like his contemporaries, to see China's problems not as unique or isolated but rather global in nature and solution. Already in the inaugural essay he had identified "international might" (*guoji de qiangquan*) among those repugnant structures of authority, naming Japan explicitly as one of those powers to be resisted and overthrown by the people.[59] By the time of his writing of "The Great Union" several weeks later, Mao was ready to press his internationalist theme harder. In a world in which the unity of the powerful, the nobles, and the capitalists had reached an extreme, countries had been ruined, humankind made bitter, and society closed in darkness.

The natural outcome of this imbalance—both within and among nations—was revolution, resistance, and popular unity. Mao claimed to see the first signs of this process not in China but abroad. It was dramatically evident, he contended, in the "Russian socialist revolution." In central Europe the revolutionary impulse was already finding an additional outlet. Germany, its international and political power broken, would soon become a communist republic, and then it would unite with Russia, Austria, Hungary, and Czechoslovakia. The strongholds of counterrevolution—France, Britain, and the United States with their strong societies and economies—might seem impregnable, but even in those countries labor unrest had already confronted the powerful officials and financial magnates with an unwelcome distraction just as they sought to concentrate on the Paris conference and control of defeated Germany and Austria. And in time those elites too would find their countries convulsed by class wars. Over the next ten to twenty years Mao saw Germany rising on the tide of revolutionary socialism, France sinking, and western Europe becoming an integral part of a global transformation.[60]

Mao was scornful of those Allied leaders who hoped to stem this tide. They were no more than a bunch of robbers bent on securing territory and indemnities. They cynically championed self-determination at the peace conference but denied it in practice. Mao urged his readers not to overestimate those strutting and proud gentlemen. Soon enough their victory would prove Pyrrhic. Mao confidently predicted from his Changsha vantage point the complete victory of international laboring circles and the extension of an already promising revolutionary pattern throughout the entire world, sweeping away even the most powerful resistance. In an article titled "Do Not Accept Industrial Despotism" Mao explained the simple populist key to this revolutionary success. When one person's refusal to bow down is supported by a multitude, when a soft protest turns into a thunderous one, then humanity will have reached a day of liberation.[61]

In early 1920, Mao (then aged twenty-seven and living in Beijing) confessed that he was still confused by all the "ism's" and doctrines clamoring for attention. His one firm conviction was that the Bolshevik revolution pointed to the future. He described Russia as the most civilized country in the world, a place above all others worth going to study. Writing in September, Mao again sounded the internationalist theme, attacking "chauvinism" (*daguozhuyi*), from which sprang (he contended in his first use of the term) "imperialism" (*diguozhuyi*), oppression of small and weak nations, and colonialism. Mao claimed to see many of the great nations quaking and self-determination carrying awakened peoples to independence. By the latter part of the year his admiration for the Soviet revolution was even stronger, and with it went a professed hope for a new international order and a tentative personal commitment to Marxism.[62]

On December 1, 1920 Mao wrote a remarkable letter to his friend Cai Hesen and others studying in France developing these points in more detail and even more emphatically. Mao claimed to share with his comrades in France the conviction that reconstructing China was inseparable from reconstructing the rest of the world. He deplored the tendency of most people to attend to their own country's selfish interests and to forget the collective happiness of humankind. In place of such narrow concerns, Mao advocated globalism (*shijiezhuyi*). It was understandable, he observed, for Chinese to direct their effort into the reconstruction of their own country. China was their home, and it was "relative to other places around the world more immature and corrupt." But Chinese should have a broader vision of their field of work to include other countries. "Helping the USSR in the completion of its socialist revolution, helping Korea to its independence, helping Southeast Asia to its independence, and helping Mongolia, Tibet, and Qinghai toward self-governing autonomy are all important."[63]

Mao went on to reject liberalism, anarchism, and democracy. They all sounded good in the abstract, but in reality, he had concluded, they did not work. He found most appealing an ideology that cast all people as compatriots, that asked each person to consider the welfare of others, and that was so international in its concerns that it would bear no patriotic color. As Mao understood it, these were the principles of socialism.[64]

In late 1920 and the early part of 1921 the New Peoples' Study Society and several other study societies that Mao had helped organize in Changsha served as the vehicle for his exploration of these newly glimpsed radical possibilities. Working through the New Peoples' Study Society in particular, he hoped to cooperate with comrades elsewhere in China as well as abroad, and thus all united address the questions relating to nothing less than the liberation of humankind.[65]

In three days of meetings of the society in early January 1921, Mao and his peers debated where change was to begin, what ideology was to guide change, and how rapidly it should be implemented. The members were divided, but Mao shared the dominant view that China's transformation was to be radical and internationalist and based on the Soviet model. China's problems were reflections of problems in the global system, and could be solved only through a common effort by oppressed peoples everywhere. Mao now confirmed his new found faith. He voiced his preference for the Russian model of reconstruction, and made clear his own acceptance of the radical methods of the communists (Leninism) and his conviction that the other ideologies were defective. Reform could only patch up problems, not solve them. Mao's ideological grip was (as he well knew) still weak, and so he suggested to his colleagues a six-month program of study focusing on five or six "ism's."[66]

By 1921 Mao's period of feverish intellectual exploration was drawing to a close. His sharpening political outlook had already carried him into labor organizing in December 1920 (an enterprise he would pursue for two years), and the following July he would be present at the founding meeting of the CCP. That same outlook would in years to come inform his attitudes as a revolutionary leader toward China's place in the world and the appropriate approach to external relations. And yet at the same time his acceptance of a Marxist creed as his formal faith and the ideological constraints imposed by membership in a communist party was to further complicate an already rich and varied body of thought.

Appraising the Patriotic Impulse

There are several points that are worth making by way of conclusion about the patriotism that gripped the politically engaged elite from the 1890s through the 1910s.

First and most important is the general point that political elites and political ideas do count. The patriots treated here played a pivotal role in interpreting and proposing responses to the internal erosion of social order and to the pounding administered by the powers. While domestic and international forces beyond the control of any individual or group can create revolutionary situations, it should be equally clear that the precise unfolding of the revolutionary crisis and its ultimate resolution has much to do with the guiding concerns of elites.[67] Political ideas are neither irrelevant nor merely a reflection of socioeconomic change, and thus the ends to which an elite seeks to harness the state are important to an evaluation of how a revolution unfolds.

Second, patriotism with its preoccupation with saving the state was a prominent feature of Chinese political life, considerably sharpened by the serious ills to which China was then prey. The patriots' remarkable fixation with the state derived from an imperial tradition that had inculcated a deep sense of personal and group responsibility for the collective good and made the state the prime agent of that good. We should not deprecate this concern with the state as a sign of political immaturity or national pathology. Nor should we evaluate it by standards derived from liberal cultures where the state is regarded with ambivalence and individualism is exalted.

Third, the most radical of the patriots had by the early 1920s wandered far indeed in search of the cure for their state in crisis. They had done so for good reason. They had become increasingly sensitive to the complex matrix in which that state functioned. For them the events of 1900–1919 had blasted some of the received wisdom about what it would take to save their country and led them to explore new options that might produce the sweeping change that China's case seemingly required.

On the domestic side, the network of ties between state and society seemed to doom simple political reform. The state, it seemed, could be transformed only if the program of transformation extended outward into the society. The state's ideology, its personnel recruitment, and its relations to the people and the elite would have to be rethought. But predictably those patterns of thought and interest tied to the state as it was would inspire resistance, and because the state's social entanglements were so extensive and at points deep, revolutionaries could expect the resistance to be widespread and stubborn. The growing realization of the power of this resistance to genuine revolution would in turn become the justification for ever more radical measures, further intensifying the conflict over the revolutionary road to China's salvation.

On the international side, a similar set of structural obstacles confronted patriots, and here too drove them to radical intellectual formulations. China was entangled in a global system whose dominant powers would stubbornly defend their long-nurtured interests in China, and as Chinese sought revolutionary solutions to the internal crisis, that foreign resistance would intensify. This opposition by the powers, by itself formidable, was augmented by the support of Chinese tied to foreigners economically, culturally, and diplomatically. To succeed, a revolution would need allies abroad as well as popular support at home. Thus internationalism as well as populism began to creep into the patriots' worldview to assume a strikingly prominent place by 1919–1920.

Finally, the attitudes discussed here have continued to inform Chinese political discourse. The patriots of the late Qing and the early Republican period became "ancestors" for later generations of Chinese intellectuals. Patriotism remains even today a vital tradition. Chinese still searching for

the right road continue to echo the plaints and aspirations of earlier patriots. In the following chapter we will see how the patriotic impulse carried
one portion of the political elite, the leadership of the early CCP, forward
to formulate and popularize a new, coherent view on China's place in world
affairs in the 1920s and early 1930s.

Chapter Four

The Rise of an International Affairs Orthodoxy, 1920–1934

The May Fourth era, long celebrated as a watershed in China's modern history, left its mark on foreign affairs as on other aspects of Chinese life. Consistent with that era's reputation for intellectual ferment, it should come as no surprise to find May Fourth's special foreign-affairs contribution in the realm of ideas—the coalescence of an interpretive framework that would exercise wide appeal in the 1920s, would become orthodoxy for the Chinese Communist Party, and would ultimately wield a powerful influence over the People's Republic of China. That framework of ideas was in effect a response to some of the classic questions already glimpsed earlier in the Qing and recurrent in the foreign policy of every nation. How does the international system work, and how do forces dominant within it shape, even harm, weaker members? Where in a treacherous world may reliable allies be found, and how much confidence can be placed in them? Finally, how should foreign policy serve those aspirations that define a nation's character?

By 1919–1920 Chinese across a broad spectrum of the political left had begun to articulate answers that fit neatly together. They stressed, first of all, the impact of imperialism on China—the system of domination and

The broad themes developed here were first explored in my "The May Fourth Era: China's Place in the World," in *Perspectives on Modern China: Four Anniversaries*, ed. Kenneth Lieberthal et al. (Armonk, N.Y.: M. E. Sharpe, 1991), 178–200. I am grateful to M. E. Sharpe for permission to draw on that essay.

exploitation thought to explain many of China's ills and most of its incapacity to cure them. Second, they moved toward a favorable estimate of the Soviet Union as a country whose revolutionary transformation offered a model to China at several levels. Finally, they emphasized their sense of community with other oppressed people, especially Asians, and their hopes that the collective effort of the weak could reform an international system originally defined and now dominated by the strong.

This reconceptualization of international affairs that developed during May Fourth and its immediate aftermath drew on an indigenous intellectual tradition and its strong patriotic strain. Those roots gave this reconceptualization power and durability even as the patriotic impulse took an increasingly cosmopolitan guise from the turn of the century. Chinese read translations of European writings done in Japan or by Western missionaries, and some Chinese traveled abroad to unravel at first hand the secrets of other societies that they might turn to China's salvation. In this way, old ideas and new preoccupations subtly intermingled. "The very richness of traditional political thought," Peter Zarrow has noted in his study of anarchism, "meant that Chinese intellectuals would confront Western ideologies in a spirit of creative eclecticism."[1]

A growing awareness of the Bolshevik revolution as an event relevant to Chinese aspirations helped reinforce this already pronounced outward orientation. The Bolsheviks had done for Russia precisely what many Chinese wanted for their own country; they had given Russia a strong state, a reformed society, and a new basis for foreign relations. When the Communist International (Comintern), established in 1919 by the new Soviet regime, sought Chinese allies in carrying out the world revolution, its representatives found a warm welcome, and for at least a decade they would trade on their special insights on political organization and political change, adding a fresh layer to Chinese views of the world.

Through the 1920s the new thinking on international affairs associated with the Comintern gripped the imagination of a surprising range of Chinese of diverse intellectual tendencies. Informal study groups scattered all across China explored this new thinking, while it exercised a strong appeal within the Nationalist Party led by Sun Yat-sen, most notably among the left-wing but even for a time among centrists. Even after Chiang Kai-shek reoriented the party in 1926–1927—attacking the CCP and rejecting Soviet patronage—these new views retained something of a foothold among some of his colleagues. Intellectuals operating outside any organizational framework—first anarchists and reform socialists and later Trotskyites—also embraced and helped popularize the new thinking. Even the warlords who held sway in Beijing and elsewhere employed the vocabulary associated with this radical reappraisal of international affairs.

But of all the political participants of the 1920s and early 1930s, the CCP would prove the most consistent, determined exponent of this fresh outlook. The foreign affairs orthodoxy was an important component in party formation. It helped give a struggling political movement an identity—a sense of its place in Chinese history and in the ongoing global struggle for a new order. The CCP thus could lay claim to ancestors, locate friends and potential allies from whom it might win support, and define its enemies and the relationship among them. At the same time the orthodoxy had strategic implications. If the CCP were to play a leading role in China's revolution, it had to understand the international environment that both constrained and opened opportunities for party action. Successful revolutionary strategy depended on grasping the intention and potential of the major powers in China and their links to China's class structure (and their putative military and political expressions).

The CCP formally became a party in July 1921, when delegates to its First Congress met secretly in Shanghai to draw together leftist study societies located in a half dozen major cities in China as well as Paris and Berlin. Much of the impetus, not to mention budget, came from the Comintern representative, Grigori Voitinsky. It was a slow start. The party at the time of the First Congress could claim no more than fifty members, and it did not gain even a semblance of ideological coherence and organizational discipline until the party held its Second Congress in July 1922.

The Second Congress deserves special attention for its "manifesto," the CCP's first integrated appraisal of world affairs and Chinese foreign relations.[2] That document stands in effect as the transition from earlier, intense, wide-ranging inquiry to an orthodoxy that would last into the 1950s and to some extent even beyond. The manifesto divided the world into three parts. One belonged to imperialism, which had since the Opium War steadily preyed on China. The second was given over to the Soviet Union, whose Bolshevik revolution offered a model and created a supporter for China in the battle against world capitalism. The third was made up of the national revolutionary movements, especially those in Asia, that had sprung into existence since World War I and that shared China's commitment to the overthrow of imperialism and feudalism.

The elements in the three-worlds view would stand in a strikingly stable relationship to each other through the 1920s and into the next decade. The first world of imperialism and the second of the Soviet Union would dominate in CCP commentary on world affairs, while the third world of fellow revolutionaries would occupy a decidedly subordinate place. A 1923 resolution, passed by the party leadership, nicely registered this sturdy hierarchy of concerns. It gave highest priority to battling the imperialists, especially Britain and the United States. Good Sino-Russian relations, including formal recognition of the USSR, came next on the list of ten practical concerns then entertained by the party. Attention to the revolutionary movements of colonial and semicolonial peoples was relegated to ninth place. Major statements appearing as late as 1934 continued to affirm the fundamental three-world view and to rank the constituent elements in the same order.[3]

This ranking made good political sense. Both the imperialist powers and the Soviet Union could influence the future of China for better or worse, and thus party policy and propaganda had to take them into daily, detailed account. By contrast, the weak and oppressed of other lands bore little direct relevance, for the moment at least, to Chinese political life, so they could be put on the margin of practical party concerns, even while the abasement of other peoples remained a highly charged, symbolic issue.

While the CCP that issued the 1923 resolution was ideologically precocious, it was still organizationally in transition. It struggled to measure up to the Leninist ideals of a centralized, disciplined party with a committed mass base. Hendricus Sneevliet (alias Maring), a Comintern operative, reached China in spring 1921, in time to guide the CCP through its First Congress, and then stayed on to press for tighter organization and greater discipline. But Chen Duxiu, who led the party through the first six years, chafed under Sneevliet's guidance and Comintern oversight. Largely autonomous branches in turn bridled at attempts by Chen to impose central control, each preferring instead to go its own way in efforts to win worker and peasant support. By the time of his departure in fall 1923 Sneevliet had made some headway in centralizing the party through the creation of a central bureau with real authority. On the downside, party membership was still minuscule (no more than 420),[4] its treasury empty, its leaders at odds, and its grass-roots efforts to win a mass following vulnerable to offended warlords and rural elites.

The CCP of 1923 was also about to embark on the first of a series of political experiments conceived in Comintern laboratories and carried out under the watchful eye and sometime the prodding hand of Comintern envoys, confident masters of the science of revolution. Each of these experiments would fail, repeatedly engulfing the CCP in crisis.

Sneevliet devoted himself to pushing the CCP into cooperating with Sun's Nationalist Party. For a time at least this alliance considerably enhanced CCP influence. The CCP's membership soared at mid-decade, and by 1927 the party could claim a following of 57,300. Many joined in the wake of an attack by foreign police on student demonstrators in Shanghai on May 30, 1925. As the sense of outrage spread through urban China and as the Nationalist army moved northward against warlord and foreign resistance, the CCP boosted its influence. It made its most dramatic gains as the sponsor of mass organizations, though it had yet to forge the proletarian spearhead conventionally associated with a bolshevik organization yet so elusive in practice not only in China.

Then disaster struck. Following Sun's death in 1925, Chiang Kai-shek emerged as the leader of the Nationalist Party. In 1926 he began to signal his intolerance toward Communist influence, and in April 1927 turned with ferocity on his erstwhile allies. A violent purge of CCP elements in Shanghai soon spread to other areas and severely weakened the party's grip on its urban strongholds. This costly betrayal precipitated Chen's ouster as party leader. He was followed in turn by a rapid succession of others—first Qu Qiubai, then Li Lisan and Zhou Enlai, and finally Wang Ming (Chen Shaoyu) and Bo Gu (Qin Bangxian)—each anointed by the Comintern and each constrained by Comintern policy.

By 1930 the CCP could maintain at best a furtive underground existence in the cities, and so increasingly it shifted to the countryside and a self-protective militarization. Those elements of the CCP forced to operate in the most remote, rugged terrain launched the final experiment of the party's formative years. For a time in the early 1930s this rural strategy pulled the party from the brink of extinction. By 1933 the CCP could claim 300,000 members. The highlands of Jiangxi province anchored by the Jinggang mountains emerged as the most formidable of the rural base areas. In November 1931 the party declared the region a soviet republic with its own army and government. By January 1933 the entire Central Committee had abandoned Shanghai for the relative safety of the Jiangxi Soviet, in effect conceding that the party's new center of gravity was in the countryside.

By then, however, the southern base areas were approaching their end. After four unsuccessful extermination campaigns, the Nationalist army finally succeeded in its fifth attack against the Communist "bandits," sending 80,000–90,000 party faithful in October 1934 in retreat to the west. The ensuing odyssey, known appropriately as the "Long March," would consume over a year of extraordinary hardship, winnow the ranks of the party faithful, and set off turmoil within the leadership.

Although another experiment had ended badly, the international affairs orthodoxy was paradoxically stronger than ever, at least within the party that was now left its sole organized proponent. That orthodoxy deserves closer examination with a special eye to its origins, core beliefs, and broad if uneven appeal extending for a time well beyond the CCP.

The Nature of Imperialism

At the heart of the May Fourth outlook on the world was a picture of China beleaguered by imperialism. That widely used term was taken by most who invoked it to describe a condition of economic exploitation and political and military domination imposed on China and other weak countries by the stronger states of Europe, the United States, and Japan. For many Chinese, imperialism was also associated with the ultimate, long-feared threat of territorial partition and national extinction at the hands of the major powers.

The concept had a dual appeal: it offered a systematic explanation for the workings of the international system then tormenting China, and it served as a politically effective rallying cry for Chinese deeply aggrieved by foreign encroachment and abuse. Already in the 1920s the Communist and Nationalist parties and even at times the warlord governments in Beijing had embraced the concept and used anti-imperialism to mobilize popular support against Japan, Britain, and the missionary presence. As the national revolution gained force in 1925, anti-imperialism occupied a prominent place in the political instruction for enlisted personnel and officers in the army and activists in mass organizations. Indeed, talk of imperialism could be found in the standard discourse of the politically engaged, whatever the party or region.[5] And even after the Nationalists turned on the left in the late 1920s, discussions of imperialism with a distinctive Leninist thrust continued to appear in print.[6]

Imperialism proved an easy concept for twentieth-century Chinese to embrace in part because it corresponded to a picture of the world derived from long contact with Westerners along the coast and from an even longer experience on the inner-Asian frontier. Chinese observers of the early Canton trade regularly commented on the foreigners' dependence on Chinese goods. The resulting conception of foreigners gave prominence to their economic activity and needs, even their greed and obsession with commerce. The conflicts of the nineteenth century added to this notion the image of foreigners as beasts with rapacious natures ready to devour China and the Chinese. Deepening foreign economic and cultural penetration evoked yet another facet to this picture of foreigners—as people able to turn the loyalty of Chinese. "Rice Christians" converted, so it was charged, to gain the protection and resources at the command of missionaries. Merchants operating in the treaty ports fell into the clutches of foreign companies, foreign powers, and foreign interests. Youths who went abroad to study returned bearing a disturbingly foreign imprint. Even high officials were tainted by daily contact with foreign envoys. The behavior of an alarming range of Chinese seemed to support this view of betrayal from within so popular with foreign policy militants.

The observations on foreigners also gave rise to a more self-confident view of international relations that was also to find its way into later notions of imperialism. The greed and rapacity of foreigners offered a handle that might allow Chinese to control them. The "barbarians" could either be tamed by satisfying their hunger or pitted against one another by manipulating their greed. As indicated earlier, this notion that contradictions existed among the powers and gave rise to competition for international advantage informed even early attempts at "barbarian management," and saw further development as Li Hongzhang, Zhang Zhidong, Yuan Shikai, and other late Qing officials battled to defend China's frontiers and blunt foreign penetration. A special favor granted to one demanding power might appease its greed and lead it to resist other, still more rapacious powers.

There was yet another, ambivalent reaction to foreign power that would find a place in later views of imperialism. Late Qing students of the world were fascinated by the strength and prosperity of Western countries and especially by the science and technology that allowed them to work economic and military miracles. But the very societies that worked these miracles were also marked by glaring deformities. Their political life was driven by repellant opportunism and self-interest. Religious superstition was incredibly widespread. Individualism and egalitarian behavior led to a lamentable "anarchy" in situations that called instead for a sense of ethics, ceremony, and mutual obligation. Chinese observers were left with the puzzle of how to explain economic success in societies gone so obviously wrong in other respects. Imperialism would offer a way for some out of their perplexity, reconciling the materially attractive to the morally repugnant.

These various preoccupations and convictions about foreign societies and international behavior were incorporated into the Chinese understanding of "imperialism" (*diguozhuyi*), a term that politically engaged intellectuals began to embrace around the turn of the century. They were schooled at first by liberal, socialist, anarchist, and other foreign literature that was reaching Chinese through a variety of sources.[7] These later intellectual influences did not challenge the older, indigenous notions of imperialism but rather made them "modern" by investing them with a conceptually sophisticated, "scientific" gloss.

Even so, those embracing the notion of imperialism were far from agreed on its specific meaning. The reason is simple. They combined the older perceptions of foreigners in a variety of ways, and they, moreover, made different uses of the foreign literature on imperialism. The divergent understandings of imperialism that resulted served in a sense to update an older argument between militants determined to turn back the foreign threat at once and at all costs and moderates given to temporizing in foreign affairs, the better to concentrate on a long-term strategy of internal strengthening. By 1905–1907 those persistent differences were reflected in a debate between reformers and revolutionaries that turned in part on the significance each assigned imperialism and the most appropriate response to it.[8]

Speaking for the reformist outlook, Liang Qichao saw imperialism as a formidable threat. Arising from foreign economic needs, it was (he contended) having a destructive impact on China. By 1904, after residence in Japan and travel through the United States, Liang had identified the great industrial trusts that had arisen in the major Western countries as the new motor driving the major powers to compete for effective control of yet untapped markets and sources of raw materials. When the trusts failed in their attempts to control overproduction, the imperialist powers moved to secure those markets and raw materials essential to their economic stability and survival. In some cases they established their control through direct rule as the United States had just done following its conquest of the Philippines or as the British had done against the Boers in South Africa.

But as he looked at China, Liang recognized the danger that imperialists might secure their control just as effectively by indirect means, so that economic advantage could be had without the burden of colonial administration. He saw the imperialist powers using their excess capital to bring the Chinese government under their sway. This influx of foreign money also carried the danger of enslaving the Chinese economically and replicating the social ills already evident in capitalist countries. Chinese had to unite against this threat, Liang contended, and support their own capitalists using cheap labor and Western techniques "so that enterprises can develop and oppose the foreigners."[9] Liang argued that if Chinese turned against one another in revolutionary violence, they would only create new opportunities for further imperialist gains.

Hu Hanmin, a close associate of Sun Yat-sen, responded for the revolutionaries. They played down the imperialist danger consistent with the priority the United League (*Tongmenghui*) placed on the overthrow of the Manchu dynasty. Hu himself disagreed with Liang on two key issues of enduring significance. First, foreign capital and trade were not inherently dangerous to China. Trade could be mutually beneficial, and a China that could not (according to Hu's calculations) generate internally the capital needed to create a modern industry had to look abroad for financing. Second, Hu rejected the economic interpretation of imperialism. To be sure, in his opinion Chinese had to bring the foreign presence under control and reclaim lost rights, but this was a political problem that could be resolved through a negotiated readjustment of Sino-foreign relations. The high costs to both Chinese and foreigners of a prolonged conflict left as the only reasonable course economic cooperation and political accommodation between China and those now prone to imperialist behavior. Such at least was Hu's conclusion.

Sun and his aides in the Nationalist Party retained views through the 1910s and into the early 1920s consistent with the position that Hu Hanmin had staked out.[10] Imperialism was fundamentally a political phenomenon and by no means an inevitable stage in the development of capitalism. Imperialism stood in their view not as an expression of the needs of a dominant economic class within the major powers but rather as a reflection of those conditions of domination and abuse that arose from inequalities of power among states. The strong, driven by a nationalist dread of insecurity or the desire for aggrandizement, would lord it over the weak, seizing their territory, interfering in their politics, and exploiting their economy.

But because imperialists were guided by political calculations of self-interest, they could be reasonable. As long as aggression remained a paying proposition, they would persist. If, on the other hand, the dominated fought back and thereby raised the cost of domination or offered attractive concessions and thereby raised the benefits of accommodation, then the imperialists would adjust their positions. Just as Sun saw imperialists susceptible to suasion and averse to conflict, he saw a strong and united China as the ultimate antidote to the imperialist threat. China would "no longer be humiliated and partitioned by other nations," and would then rise to the ranks of the world's great powers, so Sun had observed in 1912 while promoting a grandiose railway development plan.[11]

Sun and his immediate associates thus rejected the view that the economic drive of the imperialists was inherently dangerous. Once the Chinese state could regulate and police foreign enterprise, the former imperialists could be made to serve China's economic development, while earning a reasonable profit for themselves. Sun cited the experience of Japan as well as North and South America to support this view that foreign investment could be beneficial if properly controlled. In any case China had no other road to rapid industrialization. "Everywhere in China, production is not yet developed, our people are unemployed," Sun had complained in 1912 as he laid out a plan for attracting foreign investors. "If we can introduce foreign capital, create employment, then Chinese need no longer be hired laborers for others, while our domestic production will be greatly multiplied."[12]

This conception of imperialism gave Sun and other Nationalist leaders, long frustrated in their pursuit of power, a valued degree of political flexibility in seeking international backing. By thinking of the links between imperialism and capitalism as loosely drawn, Sun embraced a relatively positive appraisal of the foreign presence. A cooperative, open-door foreign policy could contribute to China's modernization and defense. Sun's position had the practical virtue of signaling an interest in accommodation to powers who continued to exercise considerable influence in Chinese politics and hence over the fate of Sun's movement. It also served to sanction the concessions to foreigners that Sun had made a political stock-in-trade. To win fresh resources to overcome his domestic rivals, Sun regularly held out the promise of some economic contract or advantage to be granted once his movement triumphed. Knowing that the political enemy, imperialism, could be made into an economic friend made such seemingly opportunistic attempts to buy foreign support more defensible.[13]

The Nationalist Party's conception of imperialism, never theoretically or systematically developed, moved leftward in the mid-1920s when Sun accepted Comintern support. In 1923–1924 formal party statements pictured China as a victim of "foreign economic imperialism." Backed by an aroused popular nationalism, the Nationalist Party committed itself to liberating China from foreign control through a sweeping program of treaty revision and nationalization of strategic sectors of the economy. Those party statements also blamed warlords, who were blocking the Nationalist way to power, for collaborating with imperialists, sowing chaos, and inhibiting economic development.[14]

In January 1926, in a further swing toward the Comintern position, the Nationalists formally embraced a more emphatically economic understanding of imperialism. Capitalist societies were in crisis and proletariat forces were arising around the world. "Imperialism has now approached its end and the time of its collapse is in sight."[15] Consistent with these themes, the Nationalist Party gave greater play to imperialism as a target of mass mobilization during the northern expedition.

All that changed after Chiang Kai-shek turned on his Communist allies in 1927 and completed the northern expedition in 1928. He was thereafter to play down mass movements as an instrument of foreign policy and to conciliate the Western powers the better to pursue state-building and limit Japanese demands. This gradualist and accommodating approach, restraining even the campaign to end the unequal treaties, reflected a conception of imperialism consistent with Sun's. Chiang's preoccupation with restoring moral standards and regaining cultural moorings left little room for an economic, class-based interpretation of China's debasement, division, and demoralization at the hands of foreigners. The left-wing of the party attacked Chiang for his caution, and fought a rear-guard defense of the principle of popular anti-imperialism previously so important to the Nationalists. An organized Chinese people were "an invincible force and will easily destroy all imperialist powers," one prominent left-winger contended in 1928. But by 1931 the left had lost its fight.[16]

The conception of imperialism that would prevail within the CCP was more emphatically economic, considerably more schematic, and decidedly more durable than the views that prevailed in the ranks of its rival. The CCP moved quickly in its early years to define and promote an economic conception of imperialism aided by a multifaceted educational effort on the part of the Comintern.

In this ideological effort the CCP's first generation did not start from zero. As we have seen, the term *diguozhuyi* had already begun in the May Fourth period to find its way into the vocabulary of those prominent in the early CCP. The Marxist study groups that had sprung up in Shanghai, Beijing, and other cities immediately following the May Fourth demonstrations took the next step, working through the available fragments of the Marxist-Leninist canon, sometimes with the help of newly arrived Comintern envoys.

By 1922 the CCP had formally taken as its own a thoroughgoing, theoretically grounded, economically deterministic conception of imperialism. The manifesto adopted at the Second Congress announced that millions upon millions of people in the major capitalist countries "were severely oppressed by an extremely small number of bankers, industrialists, and their government." Plagued by overproduction and haunted by social revolution, those powerholders had for their survival to look abroad to intensify their exploitation of "the resources and labor of the colonies and small and weak nations." At the same time each of the powers had to accommodate to the other, equally pressed capitalists in order to avoid destructive conflicts among them. This international system had made

China their joint victim, subjected to acute economic exploitation and oppression as well as deep social and political division. Not until imperialism was overthrown would it be possible for the Chinese people to reach their goal of "equality and self-determination."[17]

The CCP made a sustained effort to explore and popularize anti-imperialism as a central tenet of its faith. Party members did not gain access to Lenin's actual text until 1925 when Ke Bainian writing under the pseudonym Li Chunfan supplied the first translation.[18] But there were other authoritative Soviet sources to which they turned. Nikolai Bukharin's *The ABC of Communism*, coauthored with Evgeny A. Preobrazhensky in 1919, served as a primer for Chinese just as it had for the Soviet Communist Party. It included a brief treatment of the basic dynamics of imperialism arising out of advanced capitalism (finance capital) and pointed to World War I as a product of intensifying imperialist rivalries. Joseph Stalin's *Foundations of Leninism*, based on lectures delivered in April 1924 shortly after Lenin's death, was another widely read text. Stalin opened with a schematic treatment, stressing the sharpening contradictions that would eventually leave imperialism moribund. One set of contradictions was marked by the struggle between labor and capital. Another was among "the various financial groups and imperialist powers in their struggle for sources of raw materials, for foreign territory." But it was Stalin's third set of contradictions to which his Chinese readers were most attuned—the battle between the "handful of ruling 'civilised' nations and the hundreds of millions of the colonial and dependent peoples of the world."[19]

The CCP made its own contributions to the educational enterprise, though working to be sure within the conceptual framework handed down by the Comintern. Party journals devoted a good deal of attention to imperialism. For example, *New Youth* between 1921 and 1926 devoted approximately forty-five percent of its articles to Lenin's notion of imperialism, either as a theoretical construct or as a way of understanding China's problems. The party's chief public voice from September 1922 to July 1927, *Guide Weekly*, featured regular, detailed commentary on the maneuvers of the imperialist powers and their machinations in China. While providing party leaders an opportunity to exercise their theoretical muscle, these accounts served to popularize among rank and file as well as sympathetic nonparty readers a Leninist understanding of China's place in the world.[20]

CCP guidelines laid down in 1925 made study of imperialism one of the major topics for party training. Both activists going through the basic course and cadres ready for more advanced study went through the same fourteen-point catechism. "What is the goal of capitalists when they unite in trusts and syndicates?" "Why does the bourgeoisie of all the countries fight for markets and colonies?" "Give concrete examples of direct exploitation and oppression of Chinese workers and the common people by the imperialists and foreign capitalists (including Christian mission schools)." A reading of Ke's translation of Lenin followed by group discussion was supposed to help party members grasp "the central idea": "(a) The development of imperialism has caused the division of the world into two big camps. In one camp are the proletariat and poor peasantry of all countries and the oppressed peoples; in the other, the bourgeoisie of all capitalist countries and their imperialist governments; (b) China is one of the oppressed peoples and the imperialists have oppressed her politically, economically, and culturally."[21]

This emerging CCP view of imperialism was substantively at odds with Sun's in two respects. Perhaps the more superficial distinction was the CCP's acceptance of the idea that imperialism was not accidental or contingent behavior but the inevitable result of capitalist development. It was not the expression of political calculation or nationalist impulses but the consequence of economic maldistribution, which left no solution to mature capitalism but to turn to foreign markets for relief from domestic crisis. But in fact this notion was a premise of CCP views, not a major proposition subjected to elaboration and illustration through detailed treatment of conditions in foreign countries. To the contrary, CCP discussions of imperialism were notable for their neglect of the wellsprings of behavior on the part of the major capitalist powers.

The other, more crucial distinction separating the CCP from the Nationalists was the former's antipathy, developed well before 1921, for what were seen as the pernicious effects of imperialism on China. It divided and degraded the Chinese people, and hence accommodation of the sort that Sun envisioned was difficult to stomach. One obvious source of this conviction was Comintern gospel. The other was Chinese patriotism reinforced daily by a visceral reaction against the foreign impact in Shanghai and other large treaty ports. Foreigners dominated the coastal economy and exploited Chinese workers, leaving the many in squalor while a few enjoyed great wealth. Foreigners controlled the local government. Foreigners ran the modern schools. Chinese merchants, students, politicians, and warlords all flocked to embrace foreign ways and accept foreign direction. One party notice in 1929 neatly articulated what had become a truism about foreign seduction and indigenous betrayal: "Whichever one of the imperialists wants to dominate China must collude with one of China's factional forces; whichever one of China's factional forces wants to maintain its rule must tap the secret support of one of the imperialists."[22]

By mixing patriotism (perhaps even xenophobia) with Marxism-Leninism, this Communist view created an internal tension familiar from the history of other communist parties.[23] On the one hand, imperialism was supposed to serve an important historical role as a powerful force for progress among colonized and dependent peoples. CCP members seeking solid theoretical grounding in Soviet works could have little doubt on this point. One of the texts used for the education of CCP cadres in Moscow, Nikolai Bukharin's *Historical Materialism: A System of Sociology* (first published in 1925), described China in its only reference to that country as "a stagnant civilization" that capitalist technology would energize. Stalin's well-known exegesis echoed this point in more emphatic terms: Imperialism inevitably brought railroads, factories, and mills to feudal societies, created industrial and commercial centers, and gave rise to "a class of proletarians, the emergence of a native intelligentsia, the awakening of national consciousness, the growth of the movement for emancipation."[24] By tearing down feudal institutions and values, encroaching foreign capital prepared the way for a more economically advanced, capitalist China and planted the seeds for socialism. Only through imperialist penetration could China develop its own bourgeoisie and prepare the transition to the next stage of proletarian domination.

On the other hand, imperialism had the great disadvantage of bringing progress at a distressingly slow and uneven pace and through the agency of foreigners. So economically and politically destructive was this process, so socially divisive and nationally humiliating were its effects, and so feeble were its measurable contributions to China's progress that members of the fledgling CCP recoiled at imperialism wreaking havoc all around them. With their gorge rising, they could see Stalin's general condemnation of imperialism mirroring their own particular plight. It was, he wrote, a system of "the most barefaced exploitation and the most inhuman oppression of hundreds of millions of people inhabiting vast colonies and dependent countries."[25]

The result was that party leaders found themselves in the theoretically uncomfortable position of condemning as antithetical to China's economic development and hence trying to frustrate the very force that Marx had made their country's best long-term hope of moving to higher stages of historical development. At heart they were not ready to suffer pain inflicted by foreigners in the name of progress. And at times they bluntly said so. For example, in November 1927 the provisional Political Bureau derided the idea that imperialists could help China complete its capitalist development. To the contrary, they would make China into a colony, a result that would in turn signal the defeat of the world proletariat revolution.[26]

Rather than wait for the frustratingly slow transformation of the Chinese economy and the generation of new class relations to carry them to power, the leaders of the CCP repeatedly succumbed to an impatient search for a shortcut that would allow them to bring imperialism to an early end and to hurry through or even skip over the bourgeois-democratic stage. One source of hope was China's predominantly peasant population, which seemed to some within the CCP caught up in a web of imperialist exploitation and control that extended from urban strongholds of foreign power deep into the countryside. Cursed with a proletariat that was small, ill-organized, and hence weak, a CCP driven from the cities had forced upon it a "discovery"—that extremely oppressive conditions could create a proletarian consciousness even in a rural environment. All it took was the peasant to fall into deep economic hardship to become a kind of proletariat (*wuchan jieji*, literally "propertyless class") or at least a leading revolutionary element able to move China beyond the current afflictions imposed by imperialists and their Chinese tools.[27]

The alternative way out was to stress the weak class consciousness of China's own bourgeoisie. Here Chinese leaders in effect borrowed a page from their Soviet mentors, who had to explain how their own proletarian revolution could triumph in a country without a well-developed capitalist class. Like the peasantry, the Chinese bourgeoisie was deeply entangled in the imperialist-dominated international economy and compromised by links to the feudal landlords. The bourgeoisie thus could not consolidate its identity or play its assigned historical role. At best it would enjoy but a brief era of control before giving way to proletarian revolution. Li Lisan developed the argument most aggressively in early 1929. He claimed to see in the consolidation of Nationalist control the full-blooded triumph of the bourgeoisie in China over both feudalism and imperialism. The task of the CCP was thus, in Li's view, to move China to the next stage by overthrowing Chiang Kai-shek as the representative of the bourgeoisie and replacing him with a soviet of workers and peasants.[28]

Some who mixed impatience over imperialist control with pessimism about China's own revolutionary potential looked for an international rescue (while also seeking to strengthen the Leninist sinews of the party). There were good theoretical grounds for looking abroad for help. Capitalist trade and finance had first created a global economy and then generated in reaction a global struggle against exploitation and oppression. Stalin's often-read *Foundations of Leninism* emphasized this point: "Now we must speak of the world proletariat revolution; for the separate national fronts of capital have become links in a single chain called the world front of imperialism, which must be opposed by a common front of the revolutionary movement of all countries." Russia had shown that the system of imperialist control would break down as the strains on it mounted. Chinese revolutionaries thus had good reason to watch for signs that the chain would snap a second time and to hope that the effects would reach around the globe to shake China. Some such as Qu Qiubai even wondered as early as 1923 if China, whose market was essential to the survival of capitalism, might itself be the crucial weak link in the imperialist chain.[29]

What actually snapped at least on several occasions was the patient watch for that distant revolutionary convulsion, prompting prominent party figures to long for blatant intervention by Soviet forces to help sweep the CCP's enemies from the field. A young Mao Zedong attending the Third Party Congress in mid-1923 is supposed to have felt so discouraged about China's faltering national revolution that he contended only such an intervention would save it. Li Lisan embraced this same deus ex machina when in May 1930 he appealed to Moscow for "common action at the right moment." He wanted Soviet forces to march across the Mongolian border and join the Chinese Red Army in striking a decisive blow against the Nationalists.[30]

However attractive to CCP leaders, these dreams of an early end to imperialism and a rapid passage over the bourgeois stage faced resolute Comintern opposition. Defending its position that China's was a national revolution against feudalism as well as imperialism, Moscow pronounced anathema claims that China was engaged in a proletarian revolution against the bourgeoisie. Party leaders who fell prey to the "petty bourgeois illusion" that the protracted process of social transformation could be cut short or hastened could expect a quick call to heel. The Sixth Party Congress held in 1928 near Moscow and stage-managed by the Comintern bluntly reminded an errant CCP that China's was still a bourgeois democratic revolution even if its main force consisted of peasants and workers. Only Trotskyite heretics asking for trouble would claim the contrary. Similarly, the Comintern quickly blew the whistle on Li Lisan, compelling a contrite party center to concede that the bourgeoisie was weak, not strong, that feudalism was strong, not weak, and hence that China was not near the socialist stage but far from it. The CCP now told the Comintern and Stalin what they expected to hear: the task of China's worker-peasant revolution remained expelling imperialism and eliminating feudalism, and it expected to carry the burden by itself.[31]

But beyond the limits imposed by Moscow, the CCP's search for a way out of China's developmental dilemma was hobbled by the perplexity and confusion that attended the party's appraisal of a complex imperialist system made up of tightly interlocking and dynamically interacting governments and social classes. Imperialist powers waxed and waned in their relative importance with bewildering suddenness and frequency. At the time of its founding the CCP ranked Japan, Britain, and the United States as the premier imperialist powers followed by France and Italy. Then for a time the United States edged toward hegemony. The May 30th movement, beginning in Shanghai in 1925, at first restored the balance among the "big three," and finally pushed Britain to the fore as the main counter-revolutionary. In early 1927 Japan took the lead (as a result of a clash with Japanese troops in Jinan) only to give way to the United States in 1928–1929. The Manchurian incident in 1931 helped restore Japan to prominence, and the CCP commentary returned thereafter to its old picture of the "big three," a view that would persist down to the end of the Jiangxi Soviet.

Moreover, the nature of the crises afflicting imperialism was subject to equally bewildering shifts. Up to 1927 CCP commentary stressed the multiple strains building within the imperialist system—class conflict within each of the capitalist powers overlaid by a shifting pattern of rivalry among them. In 1928 the CCP learned from the Comintern that the imperialist powers, gripped by a counter-revolutionary fervor, had gone on the offensive and begun to plot attacks on the Soviet Union. This imperialist collusion against the USSR added a new dimension and degree of complexity to the international system still marked by tensions within and among the imperialists.

For CCP leaders trying to anticipate international trends the better to identify friends and foes, gauge relative strengths, and shape an effective strategy, this model constructed by foreigners at the head of the Comintern six thousand miles away was of little help. The model was intricate not only because it had to be theoretically informed but also because it had to smooth over past mistakes and hedge bets against unexpected developments. The model was set within an analytic framework prompted by Soviet concerns and altered periodically as those concerns changed. Finally, the model was based on information available to the Comintern in Moscow, always limited, sometimes contradictory on the subject of China, and in any case selected to fit the current interpretive framework. The CCP thus worked from forecasts and practical guidance made in Moscow for Moscow.

At no time was confusion more dramatically evident than in the three years following the split with the Nationalists. Conflict within the imperialist system was a certainty, but assessments of how the big three would divide and when and where they would fight swung crazily like a compass over a table of iron filings. At the same time the CCP noted that the imperialists seemed prepared to crush the USSR but they inexplicably faltered. Would China be engulfed by a Pacific war between the United States and Japan? Would the bourgeoisie and especially Chiang's regime fall under the sway of the United States or Japan? How readily might Chinese reactionaries—regional warlords or groups of merchants—swallow the imperialist hook, and how far might they go in abetting an assault on the USSR? Policy-relevant prediction became even more difficult with the proliferation within the CCP analyses of ill-defined social categories—despotic gentry (*haoshen*), petty compradors, comprador landlords, soldiers, the urban poor, artisans, revolutionary intellectuals and students, and the like—each with its own particular stance vis-à-vis imperialism and by extension China's revolution.[32]

Seemingly driven to distraction by this analytical schema, the central committee's guidance at times turned to mush. A resolution from 1931 provides a stark illustration of how perplexing this world under the imperialist sway could be—indeed how much it abounded in paralyzing paradoxes. According to this resolution, the imperialists were divided against each other yet united in their hostility to the Soviet Union; Chiang Kai-shek, in reality a tool of imperialism, was effecting a diplomatic rapprochement with the Soviet Union; and his government was riven by factions, each tied to one of the rival foreign powers, yet it posed an intensifying threat to the CCP.[33]

Finally, the very exigencies of survival in the early 1930s forced the CCP to curb its antagonism and move toward a limited accommodation with the hated imperialist presence. The CCP-sponsored Soviet Republic by then controlled substantial territory, and despite its remoteness, foreign mission stations and foreign business came within its administrative purview, and foreign gunboats came within the sights of its guns, while foreign loans and military assistance bolstered its enemy's encirclement campaigns. Some within the party called for unyielding anti-imperialism, giving no ground to foreigners in economic and political, not to mention military, affairs. But the ascendant view, endorsed by the Comintern, opposed a provocative, radical policy of outright confiscation of businesses and banning of missionary operations. The third plenum of the sixth Central Committee,[34] meeting in September 1930 in Shanghai, stressed that contacts with the imperialists did not amount to capitulation and need not undermine the anti-imperialist spirit of the masses. While entertaining no illusions about the ultimate goals of the imperialist powers, the Central Committee contended that some concessions might attenuate their hostility, aggravate contradictions among them, and give the lie to their propaganda about revolutionary "killing and burning."[35]

Authorities within the Soviet base area issued preliminary instructions on handling the imperialist presence in November and December 1930, followed by more formal and detailed rules in 1931 and 1934. They permitted foreign businessmen and missionaries who respected regulations and Soviet political authority to remain active in the Soviet area and cautioned against random firing on foreign ships.[36] A party animated from the start by a stark, impatient anti-imperialism was beginning to come to terms with the practical as well as the analytical limits of its faith and to temper its hopes for a complete and rapid overthrow of the old, foreign-dominated order.

The Special Soviet Relationship

The second of the essential elements making up the May Fourth view on the world was the belief in a special relationship with the USSR. The development of this special relationship marked a sharp historical turn. Czarist policy toward the Qing had been characterized by opportunism and betrayal. While pretending to mediate between China and threatening Anglo-French forces, Russia had at mid-century extracted sweeping territorial concessions. In the mid-1890s Russia gained a foothold in the northeast and then expanded it as the price for moderating Japanese demands and for granting China an alliance. The Boxers gave the Czar's forces an excuse for the brutal occupation of all of the northeast, and even after Japan had curbed the Russian appetite and limited Russian influence to the northern portion of that region, Russia stubbornly held on, striking a deal with Japan to hold off Chinese claims. If Russian policy thereafter grew milder, it was not because of a change of heart but because of growing internal unrest from 1905 and the distraction of the military conflict with Germany after 1914.

The Bolshevik revolution exercised a powerful appeal that pushed to the background, for a time at least, accumulated Chinese resentment and suspicion. As we have seen, May Fourth intellectuals turned to that revolution as a beacon in dark times. Events in Russia, to begin with, inspired hopes for an imminent, major shift in world affairs. The leaders of the new Russia had broken with their own country's aggressive past and with the community of imperialist states by announcing they were setting their foreign relations on a new footing, and then they withstood intervention by the capitalist powers intent on bringing the new regime down.[37]

Moscow confirmed this new anti-imperialist turn of policy by aligning with revolutionary change in China as in other countries under imperialist domination. Immediately following the October revolution, Leon Trotsky had in the name of the new Bolshevik regime denounced the secret treaties concluded by the wartime Allies and endorsed the principle of self-determination. This sweeping proclamation became more credible with the issue of the first Karakhan manifesto in July 1919. It set the USSR on record as ready to renounce all Czarist privileges and interests in China and to abrogate all secret and unequal treaties acquired under the old regime. The new Soviet state urged the Chinese people to "understand that their only allies and brothers in the struggle for freedom are the Russian workers and peasants and their Red Army."[38] News of this announcement caused a considerable stir when it finally reached China in March 1920.

By the 1920s the USSR had in addition begun to command respect as a model for China's renovation and hence as the fountainhead of revolutionary doctrine and direction. The Bolsheviks had taken a state in collapse, threatened by domestic chaos and foreign armies, and made it secure and strong with limited resources and stunning speed. By study and emulation Chinese might match the Soviet achievements. Here was an appealing source of guidance and support for Chinese in despair over the defects in their own culture and at odds with hostile imperialist powers. Here was a strategy for gaining power and dramatically transforming a country that was, like Russia, agricultural, poor, mired in tradition, and only recently rid of monarchy. Finally, here was hope that China, strong and progressive, might jump from feudalism to the forefront of the international community.

As the new Rome of the international communist movement, Moscow sent its emissaries to China as missionaries of a new secular religion. Chiefly representing the Comintern or the Politburo of the Soviet Communist Party,[39] they preached the word, distributed literature to the curious and discontented, and drew potential converts into the bands of the faithful. Voitinsky arrived in March 1920, followed by Sneevliet, Mikhail Borodin, M. N. Roy, Besso Lominadze, Pavel Mif, and Otto Braun. True to the missionary tradition, all were busy, confident men.

Though Communists and even for a time Nationalists brought enthusiasm and high expectations to the Sino-Soviet relationship, unsettling questions prompted by practical experience kept arising. Just how reliable was Moscow as a supporter of China's anti-imperialist revolutionary struggle? Had the USSR set aside the traditional Russian interests in China, especially along the common border? Could Soviet doctrine be imported into China intact and applied wholesale without significant adjustment to Chinese conditions and attitudes? Indeed, just how appropriate was the Soviet Union in general as a model for Chinese to study and emulate?

The Nationalists were the first to embrace the special relationship—and the first to break off. Sun Yat-sen turned to the USSR in 1923 for want of alternative sources of foreign support. He died in March 1925 still endorsing cooperation. Sun's deathbed appeal to the Soviet government, prepared by Chen Youren (Eugene Chen) in consultation with Borodin (the Soviet adviser to the Nationalist Party), expressed "the hope that the day is approaching when the Soviet Union will greet in a free and strong China its friend and ally, and that the two states will proceed hand in hand as allies in the great fight for the emancipation of the whole world."[40] Even so, Sun resisted the full embrace of the Comintern (though for some within the party even his cautious approach went too far). He took its material aid and accepted its political and military advisers, who tried to help him transform the Nationalist Party and its army along Leninist lines. But the Soviet Union did not become his model, nor did Marxism-Leninism become his faith, nor did Soviet advisers dictate his policy.

Close cooperation with the USSR barely outlived Sun. It survived the balance of 1925 and momentarily in 1926 the Nationalist Party elevated the USSR to the status of "a revolutionary trail blazer" and ally in the struggle of oppressed peoples.[41] But the emergence of Chiang Kai-shek as party leader brought an end to such effusions. Chiang shared Sun's view that the Comintern was a tool to serve practical needs. (Chiang regarded with special interest the success of Soviet economic planning and the efficiency of the Soviet party system.) Despite his suspicion of the red menace and his 1927 break with both foreign and native-born Bolsheviks, he did not embark on a simple ideological crusade. The weakness of the Nationalist regime as it struggled against its enemies at home and abroad forced on Chiang an opportunistic, three-sided approach to the USSR. It was a presence along the border in Mongolia, Xinjiang, and the northeast that needed to be managed and where possible neutralized. It was, moreover, a source of support against Japan that took on added importance in the late 1930s as Chiang's German connections began to fray. It was, finally, the apparent master of the Chinese Communists and hence might be induced to keep them on a short leash.

For the Chinese Communists struggling to get organized the special relationship with the USSR was an article of faith. Already in November and December 1920 the inaugural issue of the journal *Communist* had focused attention on the exciting developments in Russia. Despite a relatively backward environment, well-organized socialist revolutionaries had gained power and launched a great, promising economic experiment—while elsewhere the capitalist alternative, with all its ills, drifted toward collapse.[42] By the time of the 1922 Party Congress, animated interest had turned to adulation. The delegates formally declared that as world capitalism tottered, "Soviet Russia of the workers and peasants" stood firm, "the mainstay of revolutionary power for the world's toiling masses." The October revolution had, the congress declared, ignited the struggle of the proletariat throughout Europe, in the United States, and even in Japan, and it had given impetus elsewhere in the world to the rise of national revolutionary movements. But as the Soviet Union gave, so should it receive. As "the vanguard in the liberation of oppressed nations," it deserved the protection of the awakening masses in China no less than elsewhere.[43]

The CCP publicly celebrated the Soviet Union's achievements and its symbolic significance to the Chinese revolution—at no time more devoutly than on the anniversaries of the Bolshevik seizure of power. In November 1922 at one of the first celebrations Li Dazhao proclaimed the USSR the "fatherland, forerunner, and fortress for the entire world's worker and peasant masses," while Chen Duxiu praised Russia for opting out of the imperialist system, and urged the Chinese government to recognize the USSR as the first step toward resolving outstanding territorial, commercial, and other issues hanging over Sino-Soviet relations. Exactly a year later the CCP's Central Executive Committee urged activists to present the Soviet Union as a friend of China's national revolution whose support could offset the hostile influence of the imperialist powers.[44]

After mid-1927 the special relationship was not only a staple of basic party orthodoxy; it was also the CCP's exclusive property whose real value skyrocketed for cadres suddenly thrown on the defensive and into the wilderness. In late 1927 the CCP flogged the Nationalists for turning against the USSR, the fatherland of world revolution and the first to abolish the unequal treaties. The Sixth Party Congress in 1928 provided an opportunity to offer a paean to its hosts' achievements in ten years of socialist development and their power to support and guarantee the ultimate triumph of China's proletariat. Agitational work, continuing into the Jiangxi period, returned time and again to fixed themes—the achievements of the USSR, that country's friendship for China, and the consequent obligation to do whatever possible to frustrate attacks on the Soviet Union by the imperialists and their Chinese allies. Even as the Chinese Soviet entered the last phase of its defense, the party center called for redoubled effort to cultivate popular goodwill toward the USSR, the brotherly ally of China's toiling masses.[45]

Internationalist support for the USSR proved for the CCP a harder sell than patriotic defense of China against the imperialists. Some, the party center complained in 1925, regarded praise for the USSR as a "taboo" topic. The inadequacy of the internationalist message in grass-roots party propaganda was a cause for repeated Comintern complaint—at no time more insistently than the latter half of 1929, after a Soviet dispute with the Nationalists over control of the Chinese Eastern Railway in the northeast had escalated into border clashes. The party center sought to raise the volume of its praise for the USSR in order to mobilize popular support that would restrain this Nationalist encroachment on Soviet interests and neutralize the outpouring of Nationalist anti-Soviet propaganda. But at least some cadres, unable to see how defense of the Soviet Union against Nationalist provocations would advance China's revolution, neglected their internationalist obligation. In June a party resolution grumbled that "many comrades still feel some difficulty in getting out of their mouths slogans about protecting the USSR." Chen Duxiu, by now deeply disaffected from the party he had founded, bluntly explained that it was no easy task for the CCP to protect the Soviet Union when the Nationalists seemed the real defenders of China's interests.[46]

The Comintern emissaries were the critical link between the emergent CCP and Moscow. Their authority was in part personal, based on their own experience as activists and organizers and their familiarity with Marxist-Leninist theory that far exceeded anything their Chinese proteges could claim. But above all, it was the credentials and funds that they carried that put them in a pivotal, intermediary position and secured them a major, at times even dominant role in the development of the CCP. Kept in touch with Moscow by couriers and wireless, supplemented from time to time by trips back to Moscow, these envoys spoke for the Comintern, passing on its directives and advice, while also interpreting for Moscow conditions and concerns of the Chinese party.

So great was their influence that these envoys left an imprint on virtually every aspect of the early CCP. Voitinsky served as midwife at its birth in 1920–1921. Thereafter Sneevliet and his successors drafted and reviewed some of the major party documents, defined the direction of party policy, and quelled doubts and dissent. As paymasters, the Comintern envoys held the purse strings for a party that might simply have gone under if left to rely exclusively on its own meager resources.[47]

Perhaps the most enduring legacy of the Comintern envoys was their contribution as teachers and talent scouts. They faced a Chinese party with a lot to learn. One student of the Comintern role in China has described the early CCP as "still under a heavy ideological influence of patriarchal national traditions and . . . little familiar not only with Marxist teachings, but even with the terminology of contemporary social, political and economic sciences."[48] The Comintern agents brought into China the first significant collection of Bolshevik literature and promoted its translation and study. As part of the long-term effort to raise the CCP's level of sophistication, they identified promising young recruits to go to Moscow, there to drink at the ideological source. Learning some Russian, studying at first hand Soviet achievements, gaining an acquaintance with party organization and norms, and laying a solid foundation in scientific Marxism and contemporary politics—all these would promote that revolutionary maturity deemed essential to the CCP's ultimate success. Those returning to China would have a better grasp of Marxist vocabulary and reasoning. They could apply the techniques of criticism and self-criticism and the propaganda skills learned in Russia. They could even bring to bear the mechanics of a purge. Most carried a Russian alias assigned by their hosts. (For example, Wang Ming became Golubev, Zhu De became Danilov, Nie Rongzhen became Zorin, Deng Xiaoping became Krezov, and Yang Shangkun became Saltykov.)

Thanks to this early educational enterprise, the Soviet Union quickly displaced France as the mecca for young revolutionaries, and the overwhelming majority of CCP leaders in the late 1920s, the 1930s, and the 1940s had had at least some schooling in the Soviet Union. The graduates of the two most prominent, Moscow-based institutions—the Communist University of the Toilers of the East and Sun Yat-sen University—make up a virtual who's who of the CCP.[49] The former school, established in May 1921, took in CCP members along with students from the eastern Soviet Union as well as Japan and Korea, but it was eclipsed by Sun Yat-sen University in the late 1920s. The latter opened its doors in September 1925 to both Chinese Nationalists and Communists, and in 1928 after the breakup of the united front was renamed the Communist University of the Working People of China and solely dedicated to training CCP cadres. By the time of its closing in fall 1930 it had trained about sixteen hundred Chinese Communists drawn from the party's European branch as well as China. For most the program of studies consisted of an intensive two years of work, and some of the best students served as translators for Soviet instructors, taught classes themselves, or participated in translation and research projects housed within the university.[50]

The students in the Soviet Union lived a relatively privileged life. Along with free education, they enjoyed regular vacations, good food and housing, and support for dependents. On the other hand, many suffered from culture shock and social isolation. Most arrived with only rudimentary Russian, and some, particularly peasant and worker recruits, required remedial education before embarking on formal studies. All had to put up with strict political supervision by the Comintern and the Communist Party of the Soviet Union.[51] They grew impatient with pervasive bureaucracy, wondered at the persisting inequalities in Soviet life, and were dismayed by continuing hardship they witnessed in rural life. They also had to put up with occasional expressions of popular prejudice against Chinese and resentment over their special privileges.

After 1927 the Soviet Union's educational effort declined in importance. The Trotskyite controversy convulsed the schoolroom, while Moscow turned its attention to the more urgent problem of salvaging a savaged and demoralized CCP. The Soviet Union stepped in to provide a sanctuary to which party members could retreat. It opened Soviet hospitals and rest houses to ill and exhausted cadres hounded by Nationalist security organs or ground down by privation in the remote countryside. And it hosted the Sixth Party Congress in mid-1928 when no place in China was safe for such a gathering.

The CCP had been gradually building its own educational program. The foundation for its effort was the early informal study societies. The Foreign Language School in Shanghai, established by Voitinsky and his wife M. F. Kuznetsova with assistance of their translator Yang Mingzhai soon after their arrival in September 1920, was an important addition, preparing promising Chinese to study in the Soviet Union. So too was Shanghai University, created late in 1923, as a rough-and-ready Marxist intellectual center where such CCP luminaries as Cai Hesen, Qu Qiubai, and Deng Zhongxia taught. As the anti-imperialist struggle of the mid-1920s swelled party ranks, the CCP responded by forming its own cadre schools as well as by staffing training institutes run jointly with the Nationalists. The CCP schools offered two- to four-week basic courses for activists and a three-month advanced course. Finally, during the Jiangxi period the party began to create even more advanced as well as specialized centers of education, including the Academy of Marxian Communism (established in 1933) as well as schools for the army, women, and workers.[52]

Moscow's sponsorship, so important in launching and sustaining the CCP, also thrust some serious impediments in the party's way. However eager, Chinese pupils brought to their lessons their own political concerns and style. Thus despite formal pronouncements singing the praises of the USSR and proclaiming an unshakable loyalty, some among the CCP leadership were irritated by the directives from a distant Comintern and by its intrusive, condescending agents. The results were occasional confrontations and outbursts, some ambivalence among even the warmest advocates of Soviet support and the Soviet model, and sometimes bewilderment among the rank and file. These tensions were inevitable. A small and weak party operating in a complicated and turbulent political context was bound to suffer setbacks, and setbacks set off recriminations.

The Comintern enjoyed but a brief honeymoon with its Chinese partner. Voitinsky, a young and likable Russian, had the relatively easy task of creating a party, at least on paper, out of the scattered leftist study societies. He was able to leave China with his reputation and Chinese goodwill intact. Sneevliet's arrival in April 1921 inaugurated a more contentious relationship. He brought with him extensive organizing experience, first in Holland (his homeland) and then in the Dutch East Indies. Although reputedly familiar with "the east," he like most envoys did not know China or speak Chinese. He also brought with him "the social superiority complex of the white man," according to one CCP leader whose views were widely shared. Sneevliet "saw himself coming as an angel of liberation of Asian people."[53]

Sneevliet's first task was to make the CCP into a genuine Leninist party responsive to Moscow. The time for bookish ideological study and academic debate had passed, he argued; the CCP should turn itself into an instrument of disciplined political activity formally subordinate to the Comintern. Sneevliet's proposals alienated those who still saw the party's primary mission as raising the ideological level of its members rather than making a premature plunge into politics. He also encountered foot-dragging from those who feared in Comintern membership a loss of organizational independence. The First Congress in 1921 would do no more than accept membership "in principle," but under continued pressure party leaders at the Second Congress formally accepted a place in the Comintern and hence subordination to its Executive Committee sitting in Moscow.

Sneevliet's other task, even more controversial, was to maneuver the CCP into the alliance with the Nationalists consistent with Lenin's view on the proper course for "eastern" revolutions. Sneevliet argued that a still weak CCP should work as a "bloc within" that stronger, emergent bourgeois party to create a mass movement powerful enough to defeat imperialism and its feudal allies within China. Sneevliet insistently pushed this proposal against resistance, not least from Chen Duxiu. Sneevliet finally secured formal backing from Moscow and invoked Comintern discipline to force acceptance at a special party plenum held in Hangzhou in late August 1922. However, resistance broke out again at the Third Congress in June 1923. Zhang Guotao, Cai Hesen, and a minority of others went on the attack. Precisely because the CCP was weak, it could not be an equal partner and should not put itself at the mercy of the untrustworthy Nationalists. They contended that the CCP would be better off cultivating its own base among the working class. But again Sneevliet prevailed against those whom he dismissed as guided by "illusions and dreams."[54]

Voitinsky returned to China in 1923 to find a CCP still chafing under the constraints of the Comintern-imposed alliance. The bourgeoisie was not proving as staunchly anti-imperialist as the Comintern made them out. An armed insurrection by Canton merchants in October 1924 planted fears that the bourgeoisie might even defect from the revolution. Both Chen Duxiu and Qu Qiubai wanted the CCP to respond with a more independent policy, mixing cooperation with class struggle.[55]

After a period of optimism that the alliance was working to the CCP's benefit, it again became a sharp bone of contention in 1926. The party's Canton branch had concluded from first-hand experience with Chiang that the alliance had become a shell and called for a more radical and autonomous role within the united front, while Chen Duxiu revived his opposition to the party's intimate, subordinate ties to the Nationalists. The Comintern's Executive Committee meeting under Bukharin's direction responded in March 1926 with an affirmation of the alliance strategy.[56] Borodin lobbied hard and effectively within the CCP against any shift in policy. Reflecting mounting impatience, Cai Hesen (the head of the CCP's delegation to the Comintern) offered a sweeping critique of the Comintern's over-reliance on the Nationalist Party and its neglect of the CCP. Borodin treated the CCP with disdain, Cai complained, using it chiefly as a pool from which he could draw translators. What the CCP needed was better financial support, better informed and more timely Comintern direction on CCP policy, and fewer advisers with more specialized skills.[57]

In late 1926 with the CCP-Nationalist alliance under serious strain, the CCP again collided with the Comintern. In late November the Comintern Executive Committee had announced that imperialism had already gone down to defeat in half of China, and the rising revolutionary tide was about to sweep it from the rest of the country. While the CCP publicly parroted this appraisal, Chen criticized it as grossly overoptimistic. It underestimated the strength not just of the capitalist powers but also of their Chinese allies. The revolution, he cautioned, had a greater distance to go and more dangers to face than the Comintern's sanguine appraisal suggested. But even as tensions with Chiang mounted, the Comintern policy held firm. Borodin insisted on conciliating Chiang and avoiding any display of worker power in Shanghai that might alarm the Nationalist leader.[58]

China's revolution and with it the CCP had by this time become hostage to Stalin's drive to crush Trotsky and eliminate his chief rival's ideological influence and personal appeal within the Soviet party. Stalin had argued for continued CCP-Nationalist cooperation in a revolution whose enemies were feudal warlords and the imperialists. Trotsky had denounced this collaboration with the bourgeoisie and called instead for the revolutionary forces to break their subordination to the Nationalists and carve out strongholds of soviet power. Although Stalin by early 1927 held the political upper hand in his domestic contest, he was not about to embarrass himself and vindicate his foe by reversing himself at this critical juncture for the CCP. As the clouds gathered, he would not let the party seek shelter. When the storm finally broke in April 1927, he insisted that the CCP continue cooperation at least with the Nationalist's left-wing represented by the Wang Jingwei regime in Hankou. A shaken CCP gamely complied, confirming at its Fifth Congress in May that imperialism in China was indeed on the ropes and that the prospects for revolution remained good.[59]

By August even forced optimism was impossible. By then even the left-wing had turned on the CCP, and a failed insurrection in Nanchang (followed by other equally unsuccessful uprisings in the fall) did nothing to improve the situation. The party center held an emergency meeting under Lominadze's supervision and under the leadership of the Comintern's new favorite, Qu Qiubai. Bloodied and isolated, party leaders not only called for a retreat from any direct confrontation with imperialism but also turned on their recent Comintern guides (while prudently sparing the Comintern and Stalin). Luo Yinong, chair of an emergency meeting held on August 7, lashed out, "The Comintern's resolutions are good, but its representatives are lousy." He argued that Voitinsky (who had just completed his third tour of duty in China) and Roy (the Indian Comintern representative whose first visit to China coincided with the CCP's slide into disaster) should share responsibility for the outcome with Chen Duxiu.[60]

News of the April 1927 coup and its painful aftermath left the students in Sun Yat-sen University in Moscow if anything even more agitated than their colleagues in China. Expecting a major revolutionary triumph, they learned instead of a terrible setback. They reacted angrily to the Soviet leadership's attempt to make Chen the scapegoat rather than accept any responsibility itself, and they demanded an accounting from Borodin on his return from China. His bland and reluctant report with no time for questions did nothing to soothe student discontent. Disaffection in general and interest in Trotsky's criticism of Stalin in particular now spread rapidly among the young Chinese in Moscow. The disaster visited on the CCP had turned what had been a largely abstract political contest between Soviet leaders into a matter of passionate inquiry and ideological commitment by at least a significant fraction of the student population. (One estimate makes twenty percent of students Trotskyites by 1930.) Other students sympathized or wavered in their commitment. Out of the four hundred students at Sun Yat-sen University at the time, some one hundred and fifty were at least sympathetic to Trotsky. Even the CCP delegation to the Comintern, led by Qu Qiubai, could barely conceal its critical view of the damage a Stalin-run Comintern had done to the party and covertly lent support to the dissidents.[61]

Predictably the virus of discontent made its way back to China, carried by student letters and ultimately students themselves. There too Trotsky's critique of Stalin's China policy had strong appeal because it helped make sense of the CCP's crushing defeat at the hands of the bourgeoisie. While Stalin's argument that China was still both feudal and dominated by imperialism struck some as implausible, Trotsky's challenge won adherents, not least Chen Duxiu, and deepened fundamental doubts about the Comintern's understanding of China. Taking up the thread of Trotsky's thesis, Chen contended that China, countryside as well as city, was so deeply penetrated by imperialism that it was well advanced into the bourgeois stage of development. China's bourgeois class, represented by the Nationalist Party and tightly tied to imperialist interests, now held the political high ground, leaving China's revolution for the moment at least in a trough. But that revolution's ultimate task was now clear—the overthrow of the bourgeoisie—not imperialism and feudalism, as the Comintern continued to claim. By the time of his expulsion from the party in late 1929 Chen was publicly charging that the CCP had surrendered its organizational and political independence to Stalin and Bukharin, whom he stingingly derided as a couple of political opportunists fearful of confronting capitalist regimes and the imperialist system.[62]

With the assistance of Bukharin as head of the Comintern, Stalin moved to quell the doubts, oust the dissenters, and assure a compliant CCP. He started in Moscow in June 1927 by placing Pavel Mif in charge of Sun Yat-sen University. Mif, a leading Soviet China expert, recruited student loyalists and with the assistance of Wang Ming secured university control. In mid-1928 the CCP's Sixth Congress, which brought many of its ranking leaders to a Moscow suburb, provided an opportunity to impose discipline while reminding them of the CCP's political immaturity and organizational dependence. Under Bukharin's watchful eye party leaders dutifully condemned Chen's "opportunistic" policy, acknowledged the Comintern's correct understanding of the China problem, and vowed to work harder to create a truly Bolshevik party—urban, mass-based, and centralized.[63]

In 1929 Stalin intensified the struggle against Trotskyite influences within the CCP. In the fall the Communist Party of the Soviet Union and the secret police laid the groundwork for a purge of the Chinese community in Moscow (carried out in the course of 1930). At the same time the CCP began its own purge in China. The Trotskyites had stirred up dangerous inner-party dissent and embarrassing public polemics. The Central Committee condemned these renegades in October 1929 and then expelled Chen and other prominent offenders in November. Even then staunch party loyalists remained privately interested in the Trotskyite critique and looked sympathetically on the expellees—as fellow revolutionaries, not the traitors that Moscow made them.[64]

The next year Stalin had to intervene in the Chinese party itself. Not only was its leadership badly fragmented but Li Lisan, the rising power in the party, was setting off on a deviation almost as serious as Chen's. Li had first strayed in early 1929, but a reprimand from Moscow had elicited a reassuring self-criticism.[65] Early in 1930 Li again went off the deep end. Encouraged by Comintern claims that the Chinese revolution was regaining strength, Li put forward a bold CCP strategy that put China right at the center of the world revolutionary struggle.

Li contended that all the basic contradictions tearing away at the imperialist system had come together in their sharpest form in China, thus supplying an unusually powerful impetus to revolution there. Once China exploded, the whole system of global capitalism would be engulfed in flames. All that was missing was a match to fall on dry revolutionary tinder. Li thought he had that match in armed urban insurrections, to be reinforced by Red Army attacks. Wuhan was to be the focal point of this effort. On June 11 the Political Bureau endorsed Li's plans, predicting that incendiary initiatives in China could "set off a great, worldwide revolution and bring about the world's final, decisive class war." Li prejudiced his case not only by putting China at the epicenter of the coming revolutionary upheaval but also by pointedly calling the Comintern to make up for its past failures of understanding and trust by giving the CCP some real support in this critical moment of extraordinary opportunity.[66]

When cautionary statements made no difference, a worried Moscow sent Zhou Enlai and Qu Qiubai back to China in August to restrain Li. In an orgy of repentance the Central Committee criticized Li and restored the USSR and China back to their proper places in the world revolution, one at the center and the other at the periphery. But the two emissaries failed to take a sufficiently firm stand in the face of Li's erroneous policy, so the Comintern now intervened decisively. In November Mif drafted the Comintern's condemnation of Li, and Mif himself arrived in December to put matters right. Meeting with the CCP's fourth plenum in January 1931, Mif dressed down members of the old Political Bureau for their "shameful" failure to check Li and heed Comintern guidance. The plenum placed the party in the good hands of Wang Ming. When he returned to Moscow in October to work for the Comintern, another of Mif's proteges, Bo Gu, assumed effective control. Li, the fallen leader, had by then done his obligatory self-criticism and after some foot-dragging had set off for Moscow for what turned out to be fifteen years of reeducation (including two years in prison).[67]

The newcomers were now securely at the helm of the Shanghai-based party center. Moscow educated and well versed in Stalin's view on the Chinese revolution, they would be guided by their habits of deference to Comintern directives and doctrines and by the messages Moscow beamed to their long-range radio equipment. But under their command the CCP would in fact proceed to groan and then sink, pulled down in part by the weight of their revolutionary platitudes, formulaic and unfocused analysis, and doctrinal boilerplate. The steady consolidation of Nationalist power, the beginning of the Japanese invasion in September 1931 and the popular anger it created, and finally the Soviet Union's policy of appeasing Japan and of rapprochement with the Nationalists all combined to put a premium on political adroitness and strategic flexibility. Singularly lacking in those qualities, the new leadership instead grimly clung to a Comintern-imposed line that downplayed the Japanese advance, abandoned the patriotic high ground to the Nationalists, failed to preserve the Shanghai underground, and ultimately lost the Jiangxi Soviet to Nationalist blockade and repeated military assaults.[68]

The Russian-trained leaders with their bolshevizing agenda had been quick to train their suspicions on the base areas, recognized even by the Comintern as the CCP's new center of gravity and the setting for a new rural phase in the revolutionary struggle. But party leaders in Shanghai worried that policy, personnel, and organization might easily be corrupted by backward rural conditions and feudal peasant values. Until late 1930 Shanghai had depended for its control over base areas on a tenuous line of communications—a radio transmitter backed up by couriers.[69] Determined to exercise more direct supervision, the Central Committee dispatched Zhou Enlai to the Jiangxi base area in December 1930. It followed with a campaign of criticism between March and July 1932. Finally, in January 1933 the Central Committee itself moved to the Jiangxi Soviet, bringing along their radio link to Moscow. This mounting pressure carried a clear message for the original base-area leaders: they had neglected "proletarian" and "internationalist" values; and they needed to teach their peasant supporters to appreciate the leadership of the USSR, to respect the insights of the Comintern, and to recognize the danger posed by imperialism as it strengthened the Nationalists, helped the Japanese, and menaced the Soviet Union.[70] The arrival in October 1933 of Otto Braun, a German Communist trained in the Soviet Union and an amateur in military affairs, rounded out the Comintern's contributions to the "sound" development of the base areas. This last of Moscow's emissaries with real clout pushed the Red Army to give up its war of maneuver and take up instead positional defenses that favored the large and well-armed Nationalist force. His imperious political style and his intervention in military strategy won him few friends within the CCP.

Within the year the Jiangxi Soviet completely collapsed. Those such as Mao Zedong and Zhu De who had established and nurtured the base areas and then found themselves subjected to the criticism and close supervision of the young Stalinists watched years of hard work evaporate, leaving only grim uncertainty. But they at least knew where to place the responsibility. The Long March would signal the beginning of a reappraisal of party policy so fundamental that it would extend to the special relationship itself. The Comintern had, to be sure, breathed life into the CCP and ensured its survival. But the Comintern was also often ill informed, its directives sometimes misguided, its advisers frequently heavy handed and condescending, and its support consistently cautious and limited. The doubts about dependency on the USSR that Sun and Chiang had faced in the mid-1920s, the Communists were beginning themselves to ponder a decade later.

The Community of the Weak and Oppressed

The third element in the May Fourth triad was a belief in the unity of the weak and oppressed. Looking out on a world dominated by Europeans, Americans, and Japanese, May Fourth activists felt a bond with "the weak and small nations" (*ruoxiao minzu*), especially those in Asia. They all had a common goal—liberation from foreign control and the elimination of the internal impediments to justice and development. By banding together, these countries might compensate for their individual weakness and through international solidarity hasten an end to their oppression. "It is no longer valid," Mao Dun wrote in *Eastern Magazine* in April 1920, "to think in terms of one particular people's progress. All must assist one another in their development of civilization."[71] Some of the participants in the founding of the CCP such as Li Dazhao and Mao Zedong felt the tug of this transnational bond quite strongly. They argued for transcending a narrow patriotism and lending a hand to other peoples also struggling for independence and liberation.

This identification with the weak and oppressed took two main forms, to each of which was attached an important qualification. One form was the generalized identification with countries dominated by Western power, especially but by no means exclusively those in Asia.

The origins of this first view can be traced back to the turn of the century, when Chinese observers of international affairs had begun to find ample and disturbing parallels between their own condition and that of other peoples pressed to the edge of extinction by the great powers. Turkey was Europe's sick man, whose internal turmoil had left it easy prey. Egypt revealed the dangerous political consequences of letting foreigners seize financial control. Poland was a sad illustration of the perils of territorial dismemberment at the hands of cynical statesmen. The experience of the Philippines was a reminder of the universal abuse conquerors heaped on their subjects. Other subjugated peoples—the people of India, the Jews, the Irish, the blacks of Africa, and blacks and Native Americans in the United States—received sympathetic treatment. The doleful fates of these "conquered nations" [*wangguo*] and oppressed peoples served as a cautionary tale to rouse Chinese patriots.[72]

For some patriots it was not enough (in the recurrent phrase of the turn of the century) "to learn from the experience of [these unfortunate] others" (*qianche zhi jian*). Those patriots also felt sympathy—and with it a righteous desire to lend support, even as the fate of China itself seemed to hang in the balance. For example, Zhang Binglin, writing under the passion of the anti-Manchu cause, saw China's place alongside "those other weak nations who are conquered, ruled, and enslaved by powerful nations." As a member of that community, including notably India, Burma, and Vietnam, "we should try to recover the independence of them all as long as we have enough strength left."[73]

Anarchists also championed the cause of the weak and oppressed, but set it in an even broader global context. More than a decade before the creation of the Comintern with its program of world revolution, they imagined a liberation struggle that would join the common people of colonial countries with those in the imperial metropole. Indeed, they wondered, as did some in the CCP later, if the destruction of imperialism's grip on the periphery might not precipitate the collapse of imperialism's various strongholds and thus constitute the first step toward global liberation. Liu Shipei, a proponent of anarchism prominent in anti-Manchu revolutionary activity, predicted that "when the Asian colonies throw off their subjugation, the imperialist powers will lose their ability to inspire awe and their own people will become aware of the fact that they do not need to fear their government." Li Shizeng, a contemporary of Liu's also committed to the cause, described the various revolutions in the colonial periphery joining with those erupting in the strong Western states as many "small streams" that would come together in a world revolution "as great as the ocean." In solidarity and a shared ideal of justice the weak could find the strength not just to save themselves but also to transform the world.[74]

This community of the oppressed was not in the post–May Fourth Chinese conception entirely egalitarian. China was not simply one, ordinary member; it was, rather, by virtue of its size, population, cultural heritage, or revolutionary experience a special country. It could play any of a variety of prominent roles. It could stand simply as an inspiration to others locked in similar struggles. It could be a repository of experience that younger political movements might draw from. It could assume a vanguard role in a pan-Asian or even global struggle against foreign domination. More ambitious still, it could be the source of a strategy of revolution or development suitable for copying by others. Most ambitious of all, it could serve the role of patron supplying material assistance and detailed advice.[75]

This concern with the weak and oppressed took a second, more immediate form—with those peoples occupying China's territorial periphery. Like the Chinese, they lived under feudal conditions and suffered from imperialist penetration and manipulation. They too needed revolution and deserved self-determination.

The sense of solidarity in this case was even more strongly qualified. An abstract feeling of sympathy collided with the far stronger spirit of patriotism. Chinese had rejected, at times even reviled, the Manchu dynasty, but at the same time they enthusiastically embraced and defended with remarkable tenacity the territorial boundaries carried to new limits by their conquerors. Chinese, in effect, made the Qianlong emperor (1736–1796) one of the fathers of their country. The great military campaigns launched during his rule brought striking gains to the empire all along the inner-

Asian frontier. Those acquisitions in Xinjiang, Mongolia, and Tibet all contained weak and oppressed peoples.

By claiming this inheritance, Chinese were caught in a bind. They could not surrender the territorial patrimony handed down from the Qing without also renouncing the dream of restoring China to a place of power, security, even greatness in the world. But they could not deny claims to self-determination along the frontier without also undermining their broad principle of solidarity with such weak and oppressed peoples.

The best way out of this contradiction was to claim for Chinese (meaning the Han) a position of superiority over ethnic and national groups along the border. From that position, Chinese leaders could pronounce with assurance that liberation and self-determination would inevitably result in the incorporation of minority peoples into a greater China.

The tension between this new-found sense of solidarity and an older sense of patriotism and superiority is evident in the outlook of Sun Yat-sen and Chiang Kai-shek. Already in the 1910s Sun had stressed China's unity with Asian revolutionary movements, and this feature of his thinking had become more marked under the influence of the Comintern in the 1920s. At the high tide of leftist influence in 1926, the Nationalist Party made much of the awakening of "the oppressed peoples in all colonies and semi-colonies" all around the world and their increasing unity. Even so, Sun insisted that China had a prominent role to play as inspiration, model, and even protector and teacher for fellow Asians.[76]

Notions of solidarity became even more problematic when Sun and later Chiang had to deal with China's own border peoples. On its founding in 1912 the Nationalist Party was resolutely imperial in its territorial claims. It then advanced as one of its basic goals "to enforce racial integration so that the various cultures within the Republic can be developed to become one enjoyed by all." Later party statements reiterated this commitment "to work for the integration of all the peoples of our country as a single Chinese nation." Stung by charges that the Nationalist Party had turned its back on self-determination, its leaders responded in a 1924 manifesto that all races "had a common interest in the national revolutionary movement" and even for a time later promised "the right of self-determination of all races within the country."[77]

Sun himself sought a way out of the contradiction by trying to distinguish China's expansion in Asia from the modern imperialism afflicting so many nations. China had exercised its influence through the cultural appeal of the "kingly way" (*wangdao*), whereas imperialism advanced through "military conquest and hegemony" (*badao*). The distinction among peoples living in China would gradually disappear, Sun contended, as the "Chinese race" pursued its "mission of realizing human equality." In time Manchu, Mongol, and Tibetan would all become part of "a single cultural and political whole." This meant in effect, Sun bluntly indicated in 1921, that the non-Han peoples would "be melted in the same furnace, to be assimilated within the Han nationality."[78]

Chiang went a step further and claimed that in effect a problem did not exist because minority peoples came from the same stock as the Han. In *China's Destiny*, published in 1943, he described the Muslim peoples, the Tibetans, and the Mongols as "clans" united to Han and Manchu by a process of continuous historical "blending" so that all five came to make up one nation. As late as 1945 the Nationalist Party was formally promising "independence and equality for all the racial groups within the country," but in the same breath stipulated that "independence" would take the form of "a high degree of autonomy" for Outer Mongolia and Tibet (both then well beyond Chinese control), and for others it meant simply "local self-government."[79]

The CCP was even more emphatic and tenacious in support of the international community of the abused, but here too expressions of support were joined to pretensions to superior standing. Once more we can turn to the Second Congress, where the party position was early and clearly staked out. It identified the "movement of national revolution" as a key part of the broader, Soviet-led revolutionary campaign to sweep away imperialism and capitalism. World War I and the example of the Russian Revolution had already spurred to resistance the oppressed nations of India, Egypt, Ireland, and Korea as well as China.[80]

Repeatedly in its early years the CCP returned to this theme in order to affirm its concern for and identity with those countries, and even its belief that China's revolution might speed the liberation of colonies and semi-colonies of the east such as the Philippines. The faith in this link grew if anything stronger in the Jiangxi period. One of the most sweeping of the claims for the global importance of China's revolution came from Wang Ming in the course of a speech to the Comintern Executive Committee in December 1933. The Chinese Soviet, he announced, had established itself alongside the USSR as a model that would exercise "an extremely great revolutionizing influence" on national revolutionary movements, not just throughout Asia— Annam, India, Japan, Korea, Taiwan, and maritime Southeast Asia—but *all* colonies and semi-colonies, even as far away as Cuba.[81]

Formal party pronouncements during the 1920s and early 1930s on the future of border areas supported self-determination in keeping with Soviet doctrine. That support was, however, usually highly qualified. One qualifying formula was to announce the right of peoples along the periphery to decide their own future and then to express confidence that they would choose some form of federation with China. The July 1922 Party Congress, the first to engage the issue formally, explicitly identified the peoples of Mongolia and Tibet and the Muslims of Xinjiang as distinct from the people of China proper. Exercising the right to self-determination, each was to organize autonomous, democratic states. They were then, the congress declared without explanation, to join with China proper in a Chinese federated republic.[82]

The alternative and ultimately more long-lived qualifying formula was to make self-determination dependent on China's minority nationalities, not only liberating themselves from feudal authorities and attitudes but doing so through the agency of the CCP. Thus self-determination was a distant goal to be achieved under the direction of a Han-dominated political party, not through well-entrenched or widely accepted indigenous elites. Speaking before a Comintern Congress in November 1922, Chen Duxiu endorsed self-determination for Mongols but then stressed the role that the CCP had to play. It was to "actively support them in the overthrow of the special privileges of the nobility and the higher-level lamas, to lay the foundation for their economy and culture, and to reach the objective possibility of true independence and autonomy for the Mongolian people."[83]

The party center would often follow with variations in language and emphasis this formula that Chen had articulated. Mongols and other minority people were both culturally distinct and participants in the national liberation movement. But their low cultural level made it unthinkable that they could stand alongside China as an equal. At the same time (so the CCP argument went) the political oppression by imperialism and warlords as well as by indigenous elites required CCP intervention to point the way and to pull these minority peoples into China's own revolutionary movement so that they could eventually determine their own fate.[84]

This blend of principle and paternalism continued into the Jiangxi period. For example, the Soviet's constitutional outline, promulgated in November 1931, was explicit and emphatic on minority right to self-determination. Peoples such as Mongols, Muslims, Tibetans, and Koreans could each if they wished move toward "separation from China" and "the formation by themselves of independent states." But reflecting its commitment to directed liberation, the Soviet promised "a considerable effort to help these small and weak people break away from the oppressive rule of imperialism, the Nationalist Party, warlords, the nobility, lamas, local headmen, and others and thereby reach complete freedom of choice." The Soviet also committed itself to "the development among these peoples of their own national cultures and national languages."[85]

A weak and dependent party could not, however, always evade Comintern expectations, especially where the interests of the USSR were involved. The Sixth Party Congress held in mid-1028 on Soviet soil was one time the CCP had to put asides its favored qualifying formula and was forced to offer instead a more resounding and unambiguous endorsement of self-determination for China's minorities. The CCP finally escaped with a resolution that delayed substantive consideration until the next party congress, providing in the interim for the study of the issue. The CCP had also been constrained din 1922 and again in 1926 to pronounce publicly its support for the independence of Outer Mongolia and to endorse the Soviet Union's assistance to that country, even though this position caused CCP members and sympathizers visible unease. Similarly in 1928 the CCP had to recognize that Taiwan's weak and oppressed people waged their liberation struggle apart from China's. But Li Da zhao's insistence that Taiwan was part of China by virtue of history and culture probably reflected the predominate sentiment within the CCP and foreshadowed party efforts to replace the Japanese Communist Party as the mentor of the Taiwan party branch following its organization in 1928.[86]

Orthodoxy in Flux

Desperate intellectuals at an impasse in solving China's crisis had eagerly embraced Comintern guidance and ideology in the 1920s. Among the consequences was a deepening understanding of Marxist-Leninist "theory" of international affairs. But with greater understanding came questions about interpreting this theory and translating it into policy. As they went about their work in the 1920s and early 1930s, CCP leaders encountered conceptual ambiguities as well as subversive subtexts that not only caused perplexity and division within the party but also led some leaders with a marked independent streak to go beyond the ready-made exegesis and roadmaps supplied by Moscow. How could they tell which imperialist powers with a stake in China or a role in China's politics bore careful watching? Would the Soviet Union really lend the CCP substantial support, and did it really understand China well enough to help? Could the struggles of other weak and oppressed nations be practically linked to China's struggle? How far could the CCP afford to go in advancing the principle of self-determination, especially for inhabitants of the border region?

When in 1936 Mao Zedong and a small fraction of those who had set off on the Long March arrived in the primitive northwest, they brought with them not only the now well-established international affairs orthodoxy but also a stubborn determination to continue to search within its parameters for satisfactory answers to these questions—answers that could help them realize their revolutionary dreams of creating a new if dimly imagined China.

PART THREE

Mao Zedong Takes Command

Chapter Five

Toward Foreign Policy Autonomy, 1935–1945

It has long been clear that Mao Zedong's rise to dominance within the Chinese Communist Party effected some important changes in the party's external relations. By the early 1930s the leading figures in the CCP had strong views on international affairs but nothing that could be called a foreign policy. Through the late 1930s and 1940s Mao would begin to lay the foundations for such a policy as he charted his own course—one directed toward implicating the Soviet Union and the United States in Chinese affairs in ways favorable to the CCP's struggle for power. Much debated in the past, the nature and significance of these initiatives are now a good deal clearer thanks to the appearance of new materials. They highlight the extraordinary degree to which the emergence and evolution of that policy was inseparable from Mao's command of the party, his understanding of party orthodoxy, and his sponsorship of a clear and compelling program that promised to carry the party out of the political wilderness.

Mao's Rise to the Top

The 1920s and the early 1930s had provided Mao his training in party politics. The first stage of his career as a party activist played out within his

Portions of this and the following chapter got their first tryout in "The Genesis of Chinese Communist Foreign Policy: Mao Zedong Takes Command, 1935–1949" (Washington: Asia Program occasional paper, Woodrow Wilson International Center for Scholars, December 1991).

native province of Hunan. After attending the CCP's First Congress in Shanghai in July 1921, he returned home to serve as secretary of the provincial party committee, and in 1922 he threw himself into labor organizing. His activism set him on a collision course with the local warlord and finally forced him to flee to Shanghai in April 1923. The following June at the CCP's Third Congress he was elected to the Central Committee, marking the beginning of Mao's half-century of involvement in the upper echelons of the party hierarchy.

In the mid-1920s Mao wholeheartedly embraced cooperation with the Nationalists. He channeled his energy into mass mobilization, including propaganda work and training of cadres assigned to the countryside, and he continued to sharpen his skills as an organizer and a propagandist. Mao's health failed in 1924, forcing him to retire to Hunan in November for convalescence. He spent the last two years of the CCP's cooperative relationship with the Nationalists studying his own Hunanese countryside and training peasant activists.

The April 1927 coup marked a distinct shift in Mao's political career. He now tried his hand at military affairs operating at county and district level. By 1930 he had assembled two army corps (totalling about three thousand men) in the area of the Jinggang mountains in what would become the main CCP base with its center of gravity in Jiangxi province. When a provisional Soviet government was established there in November 1931, Mao became its chairman. The subsequent transfer of top party leaders from Shanghai to the base area diminished Mao's authority, even though he remained the titular head of the government. He watched as Chiang Kai-shek's forces wore down the base-area defenses, and then in October 1934 he joined in the circuitous flight to the northwest known as the Long March.

The Zunyi conference, held on January 15–17, 1935 in the midst of the Long March, boosted Mao's position. In December, on the eve of the conference, the party center had issued a defense of its record, claiming that the events of the past year had confirmed not only its but also the Comintern's correct estimate of the situation in China.[1] Mao would have none of this. In advance of the conference he had carefully prepared the groundwork for an attack on the failed military strategy of those who had pushed him aside. With his support and arguments lined up, Mao easily won the contest. While the conference put one of the Russian-trained leaders in place of another as party head (Zhang Wentian succeeded Bo Gu), it did lift Mao into the Political Bureau standing committee and opened the way for his growing control of military affairs in 1935 and 1936.[2] His successful handling of the last stage of the Long March, including Zhang Guotao's challenge to central party authority in early August 1935, were in turn to establish him as the leader most likely to take the party out of the slough of military weakness and political irrelevance.

By the conclusion of the sixth plenum of the sixth Central Committee in December 1938, Mao had established his preeminent position. In September 1941 he secured Political Bureau condemnation of the political line followed by the party between 1931 and 1935 as a "left deviation," thus vindicating his own critique of that line while diminishing the standing of potential rivals within the party leadership. In March 1943 his dominance was formally registered when he gained the chair of the Political Bureau and concurrently of a Secretariat also consisting of Liu Shaoqi and Ren Bishi. By this time Mao had well under way a campaign to rectify the CCP and thereby impress on it his concerns and style. After securing the agreement of the Political Bureau in September 1941, Mao had formally launched the rectification movement in February 1942. By the end of the year rectification had been completed in Yanan. In the spring of 1943 it was extended to base-area cadres.[3]

The rectification campaign of the early 1940s climaxed by the Seventh Party Congress of 1945 set Mao beyond easy challenge. The congress itself, contemplated as early as 1931, finally edged into the realm of reality in May 1944 when the seventh plenum of the sixth Central Committee convened in Yanan to begin preparations. (It remained in session until the eve of the congress in April of the next year.) Mao along with Zhu De, Liu Shaoqi, Ren Bishi, and Zhou Enlai constituted the presidium that was to direct those preparations while also attending to daily party business normally handled by the Political Bureau's standing committee or the Secretariat.[4]

The presidium presented the party program to the 725 congress delegates assembled in Yanan between April 23 and June 11, 1945. According to party estimates, they represented 1,210,000 party members and an armed force of 910,000 regulars and 2,200,000 militia. The program formally elevated Mao's thought to the status of party orthodoxy and revised party history to legitimate his leadership. Following the adjournment of the congress, the new Central Committee met on June 19 and confirmed Mao's status as undisputed leader. It made him chairman of the Central Committee itself as well as of the Political Bureau and of the Secretariat, now expanded to include Zhou Enlai and Zhu De. Mao was now firmly ensconced at the top.

Mao and Orthodoxy

Mao began his journey toward CCP leadership with an unequivocal but strikingly uneven commitment to the international affairs orthodoxy. That this unevenness was already evident during his early years in the party is something of a surprise given his profession of faith at the time of his political conversion. Between 1919 and early 1921 Mao had evinced a deep-seated commitment to saving China from foreign domination (a condition he had then formally associated with the term "imperialism"). He had also expressed a high regard for the Soviet Union as a model and source of support and a conviction that China was part of a global community of weak and oppressed peoples. In a striking prefiguring of things to come, his views between the early 1920s and mid-1930s did not give even approximately equal attention to the elements in the orthodox triad.

Mao's anti-imperialism was particularly robust but at the same time lopsided in its development. The imperialist powers emerge from his writing in those years as pale and distant apparitions though unmistakably malignant. "Cunning" and "vicious," they had arrived at global domination driven by their economic needs.[5] Following the conventional formula, Mao took note of the internal class conflicts and the global rivalries that would together destroy them. But these features were a given, and the details of no particular moment to Mao.

What gave Mao's understanding of imperialism life and importance in his own intellectual scheme of things was a passionate identification with the problems and potential of the Chinese people struggling under foreign domination. His burning populist concerns led him to think of China's relationship with imperialism in terms of a "dialectics of disorder and oppression."[6] In those dialectics the subordinated and divided Chinese nation loomed far larger than ascendant outsiders. As imperialist exploitation and repression deranged their country, Mao argued time and again, Chinese would become increasingly radicalized. As popular commitment, numbers, and organization grew under the whip of crisis, the revolution would develop an irresistible power and momentum that would sweep away the imperialist order in China. "The whole body of the oppressed popular masses is the real master of every Chinese problem," he could declare with assurance in November 1925.[7]

In Mao's thinking on how the dialectic would play out within China, a Marxist understanding of class was considerably less important than a patriot's preference for drawing political lines according to attitudes toward foreign domination. In drawing these critical lines Mao came early to insist on the inclusion of the peasantry in his great popular, anti-imperialist bloc. "The peasant has become the central issue of the national revolution," Mao announced sometime in the second half of 1927. And he added for emphasis, "Whoever opposes the peasant movement opposes the revolution."[8] By including peasants in his revolutionary coalition, indeed by making them the main force (while formally reserving the leadership to the party of the proletariat), Mao assured the revolution massive numerical superiority over the forces defending an imperialist and reactionary order.

Giving vent to an instinctive and habitual numerology, Mao calculated in early 1926 that "the popular masses" came to 395 million (according to his precise calculations 98.75 percent of China's total population). Only a small minority of Chinese serving as tools of imperialism—the warlords, big bourgeoisie, landlords, and evil gentry—placed themselves beyond the political pale. Mao figured these collaborators with imperialism came to only 1 million (.25 percent of China's total). A somewhat larger minority—a petty bourgeoisie of 4 million (or 1 percent)—was caught in the middle, torn between fear of revolution and hostility to imperialism and reaction. At least some of this middle group, Mao contended, could be drawn into the anti-imperialist cause.[9]

Mao's reading of imperialism and its impact on China led him, like other founders of the party, to a highly voluntaristic understanding of the Chinese revolution. He was too impatient to leave the destruction of imperialist control to the operation of the universal laws of historical development. How long would it take for socioeconomic conditions to emerge that were conducive to a bourgeois revolution? And even after the final victory of the revolution, how much longer would it take to reach the stage of socialist transformation? Rejecting China's salvation as a distant dream, indeed determined to see emancipation from foreign control in his lifetime, Mao placed his hope for an early victory in the sheer mass and determination of a united people.[10]

While the years of cooperation with the Nationalists were especially conducive to Mao's populist and anti-imperialist views, those views would continue to predominate even after Chiang Kai-shek's dramatic rupture with the CCP in spring 1927 and the CCP's shift toward a more revolutionary stance.[11]

As earlier, Mao's grasp of the major imperialists' general foreign policies and domestic conditions was remarkably thin. An analysis such as he offered in December 1930 of their disordered internal situation, itself unusual in Mao's commentary for its detail, illustrates the limits of his understanding. He noted then that Britain was in deep economic trouble and that Germany was in the grip of labor unrest. Japan was suffering from earthquake damage (suggesting natural disasters served a function akin to class conflict in promoting revolutionary change). While the U.S. Communist Party was a growing political force, American workers still starved alongside growing mountains of grain (prompting Mao to ask rhetorically, "Now tell me, is imperialism strange or what?"). Even this bit of reportage did little more than confirm that trouble was brewing in a system that Mao already knew was doomed. He could not connect this ferment abroad in any concrete, plausible, or practical way to China's struggling revolution.[12]

Also as before, Mao's international affairs commentary gave prominence to the impact on China of imperialist schemes and rivalries and particularly to the spur of oppression that would rouse the Chinese people (peasants not least of all) to revolutionary activity.[13] If anything his populist and patriotic appeal became even more marked in this period in reaction against Japan's occupation of the northeast provinces (Manchuria) in fall 1931 and the subsequent extension of Japanese influence over north China. Mao began to sprinkle his public appeals more liberally with phrases drawn from his own writings from the teens as well as the lexicon of the Chinese patriot. He warned that Chinese stood on the brink of becoming "slaves without a country" (*wangguonu*) and "slaves and beasts of burden" (*niuma nuli*).[14] In similarly graphic language familiar from patriotic discourse, he mocked the Nationalists as the epitome of national betrayal. They were "scavengers" of the imperialists. They were cursed with "the slavish nature of a running dog." They were "traitors to the Han."[15] This language reflected Mao's own persistent populist sensibilities as well as his growing skill as a propagandist with a knack for striking a popular chord.

Between 1931 and 1934 Japan's appetite for territory combined with the recurrent Nationalist encirclement campaigns posed so grave a threat to Mao's China and his base area that he began to tinker with two important features of his anti-imperialist faith. He proved unwilling, however, to undertake any fundamental revisions in that faith.

One point on which Mao did some soul-searching was whether the imperialists had to be treated as an undifferentiated bloc. Were they equally dangerous? Or was Japan posing such a serious threat to China's physical survival that the CCP should limit its attack to that target and seek ways to intensify and exploit the palpable antagonism displayed by the other imperialists toward Japan? Could the resentment engendered by Japan's gains be turned to the defense of China and perhaps even the reduction of imperialist support for the Nationalist campaigns of repression aimed at the CCP?

Mao's public attacks on imperialism during this period did gradually make Japan the major target. But even in the darkest days of 1934 he would not take the last logical step—to designate Japan the overriding threat to China's survival and to contemplate ways a weak revolutionary force might help save China and improve its own position by aligning with imperialists also threatened by the powerful Japanese advance. Into every statement, however emphatic it might be on the Japanese peril, Mao continued to insert somewhere a short if blanket condemnation of all imperialists.[16] They were determined to defend their interests in China. Thus, on the one hand they sought to offset Japanese gains by each carving out their own piece of territory, and on the other hand they sought to crush the threat of revolution by backing the Nationalists. Imperialists still seemed to agree that compromise within their own ranks might avert a destabilizing and destructive war and that survival of the Nationalists was the best guarantee of a quiescent China.

As if to leave no doubts about his unqualified opposition to imperialism, Mao revived warnings (first sounded in the mid-1920s) against indulging false hopes of help from the imperialists. He condemned the illusion that the United States or the League of Nations, no more than a tool of imperialism, would come to China's rescue.[17] The only kind of international united front that he could imagine with imperialist countries was not with their ruling elites but rather with their proletariat and other progressive forces. The latter could help in a small way by opposing their governments' support for Chiang Kai-shek, especially his assault on the base area. But the infrequency of Mao's appeal even to this quarter—limited to a couple of occasions in August and September 1933—suggests that Mao saw the solutions to China's problems in China itself.[18]

The other point in Mao's anti-imperialism under stress in the early 1930s was his definition of "the people." How far could the CCP go to win the middle group caught between revolution and counterrevolution? Was it possible that even the small but powerful minority making up the big bourgeoisie might be drawn into a still broader alliance with revolutionary forces against the common enemy, Japan? Mao's impulse to expand the revolutionary tent became evident in January 1933 when he linked his name to an appeal to noncommunist military forces to join the CCP in resisting Japan as well as the traitorous Nationalist regime. By June 1934 he had further extended the circle of possible allies. He wanted a "united front" that would transcend "political tendency," "occupation," and "gender."[19] But here too Mao moved cautiously, leaving vague how many of the middle groups he wished to draw in and still leaving beyond the popular pale the reactionary minority ready to compound with or appease imperialism. The united front from below still prevailed in his thinking; the united front from above would have to wait.

Mao's deep preoccupation with imperialist machinations within China and the prospects for popular resistance thrust the other two elements central to the CCP's international affairs orthodoxy deep into the ideological shadows. Mao accorded the CCP's special relationship with the USSR and the weak and oppressed only scanty treatment. A single significant comment with an internationalist flavor appeared before spring 1927: a sweeping declaration of faith in January 1926 that the ultimate goal of China's revolution was the elimination of imperialism around the world and the creation of a global alliance of freedom and equality.[20] After Chiang's coup and particularly during the Jiangxi Soviet period references became somewhat more common but were still in the main brief and perfunctory.

Through this entire period, running from the early 1920s to the mid-1930s, the only distinct, elaborated statement of the full orthodoxy came in a January 1934 report Mao offered as head of the Soviet government to a major gathering of representatives from the various CCP base areas. There he celebrated the Soviet Union's achievements in economic development and defense, and contrasted those advances with the economic hardships and social unrest afflicting capitalist countries. Seeking to save themselves from an imminent and deadly "general crisis," the capitalists were intensifying their aggressive foreign policy. The result was sharpening rivalries among them and the threat of an intra-systemic war. To avoid such a disastrous outcome, they were predictably joining together in plotting an attack on the USSR and (Mao could not resist adding) China. The strengthened position of the USSR together with the reckless adventurism of the imperialists created, he claimed, bright prospects for a world revolution. Indulging the concern closest to his heart, he predicted that China would occupy a specially prominent place in that revolution.[21]

Mao's other internationalist statements appear even more seriously compromised by his abiding and intrusive patriotism. His internationalism was thus variously ill-digested, contradictory, and even subverted. For example, in October 1928 Mao drew one of his few comparisons between the Chinese and Russian revolutions, suggesting in passing that China's 1927 revolutionary upsurge and failure resembled Russia's 1905 upheaval. Then within that same analysis he contradicted himself by contending that China's segmented rural economy and semi-colonial foreign domination made his country's position unique. Or again an equally off-handed comparison between China's revolution and the Russian experience offered in February 1930 came immediately on the heels of an unqualified claim for the exceptional character of China's Soviet.[22]

The Soviet Union as an ally rather than a model figured more prominently but no less problematically in Mao's thinking. In January 1929 a declaration issued under his name relegated unity with the world proletariat and the Soviet Union to last place on a ten-point CCP platform.[23] The next year he shifted toward greater solicitude for the safety of the USSR, echoing calls from the party center to defend the Soviet Union by resisting mounting imperialist pressure. That year and again in September and October 1932 Mao warned that China might serve as a base for an attack on the USSR and that crushing the Chinese revolution was but a prelude to that attack.[24]

Mao's observations stopped just short of contending that the obligations of support were reciprocal, but embattled cadres would have had no difficulty grasping the implication. Mao's own formulation of the problem made clear that if the USSR lost China as an outer bulwark of the world revolution, then the main citadel would be all the more isolated and vulnerable to a direct imperialist onslaught. The logical question to ask then was why not a more vigorous effort by the Soviet Union to help the struggling CCP if for no other reason than self-preservation. Hopes for some dramatic intervention by the friendly neighbor to the north had crossed Mao's mind in the mid-1920s, and he may well have continued into the early 1930s to play with the idea of the Soviet Union launching a diversionary probe along the Sino-Soviet border that might relieve the Chinese Soviet from the repeated and ultimately exhausting Nationalist assault. If so, it was not to be the last time his thoughts would run in this direction.

A belief in the community of the weak and oppressed was easily the most anemic aspect of Mao's version of the orthodoxy. Like his views on the special Soviet relationship, it was overwhelmed by his full-bodied patriotism and commitment to China's own revolution. For example, in August 1933 when he pointed to the sorry state into which the Indian and Korean people had fallen, he was not arguing for a commonality of interests among Asians but pointing to negative examples intended to rally Chinese to save themselves.[25]

Similarly, Mao conveyed scant sense of concern with liberating the weak and oppressed peoples along China's own imperiled border. When in August 1933 he expressed worry about the future of Tibet and then in January 1934 when he explicated the Jiangxi Soviet policy toward China's minorities, his remarks revealed above all a determination to safeguard his country's periphery. He wanted to block foreign penetration (in this case British schemes to revive the Tibetan kingdom) and to reserve to China the prerogative of directing border peoples, including Tibetans, Mongols, Koreans, and Vietnamese, toward a better future. Borrowing from the widely accepted 1920s formula, Mao explained that they would all travel along a revolutionary road charted by the CCP and that ultimately the end of class exploitation within each nationality would lead to a unity of nationalities.[26] Thus as Mao conceived it, self-determination or even autonomy was theoretically possible but in practical terms unlikely.

Orthodoxy, Foreign Policy, and the Maoist Program

Mao's already idiosyncratic understanding of the international orthodoxy would continue to evolve after the Long March as he assumed increasing responsibility for the future of the CCP. Between 1935 and 1938 Mao fashioned a broad party strategy and around it built a durable consensus. That strategy was governed by practical calculations over the route most likely to carry the CCP to power. The imperatives of the old orthodoxy were rigorously subordinated to that strategy with the result that tendencies in Mao's early approach to international affairs became more marked. The party's first foray onto the foreign policy stage was thus guided by a patriot's preoccupation with saving China from foreign threat, a utopian's faith in rapid social transformation, and an opportunist's eye for manipulating other international actors.

Mao's emergent strategy reflected above all else a practical awareness, won through hard experience, of the CCP's fragility and the obstacles standing in the way of the party's advance. Already pessimistic in the mid-1920s over the CCP's limited revolutionary prospects, Mao had like others absorbed the debilitating and demoralizing blows that Chiang had delivered twice within less than a decade—first with ease in 1927 and then with greater effort in 1934. The harrowing experience of the ensuing Long March further deepened this sense of vulnerability. As Mao himself noted soon afterward, this second stunning setback had reduced party forces as well as membership from 300,000 to a few tens of thousands, destroyed almost all party organs in Nationalist areas, and cost all revolutionary bases but one.[27]

Mao and his chief lieutenants in the late 1930s and early 1940s understandably placed a high premium on devising a strategy that guaranteed immediate survival and held some promise of ultimately winning power. A popular but defenseless party, relying only on political education and mass mobilization (as it had before 1927), would fall easy prey to its armed foes, whether the Nationalists or the Japanese or both. Similarly a party, however well entrenched in remote base areas, could be cornered and rooted out if it did not cultivate broad popular support. Since either strategy alone risked defeat, Mao ultimately concluded that the party's best hope for banishing the specter of vulnerability was to pursue a delicately balanced two-track policy.

One track led to the building of new base areas. They would sustain the Red Army, essential to CCP security, while government institutions and programs within those base areas would reach an ever broader population essential to the ultimate success of the party on the national stage. These local resources would enable the CCP to hold body and soul together while preparing to make its ultimate bid for power.

Mao's commitment to the base-area side of his strategy was particularly strong, sustained by several lines of experience. During his activist days in Hunan in 1920 he had championed provincial autonomy. Like base areas later, autonomous provinces then served in Mao's reckoning as arenas in which limited change was possible when national conditions ruled out more sweeping efforts. He argued then that such local initiatives gave an important outlet for those determined to begin China's renovation at once, and might by example stir to action doubting or hesitant countrymen in other areas.[28]

Once driven in the late 1920s into the military phase of his revolutionary career, Mao appears to have begun to think of base areas as lairs in the wilderness in which the CCP units might hide and from which they might spring at the propitious moment. He first suggested this notion in an October 1928 resolution which argued the importance of a standing, effective CCP armed force ready to swing into action when China was finally shaken by global crisis. Indeed Mao's attachment to this notion is strikingly evident in his embrace of the Li Lisan strategy with its central premise that the CCP could ride to power on the waves of discontent created by a systemic crisis.[29]

While Li's plans collapsed under the weight of Comintern criticism and growing Nationalist strength, Mao seems to have held to his faith in the armed base as a staging area from which to seize ultimate victory. By 1932 his eyes had caught on a new development that might create a fresh opening for party forces to exploit. Japan's invasion of China had further destabilized an already tense set of relations among the imperialists, while the continuing domestic consolidation of the Soviet Union had fed imperialist anxieties over their own decline even as socialism advanced. These pressures within the imperialist system might precipitate intra-systemic war or a coordinated attack on the USSR. Either of these developments or even some combination of both might, Mao contended, set off a revolutionary upsurge in China as elsewhere around the world. The CCP's task was to be ready when the crisis came. Once more Mao watched and waited but still in vain.[30]

The other track in what would become Mao's general strategy led to a broad united front, critical to drawing allies to the CCP and isolating its enemies. Mao's own populist instincts made him sympathetic to the general principle of maximizing cooperation and minimizing conflict among Chinese. In the 1910s Mao had penned some striking commentary on the power the Chinese people might wield if only they were united. In the mid-1920s he had committed himself enthusiastically to collaboration with the Nationalists and to mass mobilization. Even in the period in the wilderness during the late 1920s and early 1930s he had retained his attachment to the conception of the CCP not as an isolated vanguard party but as the leader and articulator of the needs of the entire people. Even so he had then been cautious in drawing the middle elements into the ranks of the "people," while the reactionaries were unthinkable as an ally.

Whatever Mao's reservations, pressures within the party—reinforced by Moscow—pushed the united front to the fore in the mid-1930s. At first with tacit and then more forceful backing from the Comintern, Wang Ming had begun to press in the last year of the Jiangxi Soviet to replace the united front "from below" that included little room for any but the most revolutionary classes (the peasantry and the proletariat) with one "from above" that included all but the most reactionary elements. He and other advocates of a broad united front saw the future of the CCP less in terms of peasant armies operating in remote base areas and more in terms of a return to developed urban centers and a revival of cooperation with the Nationalists. The first hints of this new approach appeared in the first half of 1933 when the CCP had sought to break out of its isolation by appealing to "white" (i.e., noncommunist) armies and to all petty bourgeoisie in the Japanese-occupied northeast.[31]

In April 1934 the party center significantly broadened its definition of potential allies, replacing a class-based, distinctly internationalist criteria for cooperation with one that was genuinely patriotic. Pressed by the fifth encirclement campaign and prodded by Moscow, the CCP recognized that it had reached "a new juncture of the utmost gravity" and agreed to advertise through a patriotic front organization in Shanghai its new position. The CCP now recognized "as friends of our Chinese nation" *all* anti-Japanese elements whether in China or abroad who supported or even felt sympathy and goodwill toward China's resistance. "At the same time," it declared, "we will take as fellow thieves of the Japanese imperialists and we will regard as enemies of the Chinese people whichever country helps Japanese imperialism, opposes the Chinese people, or emulates the kind of carving up of China carried out by the Japanese bandits." In July with its territory shrinking and with much fanfare over CCP forces about to march north to resist the Japanese, the party issued a secret general notice confirming the new, more broadly defined united front.[32]

The CCP's commitment to making any enemy of Japan the party's friend was not yet four-square. Not only did it hold back from a direct public announcement, but it also continued to invoke older contradictory themes. A manifesto issued in June by the Soviet Republic stressed not the fresh possibility of great-power resistance to Japan but rather the familiar danger of the powers partitioning China. Bo Gu followed in July with a speech that served up a positive review of recent Comintern policy strongly spiced with appropriate internationalist and class themes. Standing safely before a podium in Moscow, Wang Ming reiterated those themes in November, raising further doubts about the direction of party policy.[33]

In the spring of 1934 the Comintern's Executive Committee on which Wang Ming served had begun to adopt a "people's" front, thus reinforcing Wang's tendency in that direction. In June he began to draft for review by Joseph Stalin and the head of the Comintern, Georgi Dimitrov, a declaration formally establishing the new united front in China. Delivered in August at the Seventh Comintern Congress and published in Paris in October, the new position wrote finis to the united front from below. It called for an end to domestic political quarrels the better to resist Japan and for the formation of a united government of national defense. Wang dispatched three couriers back to China with details of the shift. Party leaders, assembled in Wayaobao in December 1935, dutifully endorsed the August declaration.[34]

Mao was not at the forefront of these policy changes. His lingering distrust of former foes, especially Chiang and the Nationalist Party, held him back. So too did his preference for giving priority to building base areas.

Mao's hedged acceptance of the new united front and the concerns behind them had by 1936 set the ascendant figure within the CCP on a collision course with the dominant CCP figure in Moscow. While Wang Ming sought to open his own line of negotiations with Chiang Kai-shek (using Pan Hannian as his agent), Mao continued to depict the Nationalist leader as an unbending reactionary. Once it became apparent that the party center had reservations about the new policy line, the Comintern's Executive Committee responded with orders to give greater priority to building an anti-fascist united front even if this meant transforming the Soviet Republic into a more open Democratic Republic and acknowledging that resistance to Japan took precedence over the fight against Chiang. Between July and September the party center finally fell in line. It would henceforth attempt to unite with Chiang in the interest of anti-Japanese resistance and put pressure on him to play a more forceful part as the leader of that national resistance. At the same time Mao as well as Zhou Enlai began making conciliatory personal overtures to leading nonparty political figures, including prominent Nationalists.[35]

Mao's doubts, however, persisted and finally led him to open resistance following Wang Ming's triumphal return to China in November 1937. Wang wanted to give the united-front policy primacy at expense of the base areas. Mao responded that an unqualified policy of cooperation with the Nationalists amounted to capitulation and failed to recognize the pivotal role of the base areas as the party's only ensurance against "extermination." The party needed, Mao argued, two tracks—base areas as well as united front. Mao lost his first face-off with Wang at a party meeting in early 1938 but prevailed in a rematch later in the year. Mao carried the day with his argument that China's revolutionary path had to take account of conditions peculiar to China, including notably the prominence of armed struggle among contending political forces and hence the imperative for the CCP to build its own military force. United-front activities were important, but they served only as auxiliaries to the party's prime concern with the military and the supporting base areas.[36]

Mao would hold the CCP to this dual policy. As he time and again explained in the years that followed, the CCP would seek cooperation through a broad united front (to include even the Nationalists), but it would also retain its politically autonomous base areas and independent armed forces. Maintenance of the bases and their armies would in themselves promote cooperation by commanding the respect of the Nationalists. And if cooperation failed, a CCP that still possessed armed base areas would not be left vulnerable. Mao explained, "Today's policy of anti-Japanese national united front is not all unity denying struggle, and it is not all struggle denying unity. It is rather a two-sided policy of unity and struggle."[37] Mao would decide where to strike the balance and when to adjust it.

The rectification campaign that followed within the party in the early 1940s had among its goals promoting an understanding of this flexible, two-track strategy and an acceptance of Mao as the ultimate arbiter of policy choices. Beginning with party leaders and then moving on to the rank and file, he asked them to discard old ideological shibboleths imported from Moscow in the 1920s and instead to think in more concretely Chinese terms. He also asked them to accept a tighter organizational structure essential to implementing a strategy of maneuver. Only a unified party with a shared outlook and a responsive hierarchy stood any chance of wartime military survival and of political success afterward.[38]

The Seventh Party Congress in 1945 formally installed as party policy Mao's postwar program that rested on his two-track strategy. The congress argued against a cookie-cutter approach to revolution. To be sure, China would have its own bourgeois revolution, but it would unfold according to the particular conditions prevailing within the country. Mao and his chief associates pronounced the prospects for revolution unpromising, and thus warned that the day of victory for the worker-peasant alliance led by the CCP was still far off. This conclusion was embellished in the new party constitution. "The resistance on the revolutionary road is especially formidable and that in turn determines the uneven nature of China's revolution, the long term nature of the revolution, [and] the complicated nature of the revolutionary struggle."[39]

At the same time major congress documents optimistically envisioned a long period of peace, democratization, and reconstruction in which the Chinese revolution could safely unfold. Given the name "new democracy," this stage in China's development was the product of a new international climate, according to Mao's now widely accepted appraisal. World War II had launched a progressive tide around the world that would sweep from China civil conflict and one-party rule and clear the ground for economic reconstruction. In this new atmosphere the CCP's unity, popularity, and organizational and mobilization skills would give it an advantage over the Nationalists and would ultimately carry the CCP to power and in time China to socialism. The alternative scenario—a return to military conflict perhaps reinforced and complicated by international tensions—was not one in which the party would do well if the past were any guide.

The uncertain path ahead with its moments of potential danger required, Mao contended, the flexibility and initiative of the two-pronged strategy combining base areas with united-front work. He could expand the party's territorial base at the expense of the Nationalists, pursue cooperation with them at the national level, or even mix expansion and cooperation in changing proportions. He could employ front organizations along with military operations, and seek to set in harness together peasant and landlord as well as worker and factory owner. This strategy linked to the new democracy political program would serve as the CCP's guide to action down through November 1946, and important elements of it would persist down to victory in 1949 and even beyond.

The task of expanding and strengthening base areas, well advanced by early 1945, enjoyed priority not because it was the prelude to a military lunge at the Nationalists. Rather secure, substantial base areas were the prerequisite to implementing a political program of peaceful CCP-Nationalist competition ("democratization") and central-government reform. Party leaders feared that the Nationalists might again resort to "bandit extermination" to preserve their autocratic, one-party rule. Mao characteristically assumed that only after Chiang became convinced that the CCP—firmly in control of its own territory and effectively defended by its own army—could not be crushed or intimidated would he grudgingly accept it as a legitimate political player.

The united front still figured as an important auxiliary to base building. The CCP wanted to compete in Nationalist-controlled territory, and only a moderate program would win support there and check the more reactionary, anti-communist elements within the Nationalist Party opposed to democratization. If successful, the united front would carry the CCP to a place of national influence alongside its chief political rival. But even if cooperation failed, united-front resources could be used to sow disorder and doubt within the enemy camp.

The determination to make inroads in Nationalist-dominated areas and to attract wavering urban groups had been reflected in party-center directives as early as September 1940. Developing a strong presence in cities as part of united-front work remained high on the CCP agenda. The presidium preparing the Seventh Party Congress agenda in 1944–1945 paid particular attention to building the urban base of support essential to any postwar drive for power. Not surprisingly, party leaders in rural exile dreamed of a return to the cities and their rich resources, substantial proletariat, and advanced culture.[40]

When Mao and other leaders said that they sought long-term coexistence with the Nationalist Party and desired a nonviolent, political solution to China's problems, they meant it, and the planning into which they poured thought and resources reflected it. To take these points seriously is to run against our conceptions of Mao as a deep-dyed, impatient radical (a view shaped by post-1949 developments) and our tendency to see a CCP-Nationalist military collision as inevitable, with the CCP merely waiting for the right moment to strike. We should not let the later military resolution of the rivalry and the strong radical current after 1949 color our understanding of the first phases of Mao's policy. Nor should we assume that Mao's ultimate loyalties were not to the complete triumph of the CCP to be followed by a far-reaching renovation of his country. The circumstances in 1945 simply did not bode well for either prospect, and Mao, who well knew it, made one of those practical, calculated adjustments that seem in retrospect a hallmark of his political career.

The implications of this adjustment for foreign policy—and the international affairs orthodoxy—had by 1945 become strikingly evident. It had led on the one side to redefining the special relationship with the USSR. And on the other side it had drawn Mao toward the United States, the imperialist with a growing influence over China and the major sponsor of the Nationalists. As both the arbiter of party orthodoxy and the architect of party policy, Mao was intent on creating a foreign policy that would serve the interests of the CCP and the requirements of his dual-track strategy.

Yanan and Moscow

On the surface Mao's public response to international developments from the late 1930s would suggest a placid acceptance of Comintern direction and the overriding claims of the USSR on junior communist parties. In July 1937 on the outbreak of the Sino-Japanese war Mao raised his voice in favor of "immediately concluding a military and political alliance with the Soviet Union and closely uniting with this country most reliable, most powerful, and most capable of helping China resist Japan."[41]

From 1939 through mid-1941 Mao's own commentary on international affairs gamely justified a shifting Soviet policy beginning with the Soviet-Japanese nonaggression pact of September 15, 1938, followed by the Soviet nonaggression pact with Germany (August 23, 1939) and the ensuing attack on Poland, and continuing down to the Soviet neutrality pact with Japan (April 13, 1941). Throughout Mao defended the Soviet Union's policy of temporization, blaming the wavering stance of the United States, Britain, and France for the difficult choices Moscow made. Mao's loyalty won him praise from the Comintern's Executive Committee. The special relationship seemed alive and well.[42]

But behind the scenes Mao began in the late 1930s and continued into the early 1940s to work free of the organizational constraints that the Comintern had fastened on the CCP. No longer would Moscow call the shots within the Chinese party. Mao would alternately honor, attempt to use, or even ignore Moscow—always with an eye on advancing his own supple, even opportunistic two-pronged domestic strategy. In the process he would both call into question the old terms of the special relationship and begin the shaping of a foreign policy in which the USSR was for a time at least a notably minor presence.

The upheaval occasioned by the Long March itself created space between the CCP and Moscow. Radio contact had been lost altogether in mid-November 1934 when the bulky transmitting equipment was jettisoned at the outset of the retreat. Radio contact was briefly established for a few weeks in October 1935 until the equipment the Soviets had sent to

Wayaobao broke down. Otherwise, the CCP operated on its own with contacts with Moscow limited to occasional couriers. After the Zunyi conference Chen Yun traveled to Moscow to report on its decisions, while Lin Yuying reached Wayaobao in mid-November 1935 and gave the party center its first briefing on the Comintern's Seventh Congress. Not until sometime around June 1936 did a transmitter and codes arrive from the Soviet Union.

By the time radio contact was restored, the CCP had begun to move toward greater autonomy and self-reliance. During the Long March party leaders spurred by Mao had turned a critical eye on the military policy that had resulted in the Jiangxi defeat. The resulting critique immediately discredited Moscow's own representative, Otto Braun, and returned to prominence in party councils the base-area leaders that the newcomers from Shanghai had earlier pushed aside. Some of the old Shanghai leadership, such as Wang Jiaxiang, Zhang Wentian, and Zhou Enlai, desperate for some new approach that might bring an end to the party's long string of reverses, moved toward the side of the proponents of the militarized base areas.

Moscow made its own contributions to this readjustment of the relationship. In 1935 the Seventh Comintern Congress coupled its announcement of a popular-front policy with a call for an end to interference in the internal affairs of its party branches and for the creative application of Comintern policies to the special conditions facing each party. Stalin and Dimitrov were thereafter through the late 1930s to reiterate to the CCP the importance of making its own decisions in light of changing conditions (even while offering advice on the need for a greater proletarian presence within the CCP). At the same time they supported Mao's claims to leadership, giving him high marks as a "brilliant strategist" and a "thorough Bolshevik" even during Wang Ming's tenure as the CCP's representative to the Comintern. Dimitrov himself urged Wang Ming on the eve of his return to China to assume a deferential mien, and again in mid-1938 sent word back that Wang Ming was not to compete with Mao for leadership.[43]

As Mao came increasingly to dominate the party center, he began to draw the main lines of communication with Moscow into his own hands. He dispatched to Moscow party envoys whom he could trust to reflect his own increasingly influential views and support his claims to leadership. Wang Jiaxiang, one of the Russian-educated who had early on thrown his support to Mao, arrived in 1937 to fill the post that Wang Ming had vacated. He was followed by others who continued to secure Mao's relationship with the Comintern—Ren Bishi in 1938 and Zhou Enlai in late

1939 and early 1940. Soon thereafter (at latest by fall 1941) Mao secured direct control over the Central Committee's long-range radio linking it to Moscow. Cumulatively, these initiatives gave Mao personal oversight over dealings with the Comintern and closed off avenues for Soviet meddling in intraparty affairs.

The dissolution of the Comintern in May 1943 created even more space for the CCP. Having learned from a U.S. wire service of the impending demise of that organization, Mao proclaimed the end of an era. He declared that the Comintern had nothing left to offer the CCP—what he then described as an independent national party with a mature leadership, reliant on its own resources, and embarked on a long-term struggle under complicated conditions unique to China. When that same month Xinjiang completed its return to the Nationalist fold, the CCP lost a transit point into the Soviet Union and highlighted the degree to which Yanan was indeed on its own.[44]

The range and nature of the CCP's contacts with Moscow were now taking on the qualities of conventional interstate relations. In May 1942 the chief Soviet representative, Peter Vladimirov, arrived in Yanan, and he stayed on until November 1945 in his guise as a TASS correspondent. He relayed for the CCP leadership earnest if vague messages meant to reassure Moscow while privately penning his own indictments of a party intent on going its own way. He complained of the anti-Soviet bent of the rectification campaign, the immobility of CCP forces in the face of the Japanese invaders, the frictions the CCP allowed to develop in its relationship with the Nationalists, and the CCP's general failure to focus on the war against Japan. Dimitrov, the former head of the now defunct Comintern, took it upon himself to make these very criticisms directly to Mao—though without any discernible effect. Mao remained in control of communications with the Soviet side. He determined what went out and how to handle what came in, so that he could contain these Soviet complaints and manage the CCP response.[45]

The rectification campaign, carried to a conclusion in 1944, sought to impress on party leaders and ultimately the rank and file a consciousness of a distinct CCP identity and style. It thus sought to put to rest the view (as Mao himself phrased it) that revolutionary strategy came from heaven or from countries other than China.[46] Already between 1937 and 1941 Mao had begun to attack "dogmatic" and "formalistic" application of Soviet approaches, analysis, and models in what was a barely veiled critique of those inclined to make the party subservient to Moscow. Wang Ming, whose ponderous scholasticism better suited him to Comintern committee meetings than making rural revolution, was the epitome of that tendency.

The Seventh Party Congress served as the culminating demonstration of the wartime CCP's determination to find its own way. Mao, not Moscow, would set the course. At the congress itself Liu Shaoqi celebrated "Mao thought" as "an admirable model of the nationalization of Marxism," while also announcing that Mao himself stood unchallenged as "the greatest revolutionary and statesman" and "the greatest theoretician and scientist" in the entire Chinese historical record. For the first time in its history the CCP had begun a congress without Moscow's imprimatur and proceeded untroubled by promptings or guidance from Moscow's representative. Though disturbed by what he saw, Vladimirov could only watch at a distance, and not until after the final ceremony did Moscow hand out its seal of approval for Mao's major address, "On Coalition Government," and for the general program for democracy in China.[47]

This growing CCP autonomy had practical policy implications first reflected in differences in the late 1930s and early 1940s between Yanan and Moscow over how completely to commit base-area forces to the antifascist struggle and how fully to accept Nationalist leadership and direction in the anti-Japanese united front.

The role of the base areas was the fundamental issue. While Stalin wanted CCP military forces to tie down Japan and prevent an attack on Soviet Asia, Mao was primarily concerned with husbanding them to assure the party's survival. In the fall of 1940 and January 1941 it became clear how little those forces might actually weigh in the strategic balance and how easily they could be crushed. The Hundred Regiments' campaign conducted by the Eighth Route Army between August and December 1940 demonstrated the CCP's will to resist. But Japanese forces inflicted heavy losses at the time and in their counterattack in North China the next year. In January 1941 the crushing defeat of the New Fourth Army at the hands of Nationalist forces in the south offered another sharp reminder that the CCP still lived on the margin of security. Indeed, the margin was so close that party leaders could well conclude that if anyone needed help it was less Moscow from the CCP than the reverse.

This need for Soviet support was a point that Mao made personally, publicly, and repeatedly in a variety of contexts from November 1935 onward. In that month he cast China in the familiar role, the base for attack north into the Soviet Union or the Mongolian People's Republic. In such an event the CCP would, he promised, rush to the defense in what would become (he hopefully imagined) a single battlefront. In mid-1936 he stressed the likelihood of Soviet intervention in China's behalf, and in September actually got a Comintern promise of aid if the CCP could consolidate its position somewhere along the Gansu-Ningxia border with the USSR. The following May, Mao asserted that "China and the USSR ought to get together" in the face of a Japan threatening to both. In November 1937 he confidently predicted that the Soviet Union, the decisive source of external assistance, was about to supply aid to China. While these comments usually referred broadly to China and not just the CCP as the recipient of Soviet help, Mao well knew that any enhanced Soviet role in China could serve to strengthen his party's position.[48]

By 1939 Mao's interest in the prospects for Soviet assistance had become unprecedentedly keen and explicit. For example, in February he praised the Soviet Red Army, noting that it had the skills and resources to overcome the deficiencies from which CCP forces suffered. Later in the year he tried another tack by stressing how the USSR's geographical proximity made it the prime source of support against Japan. While Mao's comments were, formally at least, directed at audiences within the CCP, he could be certain that the message got back to Moscow.[49] But aid for basearea forces never arrived in significant quantities despite a major military assistance program for the Nationalists that Moscow inaugurated in the latter half of 1937.

Disappointment was compounded by continuing contention over the proper use of CCP forces. Immediately in the wake of the German invasion of the USSR on June 22, 1941, Stalin sent through Dimitrov a request for armed action by communist parties to relieve some of the pressure now acutely felt by the USSR. Mao deflected the request, suggesting in a directive of June 23 and a July party declaration that the CCP would have to chart its own course and that the short-term interests of the Comintern might diverge on occasion from the long-term interests of the CCP. Now apparently was one of those occasions.[50]

During his early years as leader Mao also differed with Moscow over the proper role of the united front in China. Stalin wanted the united front to submerge political differences so that all Chinese would devote themselves wholeheartedly to pinning down Japanese forces. Stalin saw Chiang's Nationalist regime as the bulwark of that resistance, and hence the CCP was to make sacrifices and avoid frictions that might prove divisive or weaken the Nationalists. Mao on the other hand saw the united front accommodating a greater degree of friction between the two parties as well as continued CCP political, territorial, and military autonomy. Otherwise, the CCP would render itself vulnerable to attack by "reactionaries" within

Chiang's party, and it would forfeit the opportunity to organize within Nationalist-controlled areas revolutionary elements and the middle-of-the-roaders that together might form a potent popular coalition against reactionary influences there.

The differences between the two views generated considerable friction within the CCP between the fall 1935 meeting of the Political Bureau and the December 1938 meeting of the sixth plenum of the sixth Central Committee. At issue was how far the CCP under the banner of the united front should channel its resources into the cities (to the neglect of the base areas) and how far to go in cultivating good relations with the Nationalists (to the detriment of military readiness and organizational autonomy).

To the CCP it was clear that the USSR was more intent on strengthening than restraining or reforming the Nationalist government. Following the August 1937 Sino-Soviet nonaggression pact, Moscow began to support the Nationalists with loans, military advisers, and a "volunteer" air force. At the same time it pressured the CCP to seek greater cooperation with its rival, to follow Chiang's military directives, and to merge the two party organizations. While Soviet aid went largely to keeping the Nationalists in the anti-Japanese front, the Comintern provided only minimal financial support for the party. For example, Wang Jiaxiang returned in 1938 with a $300,000 appropriation from the Comintern's foreign currency fund.[51]

In December 1938 Mao at last secured inner-party agreement on the need to combine elements of class struggle with the united front. At one level Mao had overcome Wang Ming and his insistence on subordinating all party activities to a Nationalist-led united front. Mao prevailed thanks in part to the failure of Chiang's regular forces to stop Japan and by the simultaneous successes of the Eighth Route Army. At another level Mao had deflected Comintern pressure on the CCP to subordinate itself to the Nationalists. Here too Mao would not allow the short-term interests of an embattled and isolated USSR to supersede the long-term interests of his own party, which depended above all on strong base areas, independent organization, and popular support, not the good will of its political rival.

With the united-front issue as with the base areas, the German attack on the USSR proved a watershed. Entanglement in a desperate conflict with Germany sharply curtailed Soviet leverage in Chinese politics. Moscow could neither provide direct support to the CCP nor restrain the Nationalists. Absorbed in its own war effort and forced to trim its international position to accommodate its capitalist allies, the Soviet Union was short on material aid for China and cautious in its dealings with the Nanjing government, whose anti-Japanese stance now became all the more important in tying down Japan.

After 1941 the party center's expectations of Soviet aid steadily declined. The Soviet neutrality agreement with Japan in April and the German invasion in June dimmed the prospects for support. As a result, Mao was early in 1942 notably restrained in his discussion of the role that Soviet forces might play in China. News of the heavy Soviet losses and the bloody combat around Stalingrad further dampened his expectations. Yanan calculated that the Soviet Union would not even be able to participate in the final phase of the Pacific war, and for the long run, party leaders were already wondering what practical assistance a devastated USSR would be able to give China. When in September 1944 Mao raised the question of training CCP forces in Siberia, he conceded that the war had put the Soviet Union in a difficult position. At best the Soviets would play only a limited role in restraining the Nationalists in the postwar period.[52]

These deepening doubts within the CCP leadership lifted a bit in the first half of 1945. Stalin's commitment made at the Yalta conference in February to enter the Pacific War within three months after the defeat of Germany appears to have reached Yanan, most likely through Chongqing but perhaps from Moscow as well. As a result, in late February and in March the party center indicated that it was looking, indeed hoping for, Soviet involvement in the concluding phase of the war, and decided to hold elements of the Eighth Route Army in reserve to take advantage of any Soviet advance against Japan. But rekindled hopes battled against old fears that the USSR had lost so heavily in the conflict with Germany that its involvement in the Pacific conflict would be at best limited. While the main direction of CCP military strategy remained southward (where it would stay until war's end), the sudden reemergence of the USSR into the strategic picture raised troubling and urgent questions about the terms of cooperation with any arriving Soviet troops. And that in turn raised even more unsettling questions about the nature of the special relationship that Mao's devotion to his own two-track strategy had bit by bit unsettled. If Mao then knew of the Yalta provisions on Mongolia and China's northeast, in both cases advancing Soviet interests at the expense of China's, the future of those relations were even more uncertain.[53]

Mao's comments at the Seventh Party Congress in the spring revealed the cross-currents now muddying the special relationship. Mao hinted that the northeast might become an important base area for the CCP, presumably because having Soviet forces by its side or the Soviet border at its back would facilitate the task of base building. But at the same time Mao made clear the need for the CCP to guard against foreign ideological influence that might plunge the party into another bout of "formalism" inimical to its survival and growth. Cooperation was a welcome prospect, but it also carried dangers.[54]

Yanan and Washington

Just as Mao's policy unsettled the special relationship with Moscow, so too did it force a revision in the old, simple reading of imperialism's nefarious role in Chinese affairs. Rather than rehash orthodox condemnations, Mao sought instead to close the distance between Yanan and Washington. While the notion that the capitalist countries, above all the United States, might be enlisted in the service of the CCP was unprecedented in Mao's thinking, it nonetheless proved irresistible as the Soviet Union receded from the picture. An American link might both shore up base areas and reinforce united-front pressure on the Nationalists.[55]

Mao's revised view of imperialism did not take firm hold until after the dramatic recasting of international relationships through the second half of 1941. Reaching that view had been for him neither easy nor straightforward. Indeed, in the immediate aftermath of the Long March Mao had reaffirmed in unequivocal terms his old views on imperialism. He gave a cadre meeting in November 1935 a dose of the old-time religion replete with references to a coming war within the imperialist camp and the growing strength on the revolutionary side. He duly noted the ever more secure position of the USSR, the upsurge of unrest among the proletariat and popular masses in the capitalist countries, and the mounting anti-colonial movements in Abyssinia, China, and the Anglo-American possessions. The party could thus look forward, he promised, to "a new period of global revolution and war."[56]

In the years that immediately followed Mao regularly condemned the desperate maneuvers of British and American leaders to embroil the USSR in war while avoiding it themselves. But his commentary in these years hinted at other possibilities—that the major capitalist countries might be enlisted in the service of the CCP. As early as July 1937, Mao publicly declared that he sought help from those powers as long as such help did not cause any "loss of our territorial sovereignty." The same economic interests that led the Anglo-American ruling elites to appease Japanese imperialism might, he also noted, be engaged in China's side in defense of their trade and investment.[57]

A month earlier in a candid confidential comment, Mao had argued that not to recognize the divisions among the imperialists and not to play upon their economic needs would be foolish. A weak China facing a formidable Japan had to be flexible in looking for allies, he explained. And if that meant working with Anglo-Saxons driven by fear of Germany and Japan, then so be it. Mao was not denying the nature of imperialism, only making use of it. "The ultra-revolutionary course is to fight every imperialist country and all imperialist countries; but in fact to do so would only make a net to catch oneself."[58]

Mao's shift in his approach to the United States as well as Britain was facilitated by a fairly simple, schematic picture of a bourgeois ruling class divided on international issues. Essentially it was torn in two directions— one "reactionary" and the other "progressive."[59] Changing foreign policy registered the shifting relationship between those two fundamental domestic impulses. In the late 1930s Mao saw on one side reactionaries with worrisome fascist-leaning, appeasement-minded tendencies. They carried an "isolationist outlook that does not understand that if China is defeated, England, America, and the other countries will not be able to enjoy peace and quiet." On the other were the "popular" forces sympathetic to China's struggle.[60]

As the progressives gained the upper hand, particularly in the United States under Franklin Roosevelt's leadership, Mao wondered if the CCP might secure political recognition as well as military and economic support. The Americans, he was hopeful, could also restrain Nationalist "diehards." Finally, cooperation between China and the capitalists against Japan would lay the foundation for mutually advantageous postwar economic ties. That capitalists needed markets and China needed development was a point that Mao continued to make.[61]

After a period of growing optimism between 1936 and early 1939, Mao entered a time of doubt and gloom. An emerging pattern of Anglo-American appeasement of both major fascist powers revealed that the reactionaries were once again in the saddle in London and Washington. His mutterings against the treacherous imperialists became pronounced in the course of 1939 and turned to foreboding by the end of the next year. Mao contemplated the prospect of a Japanese-American war that not only might end in total U.S. victory but also confer on Washington near complete command of the Pacific. China would then cease to be Japan's colony only to become a U.S. colony.[62]

The first half of 1941 was marked by equally unrelieved pessimism. Looking into his crystal ball, Mao saw a U.S.-Japanese agreement that would draw in the Nationalists and lay the groundwork for an anti-CCP, anti-Soviet, and anti-German coalition—what he called a Far Eastern

Munich. Mao grumbled that the United States and Britain continued to hatch anti-Soviet plots, particularly to turn Hitler east, and Roosevelt seemed intent on appeasing Japan at the expense of China. But at least, he noted with relief, the anti-Soviet element in Germany had lost out, ensuring that Soviet-German relations would continue to grow steadily better (this on the eve of the German surprise attack!). In these treacherous waters China's interest was best served by a close alignment with the USSR, though Mao confessed that he was not prepared to give up entirely on the British and Americans.[63]

The German attack on the USSR in June followed by the Japanese attack on Pearl Harbor in December gave the lie to Mao's predictions and jumbled his foreign-policy calculations. Following the German surprise attack, Mao was at first uncertain what to make of the future British and American role in this rapidly changing world scene. (He may have even feared that they would join the German assault on the USSR.) In August the clouds began to lift as a result of the Churchill-Roosevelt meeting off the coast of Newfoundland. Mao welcomed the public commitments the two leaders made there to create a new world order and to support an embattled Soviet Union. That the capitalists had finally abandoned their plots and joined in the struggle to overthrow fascism showed Mao that the political progressives had indeed defeated their reactionary opponents. The conference, Mao proclaimed, "marked the opening of a new stage in the history of the world," and guaranteed victory for China and the USSR.[64]

Japan's attack on the United States at the end of the year completed the international realignment. Yanan claimed to know that it was on the winning side, and Mao even predicted Hitler's defeat within a year with Japan's fall to follow the next year.[65] Mao was ecstatic about the fresh possibilities. He envisioned a broad Pacific anti-Japanese and anti-fascist united front and an anti-Japanese military alliance that included China alongside Britain and the United States. The new lineup of anti-fascist powers might provide the support that Mao had failed to get earlier from the USSR. These new allies might help in part by constraining the Nationalists to stay in the war and to limit their attacks on the CCP, and for the rest by directly assisting the CCP in its battle with Japanese forces. Mao promised that the CCP for its part would cooperate to enhance Anglo-American fighting power and strengthen China's unity and resistance, while a Central Committee directive put special emphasis on working with American and British nationals in China.[66] Mao might be imagining a relationship with the capitalists of unlikely intimacy, but doctrinal consistency mattered little if in fact he could use them to give the CCP a boost.

While Mao's hopes for direct military support and an early defeat of the Japanese is easy to understand, his conviction that the Americans might be enlisted to serve as an important auxiliary in the CCP's united front may be more puzzling. This latter facet of his thinking is better understood if set in the context of his long-held populist fixation with the grip of imperialism on China. In his view, the international anti-fascist united front and the one in China were intertwined precisely because China had been deeply penetrated by capitalist powers. A complex transnational web spun by international capitalism and imperialist ambitions reached deep into China and entangled many Chinese. From the orthodox perspective this web was entirely harmful in its effects.[67]

But the Pacific war began to transform that simple view. No longer were the capitalists intent on using Chiang Kai-shek's regime to suppress the Chinese revolution. Rather they seemed to want from him much the same thing the CCP did—political reform and military cooperation. Chinese reactionaries resistant to these goals would face disapproval by the capitalist powers and would thus have to curb their hostility to the CCP and its program of national reform and anti-Japanese resistance.

Although Mao's wavering hopes for help from the capitalists had not finally been vindicated until late 1941, he had well before then launched a series of initiatives intended to turn those hopes into reality. Those initiatives may not have constituted a full-blown foreign policy, but they were at least the seeds of one. Mao first tried his hand at people-to-people diplomacy in an approach that stayed with him until his death. His goal was to make CCP views known in the ruling circles abroad, to mobilize progressive forces in behalf of assistance programs, and even to use foreigners as a conduit for reaching a broader audience in China.

Mao and his comrades devoted themselves to hours of patient work between 1936 and 1945 cultivating a string of foreign visitors. Hardly had the CCP settled into the northwest than it brought in Edgar Snow in mid-1936. He was followed by other Americans and British journalists, scholars, and soldiers known to be sympathetic to the CCP—such as the U.S. marine officer Evans Carlson, the British journalist James Bertram, the journalists Helen Foster Snow, Philip Jaffe, and Agnes Smedley, and the scholars Owen Lattimore and T. A. Bisson.[68]

The results of these outreach efforts were encouraging. Foreigners in China subjected to the CCP charm treatment did, as hoped, make the party better known and lent it a degree of political legitimacy. Edgar Snow's *Red Star over China* was easily the best known of a stream of writings introducing the CCP for the first time to foreign as well as Chinese audiences. Out of these contacts also came the first aid program promoted by the International Committee on Industrial Cooperatives (Indusco) based in Hong Kong. It was organized and directed by the Australian Rewi Alley, Edgar Snow, and Chen Hansheng and sponsored by such prominent Chinese progressives as Song Qingling and the Hong Kong banker Zheng Tieru. This program collected overseas money and goods in excess of $10 million and directed medical supplies and production facilities to the base areas and other regions behind Japanese lines.[69]

The conclusion of formal CCP-Nationalist cooperation in mid-1937 loosened the Nationalist-imposed blockade on Yanan and made it possible to expand the range of contacts. In the temporary Nationalist capital Hankou, the CCP's Yangzi Bureau headed by Wang Ming and seconded by Zhou Enlai devoted itself to cultivating foreign friends, including notably British and American officials. When the Nationalists had to move their capital further inland to Chongqing, Zhou followed. There he directed the party's Southern Bureau in giving foreign reporters, diplomats, soldiers, and scholars the same careful attention that Yanan was showing.[70]

Not content to limit its initiatives to Yanan and Chongqing, the CCP also sought to establish its own presence in the United States to serve (much as an embassy might) as a source of publicity and information. A Chinese bureau within the U.S. Communist Party, in existence as early as 1935, was one such line of influence and intelligence. It was initially headed by Ji Chaoding. He returned to China in 1941 to work for the Nationalist government while reporting to Zhou Enlai. In 1946 the CCP sent Chen Hansheng to take his place.[71] This fixed party presence was supplemented by the dispatch of delegations to increase support for resistance forces and promote the CCP program. For example, following the establishment of the Chinese branch of the International Anti-Aggression Congress in Hankou in February 1938, the CCP sent delegates to the United States to promote the impression of CCP military efficacy and determined anti-Japanese resistance and to stress the sorry Nationalist record.

These efforts to win foreign sympathy and to strengthen the international united front served as a prelude to CCP planning to make the most of the Allied presence during the closing stages of the war and gain the best possible postwar position. In late 1942 and early 1943, just as it was becoming clear that the USSR was bogged down in a long and costly conflict with Germany, Mao noted with approval the growing military resources that the British and the Americans were mobilizing for the European war effort. While he chided London and Washington for the delay in opening a second front, his treatment of their commitment and contributions was ever more glowing.[72] The successful Teheran conference, the German retreat from Stalingrad, and the American advance across the Pacific were harbingers of a global victory, he contended. Mao saw ahead a postwar era of great-power cooperation and progressive influence around the world. By mid-1943 Mao was focusing on the prospect of direct allied aid to the CCP in the final stage of the war, and in May 1944 the presidium handling day-to-day party affairs as well as the upcoming party congress took up in earnest how to link each side of the CCP's two-track strategy to wartime cooperation with the capitalists.[73]

From July 1944 into early 1945 Mao and his associates worked on ways to implicate the United States in support of the most important track of their domestic program, fortifying and extending the base areas.[74] The result was an audacious plan, formalized at the Seventh Party Congress, that envisioned linking aggressive expansion of base areas with the landing of American forces on China's coast in the closing phase of the Pacific conflict. The CCP saw its primary line of advance to the south. Already in February 1945 Yanan had directed the Central China Bureau to assemble forces in southern Anhui, eastern Zhejiang, and southern Jiangsu and to prepare for an American landing on the southern coast. Party leaders expected that landing sometime in the year or year and a half that they thought left before Japan's defeat.

According to CCP plans, its forces in newly created or expanded base areas and behind Japanese lines would cooperate with the Americans, gaining in the bargain international recognition as well as sorely needed military supplies. Having gotten a jump on the Nationalists, these party forces would extend control into Japanese-occupied areas of Fujian, Zhejiang, and Jiangxi with the ultimate goal the seizure of major urban centers such as Shanghai and Canton and important lines of communications. Thus strengthened, the CCP could secure its postwar influence and negotiate advantageous terms of cooperation with the Nationalists.

As a first step to that end, the CCP military was to get a foothold in the Nanjing-Shanghai-Hangzhou triangle. Yanan told forces in the south that they had six months to organize the regiment-sized units needed to link up with and work alongside allied units landing on the coast. While focusing on the south, this strategy of expansion had by early 1945 come to include secondary targets in the north. The Eighth Route Army was to begin to undercut Yan Xishan and stand ready in case of intervention by Soviet forces in the war against Japan.[75]

Mao anticipated drawing the United States into a no less important, long-term role in support of the united-front side of his domestic strategy. His reasoning followed familiar lines. Virtually alone among the powers, the United States had the leverage to force the Nationalist government to accept domestic peace and reform in the aftermath of the Pacific War. Moreover, only the United States had the economic resources to assist China with its massive task of postwar reconstruction.

Beginning in 1943 and carrying down to June 1945, Mao conducted a propaganda campaign to destroy any American illusions about the Nationalists and to neutralize any American reluctance to accept the CCP as a major political player in China. In mid-1943 he started playing up the failure of the Nationalists to sustain resistance, hoping that disappointed Americans would end the Nationalists' monopoly of U.S. aid to China. By 1944 and continuing into 1945, Mao extolled American political values, which he asserted were shared by the CCP but not by the reactionary Nationalists. In one of those exercises, on July 4, 1944, the CCP paper in Yanan claimed, "The work which we Communists are carrying on today is the very same work which was carried on earlier in America by Washington, Jefferson, and Lincoln; it will certainly obtain, and indeed has already obtained, the sympathy of democratic America."[76] Mao intended by these public performances to sway U.S. representatives in China and through them their government. But he also sought by his sniping at Chiang's regime to win a following among educated, pro-U.S. Chinese in Nationalist-controlled territory.

Mao's diplomacy of cultivation and suasion by which he hoped to lead Americans to play these several critical roles—military in the short term, political and economic for the long haul—went into high gear in 1944 and 1945.[77] He used a visiting delegation of foreign as well as Chinese journalists in June 1944 to get the CCP program past Nationalist censors and to make the case for the success of his policies and for the effectiveness of his military forces. American military and diplomatic representatives (the so-called Dixie mission), a project on which Zhou began work in May 1942, arrived in July. It offered Mao an audience even more directly linked to Washington and more time to make his case for immediate military cooperation and postwar political and economic relations. The arrival of Ambassador Patrick Hurley in Yanan in November 1944 brought Mao even closer to direct access to American policy. They sat down to work out a deal that would give the base areas support while keeping pressure on Chiang's government to accept reform and the CCP's legitimacy.[78]

Hurley would quickly prove a disappointing diplomatic partner. After presenting to Chiang the agreement reached in November with Mao, Hurley immediately made major concessions to the Nationalist leader on key points. At the same time Hurley publicly announced exclusive American political, economic, and military support for the Nationalist government. He would go on to initiate a full-scale purge of the U.S. government's China experts, whom Mao and his colleagues had carefully cultivated.[79]

For the moment Mao withheld public criticism, hoping somehow to work around Hurley if not convert him. Mao sought early in the new year to open a direct line of communications with President Roosevelt, but Washington turned aside his appeal for direct, high-level contacts. Mao was thus left with no choice but to conduct desultory talks with Hurley and the Nationalists. Zhou Enlai left the Chongqing talks on February 15, 1945 with nothing to show for his efforts while still praising the American mediator for his "zeal" and his "unceasing effort." Mao then dispatched to San Francisco a party delegation led by Dong Biwu and including Zhou's secretary Chen Chiakang. They were to help represent China at the founding of the United Nations, but they also probed for new diplomatic openings and sought to line up support within the U.S. Communist Party and among American progressives.[80] The upsurge in what Mao took to be reactionary sentiment in Washington following Roosevelt's death in April and the arrest in June of John Service, one of the China experts purged by Hurley, would add to his worry over the unfavorable direction in which American China policy was moving.

By the time of the Seventh Party Congress Mao's overtures were largely barren of results and Hurley in decidedly bad odor. But the future Soviet role in China was still not clear; American influence was still on the ascent; and the struggle to drive out the Japanese, Mao had repeatedly predicted through the first half of 1945, would prove prolonged (he thought at least another full year).[81] So he held to his basic calculations—he would have to deal with the Americans, albeit with vigilance.

In a long, informal talk at the party school in February 1945 in the wake of the Yalta conference, Mao conceded that points of tension would inevitably arise among the Allies. Indeed, anti-communist elements in the United States and Britain as well as China were already thinking about following the defeat of the fascists with an assault against the left. However, he was confident that cooperation and unity would not only survive the last phase of the war but also continue into a postwar period of peace and progress. The crises of the war had greatly raised popular consciousness in all the allied countries. He saw the whole world awakening (in something of a reprise of his views just after World War I). Everywhere the people would push their governments in a progressive direction, leaving the reactionaries out in the cold. Mao thus predicted that the CCP could look forward to favorable conditions, but it should not be impatient. It had gone twenty-four years without victory and a good deal more time would be needed to triumph in so large and populous a country against so many enemies. The party's immediate task, he explained, was to make the most of the remaining years of the war (at least two and maybe more, he guessed on this occasion) by expanding its base areas and armed forces and upgrading its urban work.[82]

This February talk proved a dress rehearsal for Mao's performance during the Seventh Party Congress and the meeting of the new Central Committee that followed in June. Perhaps the most striking statements came not in the well-known formal address on "coalition government" intended for circulation in Nationalist-controlled areas but in more informal remarks where he vigorously defended his earlier optimistic reading of the postwar scene, characterized by cooperation both within China and among the victorious powers. He still imagined popular forces gathering strength all around the world and by degrees gravitating to the successful Soviet political and economic system. In the short term the United States would remain economically vital—a marvel of prosperity. While Mao stressed in "coalition government" the prospects for drawing on this still vital capitalism in developing postwar China, privately he noted that inevitably the laws of historical development would have to kick in. Mao guessed that within a decade the United States would at last be engulfed in that long-anticipated economic crisis. The premier capitalist power would then in effect have to cede world leadership to the socialist USSR.[83]

In June in the aftermath of the congress Mao expressed worry that the United States was showing both a marked preference for propping up Chiang against the CCP and a visible apprehension about the Soviet Union. And the next month he was noting with concern that British forces moving rapidly up through Southeast Asia might arrive before the Americans could shift their forces from Europe and launch their own south China operations. But at no time in mid-1945 did Mao give any indication of abandoning military cooperation with the Allied forces in the final stage of the war. He continued to believe that the Pacific war would last at least another year, giving him ample time to implement his plan reiterated in now familiar terms. As the American offensive finally swept across coastal China, Washington would be forced to turn from its political favorite, the militarily impotent Nationalists, and instead emphasize military cooperation with the CCP. By thus harnessing the American military drive in the Pacific and the consequent American political ascendancy, he would build up the CCP position to the south. To that end he remained in touch with U.S. military representatives in June even after the Seventh Party Congress, and CCP force deployment remained oriented toward the coast.[84]

Moreover, Mao remained adamant that the CCP must ready itself for a postwar period of peace and reform in which political competition could predominate and armed forces would serve as insurance against collapse of the political process. A *Liberation Daily* editorial, issued just days after Mao's closing remarks at the congress and likely reviewed if not written by Mao himself, captured the mingled sense of optimism and vague foreboding. "There can be absolutely no doubt that the Chinese nation's enemies will be wiped out and the Chinese people's liberation will be victorious. But the future still holds many, many difficulties and many, many dangers."[85]

Mao and a Flexible Foreign Policy

Mao had carried the CCP through a major reorientation of its external relations, setting in motion what was in effect the party's first foreign policy foray. Behind that reorientation was a newfound determination to put a premium on caution and maneuver, both qualities deemed essential to prosper or at least survive under the complex and rapidly changing conditions of wartime China and a world at war.

These concerns carried Mao toward a policy profoundly at odds with his earlier vision. Now rather than driving capitalists out, he was inviting them in. Now rather than assuming a rapid transition to socialism, he was ready to bolster the influence of the capitalist powers in China and thus give China's own capitalist class a new lease on life. These differences testified to Mao's capacity as a political leader to adjust to the completely unexpected direction that the Pacific War had taken. The adjustment also reflected his own and his colleagues hunger to end nearly two decades of exile in the countryside and to exploit this tempting opportunity to assure for themselves and their party a meaningful national political role.

Mao's quest for foreign affairs autonomy—reflected in a distancing from Moscow and an attempted rapprochement with the United States—had set the old international affairs orthodoxy in limbo. But as the war approached its end, doubts were beginning to hang over his choices. His hopes invested in the United States had yet to yield any significant returns, and there were hints that the USSR might reemerge as a major player on the China scene. Events surrounding the Japanese surrender in August would deepen these doubts. Stiff-armed by one power and surprised by the sudden reemergence of the other, Mao had to scramble to redirect foreign policy. Having undercut the old special relationship, he would have to find a basis for a new one. Having transcended his old suspicions of imperialists, he would have to decide how far and how fast to restore the old demonology. As earlier, Mao had no rigid plan; much would depend on his reading of the fluid circumstances that defined postwar China and postwar international relations.

Chapter Six

The Trials of Adversity, 1945–1951

Mao Zedong entered the postwar period with a clearly elaborated general strategy and the means, the base areas and the united front, to carry the Chinese Communist Party to power and China to a new stage of peaceful and democratic development. But future prospects were already clouded by CCP uncertainty over the U.S. and Soviet roles. Washington followed an apparently unstable policy, while Moscow kept veiled its intentions in the closing stage of the war and in the immediate postwar period. On top of all this the CCP was thrown off balance by the unexpectedly early end to the Pacific War. As one surprise followed another, Mao struggled to hold to his earlier defined course. By the end of 1946, he abandoned all hopes for postwar accommodation. Mao unambiguously embraced civil war, relying on the strength of his base-area forces to carry the CCP to power.

But even in victory Mao encountered more adversity. American anticommunism gave rise to a policy of support for the defeated Nationalists, who had taken refuge on Taiwan, and then prompted military engagement in Korea. American forces marching up the Korean peninsula toward China removed any particle of doubt about the hostility of the premier imperialist power. At the same time the Soviet relationship was difficult to forge, slow to harden, and brittle under the hammer of the Korean conflict. Mao had come into his own as a policymaker, in command of the resources of a revived and unified China. But like his counterparts in other lands, he was finding that the world remained recalcitrant to his will and defiant of his expectations.

Mao's Policy Misfires

As the Pacific War moved to its final stage, the interlocking foreign and domestic policy that Mao and his associates had patiently and carefully shaped looked good on paper. Inner-party directives as well as public statements hewed to that policy well into the summer of 1945.[1] Put to the test, however, the CCP's political and military strategy for securing power proved a near disaster that had by late fall left the party vulnerable and Mao's political judgment in question.

Mao was victimized, in part, by that most predictable of elements—the very unpredictability of war itself. On August 10 Japan indicated a willingness to surrender. Suddenly the war that he counted on continuing well into 1946 and bringing American forces to the China coast was over. Just as suddenly the southern strategy of expansion lay in shambles. There would be no American landings with which party forces could coordinate. And there would be no long period of wartime preparation during which the CCP would be relatively secure against Nationalist attack. Now CCP forces would have to jump into their contest for position before the party's postwar plans had gotten well underway.

Having invested so much in the southern strategy, Mao at first held to it, hoping still to reap a handsome harvest of Japanese weapons and perhaps even gain control of some urban centers and communications lines. Mao called for haste in the conversion of party forces into large-scale units the better to force surrender of Japanese and puppet troops as well as hold off Nationalist pressure. To make the most of the American military presence and preempt a close U.S. alignment with the Nationalists, the party center directed efforts to seek cooperation with American units arriving in China, to rescue American fliers, to moderate criticism of U.S. as well as Nationalist policies, and to appeal to the strong progressive sentiment both within the U.S. government and the broad American public. Consistent with this approach, the Central Committee instructed local forces to treat with solicitude foreign establishments, whether schools, humanitarian organizations, religious bodies, or economic enterprises.[2]

By October it had become clear to Yanan that the fruits of victory to which it laid claim by virtue of its sacrifices in the resistance were slipping away. Party units had failed in their attempt to play a major role in the surrender process. Chinese puppet forces and Japanese troops had simply refused to make their peace with the CCP, turning personnel, weapons, and cities alike over to the Nationalists instead. The result was a serious loss of resources that the CCP was desperate to have. The only exception had been in the northeast provinces, where CCP forces arrived with Soviet assurances of access to Japanese arsenals. And even there the Soviets soon reversed their position with the result that only a small portion of the available supplies passed into CCP hands.[3]

At the same time Mao was finding U.S. policy increasingly wayward. His concerns about American intentions had already been pronounced at the Seventh Party Congress in the spring. To bring the Americans back into line he had fired off a salvo of criticism in what amounted to diplomacy through propaganda. Mao used the party press in July to lambaste the American ambassador and thereby to awaken sympathetic Americans to the dangers of Patrick Hurley's reactionary line and to arrest any shift in American policy toward stronger support of Chiang Kai-shek. In the first of a series of anonymous newspaper pieces on July 8, Mao identified Hurley as "an imperialist element" and saw American policy falling under the influence of a "reactionary clique" committed to propping up the Nationalists.[4]

The sudden end of the war in August did not bring a softening of U.S. policy but rather what Mao feared—a continuation of support for Chongqing. The CCP noted with mounting alarm that Washington was still funneling to Chiang substantial financial aid as well as military equipment (including some six hundred immediately available aircraft). No less threatening, American aircraft and navy transports began moving Nationalist forces into Japanese-occupied areas, while American forces began securing communications lines and strategic points along the northern coast such as Tanggu, Tianjin, Tangshan, and Qingdao, evicting the CCP, and obstructing party forces making their way to the northeast. By late September and October the CCP recognized that its own advance, by then reoriented to the north, was not faring well. Thanks to U.S. help, the Nationalists were penetrating the northeast more rapidly and more deeply than anticipated. Meanwhile, the CCP had managed by November 1 to get only thirty thousand of its own troops into the area, and they were arriving fatigued. Many had left their old gear behind, expecting to find new Japanese equipment. The Soviet refusal to release that equipment left them particularly unfit for combat. Mao was becoming increasingly anxious about the safety of this hastily deployed, ill-equipped force now facing a Nationalist army resolutely backed by the United States.[5]

Just as the CCP's American military gambit was proving a colossal miscalculation, the USSR had suddenly reappeared on the Chinese political horizon. But confirming past experience, the CCP found Joseph Stalin not a generous and direct internationalist solicitous of his Chinese comrades. He operated instead from a seemingly complex and shifting calculus in which solicitude for the Chinese party was only a part. Yanan thus entered the postwar period with renewed if guarded optimism about Soviet support, and even that would in late 1945 and 1946 begin to evaporate as Moscow sprang a series of unpleasant surprises.[6]

The first of those surprises had come even before the end of the Pacific War. Mao had then found himself distinctly an outsider looking in on the major diplomatic parleys dedicated to coordinating Japan's defeat and defining the postwar world. Exclusion from the Big Three meeting in Potsdam was understandable, and in any case Chiang was not there either. More galling, however, was being left on the sidelines while a Nationalist delegation led by Song Ziwen (T. V. Soong) traveled to Moscow to negotiate a new Sino-Soviet treaty. Mao's own assessment, offered on July 22, was that any Soviet-Nationalist treaty would enable Chiang to turn all his attention to preparations for an anti-CCP campaign, "making the dangers of a civil war unprecedentedly grave." The implication of Mao's analysis was that Moscow no less than Washington was cutting out the ground beneath the CCP.[7] Mao's fears were borne out by the treaty concluded on August 14 in which the USSR sought to consolidate its position in China while both supporting and restraining the Nationalist government.

Closely linked to the treaty with the Nationalists was a second August surprise—the unheralded Soviet entry into the Pacific War. The sudden appearance of Soviet forces in the northeast not only introduced another unexpected element in an increasingly fluid and confusing situation but also added to the CCP's discomfiture. To all appearance Stalin had given the CCP no prior warning, so party forces, heavily oriented to the south, were in no position to make the most of the fresh opportunity opened by the Soviet occupation of the northeast. On August 9, 1945 Mao and Zhu De publicly cabled Stalin, welcoming the Soviet war declaration and expressing their desire for a coordinated strategy with Soviet and other Allied forces against Japan. But Yanan realized that Soviet cooperation would be limited by the bargain Moscow had just struck with the Nationalists. Soviet forces would formally at least have to cooperate with Nationalist forces bent on extending government control to the northeast and preempting the CCP bid for a firm regional foothold.[8]

In what amounted to a third August surprise, Stalin applied pressure on Yanan to enter at once into negotiations with its powerful domestic foe even before the CCP had had a chance to strengthen its postwar position. In two personal messages to the party center, Stalin warned against the renewal of conflict in which the Chinese nation would risk annihilation and the CCP would risk loss of foreign sympathy, perhaps even destruction.[9] The CCP opened formal talks with the Nationalists in Chongqing on August 28, consoling itself with the thought that now that the Soviets had won some leverage in Chongqing perhaps a compromise among the rival parties would come more easily. Mao himself led the party's delegation, although he left the details of the talks to his colleagues, Zhou Enlai and Wang Ruofei.

The talks droned on inconclusively. There was no sign that Chiang had any serious interest in a peaceful resolution of the tensions between the two rival parties or that either Washington or Moscow would, as the CCP had hoped, press him to make concessions. After spending six weeks in Chongqing, the best Mao could bring back to Yanan was a set of vaguely worded accords. The party leader contended on his return on October 10 that although the talks had been a step toward peace, a large number of substantial but localized military collisions lay ahead. He reasoned that if the CCP could beat back Nationalist military pressure, then renewed negotiations would have a chance for success. Zhou Enlai stayed behind seeking cooperation. When his efforts proved fruitless, he broke off talks and returned to Yanan on November 25 for "consultation."[10]

Stalin still had one more surprise up his sleeve, this one held in reserve for CCP military strategists struggling to extract at least some advantage from the unexpected Soviet arrival in the northeast. Already in late August they had begun to make adjustments. With Mao away in Chongqing, it fell to Liu Shaoqi to supervise the details of the shift. Into September he steadily redirected attention to the north. Party forces began moving into Rehe and Chaha'er, which lay outside the scope of the Soviet agreement with the Nationalists. In the northeast itself the Soviets would, Yanan hoped, take a sympathetic attitude as long as party forces behaved with discretion. Aside from ordering cadres into the main cities, the party center instructed troops from Jin-Cha-Ji and Shandong to slip quietly into the region, consolidating control before the arrival of the Nationalists. But those troops were to make no formal contact with Soviet authorities, avoid big cities and main roads, not infringe on Soviet treaty obligations to the Nationalists, and pretend to have local or popular standing to hide their outside origins. To serve as the main contact with Soviet occupation forces, the head of the new Northeast Bureau, Peng Zhen, flew on September 17 from Yanan to Shenyang on a Soviet plane. Yanan for its part stayed in touch with Moscow via long-range radio.[11]

On September 19–21 the party center completed this shift in strategy. The major direction of base-area expansion would now be northward, while in central China the CCP would go on the defensive with some units to come north to support the new line of advance. For this task the CCP would need not only to expand the Eighth Route Army and the New Fourth Army into mobile field armies but also to give priority to increasing the size of the army by several hundred thousand troops by December. The immediate goal was control of Rehe and Chaha'er and ultimately all of the northeast. From the base areas extending across north China and the northeast the CCP would (it hoped) be able to push reactionaries within the Nationalist camp into accepting peace and democracy, to stimulate popular struggle within Nationalist-controlled areas, and to beat back the attacks that the Nationalists could now be expected to unleash.[12]

This late-September shift had envisioned party forces following a peripheral strategy in the northeast. Consistent with the desire to avoid embarrassment to the Soviets, the Military Affairs Committee instructed units already in the region to organize in the less populated, outer reaches of the northeast. But then on October 19 the party center reversed itself in favor of a more aggressive military strategy. Forces in the northeast were to concentrate in the southern part of the region to block advancing Nationalist troops. On November 1, 1945 Yanan affirmed the new plan for fighting on interior lines and holding Shenyang.[13]

Finally in November with the new northern strategy well underway, Stalin sprang his surprise. He demanded that CCP cadres and forces abandon the major cities of the northeast, leaving railroads, factories, and equipment intact. This ejection from centrally located and resource-rich urban strongholds astride the main communications lines dealt a fatal blow to the CCP's preferred strategy of confronting the Nationalists from strong inner lines of defense. Now CCP troops and supporting cadres would have instead to retreat to the region's poorer and sparsely settled periphery. They would have to create their base of operations along the Rehe, Outer Mongolia, Soviet, and Korean borders, and from there pursue their long-term goal of seizing the Southern Manchurian Railroad and the cities along it. Only some cadres were allowed to stay behind to maintain a secret party presence in and around the major Soviet-occupied cities.[14]

Both the Central Committee and the authorities in the northeast groped for a convincing rationale for this abrupt, damaging Soviet order. The Northeast Bureau was blunt and fatalistic: while the United States actively backed Chiang's regime, the Soviet Union could not do the same for the CCP and in some ways was proving a hindrance. The best explanation it could offer to the riddle of Soviet behavior was that the United States and Chiang had undertaken a general diplomatic offensive that had somehow forced the Soviet Union to make concessions. Perhaps giving way in the northeast was the price Moscow had to pay in order to avoid sharpening international tensions and to remove an excuse for U.S. intervention in China's internal affairs.[15]

By late fall the program laid down by Mao the previous spring had been badly battered. The Nationalists, backed by the Soviet Union as well as the United States, had hemmed the CCP in territorially, outmaneuvered it diplomatically, and was on the march militarily. As early as September 28 the Military Affairs Committee had judged the long-term military situation unfavorable. By December 12 the party center was painting a grim picture of imminent Nationalist assaults intended to carve up base areas and force the CCP to accept harsh peace terms. Yanan urged base areas and field armies to hasten their defensive preparations.[16] These directives did little to dispel the confusion among the party rank and file and the demoralization in the armed forces after a season of dizzying policy shifts, Soviet betrayal, and disappointed hopes for either peace and a return to the cities or a quick trial of strength with the enemy.[17]

Even though on the defensive at home and isolated internationally, Mao refused to abandon his basic Seventh Party Congress position. The CCP should keep up pressure on the Nationalists to accept the new era of peace and democratization while continuing expansion now directed northward. Localized tests of arms with Chiang's forces might be necessary to demonstrate CCP will and power, Mao explained, but those collisions should be managed to encourage, not endanger, political cooperation and a spirit of compromise on the Nationalist side. Continued united-front work promoting nationalism and democracy in Nationalist-controlled cities would add to the pressure by isolating Chiang's party and drawing moderates to the CCP. Finally, international cooperation remained central to realizing reform and peace in China. The party center time and again through the fall insisted on the importance of cultivating American opinion, respecting American interests in China, and avoiding collisions with American forces occupying the northern coast.[18]

Spinning from this string of reverses, Mao regained his balance with the help of Stalin and unexpectedly from the U.S. government. A late-November communication from Stalin convinced the Central Committee on December 1 that the USSR would at least seek to check the American involvement in the struggle for the northeast even if Moscow would not directly aid the CCP there.[19] On the U.S. side Ambassador Hurley's resignation on November 26 forced on President Harry S. Truman a reappraisal of China policy. On December 15 the Truman administration announced that it was sending a mission led by General George Marshall (serving as the president's special envoy) to help avert civil war. A short time later the communiqué issued at the end of the Moscow meeting of the allied foreign ministers further dispelled the cloud of gloom hanging over Yanan. U.S. Secretary of State James Byrnes and Soviet Foreign Minister Vyacheslav Molotov called for the rival parties to seek a negotiated solution of their differences, and promised that aside from supporting peace talks their respective countries would not intervene in China.

These developments delighted the party leadership and at last vindicated Mao's contention that the powers would act to restrain Nationalist diehards now spoiling for a fight. Once again affirming the Seventh Party Congress framework, the Central Committee insisted that China was in transition from the period of anti-Japanese resistance to a new era of peace and development. To speed that transition, the party center called for using the Soviet-American intervention to get talks with the Nationalists restarted and to negotiate an agreement legitimating the base areas and laying the groundwork for the creation of a coalition government and a single national army. Marshall's dispatch to China seemed to the CCP especially important because it registered the failure of what the CCP termed the "Hurley policy" (meaning full support for the Nationalists and American military intervention in the civil war). Marshall's mission, taken to reflect the triumph of American moderates, would give the CCP another chance at swaying U.S. policy.[20]

Yanan acted quickly to take advantage of this piece of good fortune. Zhou left for Chongqing, where on December 27 he resumed talks with the Nationalist delegation led by Zhang Qun. At the same time orders went out to party forces to continue to build up the northeast base area and defend it (even at risk of serious collision with Nationalist forces). CCP forces elsewhere were told to hold their ground. Meanwhile, party diplomacy and propaganda tried to evoke popular opposition in the United States and in China against the drift toward civil war.[21]

Mao's hopes for a political accommodation under Soviet-American sponsorship seemed for a time within reach. Chiang Kai-shek succumbed to pressure from Marshall, and threw his support behind a bargain with the CCP. The two Chinese parties concluded a cease-fire agreement on January 10 covering all of China except significantly the northeast. It provided for an executive committee consisting of Marshall, Zhou, and Zhang that was to supervise the field teams (also tripartite) charged with implementing the truce. Even more startling and encouraging was the conclusion of a step-by-step plan for implementing political reform and forming a coalition government. The agreement also stipulated that the military on both sides would be removed from party control.

In a directive of February 1, 1946 the Central Committee expressed its euphoria over this breakthrough. "This is the first great victory for China's democratic revolution." The new accord promised "to begin the destruction of the system of Nationalist one-party dictatorship" and at the same time to "advance our party as well as the armed forces and the base areas created by our party toward legalization." For the first time in nearly two decades the party could operate openly. But peace, the Central Committee warned, carried a price—opening base areas to political competition and handing over the party's army and self-defense forces to the control of a reorganized central government. "Party branches, political commissars, party affairs committees, and so forth will have to be dissolved within a reorganized army, and the party will have to give up direct leadership of the army." Yanan indicated that even so those in the army would retain their party membership, and political cadres would stay with their units and strengthen their political work. Party members had to adjust to new conditions and learn to respond to central leadership without the advantage of direct, formal guidance. The party center conceded that "many in the CCP don't believe that civil war can really be stopped and peace actually realized, and they don't believe that Chiang Kai-shek's Nationalist Party can under pressure from all sides carry out democratic reforms." The Central Committee warned that those who took this position were guilty of a "parochial closed-door" approach.[22]

As the CCP maneuvered toward an accommodation with the Nationalists in early 1946, the United States loomed larger than ever in party calculations. Americans had to keep Chiang in line and receptive to reform. To ensure that they played that constructive role, the CCP had to continue its policy of cultivating American opinion, and it had especially to pay close attention to George Marshall himself. Viewed as a fair and reasonable figure who could not quite shake off his anti-communist paranoia, he followed a policy that seemed to the CCP essentially favorable to the Nationalists. But Yanan reasoned that the Americans had learned from Hurley's failure and would thus try "to stand above Nationalist-CCP contradictions in order to manipulate the two sides." Directives coming out of Yanan, even as late as mid-May, put great stress on Zhou's turning the tables and manipulating Marshall to advance the peace process. To that end Zhou was to avoid any personal criticism that might alienate the American envoy.[23]

The United States also remained important in party plans for strengthening base areas and pushing forward China's economic development in the coming period of political cooperation. An extraordinary Central Committee directive, sent out on May 3, 1946, reveals how the CCP clung to hopes for good relations with the United States. "We ought to adopt a plan of carrying out trade and economic cooperation with the United States as well as Britain and France." The United States in particular would inevitably, the directive contended, exercise an enormous influence on postwar China. While the Soviet Union would have nothing to offer except perhaps for some trade, "American capital will control China (including the liberated areas)." The CCP should seek to benefit from this American presence but also exercise a degree of oversight over the expansion of American enterprise in liberated areas. Shandong with its sizable American presence was a good place to begin "drawing in foreign capital . . . , establishing factories, developing transport, carrying out foreign trade, and promoting agriculture and handicrafts." Some cultivation of American opinion was in order, the directive argued, to dispel Washington's doubts that "the CCP can carry out long-term economic cooperation" and to overcome Washington's suspicions that "we want to advance economic cooperation with the USSR in order to restrict the United States."[24]

The Soviet Union, for its part, resumed what seemed to the CCP its wayward policy after giving a helpful, initial push to the Marshall mission. Soviet support for Yanan was proving negligible—and in some ways Soviet cultivation of the Nationalists was hurting the CCP. Stalin had agreed to Chiang's request to keep his troops in the northeast, giving the Nationalist army and officials time to prepare to take over and effectively shutting the CCP out of the cities. One Central Committee directive early in 1946 flatly stated, "The USSR cannot help us in a northeast civil war." Another Central Committee telegram ruefully indicated that if the Americans came to the northeast they would see that the Soviets have not in fact been helping the party. Yet a third conceded that the party position in the northeast was weak because the Soviets could not be seen assisting CCP forces lacking in legal status, while the Americans were able to justify their support for the Nationalist armies there. The Soviets were judged no more helpful in pushing Chongqing toward peace and reform. They would have to pretend to be impartial, the party center observed, and might even seek to extract concessions from the CCP in order to establish their fairness. It thus might be best, Yanan concluded, that the Soviets hold back diplomatically. Not until late March did Soviet forces in the final stage of their occupation of the northeast (ended on May 3) finally redeem the damage done the CCP the previous November. A more benevolent Soviet stance prompted the CCP to launch a strategy of seizing the northern part of the region, including Changchun and Harbin, before Nationalist forces arrived.[25]

Once more, Mao's program seemed poised on the edge of success only to fail. No sooner had the January agreements been concluded than they began to unravel. Chiang, who had made concessions with hope of gaining time for military preparations, took the offensive in March in anticipation of Soviet withdrawal from the northeast. He unleashed his forces there, while carrying out an effective program of anti-communist propaganda that played up the misbehavior of the Soviet occupation army. By the end of June the Marshall-sponsored talks had come to a dead end. Marshall had insisted on cease-fire terms distinctly disadvantageous to the CCP, while at the same time he ignored the increasingly belligerent Nationalist behavior in the northeast, indeed seemed to encourage Chiang by continuing to provide support for the Nationalist forces in the region. A confident Chiang was now ready to press his military advantage in a general offensive against CCP forces (launched in July).

Mao tried not to let what struck him as a resurgence of reactionary sentiment on the Nationalist side upset his search for a political solution. Still clinging to the assumption that the road to "new democracy" might be complicated, he settled into what he assumed might be a prolonged period of military testing. To demonstrate CCP resolve and strength, Mao instructed Lin Biao on March 24 to stand his ground against advancing Nationalist forces in the northeast. Lin had favored mobile warfare over defense of cities or fixed positions, but Mao now overruled him. Attacked at Sipingjie, CCP forces fought a set-piece battle that turned into a rout. Mao finally on May 19 gave the spent army permission to retreat. Meanwhile, Yanan viewed with considerable concern Nationalist pressure on the CCP in other areas and urged commanders to ready their forces for the coming blow. By late May the party center was privately blaming Marshall for letting the Nationalist "diehards" stir up a military conflict, sow political terror, block democratic reforms, and in general undercut the Moscow conference decision in favor of peace. Even Mao himself conceded privately on June 1 that "the United States and the Nationalists are being extremely odious toward us, and a full-scale civil war is unavoidable."[26]

Mao now grasped the levers of the party propaganda machinery hoping to stir up international opposition to Nationalist attacks. By late June he had sharpened criticism of the United States, attacking the "imperialist elements" that had gained control of U.S. China policy. He described General George Marshall's efforts at mediation as "a fraud" and "a smokescreen for strengthening Chiang Kai-shek in every way and suppressing the democratic forces in China." Behind Marshall was the Truman admin-istration, "a reactionary capitalist clique" which had set its face against the Chinese revolution and which was putting in peril "the glorious friendship between the two great nations of China and the United States and the prospects for Sino-American trade development."[27]

Even so, the military battering administered by the Nationalists inten-sified in July, and none of the powers stepped forward to stop it. Mao still clung grimly to his faith in the Seventh Party Congress formula. In China as in the world the trend toward peace and democracy was still strong, he claimed. A resolute stand by the CCP would eventually force Chiang to back down. As before, Yanan ordered party forces to defend themselves if attacked; however, they should not behave as though the CCP sought an all-out military confrontation with the Nationalists. Mao estimated that it might take several months of military resistance supplemented by growing popular resentment and by prodding from the United States and the USSR before Chiang would "retreat after recognizing the difficulty he was in" (*zhinan ertui*)—in other words, resume negotiations in good faith.[28]

Mao's brave words and promises left some in the higher echelons of the party unconvinced. Two such doubters, Li Fuchun and Huang Kecheng, both then serving in the northeast, advanced the pessimistic argument in early July that progressive forces were weaker both within China and inter-nationally than Mao had been contending. Mao in response defended his favorable appraisal of the political environment in which the party oper-ated. Revolutionary power was much greater after World War II than it had been after World War I. He criticized Li and Huang's failure to grasp the difficulties afflicting both the reactionaries in the Nationalist camp and the American imperialists. Mao concluded with a defense of his policy of mixing concessions to the United States and the Nationalists with resis-tance and struggle against them.[29]

In a remarkable display of tenacity, Mao continued to cling to his pro-gram through the late summer and into the fall, even as fighting increased in intensity and spread throughout China. He had to concede that getting back to talks on a political settlement might take longer than earlier antic-ipated. But the party was to continue to cultivate Americans in China and not give up on the possibility that Marshall might play a useful role. The party was also to continue to seek the support of American progressives both in and outside the government. A propaganda directive cautioned, "We don't want to be sweeping in opposition, and even more we don't want to be sweepingly anti-American." Mao still insisted that CCP resistance, combined with American restrictions on Chiang, would eventually bring the Nationalists into line. The cross-currents in U.S. policy helped sustain Mao's optimism. While Washington continued its material support for Chiang dating back to fall 1945, Marshall made clear that the United States would not intervene directly in China. Moreover, he made no secret of his dissatisfaction with Nationalist pugnacity and sought between April and September to use American aid as a brake on the Nationalists.[30]

Finally, on November 21 Mao broke under the pressure and revised his basic policy. Meeting with Zhou Enlai and Liu Shaoqi, he concluded that determined CCP resistance on the battlefield had not shaken Chiang's commitment to a military solution. Nor had pressure, cajolery, appeals, and words of reassurance brought an improvement in U.S. policy. Frustrated in their search for peace and reform, the party's leaders decided to seek a decisive military victory and to reject any offer of American mediation. This November 1946 decision to wage all-out war was reviewed and confirmed at a Central Committee meeting on December 25–28, 1947 in Yangjiagou in northern Shaanxi, but it was not made public for a year to avoid antagonizing a war-weary nation and creating confusion in propaganda work. Similarly, the CCP did not openly indicate it would reject American mediation. Nonetheless, Yanan had set off down a new path to power.[31]

Mao would now assume personal responsibility for coordinating the far-flung military operations against Nationalist forces far larger and better equipped than his own. He would win on the battlefield the decisive victories that had eluded him at the peace table.[32]

Civil War and the Powers

While the late November 1946 decision thrust the party military forward as the main instrument of Mao's policy, the management of the United States and the USSR remained important. Proper handling of those two powers could help pull down the Nationalists, fend off a last-minute, direct U.S. intervention, ensure a secure and stable base for the new regime, and promote economic development in the post-liberation period.

Despite the importance of the November policy shift, it only partially redrew the picture of the international scene. Already the previous August Mao had revealed in a carefully vetted interview with the journalist Anna Louise Strong that he was rethinking his views on the world situation. He held to his earlier, often reiterated contention that progressive forces were in the ascendance all around the world and would create a global environment conducive to CCP success. But he had to concede that reactionary power, above all in the United States, had reached unprecedented heights. The Truman administration had embarked on a Cold War policy that was anti-Soviet at least in its rhetoric but that in fact seemed to Mao to set Washington on a direct collision course with the American people, the other capitalist countries, and the nations of the Pacific. The USSR stood, to be sure, in the way of any ultimate U.S. bid for global hegemony, but the most immediate obstacle confronting the Americans was Britain, France, and China, so Mao now contended. In the memorable phrase from this later widely publicized interview, the American reactionaries were only a "paper tiger," notably weak compared to the popular progressive forces now gathering strength around the world.[33]

In separate statements following the November decision, Mao and Lu Dingyi, then head of the Propaganda Department, publicly stated the CCP's modified view of postwar international affairs.[34] They conceded that imperialist influences had revived and that the system of great-power cooperation was dead. However, both insisted that progressive forces generally and the Soviet Union in particular had emerged from World War II stronger than ever and that those forces were still in the ascendance. They rejected the notion that the world order was defined by direct confrontation, either between the United States and the USSR or between the capitalists states and the USSR, and they denied that a new world war was on the horizon. Rather they located (as Mao had in his interview with Strong) the focal point of conflict within the United States, between the United States and the other capitalists, and between the United States and China's revolution.

Lu's statement was especially important for filling out the notion of the intermediate zone first suggested by Mao in August. Lu defined this zone to include colonial and semi-colonial countries as well as capitalist countries stretching from Europe to Africa and Asia. China fit prominently into this picture as a major front (alongside Britain and Western Europe) of resistance to American aggression and as the head of the anti-imperialist struggle developing in such far-flung points as Indochina, India, Iran, and Greece. An international united front made up of democratic forces enjoying the backing of the USSR would defeat U.S. reactionaries and their allies, Lu reasoned, because those reactionaries were daily more isolated and because they faced an imminent and disabling economic crisis. In this promising environment China's revolution would achieve victory in three to five years, he predicted.

From this point the CCP appraisal of U.S. policy remained negative, influenced above all by the possibility of a U.S. invasion undertaken in a last-minute bid to save the Nationalists and keep China's main ports out of the hands of advancing CCP armies. The invaders could expect help from remnant Nationalist forces on the mainland (estimated still as high as 1.5 million in late 1949) and local bandits (thought to number as high as one million). These forces of disorder and anti-Communist resistance, strongest in southeast and southwest China previously beyond CCP control would for some time continue to attack local government officials and party cadres, blockade or seize towns and villages, disrupt communications, carry out looting and robbery, commit sabotage and assassinations, and attack scattered military units.[35]

Through late 1948 and well into 1949 as CCP forces swept into the Beiping-Tianjin area, crossed the Yangzi River, and then moved farther south, Mao worried about this two-sided strategic danger with domestic reactionaries on the one side and the U.S. invaders on the other. A January 1949 Central Committee directive that he drafted offered assurance that as "the strength of the Chinese people's revolution gets ever more powerful and ever more resolute" the opportunities for such a direct intervention would diminish. But at the same time Mao used the directive to caution against being "caught unprepared in case something unexpected were to happen as the situation unfolds." The CCP posted a close watch on American activities along the coast for signs of intervention, and Mao designated a reserve force to counter any landings on the coast. He confirmed his concern in May by ordering the Second Field Army to stand ready against the possibility of an American invasion, and into the fall he was still deploying his armies with one eye on the threat to the coast.[36]

Looking beyond the military contest, Mao offered his general views on handling the imperialists to the second plenum of the seventh Central Committee on March 5, 1949.[37] The step-by-step defeat of the Nationalists, he explained, was dealing a severe blow to Washington, no longer able to depend on the Nationalists to defend its dominant position in China. "But the economic and cultural establishments run directly by the imperialists are still there, and so are the diplomatic personnel and the journalists recognized by the [Nationalists]." Bringing this remaining foreign presence under control was, he pointed out, the next concern of CCP foreign policy.

In general terms, Mao explained, his approach to the foreign establishment in China was straightforward. The CCP would not concede a privileged status to diplomats accredited to the Nationalist government, nor would it recognize objectionable treaties concluded by that government. The party would close down all imperialist propaganda outlets in China. Foreign trade would come under government control. So too would the customs system, the century-old product of a now moribund imperialist order. Only after the completion of these tasks, Mao declared, could it be said that the Chinese people had "stood up in the face of imperialism."

These guidelines laid down in early March reflected Mao's dark view of U.S. policy. But they also left room for some flexibility in case of a shift in that policy, a possibility consistent with Mao's belief that World War II had broken the dam holding back powerful progressive forces around the world. Even in the United States progressives might yet win power, perhaps boosted by the economic crisis always about to shake the capitalist system. Alternatively, growing international opposition to U.S. policy might force Washington to moderate its approach to China and seek a reluctant accommodation with the CCP.

Mao's general framework left ample room for diplomatic relations with a United States that would treat China as an equal and respect Chinese sovereignty. The language used self-consciously followed the terms laid down by Chinese revolutionaries in the 1920s. As early as July 1947 the CCP had publicly established the principles of equality and mutual benefit as the basis for dealing with other countries whether capitalist or socialist. In late November the next year the Central Committee again publicized its wish "to establish equal and friendly relations with all foreign countries, including the United States"—but on the condition of full respect for China's territorial sovereignty.[38]

By the time of the March 1949 meeting Mao saw little chance that the Truman administration would meet his basic preconditions. "The imperialists, who have always been hostile to the Chinese people, will definitely not be in a hurry to treat us as equals. As long as the imperialist countries do not change their hostile attitude, we shall not grant them legal status in China." If Washington could handle diplomatic ties on a "wait-and-see" basis, then so too could the CCP.[39] Mao nonetheless quietly probed Washington's intentions. Progress on the diplomatic front would be well worth the effort if it would help isolate the Nationalists, neutralize the threat of an American-sponsored intervention, and facilitate access to technology and trade.

No sooner had his triumphant forces crossed the Yangzi River in late April to take control of the Nationalist capital of Nanjing than Mao had the military issue a statement reiterating the now familiar formula defining the basis for diplomatic relations. That statement reflected the party center's judgment that neither the United States nor Britain was seeking confrontation. Indeed, both were indicating an interest in contacts. The Americans in particular seemed to be edging toward diplomatic overtures, having recognized the bankruptcy of their old policy of support for the

Nationalists against the Communists. The CCP's preconditions for normalization remained the same: the United States as well as Britain breaking relations with the Nationalists.[40]

When the American ambassador, John Leighton Stuart, remained behind following the Nationalist flight, Mao saw a golden opportunity to get an authoritative reading of U.S. intentions and perhaps even to influence U.S. policy. He authorized Huang Hua, the official placed in charge of foreign affairs in Nanjing, to make private soundings. Huang was an ideal intermediary; he had been a student at Yenching University when Stuart was president, and they had renewed their acquaintance in 1946. In May Huang made direct contact with the ambassador to discuss diplomatic and economic relations, and in June passed on the party center's invitation to come north for a quiet exchange of views.[41]

With these exchanges underway, Mao on June 15 once more publicized his own guarded and conditional interest in diplomatic contacts. He observed that the imperialists, plagued by crisis, were flailing about in a mad effort to save themselves. But the CCP, he also stressed, stood ready to discuss relations with anyone on the basis of equality and mutual respect for territorial integrity and sovereignty and on the condition they sever relations with the Nationalists. He also expressed his continued interest in resuming and expanding foreign trade. However, the Truman administration would not acknowledge communist victory, and so could not meet Mao's terms. So when Stuart asked Washington for a chance to go north to talk, Truman himself at once rejected the overture. On July 2 Stuart communicated the negative response to Huang. A month later Stuart was on his way home.[42]

By mid-1949 Mao had reached a deadlock with the Truman administration over diplomatic relations. He was determined to overturn the old rules, which allowed the powers to define their position in China. His stance set him directly at odds with the U.S. government's claim to diplomatic privileges while simultaneously refusing to recognize the official standing of CCP authorities where they exercised de facto control. In the latter half of 1949 and early 1950 the Truman administration made matters worse by giving its blessings to Nationalist bombing and a blockade disruptive to a coastal economy struggling for recovery.

The CCP made its own contribution to bad feelings by its decision in mid-1949 to press an espionage case against American diplomats in Shenyang. Contacts between Consul General Angus Ward and the local authorities had begun cordially after the first U.S. diplomatic post fell under CCP control in November 1948, but quickly turned sour when

Ward refused to surrender a transmitter that compromised military security and when the Soviets expressed their distaste for a capitalist diplomatic presence in the region. CCP officials then cut off the consulate and finally on June 19, 1949 publicly lodged charges of espionage. The incident ended with the trial of Ward and his subsequent expulsion along with the rest of his staff in December. In this atmosphere of ill will, Mao publicly traded verbal jabs with Secretary of State Dean Acheson, first in August 1949 and then again in early 1950.[43]

Even so the founding of the People's Republic on October 1, 1949 brought a reiteration of the standard conditions for diplomatic ties—an acceptance of "the principles of equality, mutual advantage, and reciprocal respect for territorial sovereignty." In the months immediately following, the socialist-bloc states and some Asian neutrals such as Burma, India, and Indonesia as well as the British, Swiss, Dutch, and Scandinavians granted diplomatic recognition. But the Truman administration maintained a studied aloofness, and tried to keep its Cold War allies in line on nonrecognition. When Beijing sought with Soviet encouragement to knock on the door to the United Nations, once again the United States played the spoiler, keeping the PRC out and the Nationalists in China's Security Council seat. Finally, Beijing provoked the American government to liquidate the last of its diplomatic presence in China by seizing barracks used by the U.S. legation guard ever since the United States had helped repress the Boxers at the turn of the century. Mao, then in Moscow, both approved the seizure and expressed pleasure at the removal of this diplomatic thorn in his side.[44]

As it became clear that a diplomatic bridge to Washington was too weak to carry any traffic of value, Americans in China were left as the only remaining avenue for whatever contact Mao's China would have with the United States. In early 1948 and again in early 1949 the Central Committee had laid down moderate ground-rules for treatment of residents from the United States and other capitalist countries. And Mao confirmed those rules in his March 1949 comments on the future of imperialist economic and cultural establishments. "They can be allowed to exist for the time being, subject to our supervision and control, to be dealt with by us after country-wide victory. As for ordinary foreign nationals, their legitimate interests will be protected and not encroached upon."[45]

The prospects for even this remnant of the foreign establishment steadily dimmed, its chances compromised in substantial measure by the tensions between the CCP and the American government. In late 1948, just entering the initial phase of state-building, the CCP leadership showed growing concern with the potential political and cultural threat posed by the imperialist bloc. Consequently the party center moved toward increasingly stringent control of citizens from unfriendly countries who might serve imperialist policy or promote values subversive of China's new order. Foreign journalists and news agencies with their wireless facilities and their ability to spread what the CCP regarded as false information fell under special suspicion as potential propaganda tools with a marked class nature. Missionaries had the best chance for holding on to judge from the regulations the CCP was promulgating, but even they were hostage to international tensions.[46]

Despite gathering pessimism about official U.S. intentions and suspicions of Americans in China, party officials still had a strong incentive to develop economic ties with the capitalists (even without diplomatic relations). The civil war and the Japanese invasion had left China's economy in a shambles. The modern industrial sector, which the CCP accorded high priority, was in desperate need of help. Restoring production was important not only to quickly meet the material needs of the Chinese people but also in the long term to realize the vision of an ultimate transition to socialism. It was thus imperative that the forces of production receive strong, immediate stimulus, especially in the capital-intensive, technologically advanced modern industrial sector along the coast and in the northeast. The Soviets, Mao and his colleagues had long recognized, could give but limited reconstruction aid. And even if the Soviet purse were wide open, Mao was not sure how deeply he could dip in without incurring unwanted dependence.

Mao had in March 1949 affirmed the CCP's previous commitment to trading with all foreign countries, capitalist no less than socialist, guided by the usual principles of equality and mutual help. Mao himself confirmed that "wherever there is business to do, we shall do it and we have already started; the businessmen of several capitalist countries are competing for such business. So far as possible, we must first of all trade with the socialist and people's democratic countries; at the same time we will also trade with capitalist countries."[47]

There followed in the spring soundings on the prospects for American financial and technical aid as well as trade that stood in counterpoint to the Huang-Stuart exchanges. Yao Yilin, the Minister of Industry and Commerce in the north China provisional government, made the opening overtures in April, and Chen Yi in Shanghai, Qiao Guanhua in Hong Kong, and Huang Hua in Nanjing each made their own inquiries in June. By July it was clear that those prospects were poor, or at least that the Truman administration was not going to encourage economic ties. Nevertheless, the new regime was founded in October on the basis of a document endorsing the restoration and expansion of trade relations. And shortly thereafter, while in Moscow, Mao himself indicated to his comrades that he still anticipated trading in 1950 with the United States and other capitalist counties.[48]

U.S. hostility left the CCP ever more reliant on the USSR, and posed for Mao the ever more pressing task of solving the riddle of Stalin's intentions. Mao and other party leaders retained in the late 1940s a faith in the identity of the general political values binding the CCP to the Soviet Union. They expressed that faith in a language—rhetoric, terminology, images, and so forth—learned from the Comintern in the 1920s and still shared with Moscow and others in the international socialist community.

However, past friction and disappointments had strained these bonds. The tension between ideological fraternity and divergent national styles and concerns was an old one in the history of the CCP-Soviet dealings. Moscow had shown a consistent preference for dealing with the Nationalists dating back to the 1920s. Its most recent manifestation was the hastily concluded August 1945 treaty. Bound by his bargain, Stalin vacillated over how to handle the CCP presence in the northeast and maintained a cautious diplomatic stance during the Marshall mediation. Now in the late 1940s as on earlier occasions Stalin dealt with the CCP opportunistically. He was ready to finesse its interests in order to calm American anxieties as he had been earlier to ask it to go into battle in defense of the Soviet state. And while Mao had succeeded in moving the party away from a mindless modeling on the Soviet pattern, he could not be certain that Stalin had lost all inner-party leverage or that intellectual tendencies of a Wang Ming type might not revive to compromise the CCP's hard-won autonomy.[49]

With CCP forces positioning themselves for the decisive campaign against the Nationalists in summer 1948, Mao began to consider the state-building task ahead—and by extension the role that the USSR might play in defending and building the new China. In May he stressed to Stalin China's need for help with the enormous economic tasks that loomed before the CCP. In September Mao contemplated a visit to Moscow to establish an understanding if not the rapport with Stalin so strikingly absent to this point. Though Stalin had not included the CCP, or for that matter other non-European communist parties, in the Communist Information Bureau (Cominform) organized in September 1947, Mao himself went out of his way in the latter half of 1948 to underscore the CCP's membership in the socialist community. He sent public messages to the

Italian and Japanese parties, offered condolences on the death of prominent Soviet Politburo member Andrei Zhdanov, sent congratulations on the founding of the North Korean state, and pointedly joined in celebrating the thirty-first anniversary of the Russian revolution. At the same time the CCP demonstrated its fealty to the socialist bloc by condemning Yugoslavia's President Josip Tito. Immediately following the Cominform's decision in June to expel the renegade Yugoslav party, the CCP Central Committee passed a resolution endorsing the measure, and in November Liu Shaoqi offered a lengthy public exposition of the CCP's loyalist position. But the hoped for face-to-face exchange with the Soviet leader succumbed to the difficulty of travel and the press of military affairs, both of which limited Mao's mobility, while Stalin for his part was not yet ready for a public embrace of the CCP.[50]

Dramatic CCP battlefield successes through 1948 finally forced a cautious response from Stalin. Mao's May 1948 request for economic assistance moved Stalin to dispatch a team of three hundred specialists to put the rail lines in the northeast in good operating order. Then in early 1949 he sent Politburo member Anastas Mikoyan on a secret mission to check out the Chinese party, which had defied the odds and Soviet expectations. His task was to listen, not talk; there would be no firm commitments of assistance. In the meetings held at Xibaipo between January 31 and February 7, Mao explained to the reticent Soviet envoy the nature of the new democracy political program (which had stirred doubts in Moscow), stressed his hopes for economic recovery and development (to which the Soviets could make a signal contribution), and called for simultaneously demobilizing and modernizing the CCP military (to which the Soviets could also make a contribution). In foreign affairs Mao spoke of moving at a slow pace while China straightened out its domestic affairs. Mao returned several times to the theme of true and false friends. The former, he made clear, would be the early arrivals who would help the CCP put its new home in order. For the moment true friends would not, he told Mikoyan, stand in the way of pressing the civil war to a victorious conclusion. Only the United States, certainly no friend, was likely to constitute a significant obstacle, and even the Americans, he assured the Soviet envoy, were not willing to take direct action.[51]

Mikoyan's visit did nothing to slow the CCP military advance or prevent the crossing of the Yangzi in late April. But even in the wake of these new CCP successes Stalin would not cut his ties to the Nationalists. The USSR alone among the powers appeared willing to throw Chiang a lifeline as his regime sought outside mediators in early 1949, and the Soviet ambassador clung to the discredited Nationalists, eventually following them in flight to Canton. Stalin's own advice to the CCP at this time revealed a similar caution: develop ties with the capitalist powers through China's bourgeoisie and explore diplomatic relations even with the United States.[52]

Only in the latter half of 1949—with CCP victory assured, state-building well underway, and relations with the United States festering—did the Sino-Soviet connection finally take form. Mao's speech "On the People's Democratic Dictatorship" delivered at the end of June was a major personal bid to win Stalin's support as well as to resolve any confusion at home over the new China's international orientation. "It is not possible to sit on the fence and there is no third road," Mao announced. He placed China firmly in "the anti-imperialist front headed by the Soviet Union, and we can look for genuine, friendly assistance only from that front, and not from the imperialist front." Moscow could now put away its fear that the CCP was allowing too wide a circle of nonparty people, especially nonparty politicos with an Anglo-American orientation, a political role in the new regime and that China might follow some kind of neutralist or, worse still, Titoist path. But the speech was also meant to remind Stalin of the obligations of bloc leadership. Assistance "from the international revolutionary forces" was, Mao insisted, absolutely essential "to consolidate" the CCP's victory.[53]

Just days after Mao's speech Liu Shaoqi, the second-ranking party leader, left for Moscow. Like Mao's speech, Liu's visit was the product of a May Central Committee decision on promoting high-level talks in order to secure help in China's reconstruction and a strategic commitment to deter intervention. Sent off with last-minute instructions from Mao himself, Liu was accompanied by Li Fuchun (moving from the northeast to national economic policy) and Gao Gang (representing the interests of the northeast). Liu arrived in Moscow on July 10. He found Stalin not only accommodating but actually full of praise for the CCP and insistent on giving the CCP greater but unspecified responsibility for revolutions in the East. For his part Liu offered one more explanation of new democracy, emphasizing that China's national bourgeoisie would figure prominently in economic development plans for another ten to fifteen years. Turning to foreign policy, he noted that the CCP aimed not only at destroying imperialist control but also exploiting contradictions among the capitalists. The new government would stand next to the USSR in the anti-imperialist camp, but it would also try to expand foreign trade and conclude diplomatic relations, even with the imperialists.[54]

Before his departure on August 14 Liu had won substantial Soviet support. The basis for a wide-ranging working relationship was evident in promises of technical assistance in such areas as transport and administration, help with educational reform, the immediate dispatch of two hundred advisers, a program of study visits by Chinese delegations and students, a $300 million loan, trade agreements, support in creating an air and naval force essential to taking Taiwan, and elaboration of interparty liaison. Stalin also agreed to shift Soviet air defense units from Lüshun (formerly Port Arthur) to defend Shanghai against Nationalist air attacks. After the meeting Wang Jiaxiang remained in Moscow to coordinate an increasingly complex Soviet aid program and to serve as interparty liaison.

Liu's visit in turn set the stage for Mao's own two-month pilgrimage to Moscow, the climax of a year and a half of diplomatic effort to win the security guarantees as well as the economic support the PRC needed. Stalin still seemed a reluctant host, but Mao felt compelled to deal directly with this jealous guardian of Soviet China policy. Mao had had to press twice in the fall before finally eliciting in early November the invitation he sought. Following his arrival in the Soviet capital on December 16, Mao found Stalin awkward and rough-edged. To judge from eyewitness accounts, the relationship between the two remained stiff. Their first meeting got the visit off to a rocky start: Stalin tried to elicit from Mao a concrete agenda, while Mao fended him off with pleasantries and vague aphorisms. The visit quickly turned byzantine when the Soviet liaison to Mao supplied Stalin a report critical of the pro-American current within the CCP and of the party's insufficiently firm political grip on the bourgeoisie. Stalin promptly told Mao of the report and at the same time repudiated it. Subsequent encounters produced more moments of awkward silence, sullen anger, and unexpected outbursts, revealing that these giants of the world revolution lived in strikingly different cultural and psychological worlds.[55]

Mao cooled his heels in Moscow until at last in early January Stalin dispatched Mikoyan and Molotov for a business visit. This time the Chinese leader was ready. He laid out two alternative bases on which to build the new Sino-Soviet relationship: a new, full-fledged treaty of alliance and friendship or alternatively a much more modest announcement of views exchanged between the two sides. Mao made clear that he preferred the former. He explained that such a treaty would "isolate the right wing of the national bourgeoisie." At the same time the treaty would give China "the greater political capital" useful not only "to confront imperialist countries" but also "to scrutinize all the past treaties between China and the imperialist countries." Molotov at once agreed to embrace the treaty alternative.[56]

To his comrades at home Mao explained that he saw the treaty essentially as a quid pro quo. For China the treaty would provide a "guard against possible invasion." The Soviets on the other side would get PRC recognition of Outer Mongolia's independence. The other elements in the bargain were less important. The Soviet side confirmed the $300 million loan earlier promised Liu, and Mao professed to favor this limited sum in order to keep China's debt manageable. (Mao may have simply been making the best of a disappointing deal.) An aviation agreement would give a boost to China's own aviation industry. Finally, commercial agreements would link Soviet-bloc trade with China and help in the expansion of production. Mao wanted discussions of the new treaty to take full note of its advantages. "The capitalist countries cannot but accommodate to us. It will be advantageous in compelling all countries to grant China unconditional recognition, to abrogate the old [unequal] treaties, and to conclude new treaties. And it will hold each of the capitalist countries back from rash action."

On Mao's instruction Zhou Enlai, concurrently premier and foreign minister of the PRC, hastened to Moscow to help in working out the details of the various agreements. After arduous negotiations Mao finally on February 14 got his security treaty stipulating that China and the USSR would "immediately render military and other assistance with all the means at its disposal" to the other if attacked by Japan or one of its allies, a not so veiled allusion to the United States. An economic agreement signed at the same time included as anticipated a $300 million credit (at a nominal one percent rate of interest), though its precise terms would give rise to extended haggling. Finally, an agreement dealing with the northeast left the Soviets still ensconced but less secure than before. The port of Dalian (Dairen), the naval base at Lüshun, and the Changchun Railway were all scheduled to come under complete Chinese control by the end of 1952. The PRC recognition of the independence of Outer Mongolia was registered in a joint Soviet-Chinese public statement announcing the formal agreements. Talks on economic cooperation continued into late March, producing agreements on two Xinjiang joint stock companies (one for mining and one for petroleum) and a jointly operated airline. These cooperative deals did provide welcome technology transfers, although at the price of maintaining the Soviet presence in a sensitive border region. The negotiations also produced a set of secret agreements, including one barring Americans, British, and other capitalists from the northeast and Xinjiang and another coordinating intelligence activities.[57]

The Test of the Korean War*

The victory over Nationalist forces on the mainland and the conclusion of the Soviet treaty promised the CCP surcease from foreign policy crisis. Party leaders could finally look ahead to a period of calm. They could at least concentrate on the process of economic reconstruction and political renovation for which they had struggled and about which they had even longer dreamed. Already by late 1949 they had begun to deal with a daunting array of domestic problems, none more pressing than the economy. Industrial production after a decade of conflict had fallen to roughly half of its prewar peak, and agricultural output was down by a quarter. Land reform in newly liberated areas, the suppression of armed resistance, and demobilization of an army of four million were other pressing tasks. Finally, the CCP was embarked on a military and diplomatic campaign to secure China's border regions. Korea, despite its intimate cultural and strategic links to China and especially the northeast, did not figure prominently. It was instead the challenge of taking Tibet and Taiwan that preoccupied the CCP. The former posed substantial logistical difficulties, while the latter demanded even more, a naval and air force and experience with joint operations that the CCP was only beginning to develop.[58]

Quiet on the international front was shattered on June 25, 1950 by the outbreak of the Korean War. North Korean forces crossed the thirty-eighth parallel, quickly captured Seoul, and continued their advance deep into the south. Beijing may not have welcomed the timing of this dramatic military initiative by the North Korean leader, Kim Il Sung, but the attack itself was not a surprise. Kim had talked Stalin into supporting the attack early in the year. Even so, Stalin after a formal meeting with Kim in April on the details of the attack had insisted on getting Mao's approval. At a meeting the next month in Beijing Mao gave Kim a less than enthusiastic endorsement. Like Stalin, Mao approved on the assumption that the United States would not defend South Korea and that Kim would win as promised a quick victory.[59] Beijing had already helped Pyongyang to lay the groundwork for the attack by repatriating Korean troops who had fought in the Chinese civil war and who would constitute an important part of the invasion force. From the fall of 1949 into the following spring Korean forces returned home, some with their weapons and equipment. Estimates of the

---

*This section draws from my "Beijing and the Korean Crisis, June 1950–June 1951," *Political Science Quarterly* 107 (Fall 1992): 453–78. I am grateful to the journal for permission to make use of portions of that article here.

total number sent back by the eve of the war run around 50,000–70,000 and by the fall may have exceeded 100,000.[60]

What neither Mao, nor Stalin, nor Kim anticipated was Washington's strong reaction to the North Korean attack. On June 27 President Harry S. Truman announced that the United States would not only defend South Korea under the auspices of the United Nation but also "neutralize" the Taiwan Strait by sending the Seventh Fleet to block any Communist invasion attempt. The United States would also, he declared, step up aid to the Philippines and French Indochina.

Beijing's earliest public response to this far-reaching American decision, published on June 28 and 29, was notably cautious and vague. While deploring American intervention around the world and especially in Asia, Mao as well as Premier Zhou Enlai and a *People's Daily* editorial all nonetheless focused their public fire on the American attempt to deny China control of Taiwan.[61]

But the CCP began almost at once to prepare against untoward developments in Korea, inexorably slowing domestic reconstruction and by degrees turning some programs in unanticipated new directions. In early July a Chinese embassy was hastily set up in Pyongyang, nearly a year after diplomatic recognition. At the same time the Military Affairs Committee ordered a border defense force assembled along the Yalu River. By early August more than a quarter of a million troops were in place, and the Committee had resolved to put off until 1952 any decision on a possible invasion of Taiwan in order to focus on Korea. An anxious Mao pressed Gao Gang, who was responsible for party and military affairs in the northeast, to make haste in preparing Chinese forces for combat. Finally, on September 17, in the immediate aftermath of the successful American landing at Inchon, Chinese officers entered Korea to lay the groundwork for possible intervention. All the while, Beijing continued to express publicly its alarm over the advance of UN forces.[62]

China's growing alarm, reinforced by Soviet and Korean calls for assistance, gave rise to efforts to coordinate policy among the three. Stalin's insistence on keeping a low profile in Korea even in the midst of an impending disaster left the Chinese to pick up the pieces. In late September Stalin raised with Beijing the possibility of receiving a North Korean government in exile. At the same time he refused Kim's request for Soviet intervention, directing the North Korean leader to look instead to China for rescue. At the same time Stalin authorized emergency delivery of Soviet military supplies. On October 1 with South Korean forces crossing the thirty-eighth parallel Stalin and Kim both personally requested China's help.[63]

While Mao responded at once to Stalin, it was not until October 8 that he conveyed to Kim a promise to intervene. That commitment in turn led to the creation of a joint Chinese-Korean command in December and to Mao-Kim conferences in Beijing at several critical points in the tumultuous first year of the war (early December 1950, late January 1951, and early June 1951). Those conferences dealt not only with war strategy but also with friction between the Chinese "volunteers" and their Korean brothers and sisters.[64]

As China moved toward the actual decision to intervene militarily in the conflict, Mao played the dominant role. He approached the definitive commitment of his forces along two sometimes intersecting tracks. One of those tracks led to Moscow. Having announced to his colleagues his own view that China should intervene, Mao on October 2 cabled Stalin. Chinese troops would enter Korea on October 15, Mao announced, and there they would assume a defensive posture, letting the enemy forces know that they faced a new situation. Once better prepared and equipped with Soviet arms, Chinese troops could, if need be, take the offensive. Aside from equipment, Mao wanted from Stalin help in fending off possible American naval and air attacks on Chinese cities and industry.[65]

Having indicated that China was ready to shoulder the main burden of saving North Korea, Mao followed up on October 8 by sending Zhou Enlai to nail Stalin down on the details of military support. At a meeting in Sochi on the Black Sea during the night of October 9–10, Stalin revealed that Chinese forces would have to go into Korea without the air cover they so desperately needed. The Soviet air force, he explained, had to have more time before going into combat even in the defense of Chinese airspace. Zhou cabled Mao this disappointing news, but also passed on assurances that the Soviets would immediately begin supplying weaponry for twenty Chinese divisions.[66]

While dealing with Stalin, Mao moved along the second track defined by a string of high-level meetings with his colleagues. Mao's proposal for decisive action elicited doubts that he was not able to dispel either quickly or easily. Some opposed sending troops or at least wanted to delay intervention because of the military risks to the expeditionary force and the prospects of a direct, damaging attack on China. Some argued that the new Chinese state needed time to consolidate its political control, wipe out remaining Chinese Nationalist resistance, complete land reform, stabilize the economy, and upgrade the armed forces. Some pointed to the burdens intervention would place on a war-weary population. Some may also have stressed the uncertain nature of Soviet assistance.[67]

The rapidly deteriorating battlefield situation, the delays in getting Chinese troops ready for combat, and Stalin's refusal of air support subjected even Mao to gnawing anxieties about the risks of intervention. Indeed, Mao himself seems at points to have fallen prey to serious reservations. As early as October 2 in his cable to Stalin, Mao had conceded that attacking Chinese troops might fail to destroy American forces in Korea and thus become entangled in a military stand-off. At the same time American attacks could seriously damage China's economic reconstruction. Cumulatively these reverses might deepen the discontent of Chinese who were already unsettled by the CCP's revolutionary program. The Korean intervention, Mao in effect conceded, gambled the future of the PRC.

The first of a hurried and tension-filled series of meetings took place on October 1. The leadership broke away early from the public celebration of the PRC's first anniversary to discuss Kim's urgent request for military assistance. This discussion lasted until dawn, and then resumed the following afternoon with Zhu De, Liu Shaoqi, Zhou Enlai, Nie Rongzhen, and Gao Gang in attendance. Mao announced his view that troops had to intervene, and he secured agreement on October 15 as the day for Chinese forces to march. To command them Mao suggested Peng Dehuai and won general approval. Mao then dispatched his cable to Stalin, and Zhou called in the Indian ambassador to warn that Beijing "has to be concerned" (*yaoguan*) if the Americans crossed the thirty-eighth parallel.[68]

On October 4 and 5 an expanded meeting of the Political Bureau met to consider Mao's intervention proposal. Peng Dehuai arrived from his command in the northwest to join the discussions, and quickly agreed to shoulder the Korean command. On October 8, following a series of planning meetings, Mao met again with the enlarged Political Bureau and gave the orders for Chinese forces to prepare to move across the Yalu River and do battle with U.S troops then crossing the thirty-eighth parallel and threatening Pyongyang. At the same time he cabled his decision to Kim Il Sung, and Peng left at once for the northeast to take up his command.[69]

The arrival of Zhou Enlai's unsettling report of his interview with Stalin during the afternoon of October 10 provoked a second round of consultations. On October 11–12 Mao not only suspended his intervention order but also recalled Peng and Gao to Beijing to go over once more the plans for military action. The Political Bureau met on October 13 and stayed in session through the night before coming to a unanimous agreement to send troops to Korea despite the lack of Soviet air support.[70]

The October 13 Political Bureau meeting followed by a Mao-Peng

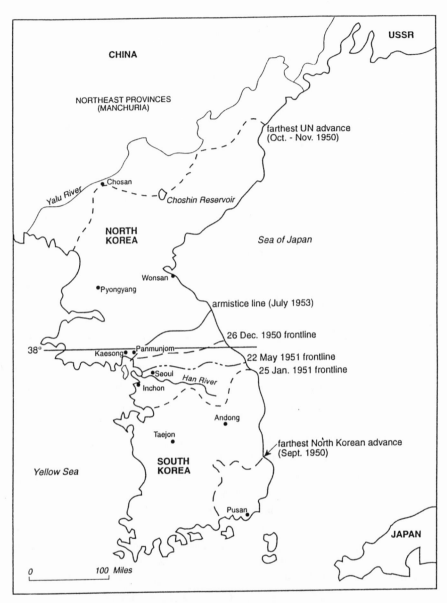

CHINA

USSR

NORTHEAST PROVINCES
(MANCHURIA)

farthest UN advance
(Oct. - Nov. 1950)

Yalu River

Chosan

Choshin Reservoir

NORTH
KOREA

Sea of Japan

Wonsan

Pyongyang

armistice line (July 1953)

26 Dec. 1950 frontline

38°

Kaesong Panmunjom

22 May 1951 frontline

25 Jan. 1951 frontline

Seoul Han River

Inchon

Andong

Taejon

farthest North Korean advance
(Sept. 1950)

SOUTH
KOREA

Yellow Sea

Pusan

JAPAN

0   100 Miles

The Korean War, 1950-1953

meeting the next day produced a consensus in favor of proceeding cautiously and avoiding a forceful challenge to the United States. The volunteers were to concentrate their attack on the South Korean "puppet" forces and to avoid hitting any but isolated American forces. The volunteers were, moreover, not to make a rapid advance but rather to establish a base of operations in the mountainous region north of Pyongyang and Wonsan. If American forces did not advance beyond those two points for six months, then Chinese forces would gain time to prepare for whatever action Beijing might think best at the end of that period. This action, the Political Bureau resolution somewhat vaguely opined, would "produce a change to our advantage." The consensus did not address the possibility that General Douglas MacArthur might continue his rapid advance, giving the Chinese force no grace period and Beijing no chance for a peaceful resolution of the confrontation. Mao now cabled Zhou, still in Moscow, the terms on which China was acting and made clear that the intervening force would consist not of the six divisions that Stalin had urged earlier in the crisis but fifteen divisions together with supporting units (260,000 troops).[71]

Now at the last moment with Kim calling for haste in the dispatch of support and Mao demanding prompt intervention, Peng's subordinates raised fresh doubts about the military operations. They reported that their forces, with few anti-aircraft guns and no air cover, faced poor odds in battle, and proposed delaying action until winter or even the following spring when they might be better equipped. On the 17th Mao called Peng and Gao back to Beijing to canvas again the precise time for moving into Korea and to hear Zhou report on the details of Soviet support. With the Americans advancing rapidly and the North Koreans in a panic, Mao finally thrust aside all hesitations and fears and insisted on immediate action. On his orders the first major body of Chinese troops advanced into Korea at twilight on October 19, setting in motion the events that would soon bring war with the United States.[72]

Any effort to pin down the exact motive behind Mao's decision to intervene must enter a mind as complicated as the crisis it wrestled with and must keep in sight the hesitations or objections that he encountered. His cable of October 2 to Stalin nicely illustrates the point. Mao contended that he felt an internationalist duty to rescue the beleaguered Korean revolution and to help maintain revolutionary morale around the world in the face of a counter-offensive launched by American reactionaries. The dangers of a revival of reactionary sentiment in China and elsewhere in Asia was for him equally troubling and demanded a decisive response. If China meekly acquiesced while the Americans occupied all of Korea and dealt a heavy blow to the Korean revolution, "then the American invaders will run more rampant to the detriment of the entire East."[73] While giving considerable weight overall to the dangers of appeasement and the opportunities for creating an international environment favorable to revolutionary change, Mao also invoked a narrower, more conventional concern with China's security. He had to act, he argued, to preempt a possible American offensive into China itself.

The discussions within the Political Bureau found Mao thinking in an internationalist framework—but now with the CCP decidedly at the center. In the meetings of October 4–5, he expressed fears of China being thrown on the defensive if it did not now deal the Americans a blow. An unchecked American advance in Korea would draw wavering countries and classes to the side of the United States, strengthen the resolve of reactionaries at home and abroad, and encourage the United States to send troops to other points along China's border.

The final consensus reached at the meeting of October 13 seemed to reflect this combination of concerns. According to Mao's summary of that consensus, military intervention was necessary above all to prevent the enemy from dominating the Yalu River and thus posing a constant threat to the northeast. But intervention was also important for guaranteeing the North Koreans a secure base of operations and for denying imperialism a victory that would fan counter-revolutionary sentiments in China and also elsewhere around the world.

The risks and uncertainties of intervention may have frightened Mao away from a precise formulation of his goals. His cables to Zhou, sent in the immediate aftermath of the October 13 Political Bureau meeting, reflected this reluctance to be pinned down. Chinese troops might win a decisive battlefield victory that would force the American-led coalition to abandon the peninsula. Even a limited military success might send a wake-up call to Washington, making clear China's determination and hence the dangers of a more costly Korean conflict. Once rudely shaken, Washington might reassess its goals in Korea; the pause in Chinese military operations following the initial entry into Korea would give the Americans time to indicate their interest in a peaceful resolution of the conflict. If, on the other hand, Washington held to its aggressive course, then Chinese troops, by then better prepared for combat, could take the offensive in a renewed test of strength. Mao must have played out in his mind each of these scenarios in the anxious days before the crossing of the Yalu. But they amounted, as he and his Political Bureau colleagues must have realized, to nothing more than a pious hope that an early blow might produce a turn for the better on the peninsula.[74]

The prospect of a U.S. nuclear strike appears not to have stood at the top of Beijing's concerns at this time. Publicly at least the new Chinese government was dismissive, arguing that a lightly industrialized and heavily rural, agricultural China was not a particularly fruitful target for nuclear attack, and that nuclear weapons were not suitable as an actual tool of land warfare in Korea. Mao himself in a September 5 talk to the Council of the Central People's Government raised the atomic threat only to downplay its significance. Even so, Mao was concerned enough about popular fears of atomic bombing that he had the wartime mobilization campaign address them. On the off-chance that the United States did attack from the air, the leadership ordered bomb shelters prepared in cities, some industrial plants removed from vulnerable urban sites, and civil defense education set in motion.[75]

Once embarked on intervention, Mao involved himself deeply in the actual planning and execution of the first three campaigns, beginning in late October and running to early January. Mao's role here, as in the high-level decision to take a military stand, was central and controlling. For example, through October Mao appears to have focused on the Korean crisis to the exclusion of other pressing issues facing the new government. His preoccupations, even anxieties, are evident in the drumbeat of advice directed at the commander of his forces in Korea.[76] The Mao that appears here is a confident figure, keenly attuned to the political dimensions of warfare by long experience with the party's armed struggle.

Mao would brook no Chinese MacArthur, and Peng Dehuai, a dutiful field commander, did not attempt to play that role. Even so, Peng did at crucial junctures question his superior's strategy. For example, in late November and early December he proposed a halt at the thirty-eighth parallel and a rest through the winter months to prepare his forces for a spring offensive. Determined to exploit the vulnerability of the disorganized and demoralized enemy, Mao ordered another round of campaigning, ruthlessly driving forward his own exhausted peasant army, inadequately fed and clothed and freezing on the battlefield. Unable to bring Mao to accept a more cautious course, Peng loyally continued the headlong assault.[77]

Once deeply and successfully engaged in the Korean conflict, Mao resolved the ambiguities in Chinese war aims in favor of bold, far-reaching goals and without any apparent formal consultation with his Political Bureau colleagues. The resolution came in late November and early December. As Peng's drive south gave increasing promise of a sweeping victory,

Mao in effect fell victim to military opportunism. On December 4 he ordered reconnaissance in force against the clearly panicked U.N. army now retreating across the thirty-eighth parallel into South Korea. The next day Pyongyang fell amid hints that the Americans might altogether abandon Korea. On December 13 he ordered the advance to continue beyond the parallel, and he reiterated that position as late as December 21. Bolstered militarily, Beijing publicly linked peace on the peninsula to the withdrawal of all foreign troops, U.S. disengagement from Taiwan, and a place for China in the United Nations.[78]

From this high point of optimism, Mao began a retreat toward a more sober appraisal of the military situation and toward more modest goals. He took the first step back on December 26 and 29 when he began to concede the seriousness of the supply and morale problems afflicting his army. From the field Peng was again calling for a rest for Chinese forces, and Nie in Beijing endorsed the proposal. But Mao insisted for political reasons on launching another attack. The third offensive thus began on December 31. A month later Peng once more proposed a rest for his forces, this time in preparation for renewed offensive action in March. With his troops exhausted, short on supplies, and harried by the enemy, Mao now at last conceded in early February that he had not won a decisive victory or intimidated the Americans but instead become entangled in a war of attrition. He would have to shift to "rotational warfare" whereby Chinese armies would be trained, sent to Korea for a time, and then withdrawn in favor of fresh forces. This rotational warfare was, Mao explained to Stalin on March 1, a way of continuing the contest of wills with the United States, a contest in which inflicting casualties was the key to victory.[79]

Mao had from the beginning of this conflict seen it as a test of wills—just as he had seen confrontations with earlier opponents. But by his own calculations he was losing the test. While the resolve and condition of his own forces had declined, his estimate of the casualties needed to destroy the enemy's will had climbed steadily higher. On November 18 Mao had called for a few more campaigns and the destruction of "several tens of thousands" of the enemy in order to change the whole international situation. On December 26 he offered a revised judgment—that it would take at least 40,000 to 50,000 American and British casualties before resolution of the Korean question would be possible. Now on March 1, 1951 Mao, once more indulging his numerological fetish, set the critical casualty figure at "several hundred thousand" Americans. Only then, he claimed, would Washington see the difficulty it was in and be ready to solve the Korean problem.[80]

Deeply engaged in the conduct of the Korean conflict through the fall,

Mao seems to have abruptly put the war to one side early in 1951. He was limited by a recurrence of ill health, perhaps discouraged by the steadily dimming prospects for some sweeping battlefield success, and increasingly immersed in the campaign against domestic counter-revolutionaries.[81]

Then as suddenly as Korea had diminished in Mao's constellation of concerns, it reappeared in late May. By then the fifth major Chinese offensive had ground to a halt, confirming the military stalemate and revealing the continuing problem of supply and the fragility of Chinese units. American forces, on the other hand, were (as Mao observed on May 26) still formidable. Having failed to destroy their will to fight, he would have to shift to a defensive strategy. Mao's own willingness to concede this point and the American approach to the Soviet U.N. ambassador on May 31 set the stage for a major reappraisal of the Korean strategy. Mao met with his colleagues, and on June 3 hosted Kim Il Sung. This flurry of activity produced agreement on trying for a negotiated end to the conflict with the thirty-eighth parallel to serve once again as the dividing line between the two Koreas. On June 23 the Soviet ambassador publicly proposed talks, immediately endorsed by an editorial in *People's Daily*. Talks opened in Kaesong on July 10.[82]

As the combatants moved toward negotiations, Mao inserted himself into the policy process on a daily basis. Through Li Kenong, the vice-minister of foreign affairs, Mao closely monitored the negotiations. After reading Li's field reports on each day's developments, Mao would prepare the instructions to guide the Sino-Korean negotiating team for the next day of talks while also orchestrating press treatment in China.[83]

Reflecting back in July 1951, Mao tried to put the past year's test in Korea in positive terms. "As the ancients said, only by being able to fight is one then able to make peace."[84] But the fighting had already proven more costly than anticipated. The war of attrition in which he had become ensnared had diverted scarce resources from the domestic scene. In 1951, the first full year of the war, defense ate up forty-six percent of the national budget (up from about thirty-eight percent the previous year), leaving only thirty percent for economic development. And for two more years the talks would remain deadlocked, raising still higher the economic costs (in all $10 billion including indirect costs) and ultimately pushing the number of China's dead and wounded on the battlefield to 382,000.[85]

Populism and Mao's Foreign Policy

Mao brought to his foreign policy in these critical years a long nurtured populism that left him wary of the urban bourgeoisie. Those caught in the grip of international capitalism shared a treaty-port world of special privilege with foreigners. They betrayed a mean-spirited devotion to money making and an indifference to the plight of China and the mass of the people. Some among the intellectuals, particularly the Western-trained and oriented, assumed superior airs and foreign ways that set in doubt, at least for Mao, their patriotic commitment.

But as a populist, Mao had also sought to unite Chinese into "a great union," not divide them, drawing even segments of the bourgeoisie into the revolutionary movement. While intimate ties with imperialism put the group that he designated "comprador" (or "bureaucratic") capitalists solidly in the counter-revolutionary camp, he regarded with greater hope the wavering "national bourgeoisie" and the more reliably progressive and patriotic "petty bourgeoisie."[86]

Mao's own rise to party leadership had been closely identified with a broad united front with its goal of drawing middle-of-the-road groups into the revolutionary enterprise alongside peasants and workers. Prompted at first by Japanese aggression, this united-front policy got a new lease on life in 1944–1945 as Mao planned the CCP's postwar effort to secure an advantageous position against the Nationalists. While the program of political accommodation and reform finally foundered in late 1946, the united front survived. In December 1946 and January 1947 the party center remained interested in working with middle elements—bourgeoisie, students, and intellectuals. Their support of the popular democratic movement would weaken the Nationalists in their urban strongholds.[87]

During the civil war Mao's hopes for the bourgeoisie mingled with anxiety over its lingering attachments to the United States as well as its incomplete break with the Nationalists. Consistent with his earlier views, Mao saw progressive nonparty Chinese pulled in two directions—on the one side by their loyalties as Chinese and on the other by foreign influence and their interests as members of an exploiting class within China. Foreign powers might seek to sway them, but so too could the CCP. Political education, Mao repeatedly stressed, would raise their political consciousness and attach them to the side of the revolution. For the moment Mao regarded involvement by intellectual and nonparty leaders in political struggle in Nationalist-controlled areas and in land-reform activities in liberated areas as good first lessons. But their political education and ultimate assimilation would take a sustained, careful effort. Urging patience, Mao censured excessively "leftist" handling of this group.[88]

By mid-1948 the concerns behind Mao's united-front policy began to shift as the military conflict turned decisively in the CCP's favor. Even though Mao still expected three years or more of fighting,[89] he and his colleagues began to give some thought to the task of completely breaking bourgeois ties to the Nationalists and of assimilating the middle element of that class into the new political order.

Most immediately, the bourgeoisie was critical to facilitating control in the urban centers falling to CCP forces, beginning in the north in 1948 and culminating in May 1949 with the capture of Shanghai. The cadres accompanying the victorious CCP armies found themselves on unfamiliar ground where party organization was weak and class enemies and U.S. and Nationalist influences were still strong. The party center made clear during this period that securing the cooperation of the middle elements of the bourgeoisie was critical to isolating the CCP's foes, restoring production, reopening commerce, and maintaining administrative functions. When Liu Shaoqi discovered Tianjin authorities straying from the moderate line in May 1949, Mao personally issued a reprimand intended as a general reminder to seek bourgeois cooperation.[90]

The united front was also important in laying the foundation for the new political order. Looking ahead to the task of state-building, Mao began to recruit middle-of-the-road, "democratic" political leaders and prominent personalities for inclusion in the emergent government of the people's republic. While securing their political cooperation, Mao also saw this initiative as a way to prevent the third force from falling under the sway of U.S. interests and ideals and to soothe their palpable anxieties about CCP rule. In mid-1948 the CCP began making contacts through its Hong Kong office, and in late 1948 the first of the democratic personages reached the northeast. Though himself not on hand and in any case absorbed in military affairs, Mao pressed party representatives on the scene to engage the newcomers in a frank exchange of views, provide them party literature, put them in touch with the masses, and take any other measures that would advance their political education. In May on the eve of the Political Consultative Conference (formally inaugurated the middle of the next month) the Central Committee reiterated its commitment to education to draw as much of the middle group as possible into the political arena.[91]

Finally, the bourgeoisie seemed to occupy a secure place for the foreseeable future in the CCP's strategy for raising China's economic and educational level in preparation for an ultimate transition to socialism. The new democracy formula held that bourgeois elements commanded talents and resources critical to China's progress. Though ultimately to disappear as a class, they were simply too useful for the foreseeable future for the party center to tolerate "adventuristic" policies that would alienate them. Their treaty-port base was the most developed part of China's economy. There productive forces controlled by the middle bourgeoisie—capital, technology, and links to international markets—could be unleashed quickly, help meet the immediate needs of the people and government, and ultimately make China prosperous. To take advantage of this commercial and industrial potential, the CCP planned to encourage established entrepreneurs, to restrain labor, and to keep open channels for foreign trade essential to the recovery and growth of the coastal economy. Mao gave his imprimatur to this approach at the second plenum in March 1949. He called for preserving the commercial and industrial activities of the national bourgeoisie and even allowing them to expand as part of a mixed economy under central control.[92]

A developed educational system, also indispensable to preparing the way for the socialist stage, was no less dependent on bourgeois talent and experience. China's intellectuals were few in number, and those teachers, scientists, technicians, doctors, journalists, and artists with a strong revolutionary commitment were fewer still. For the moment the CCP could not let the fact that most intellectuals came from petty bourgeois as well as landlord and rich peasant backgrounds stand in the way of enlisting their skills. The CCP thus assigned itself the task of educating the educators and other intellectuals, thereby transforming the majority into "mental laborers" in the popular coalition.[93]

Mao's concerns with drawing the bourgeoisie into the ranks of "the people" were accentuated by U.S. policy in the course of 1949. Continuing American support for the Nationalists and a refusal to renegotiate the terms of its relationship with China brought to the surface patriotic passions—raw anger and deep shame over foreign penetration and arrogance—that had antedated and helped give rise to Mao's revolutionary career in the first place. Washington's application of economic and political pressure to undermine the Chinese revolution was a deeply irritating reminder that the heyday of imperialism might be over but that die-hard imperialists, especially in Washington, would not easily accept defeat and release their grip on China. As in the past, they would use their Chinese allies in their struggle for the status quo. When Secretary of State Acheson issued a public statement in August appealing to Chinese liberals and intellectuals, he unwittingly touched an already sensitive nerve. Just how loyal was an important part of the new democracy coalition?

Early in the year, well before Acheson's appeal, Mao had anticipated and moved to counter this familiar imperialist stratagem of boring from within. In a January directive approved by the Political Bureau Mao warned, "The mistaken view prevailing among some Chinese people as well as some of our party members that exaggerates the strength of American imperialism must be constantly watched and overcome." This illusion could prove the source of danger as the Truman administration sought to salvage American interests in China. Facing defeat on the military front, Washington would (Mao predicted) give more attention to undermining the revolution by "sending its running dogs to infiltrate the revolutionary camp and organizing so-called oppositionists." He even imagined that Washington might grant diplomatic recognition as a way of securing its influence in China the better to push this strategy of " 'destruction from within.' "[94]

Mao's late June speech, best known for its call to "lean to one side," again sounded all these themes. He repeated that the CCP was intent on using the bourgeoisie to get the economy moving again, even if it meant learning from them and working with them over the long haul. He once again stressed the importance of educating the bourgeoisie to consolidate their position within the popular coalition and to prepare for ultimate nationalization. Finally, he openly spoke of his fear that the imperialists would woo the bourgeoisie if the CCP did not. This statement would prove the prelude to an intensified effort to carry forward that education.[95]

Acheson's praise for "democratic individualism" in early August prompted Mao himself to take up the schoolmaster role. Despite the press of other business on the eve of the founding of the PRC, Mao made time to pen five commentaries. All were published anonymously in the five weeks following the appearance of Acheson's remarks and the Truman administration's China White Paper. The first two in particular radiated the special personal passion Mao had long brought to this issue. At the very start he took direct aim at "the middle-of-the-roaders or the right-wingers in People's China." Some intellectuals with no stomach for the Nationalists but reluctant to embrace the CCP "still want to wait and see." Mao worried that their continuing "illusions about the United States" left them vulnerable to "the honeyed words of the U.S. imperialists" and unprepared for the "stern, long struggle" ahead to force those imperialists to treat people's China "on the basis of equality and mutual benefit."[96]

Mao also used his commentary to dampen expectations among "the ordinary run of liberals or democratic individualists" of concrete American aid. Drawing from a classical text, Mao warned, "He who swallows food handed out in contempt will get a bellyache." He praised science and democracy, the animating ideas of the May Fourth era so formative to him as well as many in his audience, but warned each had a decided class nature. "True, the United States has science and technology. But unfortunately they are in the grip of the capitalists, not in the hands of the people, and are used to exploit and oppress the people at home and to perpetrate aggression and to slaughter people abroad. There is also democracy in the United States. But unfortunately it is only another name for the dictatorship of the bourgeoisie by itself." Even U.S. capital—available in abundance and desperately needed in China—would only go first to prop up the Chiang reactionaries and then, after they failed, to sustain a U.S. "fifth column in China."[97]

The Korean War further sharpened Mao's anxieties over Chinese still in the imperialist grip and prompted the first broad, concerted effort to mobilize the urban population and integrate the bourgeoisie and especially intellectuals into the new political order. In mid-July 1950 the CCP pulled a diverse group of nonparty leaders into a committee to sponsor popular protests in the cities of eastern China against U.S. intervention in Taiwan as well as Korea. In October, as Chinese troops crossed the Yalu River, this mobilization effort turned into the Resist-America, Aid-Korea campaign.

Lasting for the duration of the war, the campaign sought to eliminate any doubts or misconceptions about the malevolence of the international capitalist system and the damage done China by its leading power. The anti-American propaganda promoted by the campaign ranged from charges of a concerted, century-old effort to deracinate China's youth, to claims of involvement in Nationalist atrocities, and thence to evidence of a barbaric resort to germ warfare. Reinforcing the campaign's goal to root out U.S. influence, Beijing moved in late December to bring educational as well as religious and charitable organizations previously linked to the Americans under official supervision. Other sources of "illusions" such as Voice of America broadcasts and films also came under attack.[98]

These efforts most directly reflected Mao's concern to firm up the support of the petty and national bourgeoisie and intellectuals for the coming costly war effort. In December, with China and the United States trading blows, Mao made patriotic appeals calculated to calm their fears and neutralize their lingering philo-Americanism. Taking up themes from the previous fall's polemic against the U.S. secretary of state, he warned that patriots should not be deceived by American propaganda. He indicated that the war was necessary to defend the vital interests of China against renewed foreign aggression, and he urged "all patriotic industrialists and merchants" to join with the masses in a united front against this aggression.[99]

But Mao was also prompted by the more general fear (now reawakened) that the Nationalists, perhaps backed by the United States, might launch a counterattack on the mainland. Mao anticipated possible amphibious landings on the coast or an American march across the Yalu River into the northeast as the first step in an attempt at overthrowing the CCP. Accentuating these security concerns was what the CCP perceived as an alarming upsurge of counter-revolutionary activity within China itself during the first months of the war. This development raised afresh the deeply troubling prospect of a link-up between internal opposition and an invasion force.[100]

Encouraged by the American intervention in Korea and especially the Inchon landing, resistance groups appear to have intensified their harassment of the CCP in the summer and fall of 1950. Earlier reinforced by covert missions dispatched from Taiwan, they now won support from landlords, secret societies, and unemployed soldiers sensing that the political wind was shifting. They carried out widely scattered acts of violence, extending even into the northeast, the logistical base for the Korean war effort, and stirred up rumors meant to shake popular confidence and intimidate local party cadres. "You're like a frog in a well with no idea of the big picture and still in a mess. The third world war is coming and the Nationalist army will be right back."[101]

The party center responded by ordering local authorities to step up internal security measures and propaganda in order to blunt this upsurge. Past policy, an October 10 directive contended, had been too lenient in accommodating enemies of the new regime, killing too few, suspending the sentences of too many, and letting cases drag on too long. The first uncertain months of the military contest with the United States seem to have marked the high point of fear over this combined internal-external danger. Finally, on January 24 Mao offered the judgment that there was no longer a risk of an American invasion. But he did think a Nationalist invasion threat remained, so the counter-revolutionary campaign continued with Mao deeply involved in its conduct.[102]

Continued Nationalist resistance, American hostility, and the Korean conflict had all combined to feed Mao's doubts about the bourgeoisie and prompt his efforts to educate the intellectuals. But he was for a time at least constrained by the wide acceptance among his colleagues of his own earlier moderate policy of reconstruction known as new democracy. Although its precise duration was never clear, Mao, Liu Shaoqi, and Ren Bishi in statements in 1948 and 1949 had repeatedly set at anywhere from ten to fifteen years the time needed to rebuild the economy, complete the integration of the bourgeois class, and ready the transition to socialism. Speaking publicly for the Political Bureau in April 1950, Zhou set the current stage at fifteen years and stressed the need for cooperation with the bourgeoisie. As late as mid-1951 Liu was confirming that general time frame.[103]

Suddenly and unilaterally in June 1952 Mao in effect repudiated his own earlier moderate approach and announced a fundamental shift. He elevated to a new place of policy prominence the contradiction between China's working class on the one side and on the other its national bourgeoisie. The intractability of class relations in a hostile international environment had helped prepare the ground for this turnaround. Mao's own disillusionment not only with the bourgeoisie as a class resistant to assimilation but also with intellectuals and even backsliders within his own party added to his discontents and led him to override the more moderate views of at least some, perhaps most, of his colleagues. A year later he would announce an accelerated schedule for moving to socialism, and he would subordinate the contradiction between China and imperialism that had theretofore enjoyed such prominence in order to give more attention to class contradictions within China. In December 1953 the party center announced the completion of the new democratic stage of the revolution; the transition to socialism was now the main order of party business.[104]

An early transition to socialism and the concomitant liquidation of the bourgeoisie and assimilation of the intellectuals had emerged as a major policy preoccupation spurred in considerable measure by the persistence of adversity in CCP foreign relations. The last lingering element of the postwar reform program that Mao had formulated in 1944–1945 had finally fallen by the wayside, pushed aside by an impatient leader now hurrying toward his dream of a unified China (free of the last divisions produced by capitalist penetration) and of a developed China (securely located outside the orbit of international capitalism). This new phase in Mao's journey would bring its own adversities.

Triumph and Miscalculation

Mao had grounded his postwar strategy on a set of badly flawed assumptions. He began by assuming that he could establish a collaborative link with American officials in China or, as an alternative, open direct contacts with Washington. Both proved wrong. He assumed that military self-interest would turn Washington toward the CCP in the final phase of the Pacific War. He missed entirely the shift in U.S. strategy in 1944 toward island-hopping, a strategy that left China out of the main line of advance. He expected war against Japan would last well into 1946, giving him ample time to position himself for the postwar period. He was taken up short not only by the early Japanese surrender but also by Stalin's reticence as his forces occupied and then looted the northeast. In late 1945 Mao turned to Marshall as an honest broker who would compel Chiang to compromise—and grimly clung to the Marshall mediation until finally in November 1946 he abandoned all hope for an era of genuine peace and reform in China under the aegis of the United States and the USSR.

Victory in the civil war proved but the prelude to another round of miscues and reverses. In laying the foundation for the PRC Mao assumed that he had gained some breathing room. But Kim Il Sung's ill-fated initiative thrust the new Chinese regime into its first serious international crisis. When Mao decided to confront the United States in Korea, he not only promptly revealed the limits of the hard-won Soviet defense guarantees but also soon led Chinese forces into a stalemate that Mao had feared and that the PRC could ill afford. A frustrated Chinese leader, impatient with foot-dragging on the part of his own bourgeoisie and angered by stubborn American resistance to his regime, finally overturned a broad policy consensus on new democracy that he had himself constructed. He launched off on a fresh course marked by policy improvisation and growing dissension at the top of the CCP.

What is remarkable about this record is *not* that Mao made mistakes. He was not well versed in the details of international politics. Moreover, the closing phase of the Pacific War and the opening round of the Cold War placed Mao in an unusually unpredictable international environment. In any case, he had scant control over events and possessed little leverage and few bargaining chips to bring to bear on his relations with the great powers. Finally, he was plagued by recurrent bouts of illness that certainly drained his energy and perhaps at times even impaired his judgment, for example during the months just after Japan's surrender and in early 1951 as the Korean War entered stalemate.

What *is* remarkable is that Mao was, despite repeated policy reverses and recurrent doubts about his course within the party hierarchy, still able to maintain his political credibility and balance. That he was to emerge unscathed by his repeated brushes with adversity is powerful testimony to his unshakable self-confidence as well as the growing political prestige and scope for initiative that he had come, for better or worse, to enjoy in party councils.

PART FOUR

Historical Patterns and Interpretive Paradigms

Chapter Seven

Personality, Ideology, and Decisionmaking

The material presented in the chapters above leads to no simple conclusions about an "essential" approach by the Chinese Communist Party to international affairs. Rather the way that the party dealt with the world at least to the early 1950s was the product of a convergence of ideological currents and political circumstances with personality. Because ideology changed little and the people involved hardly at all, there is a case to be made that the patterns produced by this convergence proved vigorous enough to help define the foreign relations of the People's Republic of China, although the full testing of that proposition must await the appearance of fuller evidence than is now available. The goal of this chapter is to highlight those features that became manifest in early CCP foreign policy and to make a preliminary case for persistence.

The argument that the pre-1949 period was prologue has as its premise that the CCP was already a state in embryo. More than just a party with incidental foreign links, the CCP by the late 1940s had, like any state, its own territory (the base areas), its own army, and its own administrative structure. While the Nationalist government in the late 1930s and 1940s constituted the widely recognized state with all the appurtenances con-

---

This chapter and the one that follows build on a paper titled "CCP Foreign Policy: 'Normalizing' the Field," in *Toward a History of Chinese Communist Foreign Relations, 1920s–1960s: Personalities and Interpretive Approaches*, ed. Michael H. Hunt and Niu Jun (Washington: Asia Program, Woodrow Wilson International Center for Scholars, [1995].)

ventionally associated with foreign policy, the CCP was itself making a claim as an alternative focus of legitimate political authority of the sort that existed periodically in imperial times as a weakening dynasty fell back, leaving space for new authorities harboring their own imperial pretensions.

As a state in embryo, the CCP constructed a foreign policy that reveals at least in rudimentary form all the conventional features. It had an identifiable body of policymakers working within clear political structures and steadily accumulating experience. They operated from their own independent ideology. They dispatched their own emissaries and received those of other powers. They had assembled a corps of experts and posted them to key points. The genesis of CCP foreign policy was in short well advanced.

The Dominant Role of Mao Zedong

In arguing for the importance of personality to CCP external relations, we need to look no farther than Mao. He is central to understanding the CCP story, and even after we have done a better job of accounting for the role of his comrades, the influence of foreign-policy institutions and procedures, and the impact of contemporary intellectual and political currents, he is still likely to occupy an important, even dominant place.

During his rise to prominence in the early 1930s, Mao laid down a series of basic policies, each with important implications for foreign relations. In the late 1930s he took over a united-front policy ample enough to include the capitalist powers. He went on to formulate a genuinely reformist new democracy program for China that had as its foreign-policy auxiliary the harnessing of both the Soviet Union and the United States—and he stubbornly held to that course despite international as well as domestic reverses and despite growing discontent among his comrades. He in turn determined the pace at which the CCP discarded hopes for postwar great-power harmony and moved toward a view of the world dominated by two clearly defined power blocs.

By the early 1950s he had become a dominant figure, hard to resist where he threw the full weight of his considerable prestige and authority. He took China into the Korean War, subduing the doubts of colleagues, defining China's objectives in the conflict, and directing the military strategy on a day-to-day, even at times hour-to-hour basis. Finally, in the course of the war he initiated the overthrow of new democracy, a move that carried important implications for building an anti-imperialist, revolutionary China and that proved increasingly disturbing to at least some at the top directly responsible for laying the groundwork for a socialist economy.

Mao had a leadership style all his own, and it too was important to the course of CCP external relations. He was, to begin with, an obsessive worker capable of abrupt shifts in interest. This pattern is evident from Mao's youth. Later, as a policymaker, Mao tended to micro-manage one problem of long-standing concern to him before dropping it in favor of an equally intense engagement in another. During those periods of engagement his was an assertive, hands-on approach that projected assurance and secured deference from his associates. In the wide-ranging and important party work in foreign policy and in the related areas of propaganda and military affairs, Mao took a particularly strong interest. Lacking the time and energy to take charge on all three fronts at the same time, he shuttled back and forth in a hectic attempt to give the fragile party the personal guidance it needed in its passage across a dangerous and rapidly changing political and military landscape.

One can imagine the personal toll this effort took. Mao labored single-mindedly to advance the revolution against formidable odds even as comrades and family members fell one after another to political violence and personal hardship. His autobiography, related to Edgar Snow, is littered with off-handed references to colleagues lost along the way. Within his own family circle, the story was equally pathetic. His first wife and his sister faced Nationalist executioners in 1930; he had abandoned his own children on the eve of the Long March in 1934; his two brothers laid down their lives in 1935 and 1943 while working for the party; and finally American aircraft killed one of his sons in the opening phase of Chinese intervention in the Korean War. For Mao himself the rigors of leadership and the deprivations of life on the run and in remote border areas proved physically debilitating. Despite dogged efforts to keep on top of developments and the attendant flow of communications, he was slowed by illness or exhaustion during and just after the Long March, in late 1945, in early 1948, and again in the first months of 1951.[1]

However single-minded and determined, Mao was not insensitive to the importance of collegial ties. Indeed, his rise to power was attended by the careful cultivation of his associates.[2] Even with those Mao confronted on policy issues and displaced from the top of the CCP hierarchy such as Zhang Wentian, Bo Gu, and Zhou Enlai, he sought to maintain good working relations as long as they demonstrated a readiness to fall in behind the broad policy consensus that he was creating. Only former leaders such as Zhang Guotao and Wang Ming who proved adamant in their dissenting views fell entirely from his grace (and even they survived to tell the tale). This conciliatory approach not only contributed to party harmony but also helped retain the services of talented colleagues needed in diplomacy and other areas of party work.

In winning political support and building policy consensus Mao moved patiently and informally, putting in long hours in private chats that allowed him to convey to colleagues an understanding of the calculations and assumptions behind his policy. The sometimes prolonged process of private consultation also afforded Mao the chance to use his closest associates as sounding boards to test his own evaluation of unfolding national and international developments. Only after a leadership consensus had taken form would Mao seek formal endorsement from the Political Bureau, the Central Committee, or even a party congress. The priority Mao gave to the creation and maintenance of this consensus, at least in his early years as party leader, is evident in a number of important foreign-relations related cases: the redefinition of the united front, the positions endorsed by the Seventh Party Congress, and the shifting line pursued from the end of the Pacific War down to 1949.

Mao's role as a policymaker was also marked by an increasingly one-sided, "imperial" relationship with colleagues at odds with his commitment to consensus. His dominance derived from a commanding personal confidence, and it was reinforced by myth-making within the party. Success added to his preeminence. His was the politico-military strategy of base-building and the policy of national reform and resistance that gave the CCP unprecedented appeal and legitimacy and that carried it to power. Mao himself created distance by cultivating an image as an aloof, reflective figure. He also presented himself as a man of many talents—Chinese literatus, Marxist theoretician, inspired propagandist, military genius, rural sociologist, and so forth. As his stature grew and the deference shown him deepened, he more and more easily won acceptance of questionable policies and sustained them in the face of sometimes substantial doubts, high risks, and unanticipated costs. Though Mao to all appearances gave at least *pro forma* respect to collegial norms down to 1950, he also appears by that date to have established himself in theory as much as in practice as the indispensable and unchallengeable leader. The connection to the domineering, hypersensitive leader that emerged in the late 1950s may not have been direct, but the link to developments in the earlier period is nonetheless clear.

Finally, Mao the policymaker was guided by a complex and unstable set of intellectual interests that made him something of a paradox. The sources of Mao's ideas were in some ways broad. He had cultivated remarkably wide-ranging social and political interests. As a youth he read widely in

Chinese and even dipped into translated foreign literature. So eclectic are the sources of his thought that tracing them is extremely difficult.

Take for example his sources on current events. Mao read avidly from all sorts of newspapers from 1911 to his last years because, as he remarked sometime in the late teens, they were "living history" and hence an important way of gaining all sorts of knowledge about conditions foreign as well as domestic. A mere inventory of those newspapers—Chinese, Russian, treaty-port, party, and so forth—reveals an individual who, as he himself put it in 1941, felt "keenly the necessity for thorough research into Chinese and world affairs," and who lamented the CCP's "fragmentary" and "unsystematic" understanding of its increasingly complex and far-flung political environment. By the early 1940s, when Yanan had relatively easy access to outside press, Mao was subscribing to at least thirty to forty items in Chinese while reading *Reference News* (*Cankao xiaoxi*), an internally produced translation of the foreign wire services. In the 1950s as the number of items grew even larger Mao gave priority to another internally produced newspaper, *Reference Materials* (*Cankao ziliao*), as a source on foreign affairs. He would mark up the material, classify it by topic, or have it circulated and discussed among the leadership. He supposedly found the recollections of bourgeois leaders in the *Reference Materials* especially interesting for the useful insights they offered on the contradictions and struggles going on within imperialist countries.[3]

Yet Mao was also limited. He had, for example, little if any interest in science, while foreign cultures and language as well as economics were largely outside his ken. This uneven intellectual cultivation may have something to do with his belief in self-study—the autodidact's faith that knowledge can be generated through personal effort even in unpromising circumstances. Mao also suffered from his parochial, rural origins. He had had limited contact with the cosmopolitan coastal cities with their extensive economic and cultural ties to the outside world, and had shown as a youth an almost studied avoidance of the overseas experience sought by many of his peers.

The trail of failures and lost chances to see some of that world beyond China wanders back and forth across his life. The most significant lost chance for overseas exposure came in the early years, when travel might have made a considerable impact. He resisted calls that he go to France to study despite his support for the work-study program for Chinese students there. Soon thereafter he failed to follow up on his professed interest in studying in the Soviet Union. Here again Mao supported the idea of young Chinese going abroad to learn—in this case to the homeland of the revolution. He even played a role in organizing a society for the study of Russian affairs and vowed to learn Russian. But he repeatedly balked at undertaking a journey that would carry him beyond his familiar cultural or linguistic boundaries. As he explained in a strikingly defensive letter written in March 1920, he wanted to stay home because reading works in translation was easier than learning the foreign languages needed to tackle them in the original, because he wanted to master China's culture before going on to a comparative examination of Western culture, and finally because China contained a multitude of pressing problems to investigate. Decades later he made the same point: fighting imperialism meant above all grasping "the characteristics and facts of China." The world outside was distinctly secondary.[4]

His cultural and linguistic limits are evident in his approach to English. As a young man just arrived in Changsha, he had given up on study at a school of commerce because classes were taught in English. He made some efforts to learn the language but confessed that he had not gotten beyond the mastery of a toddler. Later in life—first in Yanan and then in Beijing—Mao tried again with no more success. After the Korean War he professed a desire to learn English in order to broaden his knowledge of the world. Characteristically the means he adopted defeated the ultimate purpose of the exercise. His tutor recalls that he chose to learn his English from PRC-produced textbooks, government organs such as *Peking Review*, Marxist classics such as *The Communist Manifesto* that he had already read in Chinese, and even translations of his own writings (such as volume four of his *Selected Works* and his essays "On Contradictions" and "On Practice")![5]

These deficiencies left Mao's outlook on international questions marked (and marred) by a schematic quality. Mao himself repeatedly lamented his limited understanding of the outside world. "All genuine knowledge originates in direct experience," he remarked in a philosophical work of mid-1937.[6] Lacking personal experience in the international realm, he had a shallow reservoir of knowledge to draw on. As long as he could concentrate on what he knew best (China and especially its countryside) and what aroused his passion (China's renovation), Mao proved in his early years at the helm a knowing and effective political leader. But when his revolution impinged on international relations and the concerns of the great powers, as it inevitably did with the increasing success of his political program by the mid and late 1940s, then Mao encountered real difficulties in formulating a perceptive and stable picture of friends no less than foes.

He took Marxist-Leninist theory seriously and paid tuition as a dutiful student of the lessons that the Soviet ideological system had to teach. Yet, as we have seen, he refused to bind his policy to a fixed doctrine. Indeed, he contributed significantly to the recasting of the orthodoxy handed down from the party's founding years. Mao's refusal to be pinned down to rigid formulae reflected at least in part his sense of the CCP's weakness—its vulnerability to enemies at home and abroad and its isolation from significant great-power support and hence the need to cultivate a politics of improvisation. Thus as opportunity allowed, he reached into his sack of stratagems assembled from his reading in such classics as *Romance of the Three Kingdoms* and *Chronicle of the Warring States* or in the writings of the renowned strategist, Sun Zi, showing particular fondness for coalition building and diplomatic manipulation and maneuver all so suited to the hard-pressed position often occupied by the weak. He was also guided by a strong, widely shared faith in the power of personal cultivation and personal relations to make a difference in dealing with foreigners. Even conflictual relations he saw as matters of psychology and education rather than merely contending interests to be resolved by brute force.

But above all the unpredictability of Mao's policy can be traced back to the complexity of his thought and the instability of his views.[7] Mao's thinking about the international arena (much like his views on domestic affairs) was a loose amalgam. He had long-standing and strongly populist views. Perhaps because Mao did not study in Moscow or anywhere else overseas, he knew his country well and at first hand. More than most of his colleagues and rivals he was aware of Chinese society—the opportunities it offered as well as the restraints it placed upon revolutionary activity. Born and bred in the countryside, he had carried out organizing efforts among laborers and peasants, and conducted rural surveys in the mid-1920s and again in the Jiangxi period. The lively, folksy language that he used reflected this side of his personality.[8]

Mao's patriotic instincts were equally old and central. While he never gave a single sign of doubting the importance of internationalism to the CCP (especially the support that might flow from the special relationship with the USSR), his internationalism was always firmly situated within a broader, distinctly China-centered outlook. Other revolutionary movements were without question part of a global process of transformation that was also carrying the CCP forward, but he would sacrifice for those movements only in proportion to their salience to his party's success *and* to China's revival as a nation.

This already complex outlook was deeply tinctured by a marked voluntarism. Ever since the teens he had believed in the role of will power—in the way moral and political education could transform people and constitute in its own right a historical force as powerful as any economic one. To overcome national weakness, Mao had written in 1917, Chinese needed to cultivate the martial virtues—courage, dauntlessness, audacity, and perseverance. "All were not something heaven decreed but humans worked for." Mao then held up Theodore Roosevelt as an instructive example of someone who through force of will had made a weak body strong.[9]

Voluntarism was central to his foreign no less than his domestic strategy. By developing and exercising will power, China (and the CCP) could stand up to its enemies. Conversely, a failure to stand and fight would only embolden enemies (whether warlords or Nationalists, Japanese or Americans) to continue their abusive and overbearing ways. This same voluntarism led Mao to think of China's liberation from the control of foreign imperialists and their domestic allies as an immediately realizable project. And once he had essentially completed that task in 1949, he turned with equal impatience to the task of national revival that had already gripped him in the 1910s as a young man. Once more he refused to think in terms of distant dreams; he demanded quick results and depended above all else on the great energy of the Chinese people, which he trusted to respond to his own leadership, to bring his dreams of remaking China to fruition.

It is tempting in looking back to seek an inner logic to Mao's thinking and behavior, a key that would unlock the secret of his policy. But such a quest is most likely a misguided effort, particularly for an individual as intellectually complex as Mao was. His thinking consisted of multiple strands twisted uneasily together, and his explicitly experimental style gave considerable play to combining ideas in different patterns as he faced changing circumstances. His thinking on politics and foreign policy reached periodic syntheses or reconciliations of contradictory impulses. He would for a time hold the contradictions in suspension. Then the political environment would evolve, prompting Mao to rethink his previous position and form from old notions an entirely unpredictable and fresh stance.

Mao was one of a kind, and without him Chinese foreign as well as domestic policy would, for better or worse, not have been the same. Other, more worldly party leaders might arguably have brought to CCP policy a better grasp of the details of international affairs. But they might also have stumbled where Mao moved with assurance—in inspiring confidence, maintaining unity, maneuvering a vulnerable party away from danger, and amassing all the resources needed to overwhelm even a weakened Nationalist government. Other leaders might in the end have run the revolutionary train off the track, and almost certainly they would have directed the train along lines and at a speed significantly different from the ones Mao took.

The Mao who was increasingly central to CCP policy up to the early 1950s seems no less important in the subsequent period. Policy, foreign as well as domestic, had become tied to the vision of one man and hence hostage to changes in that vision. Any treatment of PRC policy down to Mao's death in 1976 may with good justification start with the presumption that Mao either personally handled important policy decisions or set the parameters in which subordinates such as Zhou Enlai worked. This presumption may prove flawed or incomplete at points. For example, recurrent bouts of illness may have kept Mao on the sidelines at critical moments during the 1950s, and the last years of failing energy and concentration may have weakened his grip and increased his dependence on select associates. We are also right to look for ways colleagues resisted to one degree or another his increasingly frequent and dramatic violations of collegial norms and perhaps on occasion sought to subvert his directives to further their own preferences.

But in general Mao's preeminence should be taken at least as a starting point as scholars move toward a better-documented version of PRC foreign policy. As they look more closely, they may want to consider whether Mao by the early 1950s had started down the same path followed by the centralizing state-builders of the imperial past. Anticipations of Mao's imperial order were already evident before 1949. He had concentrated political power. The wartime rectification campaign and the repeated insistence on subordinate units reporting to and following the lead of the party center all reflected his concern with establishing a single source of authority. He had begun to elevate himself as the single legitimate leader with the prerogative to initiate and alter policy and intervene at will in the policy process. In 1953 he asserted the right to have the last word on party center directives, and the rest of the decade revealed a determination to dictate policy sometimes against the wishes of his "colleagues."[10]

Courtiers who voiced criticisms Mao now no longer tolerated. He instead thrust them unceremoniously aside (the fate of Peng Dehuai and Wang Jiaxiang) or openly upbraided them for their failures (Bo Yibo and Deng Zihui). In this court-like atmosphere some fell silent as prudence checked any impulse to remonstrate or argue with the great man. He had begun promoting his own notion of political orthodoxy, and pressed ahead with restoring the old imperial boundaries. The Qianlong emperor would have recognized and approved these aspects of Mao's rule.

Mao proved, however, a most unusual emperor. His patriotic and state-building impulses warred with a personal attachment to voluntarism and populism, and underlying both was a lingering anarchic strain that spelled danger to the very political order and state that he had built. Returning to a commitment vociferously voiced in 1919, he proved distrustful of the trammels, privileges, and abuses associated with authority and entrenched hierarchies at home. Nor would he suffer silently the pretense and arrogance of the great powers. His impatience at playing a subordinate role to the USSR helped bring an end to the Soviet alliance hardly a decade after its conclusion. The grandees of American capitalism riled him even more. U.S. imperialism was a standing rebuke to his vision of a new international order that dated back to the May Fourth period. Unable to reconcile himself to either superpower, Mao would in the 1960s prove ready, at least in rhetoric, to take on both at once.

Ideological Survival and Transformation

In seeking to define the body of ideas that inspired and guided the CCP approach to external relations, we recall that Mao and his associates had moved through stages, beginning with a youthful preoccupation with restoring the state that in turn gave way to a formal party orthodoxy derived from the Communist International (Comintern). That orthodoxy was itself in turn subject to constant revision, most dramatically from the 1930s. Each of these phases deserves attention.

The century of humiliation has long been a favored point of reference both within China and outside for explaining the CCP's basic stance toward foreign culture and powers. However, an explanation emphasizing China's abasement seems incomplete. Humiliation and subjugation is itself hardly unique in historical annals, and it has been the sorry experience of many peoples and cultures in the three centuries of Western colonization and domination over large sweeps of the rest of the globe. And certainly humiliation does not predetermine behavior; it may result in a range of responses from capitulation and collaboration to random, desultory resistance to persistent, organized efforts at cultural or national revitalization.

The case of China makes more sense if we add to humiliation a strong state tradition—itself a kind of ideology, which for contemporary Chinese accentuated the seriousness of foreign domination and served as an inspiration for action. The founding fathers of the CCP were witness to the prolonged crisis of the late Qing and early Republic. The recurring rounds of foreign encroachment and the near collapse of the Chinese empire haunted them. They had nightmares of national abasement, even extinction, but also dreams of discovering the sources of China's ills and by curing the disease restore the state, rescue the crumbling empire, and lift China's standing in the world.

As patriots, they at first drew from imperial political discourse to express their preoccupation with China's renovation. While nationalism came to carry pejorative connotations for these young Marxists, patriotism remained in favor. It gave expression to an old and deep-seated commitment to the state. It helped the CCP speak across political lines. And it allowed these ostensible internationalists to hold on to their empire.

The formal founding of the CCP thus did not expunge patriotic concerns but rather started the process of creating a party orthodoxy that assimilated those concerns. Patriotism itself served as a kind of bridge as the first generation of Communists, including the survivors who would lead the party to power, came to the conclusion that rebuilding the Chinese state was inextricably tied not just to revolutionizing China but to transforming the international order as well. Just as the old world order had helped bring about China's abasement, so too would the emergence of a new order facilitate the rise of a new China. Li Dazhao articulated a powerful and attractive vision when in the late teens he explicitly linked the revival of the Chinese state and nation to a regional revival that would itself in time merge into a reorganization of the global system as a "great harmony."[11]

But the orthodoxy itself was to prove unstable. For example, the very patriotism that helped prepare the intellectual ground for the orthodoxy was also to subvert it when the orthodox formula did not yield a rejuvenated and transformed China in the 1920s and early 1930s. When global commitments and foreign concepts inherent in that orthodoxy demonstrably impeded the CCP's domestic road, the leadership increasingly gave priority to the party's short-term survival and ultimately the political control on which its dreams of national revival and transformation depended. Internationalist commitments and foreign concepts that ill-served these goals came under critical scrutiny. The resulting transformation of the Comintern-sponsored international-affairs orthodoxy developed momentum as the CCP gained its footing and confidence in the late 1930s and 1940s and then secured state power in 1949. By the time of the establishment of the PRC, revolutionary opportunism and Chinese patriotism had produced an ideological sea change.

Even notions of imperialism, the most durable of the three elements in the orthodoxy, underwent change. Mao Zedong contributed significantly to reworking the 1920s orthodox view, although it should be stressed that some party leaders before Mao, as well as some of Mao's colleagues after 1935, were also drawn to a flexible, nondoctrinaire approach to handling capitalist powers and for some of the same reasons that moved Mao.

Mao himself did not use the term "imperialism" until relatively late (1920), and he appears never to have fully embraced the Comintern's anti-imperialist creed with its stress on the implacable drive and economic nature of the foreign policy of advanced capitalist countries. Imperialist penetration and anti-imperialist struggle *in* China was not some bloodless abstraction but part of the bedrock of Mao's personal experience. He was determined to put his own country at the center of the picture; what the imperialists thought and did was distinctly secondary to their effects on China. Moreover, a mechanistic and deterministic picture of imperialism in action held no appeal.

Like earlier party leaders, Mao found it disagreeable if not repugnant to think of imperialism (in the stripped down, Comintern-export model) as a disembodied global system evolving along economically determined lines, creating through its own painfully inflicted change the basis for a new, better society. The notion that the deep damage imperialism inflicted on China would somehow uplift the country was fundamentally at odds with Mao's own firm conviction that imperialism had harmed China, not helped, disrupting and deforming the economy while generating a class of traitors linked to international capitalism by training and self-interest. How could Mao listen with equanimity to calls from Moscow for patience while the slowly rising capitalist tide lifted a backward China off the rocks of feudalism? A China-centered conception of imperialism with its emphasis on the growing resistance of the Chinese people, the possibility of healing divisions foreigners had created among Chinese, and the dream of restoring China to a place of leadership in international affairs is one that Stalin's Comintern would have recognized as but a distant relation to its own.

In translating its anti-imperialist principles into policy, the CCP under Mao succeeded in challenging Stalin. Anti-imperialist policies that served Soviet interests without also clearly advancing those of China and the CCP were self-defeating. In practice perhaps the most notable feature of the CCP's handling of the imperialists was self-interested opportunism. Mao and his colleagues refused to let formal doctrine, especially one that issued from a foreign capital, constrain their approach to the formidable imperialists standing in their way. Perhaps ultimately imperialists were implacably hostile, and perhaps conflict among them was inevitable. But in practice the CCP in the 1930s took up where the left wing of the Nationalist Party had left off in the 1920s: popular resistance and diplomatic manipulation could force capitalists to moderate their goals and seek some accommodation. The result was a policy of maneuver and suasion—of private appeals as well as public scoldings, of people-to-people diplomacy no less than official contacts—tenaciously pursued despite repeated failures and setbacks.

In the early 1930s, even before Mao took charge, the party's first formal articulation of a foreign policy, laid down in the Jiangxi Soviet, rejected an uncompromising hostility toward imperialism in the interest of advancing the revolution. The shift to a broad united front led in turn in 1936 to a campaign of cultivating American and other foreign progressives, particularly those in China, with the expectation that their favorable accounts of Yanan would have an impact at home. This campaign rested in part on the premise that the United States, awash in the goods and money that threatened its capitalist economy, needed China as much as China and especially the CCP could use American capital, technology, and political support. This was the message conveyed to Edgar Snow and later John Service. It was also the message the CCP sent itself in May 1946 when a Central Committee directive argued for cooperation with a United States economically ascendant in China.

Formal party statements as well as private comments continued down through the founding of the PRC to express interest in the economic contributions capitalists might make to building a new China. While in Moscow, Mao himself indicated to comrades back in Beijing that he still anticipated trading in 1950 with the United States and other capitalist countries. A short time later Liu Shaoqi reported back to Mao his views on the economic arrangements that Mao was then in the midst of negotiating with the Soviets. Liu underlined the broader importance of those arrangements—the deals with the Soviets might serve as a basis for similar deals with organizations and individuals from imperialist countries.[12]

The CCP supplemented talk of suasion and accommodation with carefully considered, coordinated propaganda volleys intended to demonstrate the steel of resolve behind its more pliable diplomatic stance. The verbal shots of June and July 1946, for example, were occasioned by a hard-line trend in U.S. policy and were intended to stir American progressives to action and to prompt American reactionaries to reassess their course in light of the potential costs imposed by CCP hostility. From firing words it was but a small step to threatening to fire bullets, and in extremity actually pulling the trigger. China's response to the Korean War put on display the full set of its tools of persuasion from public protests in the press to private warnings through diplomatic channels and then to surprise attacks on the battlefields.

The underlying policy assumption here—that a weak CCP might influence the course of mighty imperialists—seems on the surface preposterous. But it was sustained by the faith that imperialists, however powerful they might at the moment seem, were in fact daily drawing closer to the economic crisis that would bring the ruling elite down—and with them would go the entire capitalist system. Aware of their vulnerability and beleaguered by opponents at home and abroad, the masters of the imperialist world were surely rational enough to see that accommodation, even retreat, might purchase their own salvation. Bouts of folly prompted by their ever more desperate situation would only intensify conflict with revolutionary forces in China and elsewhere around the world and thus hasten their doom. Isolating those imperialists politically and providing them a way out was thus both a politically promising and cost-effective strategy for a party struggling (sometimes against long odds) to win power.

Complicating Mao's views on imperialism was his consistent assumption that the ruling class was deeply divided over the strategy for its own salvation. The foreign policy of capitalist states was for him a gauge registering the shifting balance in that internal battle. As reactionaries and progressives contended for the upper hand, the winning side would determine not just the country's political color but also (and more to the point for Mao) its policy toward China. But that contest was not grounded in modes of production or governed by iron laws of historical development. The outcome of the struggle was unpredictable and subject to the influence (so at least Mao thought) of CCP initiatives intended to encourage progressive forces or to tie the hands of the reactionaries.

Through the Mao years this flexible, even opportunistic approach to imperialism was inextricably entangled with the handling of the united front and the repeated redefinition of the "people." Mao's reading of the major capitalist powers as well as the Chinese bourgeoisie had broad implications for his general policy. When cooperation with those powers seemed promising, Mao inclined toward an expansive definition of the united front. Conversely tension with the United States and its allies led him to narrow the range of his domestic partners. But the influence could work the other way, with a reading of domestic class relations reshaping Mao's view of international relations. Elements or classes within China that seemed engaged in outright resistance to the CCP's project of national transformation or that even seemed to be dragging their feet could heighten Mao's preoccupation with capitalist political and cultural penetration and thereby dim the prospects for international cooperation or accommodation.

Mao's highly personal, strikingly flexible, and fundamentally unorthodox approach to imperialism and the way that he linked it to domestic policy helped define the foreign relations of the PRC. For example, policy toward the premier imperialist, the United States, proved after 1949 no less than before the product of opportunism. These characteristics emerge more and more prominently in studies on the confrontations in Korea and in the Taiwan Strait, of the shift to a policy of diplomatic normalization in Mao's last years, even in the post-1979 effort to build and benefit from the economic, military, scientific, and cultural relations with its former nemesis.

This policy of twists and turns has played out against a steady fixation with imperialist influence within China. From the Korean War to the Cultural Revolution and into the open-door 1980s, Beijing has launched one campaign after another to expunge the grip that imperialism had managed to fasten on some Chinese minds. Mao himself coined the phrase "peaceful evolution" (*heping yanbian*) in 1959 to describe the ongoing, insidious imperialist strategy to undermine the revolution from within. While John Foster Dulles provoked him to speak out on this occasion, Mao drew on long-standing concern with his revolution's vulnerability to imperialist pressure and residual capitalist attitudes at home. More recently, Deng Xiaoping has stressed that if China were going to open its doors, it needed to fit them with a socialist screen to keep out the pests, above all "bourgeois liberalism" in all its troubling variety. The danger of becoming "corrupted and seduced by capitalism" was, he pointed out, an inescapable part of taking advantage of technological and scientific "cross-fertilization among different peoples."[13] While a long-lived, politically tenacious leadership has resolutely maintained these anxieties, a younger generation is not likely to think quite so emphatically of China as a victim of the international economy and thus may find diminishing appeal in anti-imperialist ideas suited to another age and another China.

A sense of solidarity with the USSR eroded even faster and suffered an even earlier demise. Soviet prestige as leader of revolutionary forces around the world had been buffeted in the 1920s and 1930s. New instances of shifting and self-interested Soviet behavior followed during the anti-Japanese war and the opening phase of the Cold War: the support for the Nationalists as the leading Chinese resistance force; insistence on expending scarce CCP resources to help pull the USSR through the German invasion; the policy reversals in the strategic northeast just after World War II; Stalin's persistent concern with the Czarist privileges and position along the inner-Asian frontier; Moscow's slow, maladroit, and ultimately unsettling response to CCP military victories in the late 1940s; and finally Stalin's reluctance to abandon the Nationalists and accept in their place the CCP as China's new ruling party and as the USSR's new Cold War ally.

The CCP leadership was all too aware of the doubts that Soviet leaders harbored about the immaturity of the Chinese party, and they had learned that Moscow's foreign policy operated on equal parts of caution and opportunism geared to the interests of the Soviet state. Each episode, each twist and turn, each surprise, each slight had ground away at the CCP's residual deference and admiration.

Between 1935 and 1953 Mao and Stalin held the key to a stable and successful Sino-Soviet relationship. Alike in their parochial background, different in their political styles, and unequal in their relative international standing, they moved in distinctly different and largely self-contained worlds. Deepening the gulf between them was the adherence of each to an imperial heritage. Each was a watchful guardian of his own country's claims across a long, common inner-Asian frontier, running from Xinjiang through Mongolia to the northeast.

The dizzying Nationalist collapse in late 1948 and 1949 and the CCP's now undisputed claim to rule China finally led Mao and Stalin to move step by cautious step toward closer contacts and mutual commitments. As we have seen, Mao's visit to Moscow got him his security agreement providing insurance against an American attack and some economic aid, but the visit also revealed a striking lack of rapport with Stalin and served to highlight the cultural and intellectual gulf separating those two "internationalist comrades." Mao later recalled that during the civil war Stalin "took us half seriously, half skeptically. When we won the war, Stalin suspected that ours was a victory of the Tito type, and in 1949 and 1950 the pressure on us was very strong indeed."[14] The Korean War brought more friction. While the Soviet Union publicly backed China and provided military support, on neither front did Stalin fully meet Beijing's expectations.

The old special relationship survived into the early PRC but in much modified form. To be sure, the hard logic of postwar Soviet-American rivalry as well as the reassuring commonalty of ideological outlook still provided ample reason for close links. Moreover, the Soviet Union remained the only available model for the state that the CCP hoped to build, the society the party wished to remake, and the economy it had to develop. Finally, while the old faith in wise, disinterested Soviet leadership may have been tarnished, Mao remained respectful of the leading role of the Soviet Union and especially of Stalin, his senior in years, political experience, and economic achievement. Mao's concerns with his own party's fate had led him to sidestep, ignore, or parry Moscow's suggestions and requests and even to refashion Comintern doctrine. Yet far from showing any signs of defiance or confrontation, Mao continued to pay tribute to the USSR as the stronghold of the socialist ideal and as a powerful force in international relations.

Even so, by the first years of the PRC the relationship had so evolved that no longer could the basic terms be imposed by one side on the other; they would have to be negotiated. Mao had contributed to this outcome by pulling the CCP away from the tight Soviet orbit in which it had moved during its first decade and a half. He had successfully established his standing as an independent, indigenous leader bent on taking his party and country along a Chinese road. The abolition of the Comintern helped Mao alter the dynamics of the relationship by eliminating the formal, organizational expression of the debilitating subordination to Moscow.

After Stalin's death relations remained, at least on the surface, fraternal. The Soviet Union took the final step toward liquidating its position in the northeast and Xinjiang. Soviet aid and advice contributed materially to China's economic and military modernization, while economic, educational, and cultural exchange drew the two countries still closer together. But proximity bred doubts if not contempt, and by the late 1950s the foundations for the special relationship had begun to crack. The various pressures that broke the relationship—from Mao's disaffection with economic development Soviet-style, to his doubts about Moscow's ability to lead the socialist world and about Nikita Khrushchev's pursuit of "peaceful coexistence" with the United States, to the specific ideological, strategic, and territorial irritants—has yet to be precisely delineated. Nor do we yet know the exact stages by which the break developed. Whatever their origins, the anti-Soviet polemics of the early 1960s marked the end of the special relationship by transforming the USSR, once the embodiment of all that was hopeful in the world, into a "social imperialist."

Identification with the weak and oppressed, the third element in the early CCP orthodoxy, held up the best of all. Into the 1930s and 1940s the CCP continued to take the position articulated by Mao himself in 1936: China's liberation would "have a deep influence on the revolutions in the East and throughout the world." A 1939 statement by the party journalist Zhang Hanfu echoed the point, making China's resistance war "a glorious example" and "the harbinger and vanguard" for others also struggling to achieve liberation and independence. Neighbors could draw on China's "experience and lessons." A decision by the Central Committee on July 7, 1940 urged contact with other struggling Asian revolutionary movements—in India, Vietnam, and the Philippines—the better to support and coordinate them. Zhang Ruxin, a well-placed party publicist and educator writing the next year, located the Chinese revolution at "the core of the national revolution struggles of all the oppressed peoples of the East" and placed the CCP in "the forefront of the revolutionary movements of colonial and semi-colonial areas."[15]

As a concrete expression of claims to regional leadership, Yanan hosted a meeting of the Eastern People's Anti-Fascist Congress in October 1941. This gathering of the Asian wing of the international united front attracted more than 130 delegates representing 18 countries (including Japan, India, the future Indonesia, the Philippines, Malaya, Burma, Vietnam, and Korea) together with representatives from Taiwan and from various nationalities within China. Mao appeared before this meeting to call for regional unity in resistance against Japan. The following December he drafted a directive stressing the same theme and pressing specifically for closer contacts with the communist parties of Southeast Asia and for greater effort to coordinate "leftist" tendencies among them that might impede anti-Japanese resistance.[16]

The CCP moved into the postwar period with its regional concerns undiminished. At the Seventh Party Congress in spring 1945 Liu Shaoqi attributed to the "Thought of Mao Zedong" the power to help in "the cause of the emancipation of the peoples of all countries, and of the peoples of the East in particular." Liu forcefully returned to this theme of regional leadership in November 1949 after his trip to Moscow. The road traveled by China under Mao's direction was "the road the peoples of many colonial and semi-colonial areas should traverse in their struggle for national independence and people's democracy." The year before, the Central Committee had already anticipated Liu's position by charging its newly created United Front Department with the task of establishing links with other Asian communist parties as well as overseas Chinese. Throughout Mao himself was more circumspect, limiting himself to occasional and brief calls for the anti-imperialist forces of the East to rally together to oppose enslavement. The major exception had been Mao's August 1946 interview with Anna Louise Strong, in which he had discussed China's special role in the intermediate zone, the scene of the most acute struggle against imperialism. And even there he had delayed release of the interview and left the first major public exposition to Lu Dingyi the following January.[17]

The CCP clung to this role as the leading Asian power down to the founding of the PRC and beyond—with explicit approval, even encouragement from Moscow. In mid-1949 Stalin confirmed the CCP's prominent position within the international communist movement as a leader of the East. When in 1951 Lu Dingyi publicly contended that leaders of revolutionary movements could learn from Mao the importance of applying

Marxist-Leninist theory to the particular conditions that each operated under, he was but stating an accepted international division of labor in which the PRC as a loyal member of the global socialist community tended the revolutionary garden on its own block.[18]

But strains within this Sino-Soviet understanding began to emerge in the 1950s as Mao's conception of his own revolution became increasingly idiosyncratic, thus rendering problematic from Moscow's perspective the wisdom of China's regional influence and its status as a revolutionary model. The Sino-Soviet split and the continuing tensions with the United States raised this community of the weak and oppressed to a new level of importance in the 1960s and 1970s in the eyes of Beijing. The struggling countries of Africa, Latin America, and Asia, along with American clients seeking greater independence (chiefly Western Europe and Canada), constituted an "intermediate zone." By bringing these "oppressed" countries of the second and third worlds together, Beijing hoped to create a powerful new international united front against the two imperialist superpowers.[19]

The PRC claim to solidarity with and leadership in the global community of the oppressed proved more than simple posturing. China provided material assistance and educational opportunities that were, especially in the 1950s and 1960s, large in proportion to the resources at hand. Moreover, in Korea between 1950 and 1953 and in Vietnam from early 1950 internationalist commitments, strongly reinforced by patriotic impulses, carried China even further—to a heavy investment in life and treasure to help resist American pressure along the frontier. Such support was, to be sure, meant to protect China's revolution and security, but it also helped make Asia safe for revolutions like China's own.[20]

At the same time elements of PRC policy toward countries along its periphery has also displayed, perhaps increasingly, a "traditional" look. Beijing has resorted to the time-honored devices of military expeditions, the cultivation of good personal relations with the ruling elite, the offer of refuge to down-and-out allies, the promotion of trade, and the grant of aid. Thus it has sought, with mixed results, to win a modicum of influence in North Korea, Japan, Vietnam, Cambodia, and elsewhere in its "sphere of influence" in Southeast Asia, the Himalayan states, and Outer Mongolia.

As the region's dominant power, the PRC has had strikingly limited success in extending a mantle of protection over overseas Chinese. On taking power the CCP was concerned with cultivating those compatriots. It wanted not only to make them feel a part of the "new China" and turn their patriotism into tangible contributions but also to counter Nationalist and U.S. influence within their communities.[21] But Beijing also realized that

Chinese resident in Southeast Asia were in a politically precarious position that exposed them to attack as unwelcome guests. They were in one sense hostages to the shifts in the politics of the host country. They were also hostages to the ups and downs of that country's relations with a resurgent China.

The very lack of naval power that stood in the way of regaining control of Taiwan also served as a check on PRC policy toward those Chinese abroad. The PRC has been able to do little more than to urge on them a prudent integration into the local culture and, in the wake of major bouts of persecution as in Indonesia and more recently in Vietnam, to bluster and take in some refugees.

Early orthodox claims of identity with and support for the weak and oppressed have proven even less substantial for non-Han peoples within China. Whatever CCP claims, those occupying China's territorial periphery posed for the CCP a special problem. Like the Chinese, they lived under feudal conditions and suffered from imperialist penetration and manipulation, so the party center argued. So they too needed revolution and deserved self-determination. This abstract feeling of sympathy and solidarity, however, collided with the CCP's reluctance to surrender Xinjiang, Mongolia, and Tibet even if each contained weak and oppressed peoples bent on independence. After 1949 no less than before it was hard to imagine allowing a minority population that was only six percent of China's total to decide the future of over half the land area at China's disposal. Arguing against such a course were Han feelings of cultural superiority, the pressing claims of frontier defense, the attractions of underpopulated and resource-rich territories, and the association of national greatness with the integrity of inherited territorial limits.

The best way out of this contradiction between internationalist solidarity and imperial dreams was to claim for Chinese (meaning the Han) a position of superiority over ethnic and national groups along the border. From that position, Chinese leaders had from the 1920s pronounced with assurance that liberation and self-determination would inevitably result in the incorporation of minority peoples into a greater China.

The process by which this incorporation was in fact achieved should be familiar to Americans or for that matter Russians from their own history of continental expansion. A policy of attraction—of drawing "backward" peoples into the cultural and economic folds of the advanced—was in theory the mainstay. But to ensure that China's unity and the process of integration was not disrupted by chauvinistic or other irredentist elements, the PRC employed time-honored techniques. Armed forces were kept at the ready; a political strategy of divide-and-rule was often effectively brought into play; and Han frontier settlement was tolerated and sometimes encouraged. The result of this successful strategy has been to make China the only major territorial empire to survive to the end of the twentieth century.

In the early 1930s hard-pressed party leaders had generally skirted the question of China's territorial claims. Once in Yanan the emergent united-front strategy put a premium on enlisting maximum support in border areas as elsewhere against the Japanese invaders. This meant downplaying traditional territorial interests in order to create close links with sinified minority elites and in some cases drawing them into the CCP.[22]

But out of the public eye party leaders were more candid and assertive. For example, in July 1936 Mao had privately indicated that although Xinjiang, Tibet, and Mongolia (including Outer Mongolia) could enjoy autonomy, they would still be federated with China. Mao's comments at that time both affirmed the long-standing CCP principle of self-determination and Mao's own confidence that after China's revolution Outer Mongolia as well as Tibet and the Muslim peoples "will automatically become a part of the Chinese federation." He made the point formally in October 1938.[23] In 1943 the party finally laid claim to Taiwan as part of China consistent with the formal allied commitment made at the Cairo conference, while also promising a measure of autonomy to the island.[24]

The abstract commitment to solidarity with and self-determination for the peoples in the border areas eroded even further in the late 1940s as the CCP took the first tentative steps toward a policy of military control and political assimilation. In January 1949 the CCP simply eliminated Manchus from the list of nationalities, pronouncing them Han with special requirements. While stressing the equality of the remaining nationalities, the CCP also emphasized that unity in the face of the Nationalists and the American and British imperialists, the common enemies of all the peoples of China, was also essential. The CCP would oppose any outlook or activity harmful to that unity. Once more privately Mao did not mince words, for example telling Anastas Mikoyan in early 1949 that the CCP intended to retake Tibet and Taiwan and gather in all nationalities in a single China. In setting up the new government Zhou Enlai stressed that its minority policy would break with the oppressive policies of previous Chinese governments, but at the same time he made clear that the minority peoples would have autonomy, not the right of self-determination, and that they would have to cling to China to ward off continuing imperialist intrigues.[25]

The process of asserting control over minority nationalities accelerated under the PRC. On both the immediate and the more remote periphery Beijing fell back on the repertoire perfected during imperial times, above all colonization and the exercise of military power.

In 1950 the PRC sent in troops to resecure Tibet, bringing to an end four decades of virtual independence for that region. Mao marked the success in May 1951 by celebrating the "fraternal unity" between Han and Tibetan after (what he described as) several hundred years of harm inflicted by the Qing, the Nationalists, and the imperialists. While he warned against "Han chauvinism," Chinese-imposed reforms nonetheless triggered resistance in eastern Tibet. The spread of resistance westward and an outburst of armed opposition in Lhasa finally led to forceful Chinese military countermeasures in 1959.[26]

Elsewhere—especially in Inner Mongolia and Xinjiang—the party also denied self-determination and instead vindicated long-standing imperial claims (even while Mao issued more warnings against Han chauvinism). In northern Xinjiang the Chinese influx had by the mid-1960s outnumbered the Kazakhs by 2.6 million to .5 million. To keep Kazakhs from combining forces with Uighurs to the south, Beijing ruled them apart from each other. The Chinese army played a prominent role in this colonization process, combining garrison duty with agricultural production and conservation, construction of factories, and development of the region's rich mineral resources. Colonization was also the preferred line of policy in Inner Mongolia. During the Great Leap Forward in the late 1950s, and again during the Cultural Revolution in the late 1960s, colonization efforts were generally intensified and an accommodating cultural policy toward the national minorities in Mongolia and elsewhere gave way to enforced sinicization. Repression in Tibet and Xinjiang, which continues today, reflects the high priority still accorded defense of the empire handed down from the high Qing.[27]

The identification with the weak and oppressed, perhaps least significant of the old international-affairs orthodoxy, proved in the final analysis problematic at two levels. First, while in rhetoric solidarity had always been important, that solidarity had always been given a hierarchical twist by patriotic impulses and attendant pretensions to regional power status. Second, expressions of solidarity have proven even more empty when measured against performance in China's border areas. The tempting conclusion to draw is that China, while proclaiming its solidarity with the weak and oppressed, has demonstrated in practice that it is more accurately a multinational empire hostile to self-determination within its own borders and determined to project its influence into adjoining countries regardless of the preferences of its neighbors.

Decisionmaking

The leadership of the CCP made its decisions within a nexus of policy-making procedures and institutions. They are critical to understand for the ways they may have either facilitated or restrained policymakers. Four notable impressions about CCP decisionmaking down to 1951 emerge from the treatment in earlier chapters. Each is worth keeping in mind for the subsequent years.

First, the CCP was governed by a bias at the top toward consultation and consensus which Mao reinforced but did not create. The party had in 1920–1921 grown out of discussion groups scattered across China. The premium placed from the outset on wide-ranging study and debate stayed with the CCP even as the Comintern pushed it toward a more centralized, disciplined structure. The crimp sometimes put on discussion and consultation during the party's first years resulted in policy inadequately understood, resented, or resisted. The 1927 coup compounded the problems. Scattered and driven underground, the party leadership fell victim to disruptive controversy and bitter rivalries. Despite this debilitating disarray, the preference for consultation and consensus still prevailed right down to one of the party's low points, the Zunyi Conference.[28] In the decade and half that followed Mao would make good use of this preference as he sought to combine centralized, disciplined decisionmaking with wide-ranging discussion and consensus building.

The consensual impulse is evident in the time and effort devoted to ensure a full airing of views over, for example, the application of the united front between 1935 and 1938, the formation of the new democracy strategy (in the making for two years before its formal implementation at the Seventh Party Congress), and the general policy line pursued from the end of the Pacific War down to 1949. We see here a complex kind of elite politics which consisted in part of informal exchanges among leading figures in advance of major meetings combined with chipping away at established policy during formal gatherings of the Political Bureau, the Secretariat, or other relatively small gatherings of twenty or fewer leaders. The result was policies that the party center created, revised, and abandoned in an incremental fashion. Mao might strain against the restraints imposed by collective leadership that he had himself assembled, but he felt for a time at least compelled to respect them.

The decision to intervene in Korea demonstrates that consensus building was still important as late as 1950. There were good reasons then for keeping discussions short. The Korean crisis fell squarely within Mao's acknowledged area of authority, military and foreign affairs, and he had himself decided on October 1–2 in favor of sending troops. Moreover, the rapid advance of American forces toward the Sino-Korean border left no time to waste. Finally, Mao brought to the crisis a political authority lifted to unprecedented heights by his success at leading the CCP to an early and decisive seizure of state power.

He nonetheless suffered through three time-consuming rounds of discussions with his colleagues. During the first (October 2–8) he secured a general endorsement of intervention but only after dealing with a range of doubts and reservations within the Political Bureau. Stalin's decision on October 10 to withhold air support agitated Beijing and forced Mao to resume the consultative process. This series of talks ended on October 13–14, with the leadership agreed on a cautiously conducted intervention. Then finally on October 17, on the eve of crossing the Yalu, military commanders in the northeast called for delay into the winter or even the spring, precipitating yet a third round of meetings in Beijing. Only after dealing with this latest bout of hesitations did Mao finally get Chinese troops moving into battle.[29]

Second, the time and care invested in creating a policy consensus, along with the difficulty in assembling the leadership in the pre-1949 period, created a marked bias in favor of inertia. Policies put together in a cautious, incremental fashion were not suddenly or easily set aside. Rather change came through a gradual erosion of established policy and the no less gradual construction of a substitute. Weaknesses in the old policy would eventually reach a critical point, finally forcing the leadership to bring forward formally the new policy already waiting in the wings.

The decline and fall of new democracy offers a good example of the durability of a consensually based policy. Having carefully constructed that policy, Mao and his colleagues clung to it despite the repeated blows to the assumptions on which it was based and despite the criticisms directed at it from within the party. The early end of the war in the Pacific wrecked plans for military cooperation with the United States, a central element in the party's new democracy strategy to gain a postwar position of strength. The collapse soon thereafter of U.S.-Soviet cooperation ruined hopes for external pressures thought critical to moving the Nationalist regime to accept a reform agenda and a coalition government. Finally, in November 1946 Mao, Zhou Enlai, and Liu Shaoqi met and abandoned the coalition-government goal pursued through Marshall's mediation. Growing irritation over philo-Americanism among middle-of-the-roaders shot a hole in new democracy's domestic united front, and the explosion of counter-revolutionary resistance following the outbreak of the Korean conflict made that hole bigger. The lack of clear aid commitments from the Soviet Union and the American-led embargo left economic policy under new democracy for a time in limbo. By the first years of the PRC a much battered new democracy had a lifespan, once regularly set by the leadership at ten to fifteen years, of doubtful duration. Finally, in June 1952 Mao made the definitive policy shift, casting aside the last shreds of new democracy in favor of an early transition to socialism.

Third, the institutional arrangements supporting CCP decisionmaking were loose and shifting, befitting a system that was highly personalistic and centralized. The impetus for organizing a distinct foreign-policy apparatus came from the Comintern in July 1928 at the CCP's Sixth Congress. A resolution adopted there called for building links with communist parties in the major imperialist countries as well as with Asian revolutionary movements. It was not until the establishment of the Soviet Republic in 1931 that an individual (Wang Jiaxiang) was singled out as responsible for foreign affairs. In January 1934 Wang took charge of the first formal foreign ministry, although the isolation of the Jiangxi Soviet in fact left what must have been a rudimentary ministry with little to do but administer regulations dealing with local foreigners.[30]

Once settled in Yanan, policymakers were supported by a variety of units and a changing cast of characters. These included the party foreign-affairs department created in January 1936 with Bo Gu in charge as well as a liaison office, which was established in March 1938 as part of the Shaan-Gan-Ning border region government to handle visitors, foreigners as well as non-party Chinese. The foreign-policy institutions would come to include as well the United Front Department, assigned responsibility for handling liaison with Asian communist parties as well as overseas Chinese when it was created in September 1948.[31] Patriotic students rallying to Yanan in the late 1930s provided a pool of talent from which this nascent foreign-policy bureaucracy could draw.[32]

Outside of Yanan the regional bureaus figured prominently as executors of policy as well as sources of information. Particularly important was the Southern Bureau, which handled international contacts in the wartime Nationalist capital, Chongqing. (Zhou Enlai's assistants there, such as Zhang Hanfu, Wang Bingnan, and Chen Jiakang, would figure prominently in the PRC foreign-policy establishment.) The Northeast Bureau— headed first by Peng Zhen, then Lin Biao, and finally Gao Gang—became equally important at the end of the war. It carried the burden of dealing with and reporting on Soviet occupation forces in the region and later led the way in handling the Soviet program of economic assistance. Before the dissolution of the Comintern, the party's representative in Moscow also had a role in policymaking. Reporters for the New China News Agency played their own quasi-diplomatic role, especially in Hong Kong and Chongqing, where they maintained a wide range of contacts and directed a steady flow of information on international developments back to Yanan.[33] Some of these "reporters," such as Qiao Guanhua, were later recruited into the foreign service. Even the military got into the game, for example by setting up an office in Lanzhou, which handled important contacts with the USSR in its heyday between 1937 and 1939.[34]

In collecting information the party center showed no more penchant for rigid procedures or fixed bureaucratic structures. It relied on all the players in the policy network as well as its own translation service (focused on international news), the Soviet liaisons attached to Mao, party leaders traveling to Moscow, and Mao's own radio conduit to Stalin. The implementation of policy similarly depended on a loose, informally linked bureaucracy. Once a decision had been reached, it might be handled by a special, ad hoc work team of three or four leaders, by the Military Affairs Committee, by the party team in Chongqing led by Zhou Enlai, or by designated diplomatic agents such as the senior Liu Shaoqi (who made the summer 1949 breakthrough trip to Moscow) or even the junior Huang Hua (who served as intermediary between Beijing and the last American envoy).

Fourth, in a pattern that would persist into the PRC, domestic concerns mingled inextricably with international pressures to produce CCP foreign policy. Decisions on foreign and domestic issues did not occupy different lobes in the collective mind of the CCP. It could not be otherwise. The party sprang from a domestically defined ideological agenda—a preoccupation with China's political and social transformation and its economic development, and these basic, long-range concerns fundamentally shaped the CCP's approach to external relations. The founding fathers of the CCP and their juniors, who would dominate the party for its first fifty-five years and in many ways down to the present, were heirs to and participants in a discourse about China's renewal going back to the nineteenth century. Like other earlier Chinese policymakers, indeed like policymakers everywhere, the leaders of the CCP were preoccupied above all by pictures of what they wanted their country to become and by the methods they thought appropriate for realizing their goals.

Party leaders from Li Dazhao onward have translated those general concerns into a set of specific issues that help us to locate them in the same intellectual generation. They were preoccupied with the stages through which China was to move as it progressed toward socialism, the duration and nature of China's capitalist interval during which the forces of production developed, and the means by which the transition to socialism was to be effected. Young Chinese in France and in Marxist study groups in China debated those questions in the teens and early 1920s. Those questions echoed in the private discussions and formal meetings of party leaders through three decades of struggle for power.

Throughout the debate on this complex of questions relating to when and how socialism would come to China, party leaders were forced to relate international conditions to party goals and to sort through the different kinds of foreign policies that might serve those goals. They wrestled with how a weak state achieves development, manages stronger states diplomatically, and controls the cultural and economic pressures those states exert on development. How much did the world impinge on China, and how much could China do to change the world? These questions discussed by the New Peoples' Study Society in 1920–1921 echoed in the making of CCP policy. Was the reform of China a step toward global or third world or Asian transformation? Did the global conditions have to be right for China's revolution to advance or survive? How tightly did China need to coordinate with international forces? How much did China need to be guided by some revolutionary center as part of a global struggle?

Mao and other party leaders saw their revolutionary enterprise buffeted by international forces and decisions just as they saw their China deeply penetrated by foreign economic pressures and ideas. This perception conditioned their understanding of and reaction to virtually every international development. Similarly, in the practical "domestic" matter of the party's short-term survival and its long-term chances for coming to power, they looked abroad as well as at home. They put a premium on manipulating foreign powers, exploiting class divisions in other countries, and winning the support of like-minded leaders and groups abroad.

This complex interrelationship between foreign and domestic developments is strikingly evident in 1948 and 1949 as the CCP's concerns with U.S. hostility, possibly even an American invasion, played off against a mounting preoccupation with the indigestibility of China's bourgeois intellectuals and the residual grip of imperialism on middle-of-the-road political leaders. The outbreak of the Korean War injected new tensions into class relations, and stirred fears in Beijing that the Korean conflict might well spill over into China and unite dissident groups with an American-Nationalist invasion force. Out of those fears developed the repression of counter-revolutionaries in a campaign that began in fall 1950 and carried over into 1951.

While it should come as no surprise that a self-consciously weak and vulnerable political movement would strive to integrate foreign policy with domestic goals, even a victorious CCP with its hold on China secured continued to link foreign and domestic policy. Mao and other party leaders still saw their revolution buffeted by global rivalries and caught in a web of international political and military pressures. Devising an economic program that would lay the foundations for ultimate transition to socialism also created for the PRC a close, complex interplay between foreign and domestic issues that is still not clearly understood. While the Soviet Union was the natural partner and guide for China's development, Moscow hesitated for a time to make clear what kind of resources China could have. However, by the mid-1950s the PRC had seemingly settled into an economic strategy guided by the Soviet model and limited to assistance from the socialist bloc.

Foreign policy and domestic development thus remained entangled—and the proper relationship between the two a matter of some dispute—even as Mao assumed a more imperial role. Mao himself turned on a Soviet model antithetical to his vision of China's revolutionary road and stirred up crises with the United States, the Soviet Union, and India disruptive of smooth and rapid economic construction. Mao's course in turn alarmed colleagues such as Wang Jiaxiang who gave priority to a foreign policy that would allow China to focus on economic growth. In the first half of 1962 Wang launched a sharp critique of foreign-policy adventurism that would finally two decades later win powerful converts. He in effect charged Mao with feeding international turmoil and tension with the result that by the end of the 1950s Mao had succeeded in alienating the economic leaders of the two major international blocs and in leaving China without a developmental patron or access to the resources of either major economic system.[35]

Hallmarks of CCP Foreign Policy

What emerges out of the three major sets of generalizations developed above is a CCP behaving in terms that we are familiar with from the foreign-policy literature of other countries. CCP policy has slipped free of interpretive straitjackets imposed by those convinced of the primacy of Marxist-Leninist ideology, the international system, or some primordial "middle kingdom" mentality. Instead we find policymakers, strong personalities, working within perceived political constraints that are domestic as well as international in nature. Or put more precisely, we find policymakers interpreting the political environment for themselves and for their followers within the framework of ideology in both its formal and informal manifestations.

Mao Zedong did much to shape the process of decisionmaking as well as its outcome in his first decade as undisputed leader. But Mao operated within a complex environment, aspects of which he warmly embraced or simply took for granted. That a revolutionary elite had the right, even obligation to guide China out of its crisis and re-create the strong state familiar from imperial times was a given. That a sustained effort at remaking China would need a supreme leader, both practical guide and potent symbol, was also a given. That the leader would need the good guidance and loyal service of a wide circle of subordinates was equally self-evident. That some shared, explicitly formulated system of belief was required to direct their political effort and mobilize their followers was also self-evident. Finally, that a revived China would be able to expunge all traces of foreign domination and erase the shame of its fall from imperial glory was a basic article of faith.

Other aspects of that environment Mao either bridled against or even sought to alter. That China's revolutionary course could be defined from abroad, whether directly from Moscow or indirectly by Soviet surrogates within the CCP, was an aspect of early party life to which Mao came to take strong exception. In time he turned his heretical doubts on this point into an orthodoxy of its own. That rigid deterministic systems, whether derived from theories of imperialism, notions of class relations, or laws of historical progress, should constrain the imagination of leaders and the energy of a people was antithetical to his most fundamental instincts. That China's renovation would require prolonged labor and careful planning, accommodation with China's wealthy and talented, and even intimate dealings with the capitalist economies was a proposition that Mao would in time reject.

Because personalities differ, because politics is a highly contingent affair, and because ideologies are not uniform, policy is never neat and predictable. Shifts in outlook, contention over goals, and misapprehension of the situation quite predictably produce a messy and disjointed policy process. These features apply as much to the CCP as other policymaking bodies and invite wide-ranging comparison, not just with other Marxist parties but also with other makers of international policy. These features also argue for giving more attention to continuity in Chinese foreign relations than we have entertained to date by setting the CCP alongside predecessor regimes. Finally and perhaps most important of all, these features make CCP foreign policy more comprehensible *and* interesting.

Chapter Eight

Constructing a History of CCP Foreign Relations

The study of the foreign relations of the Chinese Communist Party is undergoing dramatic changes that are taking it in a distinctly more historical direction. This development has essentially been driven by the appearance of an abundance of new material, the basis for the previous chapters and the subject of the guide to the literature that follows. This material is largely the product of the party's own history establishment and its mandate to transcend a simple and largely discredited party mythology in favor of a better documented and hence more credible past. The publication of documents, memoirs, chronologies, and standard historical accounts has at last made it possible for specialists outside of China to move beyond broad, heavily speculative treatments based on fragmentary evidence and to construct a party foreign-policy history marked by engaging human detail and structural complexity.

This volume is itself a good gauge of that already well-advanced if uneven reorientation. As is evident in the chapters here, the historical ground becomes more treacherous to traverse the closer we get to the present. The prehistory of the CCP (located in the opening chapters of this study in the late Qing and the early Republic) is firmly in place. From the point of the CCP's formal founding in 1921 down to its consolidation of state power in 1949–1950 (the subject of the middle chapters here) the evidence offers uneven footing that requires some caution. The most recent phase—the foreign relations of the party-state—is just beginning to pass into the historical realm (as the tentativeness of the previous chapter suggests). It will prove the most interpretively volatile as historical patterns begin to emerge for the first time from the accumulation of reliable evidence.

This trend toward a more historical treatment of the CCP's external relations has occurred at an uneven pace and taken different forms in a field effectively fragmented into two distinct parts. The work done in China is already decidedly historical though still politically constrained. Outside of China (largely but by no means exclusively in the United States) scholarship bears the imprint of the political science discipline and the closely related international-relations field, which has long dominated CCP foreign-policy studies. Historical questions and historical methods are thus at least outside of China only beginning to move from the margins to a more central position.

The purpose of this final chapter is to offer a guide to this emergent historical approach. The chapter begins with an extended look at the field's two chief geographic divisions, China and the United States. It closes with some thoughts on ways to encourage the already promising prospects for a solidly grounded and conceptually sophisticated history of party foreign relations.

Scholarship in China

Scholars in the People's Republic of China, now in many ways at the leading edge of CCP foreign-policy history, have only recently come into their own.[1] They long labored under the gaze of party representatives whose main task was to ensure that history served the party's political agenda and contributed to nationalist myths and popular morale during the international crises that marked Mao Zedong's years of power. Under these difficult conditions specialists on Chinese foreign relations did their best work by putting together politically inoffensive collections of historical materials, many of notable quality and lasting value. But in their own writing they had to serve up a thin historical gruel heavily spiced but hardly made more palatable by quotes from Chairman Mao and other sources of the official orthodoxy. This revolutionary historiography, following tenets laid down by Mao, stressed the wave of imperialism that had overpowered China. Commercial and later industrial capitalism, its diplomatic agents, and those Chinese drawn into the unsavory role of collaborator had left the Chinese people impoverished, economically subordinate, and politically in thrall. The predatory character of imperialism locked China in fundamental conflict with the powers until a popular revolution transformed China and altered China's relationship to the capitalist world.

Since the late 1970s established scholars have worked free of many of the old interpretive constraints, and joined by a younger, adventuresome generation have begun to exploit their inherent advantages in studying China's complex behavior in an often threatening and generally intrusive world. They have had immediate access to publications (some of limited circulation), and enjoyed the first glimpses into the archives. They have profited from their personal contacts with former policymakers, and brought to new sources an unmatched sensitivity to the political culture in which China's policy was made. They have enjoyed the stimulus of a large and interested audience for their writing and easy opportunity to discuss with colleagues work in progress and news of the field. As a result of these developments, the center for the study of foreign relations and the CCP has shifted back to China. A glance at the number of specialists and special research offices, the frequency of conferences, and the long list of publications would confirm this impression.

But Chinese specialists still face some notable difficulties. One of these is a patriotism that the CCP did not create but did powerfully reinforce in scholarship as in other realms of Chinese life. The mantra is familiar: China was divided and oppressed; China pulled itself together under CCP leadership; China stood up. This satisfying if somewhat simple story to which specialists on party history and foreign relations still give at least lip service constrains their examination of foreign relations, not least with the capitalist powers and inner-Asian peoples. These sensitive topics must be addressed correctly and carefully or not at all.

While the fate of non-Han people under China's imperial ambitions are simply written out of the category of foreign relations (to be treated instead as an "internal" matter), dealings with foreign powers are featured in terms of the comfortable and safe tale of struggle and triumph. For example, PRC scholars enjoying unparalleled access to source materials on the Korean conflict waged against a U.S.-led coalition have been in a position to offer the fullest account of its conduct, warts and all. Their accounts are indeed fuller but the warts are hard to spot, thus keeping alive the old heroic narrative. Patriotism, reinforced by party orthodoxy, has inspired repeated claims that the Korean intervention was a "brilliant decision" (*yingming juece*) unblemished by confusion, division, or opportunism. That very phrase appears in the title of one of the earliest of the documented accounts to appear in the PRC, and the theme persists in virtually all of the secondary studies of the Korean War published over the last decade.[2]

A second impulse, as constraining as patriotism and no less intrusive, has been the pressure to fit research findings within a linear, progressive conception of the CCP's development. Highly self-conscious of the importance of its own past to legitimizing the current leadership and maintaining party prestige, the CCP has consistently sought to explain its evolution in terms of the forces of history and the wisdom of its leaders. The result is a picture of a party that adjusted to changing social and international conditions and that consistently and correctly reassessed its own performance, distinguishing correct from mistaken policy lines. The party, at least in theory, thus developed according to a logic which left scant room for recurrent miscalculation or fundamental misdirection.

This notion of history in which all events are mere tributaries feeding the main stream itself flowing toward some predestined point is extraordinarily constraining as a look at PRC writings relating May Fourth to the CCP reveals. Chinese scholars interested in the origins of the party have tried to force a rich set of contemporary views into an orthodox framework wherein the raison d'etre of May Fourth is to serve as intellectual midwife to the CCP's birth. Their studies make the Bolshevik revolution the central and transformative event in the intellectual life of future party leaders; they underestimate that era's ideological exploration and fluidity; they minimize attachment to such heterodox beliefs as anarchism; and they downplay the influence of earlier personal concerns and indigenous political ideas.[3]

The third obstacle standing in the way of party historians is the sensitivity with which the party center continues to regard past relations with "fraternal" parties. This reticence is perhaps understandable in the case of North Korea and Vietnam. A candid look at the past can complicate dealings with parties still in power. But the reticence applies even to the now defunct Soviet party. By thus consigning interparty relations to historical limbo, the CCP has effectively set out of bounds large and important slices of its own foreign-relations record and experience.

How the CCP privately assessed the USSR as a supporter and model— surely the single most important issue for understanding the CCP's position within the socialist camp—will remain a matter of speculation if not controversy as long as the historical sources needed to arbitrate it are kept locked in Chinese archives and excluded even from restricted-circulation materials. The opening of Soviet archives may provide the first revealing, detailed picture of broad aspects of the relationship, and may perhaps even help overcome some of the squeamishness party leaders apparently feel about a candid look at this important part of their own past. Or it may take the passing of the last of party elders whose memories of dealing with the Soviets go back to the 1920s. However they get there, scholars badly need freer rein to research and publish on this long-sensitive topic vital to understanding the CCP after 1949 no less than before that date.

The last and easily the most practical problem handed down from earlier CCP historical work is the matter of the layers of tendentious documentation and personal reminiscences that have come to surround Mao Zedong. Those layers have unfortunately not only served to obscure him as a personality and policymaker but also covered over the contributions of his colleagues. Repeatedly over the last half century party officials have remade Mao, re-creating his persona to suit the politics of the times. These multiple layers baffle and distract foreign scholars no less than Chinese.

The process began in the late 1930s when the task was to reinforce Mao's claims to leadership of the party. Mao himself made a signal contribution by relating his autobiography to Edgar Snow in mid-1936. Putting aside the reticence usually so marked a feature of Chinese autobiography, Mao offered a self-portrait that highlighted his own moment of Marxist illumination and his strong revolutionary commitment. The resulting account bears an uncanny resemblance to the genre of spiritual autobiography penned by Buddhist and Confucian writers intent on making their own journeys of spiritual self-transformation and spiritual discovery available for the edification of others.[4]

But Mao's account also arose from the more practical political concern with launching a publicity campaign that would win support for the party among Chinese and foreigners and bring in much-needed contributions from the outside. Inviting Snow, a reliably progressive American, to Bao'an was part of that strategy. Mao set aside roughly two hours a night over ten evenings to tell his story. While Wu Liping translated, Snow took notes. Huang Hua then translated those notes back into Chinese for Mao to review. Snow then returned to Beiping to prepare the final account, to appear in 1938 in *Red Star over China*. The first Chinese version of Mao's story appeared the year before. That Chinese edition and others would circulate within Nationalist as well as CCP controlled areas.[5]

The second layer, associated with the "new democracy," Mao began to form in the wake of Wang Ming's defeat and in the context of the rectification movement of 1942–1943.[6] Party theoreticians had in 1941 begun to promote the importance of "Mao thought" to party orthodoxy, and a Political Bureau meeting in September and October of that year produced statements of support from Wang Jiaxiang, Zhang Wentian, Chen Yun, and Ye Jianying. (Neither Zhou Enlai nor Lin Biao were present.) For the next two years the visibility of "Mao thought" continued to rise. Zhang Ruxin, Zhu De, Chen Yun, Liu Shaoqi, and Zhou Enlai offered praise, and

Mao's writings figured prominently in the study material used in the rectification campaign. The Seventh Party Congress brought the apotheosis. A Liu Shaoqi report and a resolution passed at the congress established a Maoist historiography and proclaimed the guiding role of "Mao thought."

As early as mid-1944 the first genuine collection of Mao's writings had appeared to help consolidate his claim to ideological dominance within the CCP. This early five-volume *Mao Zedong xuanji* [Selected Works of Mao Zedong] was edited under Wang Jiaxiang's supervision and published in the Jin-Cha-Ji base area by the New China News Agency. New editions of his selected works (perhaps as many as eight, some with restricted circulation) continued to appear in the base areas down to 1948. That same year Xiao San published his account of the young Mao. Xiao had conceived the project nearly a decade earlier and proceeded with Mao's approval and the support of the party leadership.[7]

The third layer of Mao publications began to appear soon after the conquest of power in 1949. Stalin is supposed to have suggested to Mao during their Moscow summit the formal designation of an official body of Mao's writings. The Political Bureau gave its approval in spring 1950, and a compilation committee was formed at once. The resulting four volumes of this new *xuanji*, published between 1952 and 1960, burnished the image of the statesman traveling the Chinese road to socialism. This new collection, carefully revised by Mao with the help of his staff, was flanked by yet another treatment of the young revolutionary, this one by Li Rui.[8]

The next layer in the official Mao was laid down during the Cultural Revolution. Alarmed by what he saw as ideological backsliding in the USSR and the persistent bourgeois grip on China's intellectual and cultural life, Mao put forward his own ideas as the antidote. His acolytes took up the struggle, beginning with compilation of the "Little Red Book" on the eve of the Cultural Revolution. That slim but ever-present volume was but the herald to twenty-plus collections intended to define the most imposing Mao ever—"the greatest genius in the world," unsurpassed "in several hundred years in the world and in several thousand years in China." One enthusiast declared, "Chairman Mao stands much higher than Marx, Engels, Lenin, or Stalin." His thought "serves as the lighthouse for mankind," its "universal truth applicable everywhere."[9]

The latest layer took form soon after Mao's death and was shaped by the political struggle to claim his legacy and appraise his achievements. Hua Guofeng sought to strengthen his claim to leadership through the editing of volume five of the official *xuanji*, published in 1977. The other, ultimately victorious side in the succession struggle dismissed the special pleading of that volume and went off in search of its own Mao. The new image, intended to serve the political program of Deng Xiaoping and his allies, was defined after two years and considerable Political Bureau discussion. The resulting 1981 resolution, prepared by a small drafting group headed by Hu Qiaomu and supervised by Deng himself along with Hu Yaobang, made Mao bear the burden of mistakes committed in his last years, forced him to share credit for the successes with his colleagues, but let him retain full credit for his earlier revolutionary leadership. Finally, in 1986 a two-volume reader appeared defining the essence of this latest, emphatically scientific version of "Mao thought."[10]

In the new atmosphere of greater openness the party history establishment has made available a wide range of works that constitute the point of departure for anyone interested in Mao's outlook and political role. But cutting through the successive layers of Mao documentation and sorting through the mountain of writing that he left behind is a task that Chinese scholars have sidestepped. Without comment, they have let new scholarly collections pile up on top of the older ones compiled with a marked political agenda, leaving specialists outside China such as Takeuchi Minoru, Stuart R. Schram, Michael Y. M. Kau, and John K. Leung struggling to produce a full and accurate collection essential to recovering the historical figure beneath all the political mythmaking.

A variety of other difficulties stand in the way of the development of party history in its homeland. The publications process lacks quality controls, in part because there are so many party history journals with pages to fill and so many party elders with reputations to burnish, causes to advance, and scores to even. Access to archives for the entire history of the Communist Party and for the era of the PRC is tightly restricted. Some favored Chinese specialists get in; foreigners are uniformly excluded. Even the best libraries are weak on international studies generally and on the foreign relations of particular countries whose histories impinged on that of China. Opportunities are limited for research in libraries and archives outside China and for exposure to conceptual approaches prevailing abroad.

As a result, party historians in China operate in an atmosphere of caution and insularity. There is little if any interest in methodological or theoretical issues so prominent outside of China. Scholarly debates do not publicly at least go beyond brief exchanges in party history journals over such factual questions as the date of a particular document or the contents of a particular conversation. Engrossed in a clearly defined body of party history materials, researchers pay scant attention to either Chinese society or the international environment in which the CCP operated. The failure to read, not to mention engage, foreign scholarship has helped preserve the narrowness, discourage international dialogue, and close off CCP history from comparative insights.

Behind at least some of these difficulties is something that is likely to be in short supply for the foreseeable future—material resources for research and the assurance that researchers have political support or at least tolerance from a ruling party concerned to keep its historical reputation free of blemish. An attempt to circumvent these two problems by sending Chinese abroad for graduate study in history and international relations has proven somewhat disappointing. It is my impression that those studying overseas in one or another of the broad foreign-relations fields have not found training and research on China-related topics notably attractive, and dismayingly few of those who have completed their studies abroad have gone home to share their skills, knowledge, and contacts. Long-time expatriates are likely to find settling into home institutions trying and particularly frustrating after having paid a substantial personal price in making the earlier adjustment to foreign academic life.

Despite all these problems, good work on CCP foreign relations is being done in China that bears considerable relevance to historical scholarship in the United States and elsewhere abroad. Indeed, it has already had an impact here, thanks above all to the PRC scholars who have helped foreigners researching in China, who have published in English, or who have begun careers in the American university system. It seems certain that foreign historians bent on studying the CCP will ride on the coat-tails and in many cases work in close cooperation with the larger and more active group of Chinese scholars.

Scholarship in the United States

On this side of the Pacific historical work on CCP foreign relations has suffered from neglect. In the most direct sense this state of affairs is the result of indifference to the subject by historians of modern China. The paucity at least until recently of adequate sources provides the most obvious explanation for this indifference. But perhaps even more important is the fall of foreign relations from historical grace—from the position of prominence and respect it once enjoyed. As historians embraced a "China-centered" approach, they became increasingly absorbed in intellectual, social, economic, and local history. They looked back with a critical eye on the earlier historical literature with its strong emphasis on China's external relations, and they saw scant reason for interest in more recent treatments of CCP foreign policy produced in the main by political scientists.[11]

As a result, an emergent CCP foreign-policy history, like other aspects of China's foreign relations, stands somewhat apart from today's governing historical concerns. Why should specialists in early twentieth-century anarchism, urban women, or rural society care about the party's dealings with the outside world? Even specialists in party history drawn from a new generation are inclined to set foreign relations beyond their purview or banish it at best to the margins of their concerns.

But arguably to set foreign relations somewhere on the edge of Chinese history is to impoverish both. Politics and the state do matter, a point that social and cultural historians in a variety of fields have come to accept.[12] And foreign policy, the regulation of relations with the outside world, may be one of the most powerful and consequential aspects of the state's activity. Understanding the decisions, institutions, and culture associated with that activity can be of signal importance in filling out such diverse topics as the role of ideas, life in the city, or changes in the countryside. Party historians in particular run the risk of losing track of the global dimensions of the revolutionary and state-building enterprise and thereby forfeiting a chance to move toward a fully rounded understanding of the CCP. At the same time, CCP foreign relations needs the methodological leavening and interpretive breadth afforded by the history of China as it is now practiced. Foreign relations also needs the well honed language tools that historians of China could bring to mining the documentary ore now so abundantly in view.

While there is no reason to mourn the passing of the age of foreign-relations hegemony in the study of the Chinese past, the effect has been to leave the stewardship of China's foreign relations to political scientists with their own understandably distinct agenda and style. The consequence of their dominance is a literature tending in two directions, each bearing features that are worrisome because of the effect they may have in slowing and skewing the use of new materials on the CCP.[13]

One tendency, marked but by no means dominant, is a preoccupation with theoretical abstractions. What may most strike historians is how this theory-building enterprise tends to thrive under conditions that are euphemistically described by those who attempt it as "data poor" (if imagination rich). We can all call to mind efforts to construct and test high-flying theoretical formulations that get off the ground only after the perilous potholes along the evidentiary runway are carefully smoothed over. Once airborne, those formulations stay aloft only so long as no dangerous mountains of data intrude in the flight path. The virtuosity of the performance can be impressive, but it usually comes at the price of obscuring the fascinating complexity of political life with sometimes mind-numbing abstractions.[14]

The second, perhaps more pronounced tendency among political scientists is to approach Chinese policy with a stronger commitment to description and a more developed historical sensibility. Political scientists working along these lines bring to their work an awareness of the way that skimpy documentation hobbles their interpretive effort. This group also follows an old-fashioned faith in the importance of individual leader's values, style, and personality and especially Mao's.[15] But the paucity of good documentation long locked CCP decisionmaking in a black box and forced these China-watchers to find modes of analysis that would help them make sense of limited evidence and communicate their findings promptly and clearly to the broad policy community. Determined to make some sense of what was going on inside the black box, these analysts developed a variety of tools to penetrate its mysteries. However, the problematic nature of some of those tools is becoming apparent as the new CCP sources open up that box for the first time and permit comparison of past interpretations with the newer, more richly documented understanding.

The reading of public pronouncements, long a mainstay of China-watchers, is rendered particularly tricky by all the ways those pronouncements can deceive. Usually couched in explicit and correct ideological terms, they may not reflect the more direct, less jargon-ridden inner-party discussions and directives. They are, moreover, sometimes intended to manipulate foreigners, and thus are couched in terms that the party thinks will be effective on its target audience, not in terms that are revealing of inner-party calculations. Finally, they may be directed at an audience altogether different from the one the contemporary foreign reader may have assumed was the target.[16]

American observers' misreading of the CCP's propaganda line from mid-1945 to mid-1946 offers a good example of these interpretive difficulties. Inner-party documents now capture Mao Zedong as a backstage operator, carefully orchestrating an attempt to manipulate Washington into an engagement in Chinese politics beneficial to the CCP. He was not intent, as most students of the period have naturally concluded on the basis of the public record, on dismissing American contacts or rejecting American involvement.[17]

An even more complicated example of the perils of reading public signals is Zhou Enlai's interview on October 3, 1950 with the Indian ambassador. Often cited retrospectively as one of a string of crystal-clear warnings issued by Beijing following the outbreak of the Korean War, Zhou's own language in the formal Chinese record is in fact strikingly muffled and vague and does not accurately convey the depth of Mao's commitment to intervention at that moment. Zhou was apparently aware that he might be misconstrued and worked with his translator to get his point across. But U.S. China-watchers in Hong Kong had difficulty extracting a clear message from that October interview, and the puzzle still remains for historians today looking back. While we may puzzle over whether Zhou's lack of clarity was inadvertent or by design, the point remains that this critical public pronouncement is still hard to interpret.[18]

An emphasis on factions, the relatively stable groups united by some sort of overarching interest or ideology,[19] is another of the questionable shortcuts employed by China-watchers struggling to make sense of Beijing politics. The reduction of complicated political choices to stark factional alternatives reflected the analysts' need for clarity and the absence of restraints that rich documentation might impose. At first based largely on circumstantial evidence, the factional interpretation enjoyed a major boost during the Cultural Revolution when material on elite conflict became public. As a result, a variety of factional cleavages have gained prominence in the writing of China-watchers, and soon found their way back into the work on party history produced by political scientists. Perhaps the best known of the factional interpretations has arrayed "Maoists" against Moscow-oriented "internationalists."[20]

The new materials have raised two sets of doubts about the factional model. On the one hand, they offer little to support even a circumstantial argument for the existence of factions, and on the other they have set in question the Cultural Revolution evidence used to beat down former party leaders. Some of this evidence is of doubtful authenticity, and much seems torn from context to score political points.

It would prove ironic indeed if the factional model turns out to offer a no more subtle treatment of Chinese politics than does the former dependence of the CCP's own analysts on struggles within monopoly capitalism to explain American politics. Undeniably, informal networks and shifting coalitions have played a part in Chinese politics, but a compelling, carefully documented case has not yet been made that those networks have supported stable and identifiable as opposed to complex and cross-cutting political attachments. Scholars pressing factional claims bear the responsibility for being explicit about their definition of the term, marshaling reliable evidence, and setting whatever factional activity may exist within the broad political context so as to clarify the relative importance of such activity.

A final shortcut rendered doubtful by the new CCP history is the China-watchers' reliance on China's own international affairs "experts" as a prime source of information.[21] These experts, often accessible and able to speak the language (both literally and figuratively) of Western analysts, have become over the past decade understandably attractive contacts, constituting along with their foreign counterparts a transnational community of policy specialists and commentators on current international affairs.

But the new history underlines the limited insights of these experts by revealing the degree to which decisionmaking on critical issues has been closely held, the monopoly of a handful of leaders. Moreover, the new history reveals that major decisions have often been tightly guarded, not something to share with a foreigner—except where it suits the purposes of the party center to make available partial and sometimes tendentious information.

The shift toward a more historical rendering of the CCP past should have a notable impact on political-science research. Those of a more descriptive bent should welcome and benefit from the accumulation of fresh evidence that makes possible greater analytic rigor and sharper interpretive insight. The more theoretically inclined may be the more threatened, but some will accommodate to the new data, using it as ballast that will keep them closer to the safety of the ground. Indeed, it is possible that taking a longer view and looking at the implications of better documented cases may induce them to dispense with all but the most modest, commonsensical "theory" and perhaps even to enter the fray over what the evidence actually means. The theoretically enthralled may thereby rediscover in Chinese policy some of the classic and "soft" issues of international politics—the importance of personality, the contingent nature of politics, the complexity of thought behind action, and the persistence and power of political culture.

While this new CCP history should give political scientists pause, they also have important contributions to make to a more historically oriented field. Their concern with understanding the state and explaining its exercise of power has generated a repertoire of theories that may prove helpful to anyone trying to make sense of considerable new data and still uncertain of the most fruitful way to frame the issues. Moreover, the political scientists' preoccupation with contemporary questions stands as a salutary reminder to the more historically oriented of the complex relationship of past to present—of how the present may subtly influence the agenda for historical research and how historical findings may illuminate current problems.

Defining a Historical Agenda

CCP foreign policy is, as the above discussion suggests, a field distinctly in flux. Specialists have put a good deal of time and energy into coping with the recent flood of valuable documentary and other materials. The flood may be cresting, and those who have escaped drowning and reached the safety of high ground are now in a position to reflect on their future tasks.

The most obvious is to link a better documented version of CCP external relations chronologically and thematically to Chinese foreign relations in general. Qing sources, printed and archival, have long stood available, and have been recently reinforced by the opening of collections located in the PRC. Materials from the Republican era get steadily better as fresh publications appear and archives open on Taiwan and within the PRC. The new CCP material helps round out an already rich documentary base and makes all the more urgent an integrated treatment of China's external relations. Drawing on this range of sources, historians can begin to offer in-depth treatment of all the kinds of topics associated with a well-developed foreign-relations literature—from important personalities to the relation of policy to the "public." It should also convey a more complex sense of policy with features—economic opportunism, political flexibility, cultural ambivalence, strategic opportunism, and policy confusion—long associated with the better studied policies of other countries. To bring these themes into better focus, specialists will want to place the CCP's historical experience in a comparative framework and look for insight on the CCP that might emerge from juxtaposition with other foreign-relations histories.[22]

This broad agenda, good as far as it goes, neglects a fundamental and necessarily unsettling interpretive collision about to play out within the CCP foreign-relations field. Its resolution bears directly on the kind of agenda the field will follow. As historians turn to CCP foreign relations, they will bring with them an anthropological concern with culture and a postmodern sensitivity to language, both currently strong preoccupations within their discipline.[23] Those interpretive proclivities are distinctly at odds with at least three fundamental features of the established literature and discourse defined by political science. Finding ways to make fresh, thoughtful use of the new historical evidence is here as perhaps in general inextricably tied to a critical examination of older, well-worn, and often narrow channels of interpretation.

One point of conflict arises from the long-established tendency to cast policy in terms of antinomies that in effect impose an interpretive straitjacket. The literature is peppered with reference to policies that are supposed to fit in one of several either/or categories. Policies were either "idealistic" or "realistic." They were either "ideologically driven" or responsive to "situational factors." They were shaped either by the "international system" or by "domestic determinants." These alternatives confront scholars with an interpretive dilemma that they often resolve by impaling themselves on one or the other of its horns.

Of all the dualisms, none is more pervasive and troubling than the idea of the "international system" and its conceptual twin, "domestic determinants." A moment of critical reflection reminds us that the makeup of the international system is not self-evident, and those who champion its power to shape national policy differ widely on what the system is and how it works. Claims for the primacy of "domestic determinants" suffer from an equally serious problem: "domestic" is understood so narrowly and "determinants" is taken so literally that the phrase is almost drained of its significance.

The impulse to distinguish domestic and international influences may not be particularly useful in understanding the foreign policy of any country, and in the case of China draws a distinction that party leaders from Chen Duxiu to Deng Xiaoping would have found baffling, even wrongheaded. The growing availability of documentation makes it possible to argue what common sense already suggests—that discussions of Chinese policy need to transcend this and the other stark categories that narrow and impoverish our discourse.

Some scholars (including political scientists) have already begun to escape these stark alternatives.[24] They have shown not just that Mao and his colleagues operated within an international arena of Cold War rivalry and in a China of revolutionary aspirations and conflict but also that those worlds overlapped and interacted. Conclusions drawn from the behavior of the American imperialists, upheavals observed in Eastern Europe, and Nikita Khrushchev's theses on peaceful coexistence played off against internal discussions and debates about the best road for China's socialist development, treatment of peasants and intellectuals, the nature of party leadership, and China's appropriate place in a world revolutionary movement. Together the foreign and the domestic strands were interwoven into a single web, and neither strand can be removed without doing fundamental harm to our understanding of the whole.

A second point of likely conflict is an interpretive vocabulary whose unexamined assumptions exercise a quiet but nonetheless dangerous linguistic tyranny. Any reader of international relations would recognize the widely used lexicon, including prominently such terms as "national interest," "strategic interests," "geostrategic imperatives," and "geopolitical realities." Thus we get accounts that confidently proclaim China's foreign relations are "propelled by national interests" (not its evil twin, "ideology"). Other accounts seek to differentiate "pragmatic" policies (usually linked with Zhou Enlai's or Deng Xiaoping's name) from "radical" or "provocative" policies (here Mao or the "Gang of Four" is likely to appear), and hold up as an ideal a "balance-of-power" approach that secures "strategic interests," "national security," and "foreign-policy interests" in a changing "international system."

While this language most commonly appears in American writing on contemporary China, Chinese scholars writing about their country's foreign policy have been showing signs of appropriating this vocabulary. Influenced by American international relations literature as well by their own search for a usable foreign-policy past, they have emphasized the neatly formulated and smoothly executed nature of Chinese policy and held up Zhou Enlai as a model of "realism" and "expertise," while wrestling over whether to make Mao's contributions to foreign policy "realistic" or "ideological."[25]

Behind this vocabulary lurks a strongly judgmental impulse antipathetic to less universal, more culture-specific insights. Understanding policy, whatever its complexities, takes a back seat to handing down a clear-cut verdict based on what a "rational" or "realistic" actor would have done in a particular set of circumstances.

The Korean War literature starkly illustrates this point about the powerful impulse to evaluate the rationality or realism of policy. Chinese scholars have joined Americans in reporting approvingly on Beijing's reassuringly clear, unitary, and above all carefully calculated response to U.S. intervention on the peninsula. In the American literature on deterrence China's handling of the Korean War has even been enshrined as a positive model in striking contrast to the bumblings of U.S. policymakers at the time.[26] Subjected now to a closer look thanks to the new evidence, this positive characterization seems wide of the mark. Mao and his associates, it now turns out, were themselves engulfed in the kind of messy and confused decisionmaking that also afflicted American leaders. Viewed in this new light, Beijing's reaction to the Korean crisis becomes interesting not so much for the evaluative question of who did the better job but rather for the interpretive question of how do we understand the limits of cultural understanding and human control in a story strongly marked by chaos and contingency. These observations are not meant to deny rationality on the part of Chinese policymakers or for that matter on the part of Americans but to highlight the difficulty of evaluating policy rationality, especially with the help of simple, dichotomous notions of policy as either realistic or idealistic, driven by either careful calculations of national interest or by ungovernable ideological impulses.[27]

Though the critique of the rational actor model is widely made and apparently widely accepted,[28] much of the CCP literature still seems unusually preoccupied with distinguishing misguided from sound policy. This siren call to make judgments about international behavior finds a response in all of us, but answering the call carries dangers. The most apparent is the tendency for simple judgments and a polemical style to appeal most strongly when limited evidence affords the weakest supporting grounds for them. For example, it was easy to offer up an idealized Mao when his own party decided what we should know, and it was natural to move toward a negative appraisal when new revelations thrust at us serious, previously unsuspected personal flaws. As the evidence becomes fuller and more reliable for Mao as for the CCP in general, older judgments must confront previously unimagined moral and political dimensions, and what previously seemed self-evident evaluations dissolve into complexity.

But beyond the simple problem of judgments handed down on scant or skewed evidence there is a broader and more complex problem. The claim to understand and judge "national interest," "national security," and so forth rests on a fundamentally metaphysical faith that value preferences serve to settle otherwise eminently debatable issues. That claim becomes often unthinkingly universalistic when scholars discover in countries and cultures other than their own roughly comparable notions of national interest and national security—at least among policymakers deemed sufficiently skilled in the realist calculus of power. The inadvertent results of this rational actor framework are judgments that are fundamentally culture-bound or at least that employ a definition of culture so narrow as to close off potentially interesting lines of investigation. Historians more interested in understanding the past than judging it will find limited appeal in hauling CCP leaders into court and formulating a verdict on the basis of their realism.

The third interpretive impulse likely to create conflict is a notion of ideology that is ahistorical and anemic. This unfortunate approach to the role of ideas in policymaking is in part a reflection of the rigid dualisms and fixation with rationality discussed above. It is also a reflection of a broader tendency during the Cold War to denigrate ideology as a peculiar deformation of the socialist bloc, a tendency that carried over into the China field as international relations specialists, schooled in comparative communism, applied a Soviet model to Chinese politics. In their accounts a pervasive, powerful Marxist-Leninist ideology came to offer an important key to understanding Chinese policy.

The resulting notions of CCP ideology are, it would now appear, ahistorical. The use of the Soviet Union as a starting point for understanding Chinese thinking may be unwise and is certainly premature because the Soviet model is itself drawn in narrow political terms and lacks firm historical grounding.[29] Moreover, the Chinese party, which itself only recently began to come into sharper historical focus, is unlikely to offer an easy fit with any Soviet template.[30] Indeed, we may look back on this Sino-Soviet ideological model and realize that the conclusions drawn from one set of highly circumstantial studies became the foundation for another set of equally circumstantial studies.

The prevalent thin, abstract conception of ideology should not divert our attention from more subtle and perhaps powerful informal ideologies that may be of considerably greater analytic value.[31] Examining the intellectual predispositions and fundamental assumptions that constitute informal ideology may render us more sensitive to the cultural and social influences over policy. Such an approach may thus help us better understand how calculations of "interest" are rooted in social structure and filtered through a screen of culturally conditioned assumptions and how individual responses to "objective" circumstances in the international environment are profoundly conditioned by personal background, beliefs, and surroundings.

Analysts using imposed, culture-bound categories find themselves in much the same impossible situation an outsider would face in trying to understand the Australian aborigines who spoke Dyirbal. To ignore their language is to close the door to understanding their world with its unfamiliar classification: *bayi* (human males, animals); *balan* (human females, water, fire, fighting); *balam* (nonflesh food); and *bala* (a residual category).[32] This breakdown may not make much sense to an outsider, but if getting into the head of the "other" is important, then uncovering the particular categories used to constitute their world is essential. By contrast, the conceptual baggage the observer brings from home must be counted a serious impediment. Employing outside frames of reference may obscure more China-centered and China-sensitive perspectives and thereby divert us from our ultimate destination—the understanding of China's beliefs and behavior in international affairs.[33]

One promising way to get beyond simple and mutually exclusive notions of CCP ideology—for example, either making it "Marxism-Leninism" or "nationalism"—is to think of it as a fabric that we can better understand by following the strand of keywords. A close look at those keywords and the relationship among them might prove helpful in defining policy discourse over time and unlocking contending visions of China's place in the world.[34]

"Patriotism" (*aiguozhuyi*) is one of those neglected keywords examined earlier in these pages. Another is "small and weak nationalities" (*ruoxiao minzu*). It too would repay close examination, revealing complexities not easily spotted in a straightforward reading of formal party statements. Like patriotism, this term had its roots in the late Qing, and persisted in CCP discourse from the party founding through the Maoist era and even beyond, injecting into it tensions as well as unintended ironies. China at times offered flamboyant rhetorical support for its revolutionary neighbors, but it has also collided with India and Vietnam, both important members of that community to which China claimed to belong. How has the concept of "small and weak nationalities" evolved, and what has China's regional ambitions and limited resources done to reconstitute the meaning of that term?

This discussion of keywords suggests that we need a more subtle and expansive notion of ideology—one that includes more than the formal ideology that the party utilized as an organizational glue and mobilization guide—if we are to move toward a richer understanding of CCP external relations. The network of ideas that make up an informal ideology is a complex, unstable amalgam drawn from a wide variety of sources and varying significantly from individual to individual. Some party leaders had experienced formative brushes with anarchism. Others had reacted strongly against disturbing urban conditions that made capitalism the main foe. Yet others constructed from their rural roots a populist outlook. Each borrowed from a rich, complex intellectual tradition, drew from distinct regional roots, and learned from diverse political experience as youths. A more penetrating grasp of Chinese policy depends ultimately on exploring the enormous diversity of thinking that shaped its course.

The negotiation of these and other points of difference between historians and political scientists will redefine the agenda for CCP foreign-policy studies and in the process help recast a field already in the midst of important change as a result of the revival of CCP studies in China. Historians taking a more prominent place in the field will be advancing a new constellation of questions and methods. The response by political scientists will doubtless vary with those of a descriptive bent finding it easy, while those devoted to theory may well find the transition awkward. How much this interaction across disciplinary lines will lead to a new mix of concerns and approaches and how much historians and political scientists will turn their back on each other, effectively creating a schism in the field, remains to be seen. Whatever the outcome outside of China, party historians within China are for their part likely to maintain a largely autonomous community interacting selectively with foreigner counterparts. Thus this trend toward a more historical picture of CCP external relations, at work in both the United States and China, is not likely to lead to a new monolithic field. And perhaps this outcome, marked by national and disciplinary diversity, is to be welcomed if it proves conducive to the wide-ranging inquiry and lively discussions associated with a field in renaissance.

Afterword: A Guide to the Literature

This section offers a general overview of the literature on the origins and evolution of the CCP's external relations. This opportunity to share with interested readers my understanding of that literature also permits me to acknowledge the scholarly contributions of others who made my synthesis possible.

Background and General Treatments

Anyone in search of major themes in Chinese foreign relations or a ready overview should start with Jonathan Spence's elegant *The Search for Modern China* (New York: Norton, 1990), and *The Cambridge History of China*, general editors Denis Twitchett and John K. Fairbank (Cambridge University Press, 1978–). *The Cambridge History* provides good coverage not only of the period treated in this study—the nineteenth and twentieth centuries—but also earlier times. Both Spence and *The Cambridge History* volumes offer help on the relevant literature.

Of all the broad-gauge surveys of CCP external relations, John Gittings's *The World and China, 1922–1972* (New York: Harper and Row, 1974) stands out for the vigor of its argument and for the breadth of its conception. Gittings first broached the major themes later developed in the book in "The Origins of China's Foreign Policy," in *Containment and Revolution*, ed. David Horowitz (Boston: Beacon Press, 1967), 182–217. Hélène Carrère d'Encausse and Stuart Schram, *Marxism and Asia: An Introduction with Readings* (London: Penguin, 1969), also offers a long-term view of the CCP within the context of the international communist movement. A sampling of the new work and a discussion of its interpretive implications and field repercussions can be found in Michael H. Hunt and Niu Jun, eds., *Toward a History of Chinese Communist Foreign Relations, 1920s–1960s: Personalities and Interpretive Approaches* (Washington: Asia Program, Woodrow Wilson International Center for Scholars, [1995]).

Historical materials appearing in China over the last decade have dramatically broadened our window on CCP foreign relations and left somewhat dated most of the earlier Western-language literature. The most important of those materials for the period treated here is Zhongyang dang'anguan, comp., *Zhonggong zhongyang wenjian xuanji* [A selection of CCP Central Committee documents] covering 1921–1949. This collection is supposedly drawn from an even fuller body of materials extending beyond 1949, *Zhonggong zhongyang wenjian huibian* [A compilation of CCP Central Committee documents], compiled by Zhongyang dang'anguan and available on a very limited basis only in China. The *xuanji* first appeared in an "inner-party" (*dangnei*) edition (14 vols.; Beijing: Zhonggong zhongyang dangxiao, 1982–87). It has reportedly been supplemented by a two-volume addition. An open edition is now available (18 vols.; Beijing: Zhonggong zhongyang dangxiao, 1989–92). A translation of key items from this collection will appear in *The Rise to Power of the Chinese Communist Party: Documents and Analysis*, ed. Tony Saich with Benjamin Yang (Armonk, N.Y.: M. E. Sharpe, forthcoming).

There are several other general collections containing materials helpful to exploring the party's approach to international issues and its closely related domestic concerns: Zhongguo renmin jiefangjun zhengzhi xueyuan dangshi jiaoyanshi, comp., *Zhonggong dangshi cankao ziliao* [Reference materials on CCP history] (11 vols.; n.p. [Beijing?], n.d. [preface in vol. 1 dated 1979]; continued for the post-1949 period as *Zhonggong dangshi jiaoxue cankao ziliao*); Zhongguo shehui kexueyuan xinwen yanjiusuo, comp., *Zhongguo gongchandang xinwen gongzuo wenjian huibian* [A collection of documents on CCP journalism] (3 vols.; Beijing: Xinhua, 1980; "internal circulation" [*neibu*]), which covers 1921–1956; and Fudan daxue lishixi Zhongguo jindaishi jiaoyanzu, comp., *Zhongguo jindai duiwai guanxi shiliao xuanji (1840–1949)* [A selection of historical materials on modern China's foreign relations (1840–1949)] (4 vols.; Shanghai: Shanghai renmin, 1977).

Most of the major figures in the CCP have had their major writings published. The Mao collection (discussed below) is the best known, but the list extends to those who played a prominent role briefly in the mid and late 1920s (such as Qu Qiubai and Peng Shuzhi), the group that accompanied Mao to the top (such as Liu Shaoqi, Wang Jiaxiang, Deng Xiaoping, Peng Dehuai, and Chen Yun), party intellectuals (such as Chen Hansheng and Ai Siqi), notable public supporters (such as Song Qingling), and even that party black sheep, Wang Ming. These volumes appear variously as *wenji* (collected works), *wenxuan* (selected works), *xuanji* (selections), and in several cases *junshi wenxuan* (selected works on military affairs). Generally these collections, especially the ones published in the early decades of the PRC, are less revealing on foreign affairs than the more recent materials. The collected works for a few of the best-known party figures can be found in translation.

For an early introduction to these various materials, see Michael H. Hunt and Odd Arne Westad, "The Chinese Communist Party and International Affairs: A Field Report on New Historical Sources and Old Research Problems," *China Quarterly*, no. 122 (Summer 1990): 258–72. Steven M. Goldstein and He Di offer an update in "New Chinese Sources on the History of the Cold War," *Cold War International History Project Bulletin*, no. 1 (Spring 1992): 4–6. Fernando Orlandi, "Nuove fonti e opportunità di ricerca sulla storia della Cina contemporanea, del movimento comunista internazionale e della guerra fredda" (Rome: working paper, Centro Gino Germani di Studi Comparati sulla Modernizzazione e lo Sviluppo, 1994), offers the most recent, wide-ranging survey of the new literature. Susanne Weigelin-Schwiedrzik, "Party Historiography in the People's Republic of China," *Australian Journal of Chinese Affairs*, no. 17 (January 1987): 78–113, stresses the highly political nature of the party history establishment. *CCP Research Newsletter*, edited by Timothy Cheek, and the twice-monthly *Zhonggong dangshi tongxun* [CCP history newsletter] are both essential for keeping current with new publications and research projects.

There are in Chinese several major guides to party history literature. Zhang Zhuhong, *Zhongguo xiandai gemingshi shiliaoxue* [A study of historical materials on China's contemporary revolutionary history] (Beijing: Zhonggong dangshi ziliao, 1987), is broadly cast but omits limited circulation source materials and journals. A draft version of the Zhang volume containing more citations to restricted ("internal circulation") materials appeared in *Dangshi ziliao zhengji tongxun*, 1985, nos. 7–12. A partial English translation, prepared by Timothy Cheek and Tony Saich, has appeared in *Chinese Studies in History* 23 (Summer 1990): 3–94, and *Chinese Studies in Sociology and Anthropology* 22 (Spring-Summer 1990): 3–158. Zhang

Jingru and Tang Manzhen, eds., *Zhonggong dangshixue shi* [A history of CCP historical studies] (Beijing: Zhongguo renmin daxue, 1990), traces the field's development, including notably its opening up in the 1980s.

Party history journals are a treasure trove, offering fresh documentation, revealing articles, and news of conferences and pending publications. A number of the chief journals underwent a confusing set of title changes in the late 1980s, and most are restricted in their circulation. They are as a result difficult for researchers outside of China to keep straight and use systematically. Of these journals *Dangde wenxian* [Literature on the party] (published by Zhongyang wenxian yanjiushi and Zhongyang dang'anguan, 1988– ; "internal circulation") and its earlier incarnation, *Wenxian he yanjiu* [Documents and research] (published by Zhongyang wenxian yanjiushi, 1982–87; "internal circulation"), deserve singling out for their fresh documentation as well as helpful articles.

The Rise of an International Affairs Orthodoxy (1921–1934)

CCP views on foreign affairs emerged during the late Qing and early Republic out of a complex intellectual setting. This background is nicely suggested by a large body of literature: Charlotte Furth, ed., *The Limits of Change: Essays on Conservative Alternative in Republican China* (Cambridge: Harvard University Press, 1976); Hao Chang, *Chinese Intellectuals in Crisis: Search for Order and Meaning (1890–1911)* (Berkeley: University of California Press, 1987); Don C. Price, *Russia and the Roots of the Chinese Revolution, 1896–1911* (Cambridge: Harvard University Press, 1974); James Pusey, *China and Charles Darwin* (Cambridge: Harvard University Council on East Asian Studies, 1983); Mary B. Rankin, *Early Chinese Revolutionaries: Radical Intellectuals in Shanghai and Chekiang, 1902–1911* (Cambridge: Harvard University Press, 1971); Benjamin I. Schwartz, *In Search of Wealth and Power: Yen Fu and the West* (Cambridge: Harvard University Press, 1964); Harold Z. Schiffrin, *Sun Yat-sen and the Origins of the Chinese Revolution* (Berkeley: University of California Press, 1970); Li Yuning, *The Introduction of Socialism into China* (New York: Columbia University East Asian Institute, 1971); Martin Bernal, *Chinese Socialism to 1907* (Ithaca: Cornell University Press, 1976); Arif Dirlik, *Anarchism in the Chinese Revolution* (Berkeley: University of California Press, 1991); Peter Zarrow, *Anarchism and Chinese Political Culture* (New York: Columbia University Press, 1990); Chow Tse-tsung, *The May Fourth Movement: Intellectual Revolution in Modern China* (Cambridge: Harvard University Press, 1964); Lin Yü-sheng, *The Crisis of Chinese Consciousness: Radical Antitraditionalism in the May Fourth Era* (Madison: University of Wisconsin Press,

1979); Vera Schwarcz, *The Chinese Enlightenment: Intellectuals and the Legacy of the May Fourth Movement of 1919* (Berkeley: University of California Press, 1986); and Benjamin I. Schwartz, ed., *Reflections on the May Fourth Movement: A Symposium* (Cambridge: Harvard University East Asian Research Center, 1972).

Writings from the People's Republic of China offer such a constricted treatment of the CCP's May Fourth background that they are of only limited use. Broader perspectives are available in documentary collections such as *Wusi aiguo yundong* [the May fourth patriotic movement], comp. Zhongguo shehui kexueyuan jindaishi yanjiusuo jindai ziliao bianjizu (2 vols.; Beijing: Zhongguo shehui kexue, 1979); and *Shehui zhuyi sixiang zai Zhongguo de chuanbo* [The propagation of socialist thought in China] (3 vols.; Beijing: Zhonggong zhongyang dangxiao keyan bangongshi, 1985). The latter is but one of a number of documentary collections that have been compiled in China over the last decade on ideological transmission and formation around the time of May Fourth.

An accumulation of research spanning several decades offers good insight on the founding of the CCP and subsequent party-building. See in particular Arif Dirlik, *The Origins of Chinese Communism* (New York: Oxford University Press, 1989); Lawrence Sullivan and Richard H. Solomon, "The Formation of Chinese Communist Ideology in the May Fourth Era: A Content Analysis of *Hsin ch'ing nien*," in *Ideology and Politics in Contemporary China*, ed. Chalmers Johnson (Seattle: University of Washington Press, 1973); Hans J. van de Ven, *From Friends to Comrades: The Founding of the Chinese Communist Party, 1920–1927* (Berkeley: University of California Press, 1991); Michael Y. L. Luk, *The Origins of Chinese Bolshevism: An Ideology in the Making, 1921–1928* (Hong Kong: Oxford University Press, 1989); Marilyn A. Levine, *The Found Generation: Chinese Communists in Europe during the Twenties* (Seattle: University of Washington Press, 1993); and Benjamin Yang, *From Revolution to Politics: Chinese Communists on the Long March* (Boulder, Colo.: Westview, 1990). Benjamin I. Schwartz, *Chinese Communism and the Rise of Mao* (originally published 1951; Cambridge: Harvard University Press, 1966), is a classic that still commands attention.

There is good material on early party leaders. See in particular Maurice Meisner, *Li Dazhao and the Origins of Chinese Marxism* (Cambridge: Harvard University Press, 1967); Huang Sung-k'ang, *Li Ta-chao and the Impact of Marxism on Modern Chinese Thinking* (The Hague: Mouton, 1965); *Li Dazhao wenji* [Collected works of Li Dazhao], comp. Yuan Qian et al. (2 vols.; Beijing: Renmin, 1984); Lee Feigon, *Chen Duxiu: Founder of the Chi-*

nese Communist Party (Princeton: Princeton University Press, 1983); *Duxiu wencun* [A collection of writings by (Chen) Duxiu] (originally published 1922; 2 vols.; Jiulong: Yuandong, 1965); and Zhang Guotao, *The Rise of the Chinese Communist Party: The Autobiography of Chang Kuo-t'ao* (2 vols.; Lawrence: University of Kansas Press, 1971–72).

The variant views on imperialism in the 1920s emerge from A. James Gregor and Maria Hsia Chang, "Marxism, Sun Yat-sen, and the Concept of 'Imperialism'," *Pacific Affairs* 55 (Spring 1982): 54–79; Herman Mast III, "Tai Chi-t'ao, Sunism and Marxism During the May Fourth Movement in Shanghai," *Modern Asian Studies* 5 (July 1971): 227–49; Edmund S. K. Fung, "The Chinese Nationalists and the Unequal Treaties 1924–1931," *Modern Asian Studies* 21 (October 1987): 793–819; Fung, "Anti-Imperialism and the Left Guomindang," *Modern China* 11 (January 1985): 39–76; and P. Cavendish, "Anti-imperialism in the Kuomintang 1923–8," in *Studies in the Social History of China and South-east Asia*, ed. Jerome Ch'en and Nicholas Tarling (Cambridge, Eng.: Cambridge University Press, 1970), 23–56.

To form a more precise impression of CCP views on imperialism, turn to contemporary materials, notably prominent party journals such as *Xiangdao zhoubao* [The guide weekly] (1922–27) and the collections of Central Committee documents (noted above). Evidence on the general attractiveness of anti-imperialism as a tool of political mobilization can be found in *Wusa yundong shiliao* [Historical materials on the May 30 (1925) movement], comp. Shanghai shehui kexueyuan lishi yanjiusuo, vol. 1 (Shanghai: Shanghai renmin, 1981); *Sanyiba yundong ziliao* [Materials on the March 18 (1926) movement], comp. Sun Dunheng and Wen Hai (Beijing: Renmin, 1984); and *Sanyiba can'an ziliao huibian* [Materials on the March 18 (1926) massacre], comp. Jiang Changren (Beijing: Beijing, 1985).

The CCP's relationship to the Communist International (Comintern) in the 1920s and early 1930s is, despite limited, fragmentary evidence, the subject of a good range of studies. The central work is C. Martin Wilbur and Julie Lien-ying How, *Missionaries of Revolution: Soviet Advisers and Nationalist China, 1920–1927* (Cambridge: Harvard University Press, 1989), a much expanded version of C. Martin Wilbur and Julie Lien-ying How, eds., *Documents on Communism, Nationalism, and Soviet Advisers in China, 1918–1927: Papers Seized in the 1927 Peking Raid* (New York: Columbia University Press, 1956). The following are more specialized but no less important: Tony Saich, *The Origins of the First United Front in China: The Role of Sneevliet (Alias Maring)* (2 vols.; Leiden: E. J. Brill,

1991); Jane L. Price, *Cadres, Commanders, and Commissars: The Training of the Chinese Communist Leadership, 1920–1945* (Boulder, Colo.: Westview, 1976); M. F. Yuriev and A. V. Pantsov, "Comintern, CPSU (B) and Ideological and Organizational Evolution of the Communist Party of China," in *Revolutionary Democracy and Communists in the East*, ed. R. Ulyanovsky (Moscow: Progress Publishers, 1984); and Alexander Pantsov, "From Students to Dissidents: The Chinese Trotskyists in Soviet Russia," trans. John Sexton, *Issues and Studies* (Taibei), vol. 30, pt. 1 (March 1994): 97–126, pt. 2 (April 1994): 56–73, and pt. 3 (May 1994): 77–109. Once standard accounts still deserving attention include Allen Whiting, *Soviet Policies in China, 1917–1924* (New York: Columbia University Press, 1954); and Dan N. Jacobs, *Borodin: Stalin's Man in China* (Cambridge: Harvard University Press, 1981).

There are some revealing memoirs on the early CCP-Soviet relationship. Yueh Sheng, *Sun Yat-sen University in Moscow and the Chinese Revolution: A Personal Account* ([Lawrence]: University of Kansas Center for East Asian Studies, 1971); and Wang Fan-hsi, *Chinese Revolutionary: Memoirs, 1919–1949*, trans. Gregor Benton (Oxford, Eng.: Oxford University Press, 1980), are notable for their treatment of study in Moscow and its personal impact. Otto Braun, *A Comintern Agent in China, 1932–1939*, trans. Jeanne Moore (Stanford: Stanford University Press, 1982), is colored by a strong anti-Mao animus.

Among a substantial collection of general surveys in Chinese on the CCP and the Comintern, the standouts are Xiang Qing, *Gongchan guoji he Zhongguo geming guanxi shigao* [Draft history of the relations between the Comintern and the Chinese revolution] (Beijing: Beijing daxue, 1988); Yang Yunruo and Yang Kuisong, *Gongchan guoji he Zhongguo geming* [The Comintern and the Chinese revolution] (Shanghai: Shanghai renmin, 1988); and Yang Kuisong, *Zhongjian didai de geming: Zhongguo geming de celüe zai guoji beijing xia de yanbian* [Revolution in the intermediate zone: the development of China's revolutionary strategy against an international background] (Beijing: Zhonggong zhongyang dangxiao, 1992), the freshest and most detailed treatment. All three accounts carry the story into the 1940s—down to the dissolution of the Comintern and beyond.

Treatment of the CCP approach to national minorities and its support for foreign liberation movements, an important issue as early as the 1920s, can be found in June T. Dreyer, *China's Forty Millions: Minority Nationalities and National Integration in the People's Republic of China* (Cambridge: Harvard University Press, 1976); Walker Connor, *The National Question in Marxist-Leninist Theory and Strategy* (Princeton: Princeton University

Press, 1984), chaps. 4, 8–10; Frank S. T. Hsiao and Lawrence R. Sullivan, "A Political History of the Taiwanese Communist Party, 1928–1931," *Journal of Asian Studies* 42 (February 1983): 269–89; and Hsiao and Sullivan, "The Chinese Communist Party and the Status of Taiwan, 1928–1943," *Pacific Affairs* 52 (Fall 1979): 446–67.

The Emergence of a Foreign Policy (1935–1949)

The CCP's handling of the United States and the Soviet Union during the Pacific War and into the early Cold War period has been the subject of roughly three decades of serious scholarship. The appearance of new documentation has rendered much of that literature obsolete and compromised interpretations advanced as recently as the late 1980s. Several major works drawing on the fresh source materials have already appeared. John W. Garver's *Chinese-Soviet Relations, 1937–1945: The Diplomacy of Chinese Nationalism* (New York: Oxford University Press, 1988) stresses the CCP's policy of maneuver and places Mao alongside Chiang Kai-shek as a nationalist whose outlook drove him into "rebellion" (274) against Moscow. Odd Arne Westad's *Cold War and Revolution: Soviet-American Rivalry and the Origins of the Chinese Civil War, 1944–1946* (New York: Columbia University Press, 1993), sets Mao's policy in an impressively international context and pictures as largely abortive his efforts to make the great powers serve his party's cause in the immediate aftermath of World War II.

Also drawing on new material are shorter studies: John W. Garver, "The Origins of the Second United Front: The Comintern and the Chinese Communist Party," *China Quarterly*, no. 113 (March 1988): 29–59; Garver, "The Soviet Union and the Xi'an Incident," *Australian Journal of Chinese Affairs*, no. 26 (July 1991): 147–75; Michael M. Sheng, "Mao, Stalin, and the Formation of the Anti-Japanese United Front, 1935–37," *China Quarterly*, no. 129 (March 1992): 149–70; Sheng, "America's Lost Chance in China? A Reappraisal of Chinese Communist Policy Toward the United States Before 1945," *Australian Journal of Chinese Affairs*, no. 29 (January 1993): 135–57; Sheng, "Chinese Communist Policy Toward the United States and the Myth of the 'Lost Chance', 1948–1950," *Modern Asian Studies* 28 (1994): 475–502; and Chen Jian, "The Ward Case and the Emergence of Sino-American Confrontation, 1948–1950," *Australian Journal of Chinese Affairs*, no. 30 (July 1993): 149–70.

A number of studies prepared without benefit of the recently released documentation are still worth attention. James Reardon-Anderson, *Yenan and the Great Powers: The Origins of Chinese Communist Foreign Policy,*

1944–1946 (New York: Columbia University Press, 1980), stirred up debate by minimizing ideological constraints on CCP policy and by arguing for a "lost chance" at the end of the Pacific War when the CCP was frustrated in its attempt to avert Sino-American hostility and to minimize dependence on the Soviet Union.

This interpretative challenge was quickly taken up by several contributors to *Uncertain Years: Chinese-American Relations, 1947–1950*, ed. Dorothy Borg and Waldo Heinrichs (New York: Columbia University Press, 1980), 181–278, 293–303. See in particular my own "Mao Tse-tung and the Issue of Accommodation with the United States, 1948–1950," Steven M. Goldstein's response, "Chinese Communist Policy Toward the United States: Opportunities and Constraints, 1944–1950," and Steven I. Levine's two commentaries. Goldstein revisited the debate in "Sino-American Relations, 1948–1950: Lost Chance or No Chance?" in *Sino-American Relations, 1945–1955: A Joint Reassessment of a Critical Decade*, ed. Harry Harding and Yuan Ming (Wilmington, Del.: Scholarly Resources, 1989), 119–42.

These Goldstein accounts emphasize policy constraints imposed by formal party ideology. They as well as his "The Chinese Revolution and the Colonial Areas: The View from Yenan, 1937–41," *China Quarterly*, no. 75 (September 1978): 594–622, and his "The CCP's Foreign Policy of Opposition, 1937–1945," in *China's Bitter Victory: The War with Japan, 1937–1945*, ed. James C. Hsiung and Steven I. Levine (Armonk, N.Y.: M. E. Sharpe, 1992), 107–134, draw from his "Chinese Communist Perspectives on International Affairs, 1937–1941" (Ph.D. thesis, Columbia University, 1972), a pioneering effort at systematic treatment based largely on party press and other public pronouncements available to researchers at the time.

Levine's own major statement, *Anvil of Victory: The Communist Revolution in Manchuria, 1945–1948* (New York: Columbia University Press, 1987), also joined the issue by looking at revolutionary mobilization in a strategically pivotal and internationally sensitive region. It elaborates themes anticipated in his "A New Look at American Mediation in the Chinese Civil War: The Marshall Mission and Manchuria," *Diplomatic History* 3 (Fall 1979): 349–75, and his essay, "Soviet-American Rivalry in Manchuria and the Cold War," in *Dimensions of Chinese Foreign Policy*, ed. Chün-tu Hsüeh (New York: Praeger, 1977), 10–43.

Other early accounts grappling with CCP foreign-policy ideology include Okabe Tatsumi, "The Cold War and China," in *The Origins of the Cold War in Asia*, ed. Yonosuke Nagai and Akira Iriye (New York: Columbia University Press, 1977), 224–51; and Warren I. Cohen, "The Development of Chinese Communist Policy Toward the United States," *Orbis* 11 (Spring and Summer 1967): 219–37 and 551–69.

A growing body of scholarship helps situate CCP external relations in the broader context of base building, revolutionary warfare, peasant mobilization, and united-front policy in the 1930s and 1940s. Key items include Odoric Y. K. Wou, *Mobilizing the Masses: Building Revolution in Henan* (Stanford: Stanford University Press, 1994); Gregor Benton, *Mountain Fires: The Red Army's Three-Year War in South China, 1934–1938* (Berkeley: University of California Press, 1992); Kui-Kwong Shum, *The Chinese Communists' Road to Power: The Anti-Japanese National United Front, 1935–1945* (Hong Kong: Oxford University Press, 1988); Levine, *Anvil of Victory* (cited above); Chen Yung-fa, *Making Revolution: The Communist Movement in Eastern and Central China, 1937–1945* (Berkeley: University of California Press, 1986); and Suzanne Pepper, *Civil War in China: The Political Struggle, 1945–1949* (Berkeley: University of California Press, 1978). Some of the issues raised by this literature are discussed in Kathleen J. Hartford and Steven M. Goldstein, "Perspectives on the Chinese Communist Revolution," in *Single Sparks: China's Rural Revolutions*, ed. Goldstein and Hartford (Armonk, N.Y.: M. E. Sharpe, 1989), 3–33.

PRC historians have led the way in filling out the picture of CCP policy from the late 1930s down to 1949. The most ambitious account to date is Niu Jun's *Cong Yanan zouxiang shijie: Zhongguo gongchandang duiwai guanxi de qiyuan* [Moving from Yanan toward the world: the origins of Chinese Communist foreign relations] (Fuzhou: Fujian renmin, 1992). Niu locates the origins of the CCP's independent foreign policy in the Yanan years, and perhaps better than any other account—in English or Chinese—provides the supporting evidence. He builds here on his earlier work on the CCP's handling of the Hurley and Marshall missions, *Cong He'erli dao Maxie'er: Meiguo tiaochu guogong maodun shimo* [From Hurley to Marshall: a full account of the U.S. mediation of the contradictions between the Nationalists and the Communists] (Fuzhou: Fujian renmin, 1988).

Chinese specialists have published extensively in Chinese journals on various key aspects of CCP policy in this period. A portion of that work has appeared in translation. See especially Zhang Baijia, "Chinese Policies toward the United States, 1937–1945," and He Di, "The Evolution of the Chinese Communist Party's Policy toward the United States, 1944–1949," in *Sino-American Relations, 1945–1955*, 14–28 and 31–50 respectively; and Yang Kuisong, "The Soviet Factor and the CCP's Policy Toward the United States in the 1940s," *Chinese Historians* 5 (Spring 1992): 17–34.

Key sources for this period, aside from the central party documents mentioned above, are Zhongyang tongzhanbu and Zhongyang dang'anguan, comps., *Zhonggong zhongyang kangRi minzu tongyi zhanxian wenjian xuanbian* [A selection of documents on the CCP Central Committee's national anti-Japanese united front] (3 vols.; Beijing: Dang'an, 1984–86; "internal circulation"); and Zhongyang tongzhanbu and Zhongyang dang'anguan, comps., *Zhonggong zhongyang jiefang zhanzheng shiqi tongyi zhanxian wenjian xuanbian* [A selection of documents on the CCP Central Committee's united front during the period of liberation struggle] (Beijing: Dang'an, 1988; "internal circulation").

Personal accounts are useful in supplementing the primary collections. See Shi Zhe with Li Haiwen, *Zai lishi juren shenbian: Shi Zhe huiyilu* [Alongside the giants of history: Shi Zhe's memoir] (Beijing: Zhongyang wenxian, 1991); Nie Rongzhen, *Nie Rongzhen huiyilu* [The memoirs of Nie Rongzhen] (3 vols.; Beijing: Janshi, 1983, and Jiefangjun, 1984); Wu Xiuquan, *Wode licheng* [My course] (Beijing: Jiefangjun, 1984); Peter Vladimirov, *The Vladimirov Diary, Yenan, China: 1942–1945* (Garden City, N.Y., 1975), a translation that is not as complete as the Russian original, and in any case betrays a tendentious quality that invites some suspicion; and Ivan V. Kovalev and Sergei N. Goncharov, "Stalin's Dialogue with Mao Zedong," trans. Craig Seibert, *Journal of Northeast Asian Studies* 10 (Winter 1991–92): 45–76. Chen Jian has translated the portions of the Shi Zhe memoir dealing with the 1949 missions by Anastas Mikoyan and Liu Shaoqi in *Chinese Historians* 5 (Spring 1992): 35–46; and 6 (Spring 1993): 67–90.

Mao Zedong

Anyone interested in tracing Mao's evolving outlook on international affairs and his central policy role from the mid-1930s has an embarrassment of documentary riches to contend with. Indeed, a wide variety of materials have accumulated layer upon layer so that systematic research requires considerable patience. Those who press on will find as their reward Mao emerging from these materials a more complex and more interesting figure than previously guessed.

Most notable among the English-language treatments of Mao's career is the body of writing by Stuart R. Schram. See in particular Schram's classic life-and-times biography, *Mao Tse-tung* (Harmondsworth, Eng.: Penguin, 1966); the update to it in *Mao Zedong: A Preliminary Reassessment* (New York and Hong Kong: St. Martin's Press and Chinese University Press, 1983); and finally his *The Thought of Mao Tse-tung* (Cambridge, Eng.: Cambridge University Press, 1989), consisting of two essays that first appeared in *The Cambridge History of China*, vols. 13 and 15. See also Frederick C. Teiwes, "Mao and His Lieutenants," *Australian Journal of Chinese Affairs*, no. 19–20 (January–July 1988): 1–80; Jerome Ch'en, *Mao and the Chinese Revolution* (London: Oxford University Press, 1965); Frederic Wakeman, Jr., *History and Will: Philosophical Perspectives of Mao Tse-tung's Thought* (Berkeley: University of California Press, 1973); Dick Wilson, ed., *Mao Tse-tung in the Scales of History* (Cambridge, Eng.: Cambridge University Press, 1977); Robert A. Scalapino, "The Evolution of a Young Revolutionary—Mao Zedong in 1919–1921," *Journal of Asian Studies* 42 (November 1982): 29–61; He Di, "The Most Respected Enemy: Mao Zedong's Perception of the United States," *China Quarterly*, no. 137 (March 1994): 144–58; and Benjamin I. Schwartz, "The Maoist Image of the World Order," *Journal of International Affairs* 21 (1967): 92–102. The Schwartz article is notable as a pioneering effort to inject more sophistication and subtlety into the study of Mao's guiding ideas by placing earlier foreign-relations practices and experience as well as twentieth-century nationalism alongside Marxist-Leninist sources.

There is a good body of writings on Mao's early years. The starting point has long been Mao's own recital in Edgar Snow's *Red Star Over China* (originally published 1938; New York: Grove Press, 1961). The first to add to the picture was Xiao San (Emi Hsiao), *Mao Zedong tongzhi de qingshaonian shidai* [Comrade Mao Zedong's boyhood and youth] (originally published 1948; rev. and exp. ed., Guangzhou: Xinhua, 1950). A translation is available as *Mao Tse-tung: His Childhood and Youth* (Bombay: People's Publishing House, 1953). Li Rui followed with *Mao Zedong tongzhi de chuqi geming huodong* [Comrade Mao Zedong's initial revolutionary activities] (Beijing: Zhongguo qingnian, 1957). The translation prepared by Anthony W. Sariti and James C. Hsiung appears as *The Early Revolutionary Activities of Mao Tse-tung* (White Plains, N.Y.: M. E. Sharpe, 1977). Li Rui has since offered a revised and expanded version of the biography: *Mao Zedong de zaoqi geming huodong* [Mao Zedong's early revolutionary activity] (Changsha: Hunan renmin, 1980). The recollections by Siao Yu (Xiao Yü; Xiao Zisheng), *Mao Tse-tung and I Were Beggars* (Syracuse, N.Y.: Syracuse University Press, 1959), sound a somewhat sour tone. Recently a full collection of early writings has been published in China: Zhonggong zhongyang wenxian yanjiushi and Zhonggong Hunan shengwei "Mao Zedong zaoqi wengao" bianjizu, comps., *Mao Zedong zaoqi wengao, 1912.6–1920.11* [Mao Zedong manuscripts from the early period, June 1912–November 1920] (Changsha: Hunan, 1990; "internal circulation"). M. Henri Day offers translations of some early writings in *Mao*

Zedong, 1917–1927: Documents (Stockholm: publisher not indicated, 1975).

The officially sanctioned and most frequently cited collection of Mao's writings, post- as well as pre-1949, is *Mao Zedong xuanji* [Selected works of Mao Zedong] (5 vols.; Beijing: Renmin, 1952–77). It has long been available in translation: *Selected Works of Mao Tse-tung* (5 vols.; Beijing: Foreign Languages Press, 1961–77).

Aware that *Selected Works* is highly selective and politically edited, scholars outside China have subjected the Mao corpus to critical analysis, sought to supplement it with fresh materials, and prepared translations based on the most authentic originals available. The effort began in earnest with Stuart Schram's 1963 compilation and translation of key documents, *The Political Thought of Mao Tse-tung* (rev. ed.; Harmondsworth, Eng.: Penguin, 1969). The major nonofficial collection, launched in Japan under the supervision of Takeuchi Minoru, provided a reliable and considerably fuller body of Mao materials at least down to 1949. The first series appeared as *Mao Zedong ji* [Collected writings of Mao Zedong] (10 vols.; Tokyo: Hokubosha, 1971–72); it was followed by a second, supplementary series, *Mao Zedong ji bujuan* [Supplements to the collected writings of Mao Zedong] (9 vols.; Tokyo: Sososha, 1983–85). A parallel project to provide a full English-language collection, *Mao's Road to Power: Revolutionary Writings, 1912–1949*, is now underway. *The Pre-Marxist Period, 1912–1920*, ed. Stuart R. Schram (Armonk, N.Y.: M. E. Sharpe, 1992), is the first volume to appear.

Collections compiled by the party history establishment in China over the last decade have added significant, fresh light on Mao's general outlook and his emergence as a maker of foreign policy. These collections include Zhonggong zhongyang wenxian yanjiushi, comp., *Mao Zedong shuxin xuanji* [A selection of Mao Zedong correspondence] (Beijing: Renmin, 1983); Zhonggong zhongyang wenxian yanjiushi and Xinhua tongxunshe, comps., *Mao Zedong xinwen gongzuo wenxuan* [A selection of Mao Zedong works on journalism] (Beijing: Xinhua, 1983); and Zhonggong zhongyang tongyi zhanxian gongzuobu yanjiushi et al., comps., *Mao Zedong lun tongyi zhanxian* [Mao Zedong on the united front] (Beijing: Zhongguo wenshi, 1988).

The hundredth anniversary of Mao's birth gave rise to new compilations. One was a new series on Mao the military strategist: Junshi kexue chubanshe and Zhongyang wenxian chubanshe, comps., *Mao Zedong junshi wenji* [A collection of Mao Zedong works on military affairs] (6 vols.; Beijing: publisher same as compiler, 1993), which expands on Zhongguo renmin jiefangjun junshi kexueyuan, comp., *Mao Zedong junshi wenxuan* [A selection of Mao Zedong works on military affairs] (Beijing: Zhongguo renmin jiefangjun zhanshi, 1981; "internal circulation"; Tokyo reprint: Sososha, 1985). A second is the detailed and authoritative account of Mao's emergence and triumph as a revolutionary leader in Zhonggong zhongyang wenxian yanjiushi (under the direction of Pang Xianzhi), *Mao Zedong nianpu, 1893–1949* [A chronological biography of Mao Zedong, 1893–1949] (3 vols.; Beijing: Renmin and Zhongyang wenxian, 1993). A third is Zhonggong zhongyang wenxian yanjiushi, comp., *Mao Zedong wenji* [Collected works of Mao Zedong] (2 vols. to date; Beijing: Renmin, 1983–), which stands as a supplement to the well-known *xuanji* (selected works) but which is largely silent on international issues. A fourth projected anniversary collection—on Mao's diplomacy—has yet to be released. Helpful in putting Mao's role in the revolution in context are collections of central party documents and the documents on overall united front policy from 1935 to 1948 (both cited above).

For the post-1949 Mao turn to the classified series compiled by Zhonggong zhongyang wenxian yanjiushi, *Jianguo yilai Mao Zedong wengao* [Mao Zedong manuscripts for the period following the establishment of the country] (8 vols. to date; Beijing: Zhongyang wenxian, 1987– ; "internal circulation"). This series sheds new light on Mao and world affairs down to the late 1950s, and taken together with the outpouring of Mao material during the Cultural Revolution, gives us the basis for beginning to understand Mao's PRC years. The formidable task of collecting, collating, and verifying these materials has only begun. For a good recent guide, see Timothy Cheek, "Textually Speaking: An Assessment of Newly Available Mao Texts," in *The Secret Speeches of Chairman Mao: From the Hundred Flowers to the Great Leap Forward*, ed. Roderick MacFarquhar et al. (Cambridge: Harvard Council on East Asian Studies, 1989), 78–81; and Cheek, "The 'Genius' Mao: A Treasure Trove of 23 Newly Available Volumes of Post-1949 Mao Zedong Texts," *Australian Journal of Chinese Affairs*, no. 19–20 (January–July 1988): 337–44.

To make the post-1949 Mao materials available in English, Michael Y. M. Kau and John K. Leung launched a translation series in 1986. Two volumes of their *The Writings of Mao Zedong, 1949–1976* (Armonk, N.Y.: M. E. Sharpe, 1986–) have appeared to date covering the period down to December 1957. Their formidable task has been complicated by the continuing flow of new materials out of China. Translated fragments are available elsewhere—in a variety of publications by U.S. Joint Publications Research Service (better known as JPRS); in Stuart Schram, *Chairman*

Mao Talks to the People: Talks and Letters, 1956–1971 (New York: Pantheon, 1975); and in MacFarquhar et al., *The Secret Speeches* (cited above).

Zhou Enlai

Zhou deserves special attention as Mao's chief lieutenant in foreign affairs. For the moment the place to start is the archivally based biography, Zhonggong zhongyang wenxian yanjiushi (under the direction of Jin Chongji), *Zhou Enlai zhuan, 1898–1949* [Biography of Zhou Enlai, 1898–1949] (Beijing: Renmin and Zhongyang wenxian, 1989). This biography should be used in conjunction with Zhonggong zhongyang wenxian yanjiushi, comp., *Zhou Enlai nianpu, 1898–1949* [A chronicle of Zhou Enlai's life, 1898–1949] (Beijing: Zhongyang wenxian and Renmin, 1989). Zhou's early years abroad are richly documented in Huai En, comp., *Zhou zongli qingshaonian shidai shiwenshuxinji* [A collection of writings from Premier Zhou's youth] (2 vols., Chengdu: Sichuan renmin, 1979–80); and Zhongguo geming bowuguan, comp. *Zhou Enlai tongzhi lüOu wenji xubian* [A supplement to the collected works from the time of comrade Zhou Enlai's residence in Europe] (Beijing: Wenwu, 1982). These materials largely supercede the treatment in Kai-yu Hsu, *Chou En-lai: China's Grey Eminence* (Garden City, N.Y.: Doubleday, 1968), and Dick Wilson, *Zhou Enlai: A Biography* (New York: Viking, 1984).

Helpful documentation on Zhou's policy role can be found in Zhonggong zhongyang wenxian yanjiushi, comp., *Zhou Enlai shuxin xuanji* [A selection of Zhou Enlai letters] (Beijing: Zhongyang wenxian, 1988); Zhonggong zhongyang tongyi zhanxian gongzuobu and Zhonggong zhongyang wenxian yanjiushi, comps., *Zhou Enlai tongyi zhanxian wenxuan* [A selection of Zhou Enlai writings on the united front] (Beijing: Renmin, 1984); and Zhonghua renmin gongheguo waijiaobu and Zhonggong zhongyang wenxian yanjiushi, comps., *Zhou Enlai waijiao wenxuan* [Selected diplomatic writings of Zhou Enlai] (Beijing: Zhongyang wenxian, 1990). These materials go well beyond the limited documentation in Zhonggong zhongyang wenxian bianji weiyuanhui, comp., *Zhou Enlai xuanji* [Selected works of Zhou Enlai] (2 vols.; Beijing: Renmin, 1980, 1984), which is available in translation as *Selected Works of Zhou Enlai* (2 vols.; Beijing: Foreign Languages Press, 1981–89).

For an introduction to recent work in China on Zhou's diplomatic career and thinking, see *Zhou Enlai yanjiu xueshu taolunhui lunwenji* [Collected academic conference research papers on Zhou Enlai] (Beijing: Zhongyang wenxian, 1988); Zhonghua renmin gongheguo waijiaobu waijiaoshi bianjishi (under the direction of Pei Jianzhang), ed., *Yanjiu Zhou*

Enlai—waijiao sixiang yu shiyan [Studying Zhou Enlai—diplomatic thought and practice] (Beijing: Shijie zhishi, 1989); Zhongguo geming bowuguan et al., comps., *Zhou Enlai he tade shiye: yanjiu xuancui* [Zhou Enlai and his enterprises: a sampling of studies] (Beijing: Zhonggong dangshi, 1991); and Zhonghua renmin gongheguo waijiaobu waijiaoshi yanjiushi, comp., *Zhou Enlai waijiao huodong dashiji, 1949–1975* [A record of Zhou Enlai's diplomatic activities, 1949–1975] (Beijing: Shijie zhishi, 1993).

The Foreign Policy of the PRC

The new sources and studies that have refashioned our understanding of early CCP attitudes and policies are just beginning to have an impact on the post-1949 period. Until more documentary publications appear and are digested, it is likely that our understanding of PRC foreign policy will remain thin and fragmentary, and the writings in English on the topic will for the most part hold to the well-established political science approaches.

There are several good overviews that must serve for the moment. *The Cambridge History of China*, vols. 14 and 15, covers PRC foreign policy in chapters by Nakajima Mineo, Allen S. Whiting, Thomas Robinson, and Jonathan D. Pollack, while also offering helpful source essays. Samuel S. Kim, ed., *China and the World: Chinese Foreign Relations in the Post-Cold War Era* (3rd rev. ed.; Boulder, Colo.: Westview, 1994), pulls together a good range of up-to-date accounts. John W. Garver, *Foreign Relations of the People's Republic of China* (Englewood Cliffs, N.J.: Prentice-Hall, 1993), provides a thematic treatment with some attention to the pre-1949 background. Among older surveys Wang Gungwu's terse *China and the World Since 1949: The Impact of Independence, Modernity, and Revolution* (New York: St. Martin's Press, 1977) still deserves attention for its commendable stress on setting CCP foreign relations in a broad domestic context.

The PRC's exercise of control over border regions is still only poorly understood. For the moment the best places to start are Dreyer, *China's Forty Millions* (cited above); A. Tom Grunfeld, *The Making of Modern Tibet* (London: Zed, and Armonk, N.Y.: M. E. Sharpe, 1987), chaps. 5–11; and Donald H. McMillen, *Chinese Communist Power and Policy in Xinjiang, 1949–1977* (Boulder, Colo.: Westview, 1979).

The general secondary accounts in Chinese on post-1949 policy increasingly reflect the new openness in the PRC but still stick close to the official line. Han Nianlong, chief comp., *Dangdai Zhongguo waijiao* [Chinese foreign affairs in recent times] (Beijing: Zhongguo shehui kexueyuan, 1987) is the best known of these. That volume has been translated as *Diplo-*

macy of Contemporary China (Hong Kong: New Horizon, 1990) by Qiu Ke'an. It appears as a part of the series "Dangdai Zhongguo" (Contemporary China), which includes studies on the armed forces also germane to foreign policy. *Zhongguo waijiaoshi: Zhonghua renmin gongheguo shiqi, 1949–1979* [A diplomatic history of China: the PRC period, 1949–1979] (Zhengzhou: Henan renmin, 1988) is a major survey produced by Xie Yixian, who served in the foreign service before taking up teaching duties in the Foreign Ministry's Foreign Affairs College.

These accounts should be supplemented by such memoirs as Bo Yibo, *Ruogan zhongda juece yu shijian de huigu* [Reflections on some major decisions and incidents] (2 vols.; Beijing: Zhonggong zhongyang dangxiao, 1991–93); Li Shengzhi, *YaFei huiyi riji* [A diary of the Asian-African conference] (Beijing: publisher not indicated, 1986); Liu Xiao, *Chushi Sulian banian* [Eight years as ambassador to the Soviet Union] (Beijing: Zhonggong dangshi ziliao, 1986); Wang Bingnan, *ZhongMei huitan jiunian huigu* [Looking back on nine years of Sino-American talks] (Beijing: Shijie zhishi, 1985); and Wu Xiuquan, *Zai waijiaobu banian de jingli, 1950.1–1958.10* [Eight years' experience in the Ministry of Foreign Affairs, January 1950–October 1958] (Beijing: Shijie zhishi, 1983). This last item, the second volume of the Wu memoirs, is translated as *Eight Years in the Ministry of Foreign Affairs, January 1950–October 1958: Memoirs of a Diplomat* (Beijing: New World Press, 1985).

Documentary collections are beginning to open the window on PRC foreign relations. See in particular *Jianguo yilai Mao Zedong wengao* (cited above); the tightly held collection compiled by Zhongguo renmin jiefangjun zhengzhi xueyuan dangshi jiaoyanshi (renamed Zhongguo jiefangjun guofang daxue dangshi dangjian zhenggong jiaoyanshi), *Zhonggong dangshi jiaoxue cankao ziliao* [Reference materials for the teaching of CCP history] (vols. to date numbered 12–27 with 25–27 withdrawn; n.p. [Beijing?], n.d. [preface in vol. 12 dated 1985]); Xinhuashe xinwen yanjiubu, comp., *Xinhuashe wenjian ziliao xuanbian* [A selection of documentary materials on the New China News Agency] (4 vols.; no place and no publisher, [1981–87?]); and Zhongguo renmin jiefangjun dangshi dangjian zhenggong jiaoyanshi and Guofang daxue dangshi dangjian zhenggong jiaoyanshi, comps., *"Wenhua dageming" yanjiu ziliao* [Research materials on "the Cultural Revolution"] (3 vols.; Beijing: publisher same as compiler, 1988; withdrawn from circulation). The second series of *ZhongMei guanxi ziliao huibian* [A collection of materials on Sino-American relations], comp. Shijie zhishi (2 vols.; Beijing: Shijie zhishi, 1960; "internal circulation"), reads like a "white paper" with a strong emphasis on materials between 1949 and 1958, virtually all from the public domain. Two new collections are helpful in putting early PRC foreign relations in a broad policy framework: Zhonggong zhongyang wenxian yanjiushi, comp., *Jianguo yilai zhongyao wenxian xuanbian* [A selection of important documents on the post-1949 period] (Beijing: Zhongyang wenxian, 1992–); and Zhonggong zhongyang wenxian yanjiushi and Zhongyang dang'anguan "Dangde wenxian" bianjibu, comps., *Gongheguo zouguodelu: jianguo yilai zhongyao wenxian zhuanti xuanji (1949–1952)* [The path travelled by the republic: a selection of important documents on special topics since the founding of the country (1949–1952)] (Beijing: Zhongyang wenxian, 1991).

For the Korean War, Allen S. Whiting's *China Crosses the Yalu: The Decision to Enter the Korean War* (originally published 1960; Stanford: Stanford University Press, 1968) was a path-breaking study that long stood as the single, indispensable work. His account of Chinese signalling from June to November 1950 depicted Beijing as neither Moscow-dominated nor irrational but acting essentially out of fear of "a determined, powerful enemy on China's doorstep" (159). A decade later Edward Friedman, "Problems in Dealing with an Irrational Power," in *America's Asia: Dissenting Essays on Asian-American Relations*, ed. Friedman and Mark Selden (New York: Pantheon, 1971), followed Whiting in stressing the defensive, calculated, and rational nature of Chinese policy and Beijing's "complex and differentiated view of American foreign policy" (212). The theme that China was essentially responding in Korea to a danger to its security again enjoyed prominence in Melvin Gurtov and Byong-Moo Hwang, *China under Threat: The Politics of Strategy and Diplomacy* (Baltimore: Johns Hopkins Press, 1980), chap. 2., although by this point other competing concerns—domestic issues, divisions within the leadership, and strong internationalist elements in Beijing's justification for intervention—were beginning to creep into the picture and blur the interpretation.

The last few years have witnessed a flurry of publications, one after another broadening and enriching our understanding of Chinese policy and China's place in an international history of the early Cold War (while unfortunately neglecting the domestic dimensions of that conflict). Chen Xiaolu, "China's Policy Toward the United States, 1949–1955," and Jonathan D. Pollack, "The Korean War and Sino-American Relations," both in *Sino-American Relations, 1945–1955*, 184–97 and 213–37, were soon followed by Mark A. Ryan, *Chinese Attitudes Toward Nuclear Weapons: China and the United States During the Korean War* (Armonk, N.Y.: M. E. Sharpe, 1989); Hao Yufan and Zhai Zhihai, "China's Decision to Enter the Korean War: History Revisited," *China Quarterly*, no. 121 (March 1990):

94–115, which were in turn overtaken by Chen Jian, "The Sino-Soviet Alliance and China's Entry into the Korean War" (Washington: Woodrow Wilson Center Cold War International History Project, n.d. [1992?]; Chen Jian, "China's Changing Aims during the Korean War, 1950–1951," *The Journal of American-East Asian Relations* 1 (Spring 1992): 8–41; Thomas J. Christensen, "Threats, Assurances, and the Last Chance for Peace: The Lessons of Mao's Korean War Telegrams," *International Security* 17 (Summer 1992): 122–54; and Michael H. Hunt, "Beijing and the Korean Crisis, June 1950-June 1951," *Political Science Quarterly* 107 (Fall 1992): 453–78.

Treatment of Sino-Soviet relations during the initial phase of the Korean War was for a time sharply limited by the lack of documentation. Robert R. Simmons, *The Strained Alliance: Peking, Pyongyang, Moscow and the Politics of the Korean War* (New York: Free Press, 1975); Wilbur A. Chaffee, "Two Hypotheses of Sino-Soviet Relations as Concerns the Instigation of the Korean War," *Journal of Korean Affairs*, vol. 6, nos. 3–4 (1976–77): 1–13; and Nakajima Mineo, "The Sino-Soviet Confrontation: Its Roots in the International Background of the Korean War," *Australian Journal of Chinese Affairs*, no. 1 (January 1979): 19–47, were early efforts to explore that topic and especially the ways the war may have intensified strains that would eventually bring about the Sino-Soviet split. Drawing on new materials, Kathryn Weathersby treats "The Soviet Role in the Early Phase of the Korean War: New Documentary Evidence," *Journal of American-East Asian Relations* 2 (Winter 1993): 425–58.

The most detailed and up-to-date accounts of the war's origins are to be found in Chen Jian, *China's Road to the Korean War: The Making of the Sino-American Confrontation* (New York: Columbia University Press, 1994), notable for its stress on the strong revolutionary streak in Mao's foreign policy, and Sergei N. Goncharov, John W. Lewis, and Xue Litai, *Uncertain Partners: Stalin, Mao, and the Korean War* (Stanford: Stanford University Press, 1993), which depicts the two leaders as shrewd nationalists and resolute realpolitikers engaged in an intricate game of international chess with ideology counting for little.

Within the Chinese historical establishment Yao Xu, *Cong Yalujiang dao Banmendian: Weida de kangMei yuanChao zhanzheng* [From the Yalu River to Panmunjom: the great war to resist America and aid Korea] (Beijing: Renmin, 1985; "internal circulation"); and Chai Chengwen and Zhao Yongtian, *KangMei yuanChao jishi* [A record of resisting America and aiding Korea] (Beijing: Zhonggong dangshi ziliao, 1987; "internal circulation"), were the first to deal in detail with the war. Their work was in turn improved on by Junshi jiaoxueyuan junshi lishi yanjiubu, comp., *Zhongguo renmin zhiyuanjun kangMei yuanChao zhanshi* [A battle history of resistance to America and aid to Korea by the Chinese people's volunteer army] (Beijing: Junshi jiaoxue, 1988; "internal circulation"); Chai Chengwen and Zhao Yongtian, *Banmendian tanpan: Chaoxian zhanzheng juan* [The Panmunjom talks: a volume on the Korean War] (Beijing: Jiefangjun, 1989); Ye Yumeng, *Chubing Chaoxian: KangMei yuanChao lishi jishi* [Sending troops to Korea: a historical record of the resistance to America and assistance to Korea] (Beijing: Beijing shiyue wenyi, 1990); Qi Dexue, *Chaoxian zhanzheng juece neimu* [The inside story of the Korean War decisions] (Shenyang: Liaoning daxue, 1991); "Dangdai Zhongguo" congshu bianji weiyuanhui, *KangMei yuanChao zhanzheng* [The war to resist America and aid Korea] (Beijing: Zhongguo shehui kexue, 1990); and Xu Yan, *Diyici jiaoliang: KangMei yuanChao zhanzheng de lishi huigu yu fansi* [The first test of strength: a historical review and evaluation of the war to resist America and aid Korea] (Beijing: Zhongguo guangbo dianshi, 1990), the most complete and fully researched of the Chinese studies. Zhang Xi's unusually revealing "Peng Dehuai shouming shuaishi kangMei yuanChao de qianqian houhou" [The full story of Peng Dehuai's appointment to head the resistance to the United States and the assistance to Korea], *Zhonggong dangshi ziliao*, no. 31 (1989): 111–59, is available in a translation by Chen Jian, "Peng Dehuai and China's Entry into the Korean War," *Chinese Historians* 6 (Spring 1993): 1–29.

The Chinese military has made a major effort to tell its Korean War story not only in some of the general accounts noted above but also in a long string of memoirs. They include Peng Dehuai zishu bianjizu, ed., *Peng Dehuai zishu* [Peng Dehuai's own account] (Beijing: Renmin, 1981), which contains treatment of Korea prepared before the Cultural Revolution and apparently without access to personal files; Du Ping, *Zai zhiyuanjun zongbu* [With the headquarters of the volunteer army] (Beijing: Jiefangjun, 1989); Yang Chengwu, *Yang Chengwu huiyilu* [Memoirs of Yang Chengwu] (2 vols.; Beijing: Jiefangjun, 1987 and 1990); Yang Dezhi, *Weile heping* [For the sake of peace] (Beijing: Changzheng, 1987); and Hong Xuezhi, *KangMei yuanChao zhanzheng huiyi* ["Recollections of the war to resist U.S. aggression and aid Korea"] (Beijing: Jiefangjun wenyi, 1990). Peng's memoir is translated as *Memoirs of a Chinese Marshal: The Autobiographical Notes of Peng Dehuai (1898–1924)*, trans. Zheng Longpu and ed. Sara Grimes (Beijing: Foreign Languages Press, 1984).

There are abundant published source materials on the Korean conflict. Aside from *Jianguo yilai Mao Zedong wengao* and *Mao Zedong junshi wen-*

xuan (both noted above), see Peng Dehuai zhuanji bianxiezu, comp., *Peng Dehuai junshi wenxuan* [A selection of Peng Dehuai writings on military affairs] (Beijing: Zhongyang wenxian, 1988); and Zhongguo renmin kang-Mei yuanChao zonghui xuanchuanbu, comp., *Weida de kangMei yuanChao yundong* [The great resist-America, aid-Korea campaign] (Beijing: Ren-min, 1954), a collection of documents on domestic mobilization. For a selection of Korean War materials translated from *Jianguo yilai*, volume 1, see Li Xiaobing et al., "Mao's Despatch of Chinese Troops into Korea: Forty-Six Telegrams, July–October 1950," *Chinese Historians* 5 (Spring 1992): 63–86; Li Xiaobing and Glenn Tracy, "Mao's Telegrams During the Korean War, October-December 1950," *Chinese Historians* 5 (Fall 1992): 65–85. Goncharov et al., *Uncertain Partners*, 229–91, serves up a generous sampling of Chinese as well as Soviet documents on the origins of the war.

The subsequent Sino-American crisis over the Taiwan Strait and Vietnam is getting increasing scrutiny by scholars exploiting fragmentary PRC revelations and documentation. Zhang Shu Guang, *Deterrence and Strategic Culture: Chinese-American Confrontations, 1949–1958* (Ithaca: Cornell University Press, 1992), relates new information from Chinese sources to theoretical concerns with deterrence, calculated decision-making, and "learning" by policymakers. John W. Lewis and Xue Litai, *China Builds the Bomb* (Stanford: Stanford University Press, 1988), reveals how Mao's public dismissal of the American nuclear threat was belied by a high-priority program to create a Chinese bomb.

A long list of special studies helps further fill out our picture of PRC policy: Chen Jian, "China and the First Indochina War, 1950–54," *China Quarterly*, no. 133 (March 1993): 85–110; Qiang Zhai, "Transplanting the Chinese Model: Chinese Military Advisers and the First Vietnam War, 1950–1954," *Journal of Military History* 57 (October 1993): 689–715; Qiang Zhai, "China and the Geneva Conference of 1954," *China Quarterly*, no. 129 (March 1992): 103–22; Gordon H. Chang and He Di, "The Absence of War in the U.S.-China Confrontation over Quemoy and Matsu in 1954–1955: Contingency, Luck, Deterrence?" *American Historical Review* 98 (December 1993): 1500–24; Xiaobing Li, "Chinese Intentions and 1954–55 Offshore Islands Crisis," *Chinese Historians* 3 (January 1990): 45–59; He Di, "The Evolution of the People's Republic of China's Policy toward the Offshore Islands," in *The Great Powers in East Asia, 1953–1960* (cited above), 222–45; and Chen Jian, "China's Involvement with the Vietnam War, 1964–69," *China Quarterly* (forthcoming).

Our understanding of the PRC's Taiwan and Vietnam policies is, much like insights on Korea, in debt to the Chinese military. Xu Yan, *Jinmen zhi zhan (1949–1959 nian)* [The battle for Jinmen (1949–1959)] (Beijing: Zhongguo guangbo dianshi, 1992), and Zhongguo junshi guwentuan lishi bianxiezu, *Zhongguo junshi guwentuan yuanYue kangFa douzheng shishi* [Historical facts about the struggle by the Chinese military advisory team to assist Vietnam and resist France] (Beijing: Jiefangjun, 1990; "internal circulation"), are but examples from what is likely to become an imposing body of work.

Notes

1. The Pertinence of the Past

1. For a brief discussion of this interpretation emphasizing formal Marxist ideology and the "realist" or "national interest" alternative to it, see Friedrich W. Wu, "Explanatory Approaches to Chinese Foreign Policy: A Critique of the Western Literature," *Studies in Comparative Communism* 13 (Spring 1980): 52–55; and Bin Yu, "The Study of Chinese Foreign Policy: Problems and Prospect," *World Politics* 46 (January 1994): 237–42.

2. Paul A. Cohen, *Discovering History in China: American Historical Writing on the Recent Chinese Past* (New York: Columbia University Press, 1984), chaps. 1–2, offers the best introduction to the interpretation stressing the "middle kingdom" response. See also Wu, "Explanatory Approaches," 47–49. John K. Fairbank, ed., *The Chinese World Order: Traditional China's Foreign Relations* (Cambridge: Harvard University Press, 1968); and Mark Mancall, *China at the Center: 300 Years of Foreign Policy* (New York: Free Press, 1984), are prominent examples of this approach.

3. See the suggestive essay by John E. Wills, Jr., "Maritime China from Wang Chih to Shih Lang: Themes in Peripheral History," in *From Ming to Ch'ing: Conquest, Region, and Continuity in Seventeenth-Century China*, ed. Jonathan Spence and Wills (New Haven: Yale University Press, 1979), 201–38.

4. Yü Ying-shih, *Trade and Expansion in Han China: A Study in the Structure of Sino-Barbarian Relations* (Berkeley: University of California Press, 1967); Arthur F. Wright, *Buddhism in Chinese History* (Stanford: Stanford University Press, 1959); Edward H. Schafer, *The Golden Peaches of Samarkand: A Study of Tang Exotics* (Berkeley: University of California Press, 1963).

5. Ssu-yu Teng and John K. Fairbank, eds., *China's Response to the West: A Documentary Survey, 1839–1923* (Cambridge: Harvard University Press, 1954), 10.

6. The "Chronicle" (known in Chinese as the *Zhanguoce*) and the "Romance" (*San-guo yanyi*) are available in translation. See James I. Crump, Jr., *Chan-kuo Ts'e* (San Fran-cisco: Chinese Materials Center, 1979); and Moss Roberts, *Three Kingdoms: China's Epic Drama* (New York: Pantheon, 1976).

7. Morris Rossabi, ed., *China Among Equals: The Middle Kingdom and Its Neighbors, 10th–14th Centuries* (Berkeley: University of California Press, 1983); Jing-shen Tao, *Two Sons of Heaven: Studies in Sung-Liao Relations* (Tucson: University of Arizona Press, 1988).

8. J. I. Crump, Jr., *Intrigues: Studies of the Chan-kuo Ts'e* (Ann Arbor: University of Michigan Press, 1964), 30; Sima Qian, *War-Lords*, trans. William Dolby and John Scott (Edinburgh, Scotland: Southside, 1974), 90.

9. Legalism took a pessimistic view of human nature at odds with the Confucian emphasis on cultivation of virtue as the key to good rule. Thus the legalist set high store on stern rule and swift, severe punishment as the best means to preserve order and keep the state strong.

10. Hsi-sheng Ch'i, "The Chinese Warlord System as an International System," in *New Approaches to International Relations*, ed. Morton A. Kaplan (New York: St. Mar-tin's, 1968), 404–25.

11. See for example John D. Langlois, Jr., "Yü Chi and His Mongol Sovereign: The Scholar as Apologist," *Journal of Asian Studies* 38 (November 1978): 99–116.

12. The theme of power-sharing along the coast was first advanced by John K. Fair-bank, *Trade and Diplomacy on the China Coast: The Opening of the Treaty Ports, 1842–1854* (2 vols.; Cambridge: Harvard University Press, 1953). His notion of synar-chy made room for distinct Chinese and Manchu as well as foreign interests.

13. John Hunter Boyle, *China and Japan at War, 1937–1945: The Politics of Collabo-ration* (Stanford: Stanford University Press, 1972).

14. Frederic Wakeman, Jr., *Strangers at the Gate: Social Disorder in South China, 1839–1861* (Berkeley: University of California Press, 1966).

15. Population data from *The Cambridge History of China* [hereafter CHC], general ed. Denis Twitchett and John K. Fairbank (Cambridge, Eng.: Cambridge University Press, 1978–), 1: 206, 240; and Ping-ti Ho, *Studies on the Population of China, 1368–1953* (Cambridge: Harvard University Press, 1959), 10, 281. The process by which the cultural core expanded along multiple frontiers is treated in Sechin Jagchid and Van Jay Symons, *Peace, War, and Trade along the Great Wall: Nomadic-Chinese Interaction through Two Mil-lennia* (Bloomington: Indiana University Press, 1989); C. P. FitzGerald, *The Southern Expansion of the Chinese People* (New York: Praeger, 1972), chaps. 1–4; and Susan Naquin and Evelyn S. Rawski, *Chinese Society in the Eighteenth Century* (New Haven: Yale Uni-versity Press, 1987), esp. chap. 5. Arthur Waldron, *The Great Wall of China: From History to Myth* (Cambridge, Eng.: Cambridge University Press, 1990), helps demystify a potent frontier symbol, while exploring the meaning of the frontier to Chinese.

16. See Joseph Fletcher's masterful surveys of China's imperial heyday in "China and Central Asia, 1368–1884," in *The Chinese World Order*, 206–24; and in his contributions to CHC, vol. 10, chaps. 2, 7, 8.

17. Ho, *Studies on the Population of China*, 164–65.

18. This and the following paragraph on the northeast draw primarily on Robert H. G. Lee, *The Manchurian Frontier in Ch'ing History* (Cambridge: Harvard University Press, 1970).

19. Xu Nailin quoted in Thomas E. Ewing, "Ch'ing Policies in Outer Mongolia, 1900–1911," *Modern Asian Studies* 14 (1980): 151.

20. Thomas E. Ewing, *Between the Hammer and the Anvil? Chinese and Russian Policies in Outer Mongolia, 1911–1921* (Bloomington: Indiana University Research Institute for Inner Asian Studies, 1980).

21. June T. Dreyer, *China's Forty Millions: Minority Nationalism and National Integration in the People's Republic of China* (Cambridge: Harvard University Press, 1976), 22–26; Linda K. Benson, *The Ili Rebellion: The Moslem Challenge to Chinese Authority in Sinkiang, 1944–1949* (Armonk, N.Y.: M. E. Sharpe, 1990).

22. Dreyer, *China's Forty Millions*, 33–38; Melvyn C. Goldstein with Gelek Rimpoche, *A History of Modern Tibet, 1913–1951: The Demise of the Lamaist State* (Berkeley: University of California Press, 1989).

23. Mary F. Somers-Heidhues, *Southeast Asia's Chinese Minorities* (Hawthorn, Australia: Longman, 1974); FitzGerald, *The Southern Expansion of the Chinese People*, chaps. 8–10.

24. Yen Ching-hwang, *Coolies and Mandarins: China's Protection of Overseas Chinese during the Late Ch'ing Period (1851–1911)* (Singapore: Singapore University Press, 1985).

25. Jane Kate Leonard, *Wei Yuan and China's Rediscovery of the Maritime World* (Cambridge: Harvard East Asian Research Center, 1984); and the treatment of Wei Yuan by Susan Mann Jones and Philip Kuhn, in CHC, 10: 150–51, 154–55.

26. Fred W. Drake, *China Charts the World: Hsu Chi-yü and His Geography of 1848* (Cambridge: Harvard East Asian Research Center, 1975), 68.

27. Quoted in John K. Fairbank in CHC, 10: 248.

28. Yen-p'ing Hao and Erh-min Wang in CHC, 11: 172–88; John E. Schrecker, *Imperialism and Chinese Nationalism: Germany in Shantung* (Cambridge: Harvard University Press, 1971), chap. 2.

29. J. Y. Wong, *Yeh Ming-ch'en: Viceroy of Liang Kuang, 1852–8* (Cambridge, Eng.: Cambridge University Press, 1976).

30. Kwang-Ching Liu, "The Confucian as Patriot and Pragmatist: Li Hung-chang's Formative Years, 1823–1866," *Harvard Journal of Asiatic Studies* 30 (1970): 5–45.

31. Quotes from Feng in *Sources of Chinese Tradition*, ed. William Theodore de Bary et al. (New York: Columbia University Press, 1960), 708–710.

32. Mary B. Rankin, " 'Public Opinion' and Political Power: Qingyi in Late Nineteenth Century China," *Journal of Asian Studies* 41 (May 1982): 453–84.

33. Paul A. Cohen, "The Contested Past: The Boxers as History and Myth," *Journal of Asian Studies* 51 (February 1992): 82–113, makes a good case for the enduring power of a populist mythology in twentieth-century China.

34. Parks M. Coble, *Facing Japan: Chinese Politics and Japanese Imperialism,*

1. The Pertinence of the Past

1931–1937 (Cambridge: Harvard University Council on East Asian Studies, 1991); Youli Sun, *China and the Origins of the Pacific War, 1931–1941* (New York: St. Martin's, 1993); Lloyd E. Eastman, *Seeds of Destruction: Nationalist China in War and Revolution, 1937–1949* (Stanford: Stanford University Press, 1984); William C. Kirby, *Germany and Republican China* (Stanford: Stanford University Press, 1984).

35. Chen Boda quoted in Raymond F. Wylie, *The Emergence of Maoism: Mao Tse-tung, Chen Po-ta, and the Search for Chinese Theory, 1935–1945* (Stanford: Stanford University Press, 1980), 108.

2. The Crisis of the Late Qing, 1800–1912

1. Quoted in Felix Gilbert, "Machiavelli: The Renaissance of the Art of War," in *Makers of Modern Strategy from Machiavelli to the Nuclear Age*, ed. Peter Paret (Princeton: Princeton University Press, 1986), 19–20.

2. Zeng quote in Mary C. Wright, *The Last Stand of Chinese Conservatism: The T'ung-Chih Restoration, 1862–1874* (Stanford: Stanford University Press, 1957), 218.

3. Joseph Fletcher in *The Cambridge History of China* [hereafter CHC], general eds. Denis Twitchett and John K. Fairbank (Cambridge University Press, 1978–), 10: 375–85, draws attention to the inner-Asian origins of coastal policy.

4. Quoted by Kuo Ting-yee in CHC, 10: 492.

5. Samuel C. Chu and Kwang-Ching Liu, eds., *Li Hung-chang and China's Early Modernization* (Armonk, N.Y.: M. E. Sharpe, 1994).

6. Quote from Wright, "The Adaptability of Ch'ing Diplomacy," *Journal of Asian Studies* 17 (May 1958): 368. This article offers Wright's most pointed and forceful defense of late Qing foreign policy, though she makes the same salvage effort on a broader scale in *The Last Stand of Chinese Conservatism*.

7. Michael H. Hunt, *The Making of a Special Relationship: The United States and China to 1914* (New York: Columbia University Press, 1983), chap. 4.

8. Lloyd Eastman, *Throne and Mandarins: China's Search for a Policy during the Sino-French Controversy, 1880–1885* (Cambridge: Harvard University Press, 1967); Hyman Kublin, "The Attitude of China during the Liu-ch'iu Controversy, 1871–1881," *Pacific Historical Review* 18 (May 1949): 213–31.

9. Kwang-Ching Liu and Richard J. Smith in CHC, 11: 243.

10. Joseph W. Esherick, *The Origins of the Boxer Uprising* (Berkeley: University of California Press, 1987), chap. 10, offers a nicely integrated social, political, and diplomatic history of this last, most dramatic phase of the Boxer crisis.

11. Mary C. Wright, "The Rising Tide of Change," in *China in Revolution: The First Phase, 1900–1913*, ed. Wright (New Haven: Yale University Press, 1968), 1–63; Wellington Chan in CHC, vol. 11, chap. 8; Stephen R. MacKinnon, *Power and Politics in Late Imperial China: Yuan Shi-kai in Beijing and Tianjin, 1901–1908* (Berkeley: University of California Press, 1980); Daniel H. Bays, *China Enters the Twentieth Century: Chang Chih-tung and the Issues of a New Age, 1895–1909* (Ann Arbor: University of Michigan Press, 1978).

12. For a helpful survey of Sino-Japanese relations that reaches back to the late Qing, see Shinkichi Eto, "China's International Relations, 1911–1931," in CHC, 13: 83–103.

13. The following account of the turn to the United States draws on Hunt, *The Making of a Special Relationship*, chap. 6.

14. Zhang quoted in Hunt, *The Making of a Special Relationship*, 193.

15. John E. Schrecker, *Imperialism and Chinese Nationalism: Germany in Shantung* (Cambridge: Harvard University Press, 1971); Lee En-han, *China's Quest for Railway Autonomy, 1904–1911: A Study of the Chinese Railway-Rights Recovery Movement* (Singapore: Singapore University Press, 1977).

16. Ernest P. Young, *The Presidency of Yuan Shih-k'ai: Liberalism and Dictatorship in Early Republican China* (Ann Arbor: University of Michigan Press, 1977); Madeline Chi, *China Diplomacy, 1914–1918* (Cambridge: Harvard East Asian Research Center, 1970).

17. Shinkichi Eto in CHC, 13: 78–80.

18. The sketch that follows reflects the influence of the renewed interest in the state as an important and relatively autonomous political actor. See Peter B. Evans et al., eds., *Bringing the State Back In* (Cambridge, Eng.: Cambridge University Press, 1985), especially chaps. 1 and 11, and Theda Skocpol's *States and Social Revolutions: A Comparative Analysis of France, Russia, and China* (Cambridge, Eng.: Cambridge University Press, 1979), especially 1–41.

19. Figures from Peng Zeyi, *Shijiu shiji houbanqi de Zhongguo caizheng yu jingji* [Government finance and the economy in late-nineteenth-century China] (Beijing: Renmin, 1983), 123n1; and Liu and Smith in CHC, 11: 228, 238–39, 242. Morris Rossabi, "Muslim and Central Asian Revolts," in *From Ming to Ch'ing: Conquest, Region, and Continuity in Seventeenth-Century China*, ed. Jonathan Spence and John E. Wills, Jr. (New Haven: Yale University Press, 1979), 167–99, points to the Qing forward policy as the cause of this costly Muslim communal resurgence.

20. Peng, *Shijiu shiji houbanqi de Zhongguo caizheng yu jingji*, 123n1, 136. Susan Mann Jones and Philip Kuhn in CHC, 10: 144, set the cost of fighting the White Lotus somewhat lower—at 120 million taels.

21. Frederic Wakeman in CHC, 10: 212; Immanuel C. Y. Hsu, in CHC 11: 101, 108, 110; Albert Feuerwerker in CHC, 11: 65.

22. Feuerwerker in CHC, 11: 62.

23. Peng, *Shijiu shiji houbanqi de Zhongguo caizheng yu jingji*, 84, 86.

24. Marianne Bastid, "The Structure of the Financial Institutions of the State in the Late Qing," in *The Scope of State Power in China*, ed. Stuart R. Schram (London: University of London, School of Oriental and African Studies, 1985), 62–68, 75, 76; Kuo in CHC, 10: 514; Feuerwerker in CHC, 11: 62–65.

25. James M. Polachek, *The Inner Opium War* (Cambridge: Harvard Council on East Asian Studies, 1992); Sue Fawn Chung, "The Much Maligned Empress Dowager: A Revisionist Study of the Empress Dowager Tz'u-hsi (1835–1908)," *Modern Asian Studies* 13 (1979): 177–96, which attempts a partial rehabilitation; Beatrice S.

Bartlett, *Monarchs and Ministers: The Grand Council in Mid-Ch'ing China, 1723–1820* (Berkeley: University of California Press, 1991), esp. 275–78, which provides critical background on decisionmaking at the center.

26. Quoted in Esherick, *The Origins of the Boxer Uprising*, 289.

27. Zhang Zhenkun, "Qingmo shinianjian Zhongwai guanxishi de jige wenti" [Several issues in the history of Sino-foreign relations during the last years of the Qing], *Jindaishi yanjiu*, April 1982, no. 2, pp. 176–91, offers a nuanced assessment of this phase of China's relations with the powers.

28. Not until the late 1930s did the international system turn more favorable for China with the revival of active American opposition to Japan. China would continue to operate within the relatively favorable context of two-power rivalry even after World War II as Japanese-American conflict gave way to Soviet-American competition.

3. The Patriotic Impulse, 1890s–1910s

1. The long dominant tendency among historians was to see the intelligentsia around the turn of the century moving from a preoccupation with "the concept of the Celestial Empire" (or "the old cultural Sinocentrism"), to a "modern nationalism" at odds with Chinese culture, and ultimately on to "Marxism" when nationalism alone proved inadequate. While these phrases come from Lucien Bianco's widely read synthesis, *Origins of the Chinese Revolution, 1915–1949*, trans. Muriel Bell (originally published 1967; Stanford: Stanford University Press, 1971), 52, credit for helping this formulation take hold should go to Joseph R. Levenson's seductive writing, particularly *Liang Ch'i-ch'ao and the Mind of Modern China* (Cambridge: Harvard University Press, 1953), and *Confucian China and Its Modern Fate: The Problem of Intellectual Continuity* (Berkeley: University of California Press, 1958). Some recent work such as Zhang Yongjin, *China in the International System, 1918–20: The Middle Kingdom at the Periphery* (New York: St. Martin's Press, 1991), continues to work within a culturalism-nationalism framework. But other studies—notably Hao Chang's *Chinese Intellectuals in Crisis: Search for Order and Meaning (1890–1911)* (Berkeley: University of California Press, 1987), and James Townsend's "Chinese Nationalism," *Australian Journal of Chinese Affairs*, no. 27 (January 1992): 97–130—argue for giving more weight to the influence of indigenous outlooks and ideas and to the contemporary yearning for a moral order transcending nationalism than conceded by earlier studies preoccupied with the Western impact and the demise of "sinocentrism."

2. Benjamin I. Schwartz, "The Primacy of the Political Order in East Asian Societies: Some Preliminary Generalizations," in *Foundations and Limits of State Power in China*, ed. Stuart Schram (London: School of Oriental and African Studies, University of London, 1987), 1–10.

3. For helpful general introductions to nationalism, see Geoff Eley, "Nationalism and Social History," *Social History* 6 (January 1981): 83–107; John Breuilly, *Nationalism and the State* (New York: St. Martin's Press, 1982), esp. chap. 6; Benedict Anderson, *Imagined Communities: Reflections on Origin and Spread of Nationalism* (London: Verso, 1983);

Anthony D. Smith, *Theories of Nationalism* (2nd ed.; London: Duckworth, 1983); Arthur N. Waldron, "Theories of Nationalism and Historical Explanation," *World Politics* 37 (April 1985): 416–33; and E. J. Hobsbawn, *Nations and Nationalism since 1780: Programme, Myth, Reality* (2nd ed.; Cambridge, Eng.: Cambridge University Press, 1992), esp. Introduction. For recent discussions of nationalism in China: Townsend, "Chinese Nationalism," 113–19; Frank Dikötter's provocative, *The Discourse of Race in Modern China* (London: Hurst, 1992), 107–110; and Prasenjit Duara, "De-Constructing the Chinese Nation," *Australian Journal of Chinese Affairs*, no. 30 (July 1993): 1–29.

4. See for example Yu Danchu's richly researched studies: "Zhongguo jindai aiguozhuyi de 'wangguo shijian' chugao" [A preliminary examination of the "historical warnings from perished countries" in modern Chinese patriotism], *Shijie lishi*, 1984, no. 1, 23–31; and "Meiguo dulishi zai jindai Zhongguo de jieshao he yingxiang" [The introduction and impact of the history of American independence in modern China], *Shijie lishi*, 1987, no. 2, pp.60–81.

5. The wisdom of this solution is confirmed by Huynh Kim Khanh's sensitive treatment of Vietnamese revolutionaries, whose preoccupations were strikingly similar to that of the Chinese considered here. See *Vietnamese Communism, 1925–1945* (Ithaca: Cornell University Press, 1982), 26–34.

6. John E. Schrecker, "The Reform Movement of 1898 and the Ch'ing-I Reform as Opposition," in *Reform in Nineteenth-Century China*, ed. Paul A. Cohen and Schrecker (Cambridge: Harvard East Asian Research Center, 1976), 289–305, suggests that the militants of the 1870s and 1880s took an increasing interest in reform, eventually emerging as supporters of it in the late 1890s. This idea is further developed by Mary B. Rankin, "'Public Opinion' and Political Power: Qingyi in Late Nineteenth Century China," *Journal of Asian Studies* 41 (May 1982): 453–84.

7. Wang Tao quoted in Paul A. Cohen, *Between Tradition and Modernity: Wang T'ao and Reform in Late Ch'ing China* (Cambridge: Harvard University Press, 1974), 227, 229.

8. Kang quoted in Huang Zhangjian, *Kang Youwei wuxu zhenzouyi* [Kang Youwei's authentic 1898 memorials] (Taipei: Zhongyang yanjiuyuan lishi yuyan yanjiusuo, 1974), 507; and in Jonathan D. Spence, *The Gate of Heavenly Peace: The Chinese and Their Revolution, 1895–1980* (New York: Viking, 1981), 39, 49.

9. Kang quoted in Spence, *The Gate of Heavenly Peace*, 39.

10. Liang quoted in Chi-yun Chen, "Liang Ch'i-ch'ao's 'Missionary Education': A Case Study of Missionary Influence on the Reformers," *Papers on China* 16 (1962): 104–105.

11. Liang quoted in Martin Bernal, *Chinese Socialism to 1907* (Ithaca: Cornell University Press, 1976), 145. See also Chang Hao, *Liang Ch'i-ch'ao and Intellectual Transition in China, 1890–1907* (Cambridge: Harvard University Press, 1971).

12. Mary Wright, "The Rising Tide of Change," in *China in Revolution: The First Phase, 1900–1913*, ed. Wright (New Haven: Yale University Press, 1968), 1–63, emphasizes the impetus foreign policy reverses gave to domestic political developments in this period.

13. Roger V. DesForges, *Hsi-liang and the Chinese National Revolution* (New Haven: Yale University Press, 1973), offers a portrait of one prominent latter-day militant.

14. Quotes from *The Kuomintang: Selected Historical Documents, 1894–1969*, ed. Milton J. T. Shieh (New York: St. John's University Press, 1970), 1, 3. See also Harold Z. Schiffrin, *Sun Yat-sen and the Origins of the Chinese Revolution* (Berkeley: University of California Press, 1970).

15. Chen quoted in Jerome B. Grieder, *Intellectuals and the State in Modern China: A Narrative History* (New York: Free Press, 1981), 181. For a sketch of Chen, see Ernest P. Young, "Problems of a Late Ch'ing Revolutionary: Ch'en T'ien-hua," in *Revolutionary Leaders of Modern China*, ed. Chün-tu Hsüeh (New York: Oxford University Press, 1971), 210–47. The mounting discontent with Qing policy is amply documented in *JuE yundong, 1901–1905* [The movement to expel the Russians, 1901–1905], comp. Yang Tianshi and Wang Xuezhuang (Beijing: Zhongguo shehui kexue, 1979), 47–49, 60–62, 79–82, 108–109, 112–13, 134–35, 141, 154, 160–61, 163–77.

16. Michael H. Hunt, *The Making of a Special Relationship: The United States and China to 1914* (New York: Columbia University Press, 1983), 230–41.

17. Sun writing in November 1905, quoted in Shieh, *The Kuomintang*, 10.

18. Qiu quoted in Mary B. Rankin, *Early Chinese Revolutionaries: Radical Intellectuals in Shanghai and Chekiang, 1902–1911* (Cambridge: Harvard University Press, 1971), 46; and Song quoted in Don Price, *Russia and the Roots of the Chinese Revolution, 1896–1911* (Cambridge: Harvard University Press, 1974), 181.

19. Quote from Chow Tse-tsung, *The May Fourth Movement: Intellectual Revolution in Modern China* (Cambridge: Harvard University Press, 1964), 93.

20. Quote from Chow, *The May Fourth Movement*, 106.

21. "Beijing daxue pingmin jiaoyantuan" [Beijing University delegation for lecturing the common people], in *Wusi aiguo yundong*, comp. Zhongguo shehui kexueyuan jindai yanjiusuo jindai ziliao bianjizu (2 vols.; Beijing: Zhongguo shehui kexue, 1979), 1: 525.

22. Charlotte Furth in *The Cambridge History of China* [hereafter CHC], general ed. Denis Twitchett and John K. Fairbank (Cambridge, Eng.: Cambridge University Press, 1978–), 12: 382–83.

23. The list of early party figures who fit the pattern developed below could be extended. See for example Andrea McElderry, "Woman Revolutionary: Xiang Jingyu," *China Quarterly*, no. 105 (March 1986): 95–122; and Kamal Sheel, *Peasant Society and Marxist Intellectuals in China: Fang Zhimin and the Origins of a Revolutionary Movement in the Xinjiang Region* (Princeton: Princeton University Press, 1989), 145–71. There are, on the other hand, exceptions. Peng Dehuai was thrust by declining family fortunes into the labor market before even a teenager and later into the army. He thus lacked the opportunity not to mention the educational background to participate in the patriotic discourse. There is little evidence of his early political views beyond recollections in *Memoirs of Chinese Marshal: The Autobiographical Notes of Peng Dehuai (1898–1974)*, trans. Zheng Longpu and ed. Sara Grimes (Beijing: Foreign Languages Press, 1984), 22, of listening to Taiping tales told by a grand-uncle who had fought with the rebels.

3. The Patriotic Impulse

Deng Zhongxia appears to be an exception of another type. Though he attended Beijing University, participated in the May Fourth protests, and was active in the Marxist study group in Beijing, his writings in *Deng Zhongxia wenji* [Collected works of Deng Zhongxia], comp. Renmin chubanshe bianjibu (Beijing: Renmin, 1983) dating from late 1920 onward reveal an interest in labor organizing and education to the virtual exclusion of patriotic themes.

24. Chen quoted in Lee Feigon, *Chen Duxiu: Founder of the Chinese Communist Party* (Princeton: Princeton University Press, 1983), 33, 41; *JuE yundong*, 168 (for Chen's own 1903 remarks) and 173–75 (for the 1903 draft charter).

25. Chen quoted in Richard C. Kagan, "Chen Tu-hsiu's Unfinished Autobiography," *China Quarterly*, no. 50 (April-June 1972): 314.

26. Feigon, *Chen Duxiu*, 152 (quote); *JuE yundong*, 167–68.

27. Chen, "Patriotism and Consciousness of Self," November 1914, in Hélène Carrère d'Encausse and Stuart Schram, *Marxism and Asia: An Introduction with Readings* (London: Penguin, 1969), 204–206; Chen quoted in Grieder, *Intellectuals and the State*, 225.

28. *Duxiu wencun* [A collection of writings by (Chen) Duxiu] (reprint of 1922 original edition: 2 vols.; Jiulong: Yuandong, 1965) 1: 1–10.

29. Chen quoted in Zeng Leshan, *Wusi shiqi Chen Duxiu sixiang yanjiu* [A study of Chen Duxiu's thought during the May Fourth period] (Fuzhou: Fuzhou renmin, 1983), 53.

30. Deng Ye, "Shilun wusi houqi Chen Duxiu shijieguan de zhuanbian" [An exploration into the changes in Chen Duxiu's world view late in the May Fourth period], in *Chen Duxiu pinglun xuanbian* [A selection of critical essays on Chen Duxiu], ed. Wang Shudi et al. ([Zhengzhou?]: Henan renmin, 1982), 1: 379–405.

31. Li, "The Mandate of the Morning Bell," August 15, 1916, in Huang Sungk'ang, *Li Ta-chao and the Impact of Marxism on Modern Chinese Thinking* (The Hague: Mouton, 1965), 52.

32. Li, "Dayaxiya zhuyi" [Pan-Asianism], April 18, 1917; Li, "Dayaxiya zhuyi yu xinyaxiya zhuyi" [Pan-Asianism and new Asianism], January 1, 1919; Li, "Zailun xinyaxiya zhuyi" [Once more on New Asia-ism], November 1, 1919, all in *Li Dazhao wenji* [Collected works of Li Dazhao], comp. Yuan Qian et al. (2 vols.; Beijing: Renmin, 1984), 1: 450, 609–10; 2: 109–110.

33. Li, "The Victory of the Common People," October 15, 1918, in Huang, *Li Ta-chao*, 54, as well as Li, "Qiangguozhuyi" [The ideology of the strong state], March 16, 1919, and Li, "Mimi waijiao yu qiangdao shijie" [Secret diplomacy and the robbers' world], May 18, 1919, both in *Li Dazhao wenji*, 1: 668, 2: 1–3.

34. Li quoted in Maurice Meisner, *Li Dazhao and the Origins of Chinese Marxism* (Cambridge: Harvard University Press, 1967), 22–23, 27; Li, "Mimi waijiao," in *Li Dazhao wenji*, 2: 3; Li, "Xin Zhongguo minzuzhuyi" [Nationalism of the new China], February 19, 1917, in *Li Dazhao wenji*, 1: 302–303. For Li's views on the tradition of popular resistance, see Zhu Jianhua and He Rongdi, "Shilun Li Dazhao de fandi sixiang" [An exploration of Li Dazhao's anti-imperialist thought], in *Li Dazhao yanjiu*

3. The Patriotic Impulse

lunwenji [A collection of research papers on Li Dazhao], ed. Han Yide and Wang Shudi (2 vols.; Shijiazhuang: Hebei renmin, 1984), 2: 527.

35. Quotes from Li, "Dayaxiya zhuyi," April 18, 1917, and Li, "Lianzhizhuyi yu shijie zuzhi" [Federalism and world organization], February 1, 1919, both in *Li Dazhao wenji*, 1: 450, 621. See also Li, "Xin Zhongguo minzuzhuyi," Li, "Dayaxiya zhuyi yu xinyaxiya zhuyi," and Li, "Zailun xinyaxiya zhuyi," all in *Li Dazhao wenji*, 1: 302–303, 610–11; 2: 108–112.

36. Li, "A Comparative View of the French and Russian Revolutions," July 1, 1918, in Huang, *Li Ta-chao*, 50, 51; Li, "*Bolshevism* de shengli" [The victory of Bolshevism], December 1918, in *Li Dazhao wenji*, 1: 602, 603.

37. Li, "Zhanhou zhi shijie chaoliu" [Global trends after the war], February 7–9, 1919, in *Li Dazhao wenji*, 1: 627–31; Li, "The Luminous Asiatic Youth Movement," April 30, 1920, in Carrère d'Encausse and Schram, *Marxism and Asia*, 209.

38. Li Zehou and Vera Schwarcz, "Six Generations of Modern Chinese Intellectuals," *Chinese Studies in History* 17 (Winter 1983–84): 49.

39. Quotes from Zhang Guotao, *The Rise of the Chinese Communist Party: The Autobiography of Chang Kuo-t'ao* (2 vols.; Lawrence: University of Kansas Press, 1971–72), 1: 32, 87.

40. On the early Zhou years, see Huai En, *Zhou zongli shengping dashiji* [A chronological record of events in Premier Zhou's life] (Chengdu: Sichuan renmin, 1986), 1–80, and the richly documented volume by Jin Chongji, *Zhou Enlai zhuan, 1898–1949* [Biography of Zhou Enlai, 1898–1949] (Beijing: Zhongyong wenxian, 1989), chaps. 1–6.

41. Huai En, comp., *Zhou zongli qingshaonian shidai shiwenshuxinji* [A collection of writings from Premier Zhou's youth] (2 vols.; Chengdu: Sichuan renmin, 1979–80), 1: 108–112; Zhou essays from 1914–1917 in *Dangde wenxian*, no. 2 (1988), pp. 24–26.

42. Huai, *Zhou zongli qingshaonian shidai*, 1: 162.

43. The European writings are collected in Huai, *Zhou zongli qingshaonian shidai*.

44. Zhou to Chen Shizhou, January 30, 1921, in *Zhou Enlai tongzhi lüOu wenji xubian* [A supplement to the collected works from Comrade Zhou Enlai's period of residence in Europe], comp. Zhongguo geming bowuguan (Beijing: Wenwu, 1982), 71; Huai, *Zhou zongli qingshaonian shidai*, 1: 476.

45. Huai, *Zhou zongli qingshaonian shidai*, 2: 316, 321, 340–41, 359–60, 363, 387, 403–404, 408–15, 428, 432, 451–52, 459–61, 480, 483–85.

46. Nie Rongzhen, *Nie Rongzhen huiyilu* [The memoirs of Nie Rongzhen] (3 vols.; Beijing: Janshi, 1983, and Jiefangjun, 1984), 1: 4–9, 13, 22, 24, 26–29.

47. *Nie Rongzhen huiyilu*, 1: 13.

48. *Nie Rongzhen huiyilu*, 1: 26.

49. Michael Y. M. Kau and John K. Leung, comps., *The Writings of Mao Zedong* (Armonk, N.Y.: M. E. Sharpe, 1986-), 1: 268.

50. Mao quoted in Edgar Snow, *Red Star Over China* (originally published 1938; New York: Grove Press, 1961), 131. See also Xiao San, *Mao Zedong tongzhi de qingshaonian shidai* [Comrade Mao Zedong's boyhood and youth] (originally published

3. The Patriotic Impulse

1948; rev. and exp. ed., Guangzhou: Xinhua, 1950), 14–15; *Mao Zedong zaoqi wengao, 1912. 6–1920. 11* [Mao Zedong manuscripts from the early period, June 1912–November 1920], comp. Zhonggong zhongyang wenxian yanjiushi and Zhonggong Hunan shengwei "Mao Zedong zaoqi wengao" bianjizu (Changsha: Hunan, 1990; "internal circulation"), 585–86 and 590–91 (for classroom notes from November 1 and 15, 1913).

51. Mao to Xiao Zisheng, July 25, 1916, in *Mao Zedong zaoqi wengao*, 51–52.

52. Xiao San, *Mao Zedong tongzhi*, 14; Li Rui, *The Early Revolutionary Activities of Mao Tse-tung*, trans. Anthony W. Sariti and James C. Hsiung (White Plains, N.Y.: M. E. Sharpe, 1977), 44, 77, 150; Mao's testimony in Snow, *Red Star*, 132–34, 148.

53. Mao's detailed commentary penned sometime in 1917–1918 in a translation of F. Paulsen's *A System of Ethics*, in *Mao Zedong ji bujuan* [Supplements to the collected writings of Mao Zedong], ed. Takeuchi Minoru (9 vols.; Tokyo: Sososha, 1983–85) [hereafter *Mao bujuan*], 9: 19–47. Translated excerpts (misdated) in Jerome Ch'en, *Mao and the Chinese Revolution* (London: Oxford University Press, 1965), 44–45.

54. Quoted in Stuart Schram, CHC, 13: 794. Original: Mao to Li Jinxi, August 23, 1917, in *Mao Zedong zaoqi wengao*, 85–86.

55. Hsiao Yü (Siao-yu), *Mao Tse-tung and I Were Beggars* (Syracuse: Syracuse University Press, 1959), 138, 139 (quote), 193–94.

56. Snow, *Red Star*, 147–48 (quote) and 151.

57. *Xiangjiang pinglun* [The Xiang River review], July 14, 1919, in *Mao Zedong ji* [Collected writings of Mao Zedong], ed. Takeuchi Minoru (10 vols.; Tokyo: Hokubosha, 1971–72) [hereafter *Mao ji*], 1: 53–55. Full translation in M. Henri Day, *Mao Zedong, 1917–1927: Documents* (Stockholm: n.p., 1975), 81–83.

58. *Xiangjiang pinglun*, July 21 and 28, August 4, 1919, in *Mao ji*, 57–69. Full translation by Stuart R. Schram in *China Quarterly*, no. 49 (January–March 1972): 76–87, and in Day, *Mao Zedong*, 85–94.

59. *Mao ji*, 1: 54.

60. *Mao bujuan*, 1: 27–29, 91–92; *Mao ji*, 1: 65; *Mao Zedong zaoqi wengao*, 358–59.

61. *Mao ji*, 1: 58; *Mao bujuan*, 1: 47, 51, 53.

62. Mao's interest in Russia led to the formal establishment in fall 1920 of a Russia study society. Mao to Zhou Shizhao, March 14, 1920, and Mao in *Changsha dagongbao*, September 3, 1920, both in *Mao bujuan*, 1: 192–94, 217–18.

63. Mao to Cai Hesen et al., December 1, 1920, in *Mao Zedong shuxin xuanji* [Selected letters of Mao Zedong], comp. Zhonggong zhongyang wenxian yanjiushi (Beijing: Renmin, 1983), 2–3.

64. *Mao Zedong shuxin xuanji*, 8.

65. Mao to Ouyang Ze, November 25, 1920, in *Mao bujuan*, 1: 263.

66. Record of the meetings, January 1–3, 1921, in *Mao bujuan*, 2: 48, 49, 54.

67. See for example Theda Skocpol's deservedly influential *States and Social Revolutions: A Comparative Analysis of France, Russia, and China* (Cambridge, Eng.: Cambridge University Press, 1979), and the critique by Jerome L. Himmelstein and Michael S. Kimmel in *American Journal of Sociology* 86 (March 1983): 1145–54, arguing for a more voluntaristic interpretation.

4. The Rise of an International Affairs Orthodoxy, 1920–1934

1. Peter Zarrow, *Anarchism and Chinese Political Culture* (New York: Columbia University Press, 1990), 4.

2. The "manifesto" issued at the Second Congress (July 1922), in *Zhonggong zhongyang wenjian xuanji* [A selection of CCP Central Committee documents], comp. Zhongyang dang'anguan (14 vols.; Beijing: Zhonggong zhongyang dangxiao, 1982–87; "inner-party") [hereafter ZYWJ], 1: 64–79. A translation is in *The Communist Movement in China: An Essay Written in 1924 by Ch'en Kung-po*, ed. C. Martin Wilbur (New York: Octagon, 1966), 105–119.

3. "Jiaoyu xuanchuan wenti yijue'an" [Resolution on education and propaganda issues] approved by the first plenum of the third Central Executive Committee, November 1923, in ZYWJ, 1: 149. This document is incorrectly dated 1922 in *Zhongguo gongchandang xinwen gongzuo wenjian huibian* [A collection of documents on CCP journalism], comp. Zhongguo shehui kexueyuan xinwen yanjiusuo (3 vols.; Beijing: Xinhua, 1980), 1: 2–3. The example from 1934 is in *Zhonggong zhongyang kangRi minzu tongyi zhanxian wenjian xuanbian* [A selection of documents on the CCP Central Committee's national anti-Japanese united front], comp. Zhongyang tongzhanbu and Zhongyang dang'anguan (3 vols.; Beijing: Dang'an, 1984–86; "internal circulation") [hereafter KRMZ], 1: 248.

4. Membership figures cited here and below are drawn from Xiang Qing, *Gongchan guoji he Zhongguo geming guanxi shigao* [Draft history of the relations between the Comintern and the Chinese revolution] (Beijing: Beijing daxue, 1988), 255.

5. *Diguozhuyi tiedixia de Zhongguo* [China under the imperialists' iron heel] by Qi Shufen reflected the breadth of the appeal, drawing together in its preface late Qing advocates of rights recovery (Tang Shaoyi) and left-wing members of the Nationalist Party (Xu Jian) with those aligned with the CCP (Guo Moruo). The volume, first published in 1925, also appeared under the title *Ziben diguozhuyi yu Zhongguo* [Capitalist imperialism and China] and *Jingji qinluexia zhi Zhongguo* [China under economic invasion]. It had by 1933 gone through ten printings. See also Gao Ersong and Gao Erbo, eds., *Diguozhuyi yu Zhongguo* [Imperialism and China] (Shanghai: Qingnian zhengzhi xuanchuanhui, 1925), which was dominated by such CCP luminaries as Zhang Guotao, Qu Qiubai, Zhou Enlai, Zhao Shiyan, and Peng Shuzhi. On imperialism's place in schooling at mid-decade, see C. Martin Wilbur and Julie Lien-ying How, *Missionaries of Revolution: Soviet Advisers and Nationalist China, 1920–1927* (Cambridge: Harvard University Press, 1989), 672–74, 677; and Chen Hanchu, "Dageming shiqi Zhongguo gongchandang chuangli de Zhendong shehui kexueyuan" [The Zhendong social science academy established by the CCP during the great revolution], *Zhonggong dangshi ziliao*, no. 36 (1990): 254–58.

6. See for example Ma Zhemin, *Guoji diguozhuyi lun* [On international imperialism] (Shanghai: Kunlun, June 1929); the more mechanical treatment by Wu Junru, *Diguozhuyi duiHua sanda qinlue* [Imperialism's three great aggressions against China] (Shanghai: Minzhi, 1929); and *Guoji xinjumian* [The new international situation]

([Shanghai]: Beixin, August 1927) by Chen Hansheng, a respected sociologist then working secretly for the Comintern.

7. Harold Z. Schiffrin, *Sun Yat-sen and the Origins of the Chinese Revolution* (Berkeley: University of California Press, 1970), chap. 10.

8. The following account draws from Martin Bernal, *Chinese Socialism to 1907* (Ithaca: Cornell University Press, 1976), 142–47; Li Yu-ning, *The Introduction of Socialism into China* (New York: Columbia East Asian Institute, 1971), 10–14; and Michael H. Hunt, *The Making of a Special Relationship: The United States and China to 1914* (New York: Columbia University Press, 1983), 258–66.

9. Liang quoted in Bernal, *Chinese Socialism*, 145.

10. This discussion relies on A. James Gregor and Maria Hsia Chang, "Marxism, Sun Yat-sen, and the Concept of 'Imperialism'," *Pacific Affairs* 55 (Spring 1982): 66–78.

11. Sun quoted in Gregor and Chang, "Marxism, Sun Yat-sen, and the Concept of 'Imperialism'," 72n54.

12. Gregor and Chang, "Marxism, Sun Yat-sen, and the Concept of 'Imperialism'," 69n45.

13. This opportunism is an important theme in C. Martin Wilbur, *Sun Yat-sen: Frustrated Patriot* (New York: Columbia University Press, 1976).

14. *The Kuomintang: Selected Historical Documents, 1894–1969*, ed. Milton J. T. Shieh (New York: St. Johns University Press, 1970), 68, 74 (quote), 76–77, 80, 88.

15. Manifesto of the Second National Congress, in Shieh, *The Kuomintang*, 111–26 (quote from 123).

16. So Wai-chor, *The Kuomintang Left in the National Revolution, 1924–1931* (Hong Kong: Oxford University Press, 1991), 86 (quote from Shi Cuntong); Edmund S. K. Fung, "The Chinese Nationalists and the Unequal Treaties 1924–1931," *Modern Asian Studies* 21 (October 1987): 793–819; Fung, "Anti-Imperialism and the Left Guomindang," *Modern China* 11 (January 1985): 39–76; Arif Dirlik, "National Development and Social Revolution in Early Chinese Marxist Thought," *China Quarterly*, no. 58 (April–May 1974): 292–96; P. Cavendish, "Anti-imperialism in the Kuomintang 1923–8," in *Studies in the Social History of China and South-east Asia*, ed. Jerome Ch'en and Nicholas Tarling (Cambridge, Eng.: Cambridge University Press, 1970), 23–56. The left-wing of the Nationalist Party was associated with Wang Jingwei. Its foremost ideological spokesmen after 1928 were Chen Gongpo (a founding member of the CCP who had left the party) and Gu Mengyu (a Beijing University economics professor). Chiang resurrected the strong anti-imperialist theme in 1943 when he associated his name with *China's Destiny*, written at least in large part by Tao Xisheng. For a translations, see *China's Destiny and Chinese Economic Theory*, ed. Philip Jaffe (New York: Roy, 1947).

17. Manifesto adopted at the Second Congress, in ZYWJ, 1: 65, 66, 71. For an alternative translation, see Wilbur, *The Communist Movement*, 105–106, 110. For other early, key CCP statements, see ZYWJ, 1: 130–31 (July 1923), 228–31 (September 1924), 235–36 (November 1924), 317–21 (January 1925), 401–402 (November 1925).

18. Li Chunfan (Ke Bainian), *Diguozhuyi qianshuo* [An elementary introduction to

imperialism] (Shanghai: Xinwenhua, 1925); Zhang Jinglu, "Liening zhuzuo Zhong-yiben nianbiao" [A chronology of works by Lenin translated into Chinese], in his *Zhongguo chuban shiliao (bubian)* [Historical materials on Chinese publishing (supplement)] (Beijing: Zhonghua, 1957), 455. A new translation titled *Diguozhuyi lun* [On imperialism] was published by Qizhi in 1929 under Lenin's name (slightly veiled as Yil-iji or Ilyich). That edition was revised and reprinted in 1937 (publisher Xinzhi) and again in 1948 and 1949.

19. Nikolai Bukharin and Evgeny A. Preobrazhensky, *The ABC of Communism: A Popular Explanation of the Program of the Communist Party of Russia*, trans. Eden and Cedar Paul (reprint of original 1922 edition; Ann Arbor: University of Michigan Press, 1966), 100–115; Joseph Stalin, *Foundations of Leninism* (New York: International Publishers, 1939), 13–14 (quotes). Yueh Sheng, *Sun Yat-sen University in Moscow and the Chinese Revolution: A Personal Account* ([Lawrence]: University of Kansas Center for East Asian Studies, 1971), 24 and 64, comments on the circulation of *Foundations* as well as *The ABC* within the CCP in the 1920s.

20. Lawrence Sullivan and Richard H. Solomon, "The Formation of Chinese Communist Ideology in the May Fourth Era: A Content Analysis of *Hsin ch'ing nien*," in *Ideology and Politics in Contemporary China*, ed. Chalmers Johnson (Seattle: University of Washington Press, 1973), 154. Not until mid-decade was this heavy diet of writing on imperialism to find a popular appetite whetted by mounting anger against the powers. Chen Duxiu complained in a 1923 party congress report that "slogans calling for the overthrow of imperialism still have not had a great effect." Chen report of June 1923, in *Dangshi yanjiu*, no. 2 (1980), p. 43.

21. Wilbur and How, *Missionaries of Revolution*, 539–42.

22. Party center general notice no. 30, February 8, 1929, in ZYWJ, 5: 31.

23. Dirlik, "National Development and Social Revolution," 298 and 304, makes this point in relation to the theoretical debates of the late 1920s, but it applies more broadly.

24. Nikolai Bukharin, *Historical Materialism: A System of Sociology* (New York: Russell and Russell, 1965), 117; Stalin, *Foundations*, 14.

25. Stalin, *Foundations*, 14. This impatience was a strong theme in the early years of the CCP. See Arif Dirlik, *The Origins of Chinese Communism* (New York: Oxford University Press, 1989), 225–34; and Michael Y. L. Luk, *The Origins of Chinese Bolshevism: An Ideology in the Making, 1920–1928* (Hong Kong: Oxford University Press, 1990), 47–50, 64, 79–80.

26. ZYWJ, 3: 369.

27. See for example, the party center's claim in June 1922 (ZYWJ, 1: 18); Li Dazhao's remarks at the Fifth Comintern Congress in mid-1924 (*Dangshi ziliao lunji tongxun*, no. 9 (1985), p. 40); the resolution from the Fifth Party Congress of May 1927 (ZYWJ, 3: 49–50); and the draft resolution by Qu Qiubai from the enlarged Political Bureau meeting of November 1927 (ZYWJ, 3: 389–402).

28. Li in ZYWJ, 5: 67–97, 128–29. See also ZYWJ, 1: 277–78 (Fourth Party Congress of January 1925), 3: 50 (Fifth Party Congress of May 1927).

29. Stalin, *Foundations*, 35; Luk, *The Origins of Chinese Bolshevism*, 180 (on Qu).

30. On Mao: Tony Saich, *The Origins of the First United Front in China: The Role of Sneevliet (Alias Maring)* (2 vols.; Leiden: E. J. Brill, 1991), 2: 580, 590. On Li: ZYWJ, 6: 50. Li's critics made explicit that he wanted Soviet troops to march into China: ZYWJ, 7: 24 (Pavel Mif in January 1931) and 8: 505 (Bo Gu in February 1933).

31. ZYWJ, 4: 169, 5: 205–27.

32. These observations on the shifting appraisal of contradictions among the imperialists and implications for China from mid-1927 to mid-1930 are based on ZYWJ, 4: 25, 49, 94, 110–11, 113, 148, 150, 158, 164, 167–68, 173, 178, 180, 325, 355, 458–59, 5: 18–19, 74–78, 97–98, 128, 150–51, 204–206; 6: 51, 67–68, 180–81; and *Documents of the Chinese Communist Party, 1927–1930: Party in Action During Defeat*, ed. and trans. Hyobom Pak (Hong Kong: Union Research Institute, 1971), 478.

33. Resolution, May 9, 1931, in ZYWJ, 7: 287. For another good example, see general notice no. 20 (graced with an impressively scholastic twenty-six footnotes in the original!) of November 30, 1928, in ZYWJ, 4: 457–72.

34. That is to say, the third full meeting of the Central Committee selected at the previous party congress (in this case the Sixth Party Congress of 1928).

35. Bai Deng's hardline views, in *Zhongguo Suweiai* (reprint of original 1930 edition; Beijing: Beijing daxue, 1957), 27–28; Zhou Enlai's and Li Lisan's more moderate views in ZYWJ, 6: 347–48, 365, 417.

36. ZYWJ, 6: 426–27, 470; 9: 92–93; *Zhongguo jindai duiwai guanxi shiliao xuanji (1840–1949)* [A selection of historical materials on modern China's foreign relations (1840–1949)], comp. Fudan daxue lishixi Zhongguo jindaishi jiaoyanzu (4 vols.; Shanghai: Shanghai renmin, 1977), vol. 2, pt. 1, p. 283; "Waijiao zhengce" [Foreign policy] (c. November 1931), in *Dangshi ziliao zhengji tongxun*, 1986, no. 11, pp. 16, 33.

37. Dirlik, *The Origins of Chinese Communism*, 21–52; Luk, *The Origins of Chinese Bolshevism*, chap. 1, which deal with the earliest, increasingly positive assessments of the Bolshevik revolution by anarchists and the several stripes of socialists.

38. A translation of the manifesto is in Allen Whiting, *Soviet Policies in China, 1917–1924* (New York: Columbia University Press, 1954), 269–71. The quote is from 271. Soviet authorities quickly backpedaled on this manifesto's sweeping commitment to return all concessions, thus disappointing Chinese nationalists and roiling relations with the Beijing government. Bruce A. Elleman, "The Soviet Union's Secret Diplomacy Concerning the Chinese Eastern Railway, 1924–1925," *Journal of Asian Studies* 53 (May 1994): 459–86, highlights the widening gap between Soviet propaganda and policy.

39. Other Moscow-based organizations with links to China included the Labor and Peasant Internationals and the People's Commissariat for Foreign Affairs (i.e., the Soviet Foreign Ministry).

40. Wilbur and How, *Missionaries of Revolution*, 124.

41. Shieh, *The Kuomintang*, 118.

42. *Gongchandang* article in *"Yida" qianhou: Zhongguo gongchandang diyici daibiao dahui qianhou ziliao xuanbian* [Before and after the First Congress: a selection of materials from the time of the First Congress of the CCP], comp. Zhongguo shehui ke-

xueyuan xiandaishi yanjiushi and Zhongguo geming bowuguan dangshi yanjiushi (2 vols.; Beijing: Renmin, 1980; "internal circulation"), 1: 46, 184.

43. Quotes from ZYWJ, 1: 35, 71–72. Alternative translations in Wilbur, *The Communist Movement*, 111, 118.

44. *Li Dazhao wenji* [Collected works of Li Dazhao], comp. Yuan Qian et al. (2 vols.; Beijing: Renmin, 1984), 2: 577 (quote) as well as 661 and 664 (September 1923). Chen in ZYWJ, 1: 175. Translation available in Saich, *Origins*, 1: 363, where Chen is identified as the author and November 1922 is given as the date. Resolution on education and propaganda issues (November 1923), in ZYWJ, 1: 149. See also Peng Shuzhi's comparison of Soviet achievements with capitalist problems, in *Xiangdao zhoubao* [Guide Weekly], no. 90 (November 7, 1924): 749–51.

45. ZYWJ, 3: 475–77 (December 24, 1927), 4: 171 (Sixth Party Congress at mid-1928), 7: 270 (April 1931) and 525 (December 1931), 8: 434 (January 1933) and 740–41 (November 1933); KRMZ, 1: 65 (January 7, 1933).

46. Quotes from ZYWJ, 1: 443 (general notice no. 60 of October 28, 1925) and 5: 256 (resolution of the second plenum of the sixth Central Committee held in Shanghai in June 1929). Chen's comment from July 28, 1929, in ZYWJ, 5: 340–42. See also ZYWJ, 5: 201–202, 211, 313–14, 328–30, 382–84, 507.

47. Between 1921 and 1923 the Comintern subsidy to the CCP ran about $400 a month, virtually the entire party budget. After 1927 the money was used primarily for underground work, while military units were left largely to their own devices. During the early years the actual transfer of funds was arranged by courier or effected through the Shanghai branch of a European bank in which the Soviet government had an account. Finally, in 1934 the Shanghai link was cut; an arriving bagman found the underground smashed and no one to receive the funds. Saich, *Origins*, 1: 76; Chen Duxiu report at the Third Party Congress (June 1923), in *Dangshi yanjiu*, 1980, no. 2, p. 42, which confirms heavy financial dependence; a 1989 interview with a party history specialist in Beijing.

48. M. F. Yuriev and A. V. Pantsov, "Comintern, CPSU (B) and Ideological and Organizational Evolution of the Communist Party of China," in *Revolutionary Democracy and Communists in the East*, ed. R. Ulyanovsky (Moscow: Progress Publishers, 1984), 308.

49. The first class of the Communist University included Liu Shaoqi, Ren Bishi, Peng Shuzhi, and Xiao Jingguang. Sun Yat-sen University graduates included Zhang Wentian (Lo Fu), Dong Biwu, Chen Boda, Wang Ming, Wu Xiuquan, Deng Xiaoping, Lin Boqu, Ye Jianying, Wu Yuzhang, Xu Teli, Wang Jiaxiang, Bo Gu, and Yang Shangkun.

50. The translation and publications projects, which survived the university closing, produced some literal renditions of the Marxist classics that would become standard in China. See on these two institutions, Yuriev and Pantsov, "Comintern, CPSU (B) and Ideological and Organizational Evolution of the Communist Party of China," 298–313; and Jane L. Price, *Cadres, Commanders, and Commissars: The Training of the Chinese Communist Leadership, 1920–1945* (Boulder, Colo.: Westview,

1976), 32–38, 89–99. For a guide through the shifting constellation of Soviet schools, universities, institutes, and academies attended by Chinese revolutionaries, see Alexander Pantsov, "From Students to Dissidents: The Chinese Trotskyites in Soviet Russia (Part 1)," trans. John Sexton, *Issues and Studies* (Taibei) 30 (March 1994): 97–126.

51. Chinese students were at first under the control of the CCP's Moscow branch, but student resentment led to its dissolution in the summer of 1926. The students were then screened for membership in the Communist Party of Soviet Union.

52. Price, *Cadres, Commanders, and Commissars*, 31, 38–47, 113–27.

53. Saich, *Origins*, 1: 58n (quoting Zhang Guotao).

54. Saich, *Origins*, 1: 369–71, 2: 584–85, 589–90 (quote), 781, 808, 820; Xiang, *Gongchan guoji*, 33–37; Lee Feigon, *Chen Duxiu: Founder of the Chinese Communist Party* (Princeton: Princeton University Press, 1983), 166–70. Chen's record is clouded by his formal statements as party leader in 1922 and 1923 in favor of cooperation. See Saich, *Origins*, 1: 362–63; and ZYWJ, 1: 97–103, 114–15, 128. He reputedly was more critical in private and used his close associates, particularly Peng Shuzhi, to make his doubts public.

55. John W. Fitzgerald, "The Misconceived Revolution: State and Society in China's Nationalist Revolution, 1923–26," *Journal of Asian Studies* 49 (May 1990): 330–32; ZYWJ, 1: 269–70, 272–79 (resolution at the Fourth Party Congress in January 1925).

56. ZYWJ, 1: 403; Xiang, *Gongchan guoji*, 80–87; Wilbur and How, *Missionaries of Revolution*, 259–60, 270.

57. Cai report to the Comintern, February 10, 1926, summarized in *Dangshi ziliao tongxun*, 1988, no. 4, pp. 42–43.

58. ZYWJ, 2: 327–29 (Comintern appraisal), 3: 7–11 (manifesto of January 28, 1927); Xiang, *Gongchan guoji*, 103; Feigon, *Chen Duxiu*, 186–91.

59. ZYWJ, 3: 70–80.

60. ZYWJ, 3: 292; Hans J. van de Ven, *From Friends to Comrades: The Founding of the Chinese Communist Party, 1920–1927* (Berkeley: University of California Press, 1991), 229. Luo had attended the Foreign Language School in Shanghai, and in 1921 left to study at the Communist University of the Toilers of the East. After his return to China he worked in Canton, Beijing, Shanghai, and Wuhan. Elected to the Political Bureau at this meeting, he was captured and executed by the Nationalist in 1928.

61. Alexander Pantsov, "From Students to Dissidents: The Chinese Trotskyites in Soviet Russia (Part 2 and 3)," trans. John Sexton, *Issues and Studies* (Taibei) 30 (April 1994): 56–73 and (May 1994): 77–109; Sheng, *Sun Yat-sen University*, 128–31; Wang Fan-hsi, *Chinese Revolutionary: Memoirs, 1919–1949*, trans. Gregor Benton (Oxford, Eng.: Oxford University Press, 1980), 86. Wang wrote his memoirs in the 1950s.

62. Other prominent party members who joined Chen in open revolt included Liu Renjing, Luo Zhanglong, Peng Shuzhi, and Zhang Zhaolin. Dirlik, "National Development and Social Revolution," 290, 301–303; ZYWJ, 5: 403–421, 470–93.

63. ZYWJ, 4: 174–76, 184–85; Xiang, *Gongchan guoji*, 136–37, 147–52. Here and in

general one wishes the CCP documentation had more to say about relations with Moscow.

64. ZYWJ, 5: 257, 337–40, 371–74, 394–402, 465–69; Wang, *Chinese Revolutionary*, 203.

65. ZYWJ, 5: 150–51, 204–206.

66. Quote from ZYWJ, 6: 85. See also on Li's position in the first half of 1930, ZYWJ, 6: 49–50, 67–89, 148–49, 179–94, 211–13. Xiang, *Gongchan guoji*, 152–84, develops in some detail the contrary view that Li closely followed rather than deviated from the Comintern line.

67. For Comintern censure: ZYWJ, 6: 272, 408–411, 417. For Central Committee reaction: ZYWJ, 6: 284–85, 338–41, 346–48, 361–62, 365, 481–83. For Mif's censure: ZYWJ, 7: 24.

68. Prime examples of the party center's arid approach running from June 1931 to January 1934: ZYWJ, 7: 331, 411–17, 454, 489, 552; 8: 3–15, 116–22, 140–41, 170–76, 449, 502; 9: 136–38; KRMZ, 1: 1–3, 7–8, 10, 21–22, 32–35, 111, 184–89; *Wang Ming yanlun xuanji* [A selection of Wang Ming speeches], comp. Renmin chubanshe bianjibu (Beijing: Renmin, 1982; "internal circulation"), 271–73, 284–85, 289–93; *Zhongguo jindai duiwai guanxi*, vol. 2, pt. 1, pp. 237–39.

69. Sheng, *Sun Yat-sen University*, 253. The communications difficulties appear to have been particularly acute between 1928 and 1930 to judge from ZYWJ, 4: 132, 5: 18, 6: 470.

70. ZYWJ, 7: 303–304, 306–310; 8: 116–22, 140–41, 170–76, 193–202, 253–72; KRMZ, 1: 51–57.

71. Quotes from Irene Eber, "Images of Oppressed Peoples and Modern Chinese Literature," in *Modern Chinese Literature in the May Fourth Era*, ed. Merle Goldman (Cambridge: Harvard University Press, 1977), 132. Eber offers a suggestive examination of themes in literature that mirror political commentary.

72. Yu Danchu, "Zhongguo jindai aiguozhuyi de 'wangguo shijian' chugao" [A preliminary examination of the "historical warnings from perished countries" in modern Chinese patriotism], *Shijie lishi*, no. 1 (1984), pp. 23–31. *JuE yundong, 1901–1905* [The movement to expel the Russians, 1901–1905], comp. Yang Tianshi and Wang Xuezhuang (Beijing: Zhongguo shehui kexue, 1979)—to take but one body of documentary material from that time—is sprinkled with references to the "conquered nations," especially India and Poland. See for examples 82, 141–42, 155, 166, 168.

73. Zhang quoted in Hao Chang, *Chinese Intellectuals in Crisis: Search for Order and Meaning (1890–1911)* (Berkeley: University of California Press, 1987), 113.

74. Quotes from Zarrow, *Anarchism and Chinese Political Culture*, 106 (Li) and 176 (Liu). See also 112, 173–77.

75. Steven M. Goldstein suggests these variations in "The Chinese Revolution and the Colonial Areas: The View From Yenan, 1937–1941," *China Quarterly*, no. 75 (September 1978): 595–96.

76. Shieh, *The Kuomintang*, 112 (quote), 114; Fung, "The Chinese Nationalists," 800. According to So Wai-chor, *The Kuomintang Left in the National Revolution*, 83–85,

the Nationalist left sustained this vigorous internationalism after 1927. See for example Li Zuohua's *Shijie ruoxiao minzu wenti* [The problem of the world's small and weak nations] (Hankou: Baihe, 1928). Developing Sun's outlook and invoking his name, Li offered a wide-ranging treatment of the plight of colonial people from Korea to Taiwan to the Philippines to Ireland and Iceland.

77. Quotes from the manifesto issued on the formation of the Nationalist Party, August 13, 1912; manifesto of January 1, 1923; and manifesto issued on January 30, 1930, by the party's first national congress, all in Shieh, *The Kuomintang*, 38, 68, 80.

78. June T. Dreyer, *China's Forty Millions: Minority Nationalities and National Integration in the People's Republic of China* (Cambridge: Harvard University Press, 1976), 16–17; notes on Sun Yat-sen speech, March 6, 1921, in Saich, *Origins*, 1: 225; Walker Connor, *The National Question in Marxist-Leninist Theory and Strategy* (Princeton: Princeton University Press, 1984), 67.

79. Chiang, *China's Destiny and Chinese Economic Theory*, 30–40; Dreyer, *China's Forty Millions*, 17; Shieh, *The Kuomintang*, 196.

80. Manifesto of the Second Party Congress, in ZYWJ, 1: 71–72. Alternative translation in Wilbur, *The Communist Movement*, 110–11.

81. ZYWJ, 1: 271 (Fourth Party Congress resolution of January 1925), 4: 169 (Sixth Party Congress resolution of July 1928), 6: 212 (manifesto of August 1930); *Wang Ming yanlun xuanji*, 337 (quote), where the Wang Ming speech is correctly dated (alternative dating in ZYWJ, 9: 361). See also the commentary by Cai Hesen, Liu Renjing, Chen Duxiu, and Zheng Chaolin, all in *Xiangdao zhoubao*, no. 9 (November 8, 1922), 70; no. 12 (December 6, 1922), 95; no. 36 (August 15, 1923), 276; no. 58 (March 26, 1924), 462; no. 158 (June 16, 1926), 1541.

82. ZYWJ, 1: 78.

83. ZYWJ, 1: 175–76. Translation adapted from Saich, *Origins*, 1: 364, which corrects the dating and credits Chen with the authorship.

84. ZYWJ, 1: 419 (resolution of October 1925), 5: 58–60 (letter from the party center of February 1929), 7: 70 (general notice of January 1930).

85. Quotes from ZYWJ, 7: 467. Alternative translation in Dreyer, *China's Forty Millions*, 63–64. See also ZYWJ, 8: 11 (statement of January 1932), 9: 93 (outline of the Soviet constitution of January 1934); and KRMZ, 1: 206 (resolution of the fifth plenum of January 1934).

86. On the Sixth Party Congress: ZYWJ, 4: 234 (resolution of July 9, 1928). On Outer Mongolia: *Xiangdao zhoubao*, 19–20, 43–44, 57–59, 67–68, 87, 107–108, and 116 (covering September–December 1922), 1358, 1388–90, and 1402–1404 (covering March–April 1926), and 1952 (for January 1927). On Taiwan: Frank S. T. Hsiao and Lawrence R. Sullivan, "A Political History of the Taiwanese Communist Party, 1928–1931," *Journal of Asian Studies* 42 (February 1983): 269–89; Hsiao and Sullivan, "The Chinese Communist Party and the Status of Taiwan, 1928–1943," *Pacific Affairs* 52 (Fall 1979): 446–67; Li Dazhao talk of May 13, 1924, in Hélène Carrère d'Encausse and Stuart Schram, *Marxism and Asia: An Introduction with Readings* (London: Penguin, 1969), 219.

5. Toward Foreign Policy Autonomy, 1935–1945

1. *Zhonggong zhongyang wenjian xuanji* [A selection of CCP Central Committee documents], comp. Zhongyang dang'anguan (14 vols.; Beijing: Zhonggong zhongyang dangxiao, 1982–87; "inner-party circulation") [hereafter ZYWJ], 9: 420–21 (December 1934).

2. Benjamin Yang, *From Revolution to Politics: Chinese Communists on the Long March* (Boulder, Colo.: Westview, 1990).

3. In this latter phase the campaign also took as its target those within the party thought to be political opportunists, traitors, saboteurs, informants, or provocateurs. The resulting excesses, blamed on Kang Sheng, created grievances that delegates carried to the Seventh Party Congress and that forced a public apology from Mao. Peter J. Seybolt, "Terror and Conformity: Counterespionage Campaigns, Rectification, and Mass Movements, 1942–1943," *Modern China* 12 (January 1986): 39–53; Nie Rongzhen, *Nie Rongzhen huiyilu* [The memoirs of Nie Rongzhen] (3 vols.; Beijing: Janshi, 1983, and Jiefangjun, 1984), 560–66.

4. Li Yong, "Zhonggong qida tuichi zhaokai de qingkuang he yuanyin" [Conditions and causes for delays in summoning the Seventh Party Congress], *Dangde wenxian*, 1988, no. 3, pp. 60–61; Li Yongping and He Puqing, "Zhongguo gongchandang diqici quanguo daibiao dahui gaikuang" [A survey of the Seventh National Congress of the Chinese Communist Party], *Dangshi yanjiu*, 1982, no. 2, pp. 58–66.

5. Quotes from August 1923 and November 1925, in *Mao Zedong, 1917–1927: Documents*, trans. M. Henri Day (Stockholm: no publisher listed, 1975), 159 and 196.

6. This apt phrase is Stuart Schram's from his "Mao Tse-tung's Thought to 1949," in *Cambridge History of China*, vol. 13: *Republican China, 1912–1949*, part 2, ed. John K. Fairbank and Albert Feuerwerker (Cambridge, Eng.: Cambridge University Press, 1986), 808.

7. Quote from Day, *Mao Zedong*, 199. The original is in *Mao Zedong ji* [Collected writings of Mao Zedong], ed. Takeuchi Minoru (10 vols.; Tokyo: Hokubosha, 1971–72; Hong Kong reprint, 1975) [hereafter *Mao ji*], 1: 105. See also *Mao Zedong ji bujuan* [Supplements to the collected writings of Mao Zedong], ed. Takeuchi Minoru (9 vols.; Tokyo: Sososha, 1983–85) [hereafter *Mao bujuan*], 2: 19–20 (April 1923); Day, *Mao Zedong*, 158–60 (July 1923); *Mao ji*, 1: 97–98 (August 1923); Day, *Mao Zedong*, 195–200 (November 1925); *Mao bujuan*, 9: 176 (January 1926); *Mao ji*, 1: 201–203 (December 1926).

8. Quote from *Mao bujuan*, 9: 197. For other remarks underlining the importance of the countryside, see *Mao bujuan*, 9: 165 (June 1923); *Mao ji*, 1: 151 (January 1926), 1: 239–41 (March 1927); and *Mao bujuan*, 2: 277 (May 1927).

9. The prime examples of this head-counting dating from January and February 1926 can be found in *Mao bujuan*, 1: 143–49, and in Day, *Mao Zedong*, 292–300. For Mao's views on the minority in the middle and on the right, see Day, *Mao Zedong*, 1: 199; and *Mao bujuan*, 2: 143–44, 206; 9: 197. For an influential analysis of Mao's early populism, see Stuart R. Schram, "Mao Zedong and the Role of the Various Classes in

the Chinese Revolution, 1923–1927," in *The Polity and Economy of China* (Tokyo: Toyo Keizai Shinposha, 1975), 227–39.

10. Maurice Meisner early suggested this point in "Utopian Socialist Themes in Maoism," in *Peasant Rebellion and Communist Revolution in Asia*, ed. John Wilson Lewis (Stanford: Stanford University Press, 1974), 233–41.

11. Interpreting Mao's personal views during the Jiangxi Soviet years is hindered by his official standing as head of the government and the difficulty of determining his role in the drafting of the many, largely formal governmental pronouncements and declarations (usually co-signed by his colleagues) that are the main source for this period.

12. *Mao bujuan*, 3: 193–94.

13. For some prime expressions of these themes in 1929 and 1930, see *Mao bujuan*, 3: 13–15, 131, 162–63.

14. These phrases recur in *Mao ji*, 3: 13 (September 1931), 3: 326 (August 1933); *Mao bujuan*, 4: 218, 221–22 (June 1934); *Mao ji*, 4: 369 (July 1934); and *Suweiai Zhongguo* [Soviet China] (Moscow: Foreign Workers Press, 1933; Beijing reprint, 1957), 152 (July 1934).

15. *Mao ji*, 3: 360 (April 1934); *Mao bujuan*, 4: 222–23 (June 1934); *Mao ji*, 4: 375 (July 1934).

16. This tendency is evident in a large body of writing between September 1931 and July 1934: *Mao ji*, 3: 13–15, 61–63, 107–109, 115–18, 191–93, 199–201, 209–210, 219–21, 4: 304, 359–61, 369–70, 371; *Mao bujuan*, 4: 203, 215–19, 221–23; and *Suweiai Zhongguo*, 152–55, 157–58.

17. *Mao bujuan*, 4: 217 (June 1934); *Suweiai Zhongguo*, 154 (July 1934). For earlier warnings, see Day, *Mao Zedong*, 159 (July 1923); and *Mao ji*, 1: 93 (August 1923).

18. *Mao ji*, 3: 362, 365–66, 4: 23–28.

19. *Mao ji*, 3: 183–85 (January 1933), 3: 221 (May 1933), 4: 117–19 (November 1933), 215 and 281 (both January 1934); *Mao bujuan*, 4: 218–19 (June 1934); *Suweiai Zhongguo*, 153–55 (July 1934).

20. *Mao bujuan*, 2: 144.

21. *Mao ji*, 4: 219–31, 264–69, 280–81.

22. *Mao ji*, 2: 15–16 (October 1928), 129 (January 1930); *Mao bujuan*, 3: 83 (February 1930); *Mao ji*, 3: 62 (December 1931).

23. *Mao bujuan*, 3: 15.

24. *Mao ji*, 2: 132–33 (January 1930); *Mao bujuan*, 3: 62–63, 83 (February 1930), 9: 327–28 (June 1930), 3: 160–63 (October 1930); *Mao ji*, 3: 107–108 (March 1932); *Mao bujuan*, 4: 57 (July 1932); *Mao ji*, 3: 135 (September 1932), 410 (October 1932).

25. *Mao ji*, 3: 326.

26. On Tibet: *Mao ji*, 3: 361 (for August 1933) as well as *Mao ji*, 4: 14, and *Mao bujuan*, 4: 216. For the general survey of minority policy in January 1934, see *Mao ji*, 4: 266–67. For an earlier, perfunctory endorsement of self-determination for China's minorities, see *Mao bujuan*, 3: 14 (January 1929).

27. Kui-Kwong Shum, *The Chinese Communists' Road to Power: The Anti-Japanese National United Front, 1935–1945* (Hong Kong: Oxford University Press, 1988), 57.

28. For Mao's June-October 1920 discussions of provincial autonomy, see *Mao bujuan*, 1: 218, 242; 9: 98, 108–109.

29. *Mao ji*, 2: 19 (October 1928); *Mao bujuan*, 2: 312–13 (December 1928); *Mao ji*, 2: 128–29 (January 1930); *Mao bujuan*, 3: 83 (February 1930), 9: 327–28 (June 1930).

30. *Mao ji*, 3: 107–109 (March 1933 directive drafted by Mao), 323 (report of August 1933), 4: 220–21 (report of January 1934).

31. On the early, narrow united front, see *Zhonggong zhongyang kangRi minzu tongyi zhanxian wenjian xuanbian* [A selection of documents on the CCP Central Committee's national anti-Japanese united front], comp. Zhongyang tongzhanbu and Zhongyang dang'anguan (3 vols.; Beijing: Dang'an, 1984–86; "internal circulation") [hereafter KRMZ], 1: 15, 20, 25; ZYWJ, 8: 435. On the shift in June 1933: *Zhongguo jindai duiwai guanxi shiliao xuanji (1840–1949)* [A selection of historical materials on modern China's foreign relations (1840–1949)], comp. Fudan daxue lishixi Zhongguo jindaishi jiaoyanzu (4 vols.; Shanghai: Shanghai renmin, 1977), vol. 2, pt. 1, p. 253; and KRMZ, 1: 123, 125–26.

32. Quotes in KRMZ, 1: 255, 258. See also KRMZ, 1: 244–49, 260, 342; and ZYWJ, 9: 222, 232, 323–26.

33. ZYWJ, 9: 195–96 (party center in April); *Zhongguo jindai duiwai guanxi*, vol. 2, pt. 1, p. 255 (Soviet Republic in June); KRMZ, 1: 273ff (Bo Gu); ZYWJ, 9: 374–85 (Wang Ming).

34. The following account draws on Li Liangzhi, "On Wang Ming's Role in the Establishment of the Anti-Japanese National United Front," trans. K. K. Shum, *CCP Research Newsletter*, no. 5 (Spring 1990): 25–35, and no. 6 (Summer–Fall 1990): 23–31.

35. For this extensive correspondence, see *Mao Zedong shuxin xuanji* [Selected letters of Mao Zedong], comp. Zhonggong zhongyang wenxian yanjiushi (Beijing: Renmin, 1983), 30–97.

36. See especially *Mao Zedong zhuzuo xuandu* [A reader of works by Mao Zedong], comp. Zhonggong zhongyang wenxian bianji weiyuanhui (2 vols.; Beijing: Renmin, 1986), 1: 290–94 (November 1938), but also *Mao ji*, 6: 163–240 (October 1938). ZYWJ highlights the policy differences between a verbose Wang (10: 388–97, 408–417, 444–72, 520–51, 635–80) and Mao (10: 563, 579).

37. Central Committee [hereafter CC] directive (Mao draft), December 25, 1940, in *Mao bujuan*, 9: 381.

38. For Mao's dissatisfaction in 1939 and 1940 with the ideological level of party cadres and the unresponsiveness of military and base area leaders to Yanan directives, see *Mao bujuan*, 6: 22–23, 93, 163ff.

39. Party constitution approved June 11, 1945, in ZYWJ, 13: 53. See also Mao, "On Coalition Government," April 24, 1945, in George Stuart Gelder, *The Chinese Communists* (London: Gollancz, 1946), 21, 49–51 (translation from a contemporary text); and the pre-congress CC directive, March 15, 1945, in ZYWJ, 13: 47–49.

40. See ZYWJ, 11: 489–91, 628–29, 12: 494–95, 577.

41. *Mao ji*, 5: 243 (July 1937).

42. *Mao ji*, 6: 184 (October 1938 on the Soviet-Japanese pact), 7: 9–11, 13–14,

17–19, 57–68 (September 1939 on the Soviet-German pact), 301–305 (May 1941 on the Soviet-Japanese neutrality pact).

43. Dimitrov remarks at a meeting of the secretariat of the Comintern Executive Committee, August 10, 1937, in *Dangshi ziliao tongxun*, 1987, no. 10, p. 38; Shum, *The Chinese Communists' Road to Power*, 28–29 (for quotes); Xiang Qing, *Gongchan guoji he Zhongguo geming guanxi shigao* [Draft history of the relations between the Comintern and the Chinese revolution] (Beijing: Beijing daxue, 1988), 199–200, 202–203, 228–36; Thomas Kampen, "Wang Jiaxiang and Mao Zedong and the 'Triumph of Mao Zedong Thought' (1935–1945)," *Modern Asian Studies* 23 (October 1989): 714.

44. *Mao ji*, 9: 15–24; Xiang, *Gongchan guoji*, 250. The Comintern in fact maintained a poorly understood shadow existence following its formal disbanding with Dimitrov, its former head, still offering advice to the CCP as well as other parties.

45. Peter Vladimirov, *The Vladimirov Diary. Yenan, China: 1942–1945* (Garden City, N.Y.: Doubleday, 1975); Dimitrov letter to Mao written ostensibly in a personal capacity, December 22, 1943, in *Dangshi ziliao tongxun*, 1987, no. 10, p. 39; Shi Zhe with Li Haiwen, *Zai lishi juren shenbian: Shi Zhe huiyilu* [Alongside the giants of history: Shi Zhe's memoir] (Beijing: Zhongyang wenxian, 1991), 208–224, which includes a corrective to Vladimirov's account.

46. Zhonggong zhongyang dangshi yanjiushi "Zhonggong dangshi dashi nianbiao" bianxiezu, *Zhonggong dangshi dashi nianbiao shuoming* [Elucidation of "A chronology of major events in CCP history"] (Beijing: Zhonggong zhongyang dangxiao, 1983; "internal circulation"), 105.

47. Liu speech in Hélène Carrère d'Encausse and Stuart Schram, *Marxism and Asia: An Introduction with Readings* (London: Penguin, 1969), 260, 261; ZYWJ, 13: 91. Xu Quanxing and Wei Shifeng, *Yanan shiqi de Mao Zedong zhexue sixiang yanjiu* [A study of Mao Zedong's philosophical thought during the Yanan period] (Xian: Shaanxi renmin jiaoyu, 1988), 338–52, traces the rise between 1940 and 1945 of Mao's "thought" to dominance as the party orthodoxy.

48. See for example *Mao Zedong junshi wenxuan* [A selection of Mao Zedong works on military affairs], comp. Zhongguo renmin jiefangjun junshi kexueyuan (Beijing: Zhongguo renmin jiefangjun zhanshi, 1981; "internal circulation"; Tokyo reprint: Sososha, 1985), 72 (November 1935); *Selected Works of Mao Tse-tung* (5 vols.; Beijing: Foreign Languages Press, 1961–77), 1: 170–71 (December 1935); *China Weekly Review*, 78 (November 14, 1936): 378 (July 1936 interview with Edgar Snow); *Wenxian heyanjiu* (collection for 1986), 108–118 (September 1939); *Mao ji*, 5: 190 (quoted phrase from May 1937); *Selected Works of Mao Tse-tung*, 2: 63–64 (November 1937); and *Mao ji*, 6: 66 (May 1938), 71 (June 1938), 217 (October 1938). John W. Garver, "The Soviet Union and the Xi'an Incident," *Australian Journal of Chinese Affairs*, no. 26 (July 1991): 160–62, is one of a number of accounts that have tried to reconstruct the still poorly documented, behind-the-scenes effort by the CCP to secure Soviet assistance.

49. *Mao ji*, 6: 312 (February 1939), 7: 16 (September 1939), 98 and 137 (both December 1939).

50. Wang Tingke, "Gongchan guoji de 'Sulian liyi zhongxin' yu Zhongguo geming

liyi de maodun" [The contradiction between the Comintern's "centrality of Soviet interests" and the interests of the Chinese revolution], *Zhonggong dangshi yanjiu*, 1989, no. 2, pp. 32–33.

51. The CCP also got grudging Nationalist support between mid-1937 and early 1941 and thereafter not at all. The first stipend that the Nationalists paid out to the CCP in mid-1937 amounted to $500,000. John W. Garver's *Chinese-Soviet Relations, 1937–1945: The Diplomacy of Chinese Nationalism* (New York: Oxford University Press, 1988), 37–50; Shum, *The Chinese Communists' Road to Power*, 102; Kampen, "Wang Jiaxiang," 714.

52. *Mao ji*, 8: 109 (February 1942), 172 (October 1942); ZYWJ, 13: 31, 47 (early 1945); Vladimirov, *The Vladimirov Diary*, 261–62, 346–47, 365; Nanfangju dangshi ziliao zhengji xiaozu, comp., *Nanfangju dangshi ziliao* [Party history materials on the Southern Bureau: a chronicle of events] (Chongqing: Chongqing, 1986–), 3: 114–15 (August 1944).

53. KRMZ, 3: 790 (February 3, 1945); ZYWJ, 13: 29 (February 24, 1945), 47 (March 15, 1945). Vladimirov, *The Vladimirov Diary*, 346–47, 365, notes the divisions and vacillations in CCP leaders' views on Soviet intervention in February and March.

54. *Mao bujuan*, 8: 30–31, 36–37, 43, 46.

55. The account that follows suggests greater complexity and flux in Mao's approach to the United States than most accounts concede. (See the relevant section of the concluding "A Guide to the Literature.") An important piece of the evidentiary puzzle is, however, still missing: materials from and exchanges with Moscow which may have influenced Mao's thinking either positively or negatively.

56. *Mao junshi wenxuan*, 72–73.

57. Quotes from *Mao ji*, 5: 243. For a sampling of Mao's views from 1936 into early 1939, see Chang Kuo-t'ao, *The Rise of the Chinese Communist Party: The Autobiography of Chang Kuo-t'ao* (2 vols.; Lawrence: University of Kansas Press, 1971–72), 2: 478 (comments in late 1936); Edgar Snow, "Chinese Communists and World Affairs: An Interview with Mao Tse-tung," *Amerasia* 1 (August 1937): 264–66 (interview of July 1936); *Mao ji*, 5: 181–83 (March 1937 interview with Agnes Smedley), 189–90 (outline of a report of May 1937); T. A. Bisson, *Yenan in June 1937: Talks with Communist Leaders* (Berkeley: University of California Press, 1973), 54, 59–60 (interview of June 1937); *Mao ji*, 243 (statement of July 1937); Edgar Snow Papers (University Archives, University of Missouri, Kansas City), Interviews, file 3 (Mao interview with James Bertram of October 1937); *Mao ji*, 6: 172, 234–39 (report of October 1938); and *Mao junshi wenxuan*, 205 (January 1939 preface to "On Protracted War").

58. Mao interview with Philip J. Jaffe, June 22, 1937, Jaffe Papers (Special Collections, Robert W. Woodruff Library, Emory University), Box 15. A close variant of the Jaffe interview is in Bisson, *Yenan in June 1937*, 54.

59. See the discussion in the Propaganda Department telegram of July 13, 1944, in KRMZ, 3: 718–19, and the detailed analysis in the Southern Bureau's proposal of August 16, 1944, in *Nanfangu dangshi ziliao*, 3: 110–17 for examples of this pervasive tendency in CCP views of the United States.

60. Quote from January 1939 public statement, in *Mao junshi wenxuan*, 205. Translation in Stuart Schram, *The Political Thought of Mao Tse-tung* (New York: Praeger, 1963), 269–70.

61. Mao's observation on reciprocal economic advantage appears in his mid-1936 interview with Edgar Snow, in *Amerasia*, 1: 265–66.

62. Benchmarks in Mao's views in 1939 and 1940: Edgar Snow, *Random Notes on Red China (1936–1945)* (Cambridge: Harvard University Press, 1957), 69–70 (interview of September 1939); *Mao ji*, 7: 11–16 (interview of September 1939), 218–19 (speech of February 1940); *Mao bujuan*, 6: 155–56 (July 1940 decision drafted by Mao); and *Selected Works of Mao Tse-tung*, 2: 443 (December 1940 directive drafted by Mao).

63. *Mao ji*, 7: 309 (May 1941 circular drafted by Mao), 325–26 (commentary of May 1941); *Mao Zedong xinwen gongzuo wenxuan* [A selection of Mao Zedong works on journalism], comp. Zhonggong zhongyang wenxian yanjiushi and Xinhua tongxunshe (Beijing: Xinhua, 1983), 56.

64. Quote from *Mao ji*, 8: 21–22 (August 1941 statement drafted by Mao). See also *Mao ji*, 8: 9–14 (July 1941); and ZYWJ, 11: 713 (CC directive of July 12, 1941).

65. *Mao ji*, 8: 110.

66. KRMZ, 3: 582 (Secretariat directive to Zhou Enlai, December 8, 1941); *Mao ji*, 8: 41–42 (CC directive of December 9, 1941, drafted by Mao); ZYWJ, 11: 796–99 (CC directive of December 17, 1941); *Wenxian he yanjiu* (collection for 1985), 172–73 (Mao telegram to Liu Shaoqi, July 31, 1942).

67. *Selected Works of Mao Tse-tung*, 1: 157–58 (Wayaobao report of December 27, 1935); *Mao ji*, 5: 190 (May 1937); *Selected Works of Mao Tse-tung*, 1: 331–32 (August 1937); *Mao bujuan*, 5: 260–61 (August 1937); *Mao ji*, 7: 73–76 (October 1939), 119–21 (December 1939); and *Mao bujuan*, 6: 171–72 (October 1940), offer striking examples of Mao's preoccupation with this linkage.

68. For example, considerable effort went into the Snow visit (July–October 1936) and the Carlson visits (December 1937–February 1938 and again in 1939) to judge from Cheng Zhongyuan, "Zai Sinuo 'xixing' zhi qian" [Before Snow's "Journey to the West"], *Dangde wenxian*, 1992, no. 1, pp. 94-95; and *Nie Rongzhen huiyilu*, 484–86.

69. Xie Baoding and Xing Ruojun, "Chen Hansheng tongzhi zouguo de daolu" [The path traveled by comrade Chen Hansheng], in *Shanghai wenshi ziliao xuanji* 43 (1983): 141; Wang Xi and Yang Xiaofo, comps., *Chen Hansheng wenji* (Shanghai: Fudan daxue, 1985), 458.

70. These efforts are chronicled in *Nanfangju dangshi ziliao*, vol. 1.

71. Michael H. Hunt, "The CCP's American Friends," *CCP Research Newsletter*, no. 9 (Fall 1991): 3; *Chen Hansheng wenji*, 458. To date there is very limited evidence on the role that the U.S. Communist Party may have played as a source of information and guidance for the CCP's international policy and propaganda. Here as in other instances of inter-party relations, the materials coming out of China are largely silent.

72. *Mao ji*, 8: 172, 180 (October–November 1942).

73. *Mao bujuan*, 7: 119 (July 1943); ZYWJ, 12: 235–45 (CC manifesto of July 2, 1943).

74. The following treatment of plans for military cooperation with the United States draws on CC directives, July 1 and December 25, 1944, in ZYWJ, 12: 529, 655–57; Military Affairs Committee directives, July 5 and October 14 and 24, 1944, in ZYWJ, 12: 535–36, 632, 637; and Vladimirov, *The Vladimirov Diary*, 216–17, 229–30, and 284. A Southern Bureau proposal (received in Yanan on August 16, 1944) was a notable contribution to this strategy. Its detailed analysis of U.S. politics and policy toward China was read by Mao with care. *Nanfangju dangshi ziliao*, 3: 110–17.

75. CC directives of February 24 and 27 and March 6, 1945, in ZYWJ, 13: 27–30, 33, 41–42.

76. *Liberation Daily* editorial, July 4, 1944, quoted in Stuart R. Schram, *Mao Tse-tung* (New York: Penguin, 1967), 226. See also *Mao Zedong xinwen gongzuo*, 232–33 (July 12, 1943), 104–107 (July–October 1943); and *Mao ji*, 9: 127–31 (newspaper commentary published October 12, 1944).

77. CC directive, August 18, 1944, in ZYWJ, 12: 573–76; Yang Yunruo and Yang Kuisong, *Gongchan guoji he Zhongguo geming* [The Comintern and the Chinese Revolution] (Shanghai: Shanghai renmin, 1988), 577–79; Vladimirov, *The Vladimirov Diary*, 196, 213, 216–17, 229–30, 233.

78. Mao interview with delegation of journalists, June 12, 1944, in *Mao ji*, 9: 99–103; Mao welcoming remarks on the arrival of the Dixie mission, August 15, 1944, in *Mao Zedong xinwen gongzuo*, 317–21; Mao interview with John Service, August 23, 1944, in U.S. Department of State, *Foreign Relations of the United States* [hereafter FRUS], *1944*, vol. 6 (Washington: U.S. Government Printing Office, 1967), 604–614; Vladimirov, *The Vladimirov Diary*, 252–53, 255–56, 282–84, 312–16.

79. Zhonggong zhongyang wenxian yanjiushi, comp., *Zhou Enlai nianpu, 1898–1949* [A chronological biography of Zhou Enlai, 1898–1949] (Beijing: Zhongyang wenxian, 1989), 586–603; Mao interview with Col. David Barrett, December 8, 1944, in FRUS, 1944, 6: 727–32; David D. Barrett, *Dixie Mission: The United States Observer Group in Yenan, 1944* (Berkeley: University of California Center for Chinese Studies, 1970), 77–78 (on contacts with Mao and others in late December 1944); record of CCP talks with Hurley supplied by Chen Chiakang [c. April–May 1945], in Earl Browder Papers (microfilm of collection in George Arents Research Library, Syracuse University), manuscript series, reel 10/392 and subject files, reel 4/79.

80. Barbara W. Tuchman, "If Mao Had Come to Washington: An Essay in Alternatives," *Foreign Affairs* 51 (October 1972): 44 (for Mao-Zhou appeal of January 9, 1945 to "highest United States officials"); ZYWJ, 13: 26 (Zhou quote); Mao to Earl Browder, April 3, 1945, Browder Papers, correspondence series, reel 2/45; *Mao bujuan*, 8: 31; Tung Pi-wu [Dong Biwu], *Memorandum on China's Liberated Areas* (pamphlet; San Francisco: no publisher listed, May 18, 1945).

81. *Mao ji*, 9: 161 (January 10, 1945); *Mao bujuan*, 7: 224 (February 15, 1945).

82. *Mao bujuan*, 7: 220–25, 231.

83. The material in *Selected Works of Mao Tse-tung* for this period must be used with caution. *Mao ji* and *Mao bujuan* have fuller and more accurate texts from April to June 1945, though they lack the June 11 closing address (only in *Selected Works of Mao Tse-*

tung, 3: 271–73). For the portions of "On Coalition Government" (April 24) developing Mao's international program, see Gelder, *The Chinese Communists*, 2–5, 16, 21, 49–51. The original is in *Mao ji*, 9: 183–275. For relevant sections of other Mao talks from this time, see *Mao bujuan*, 7: 279 (sometime in April), 8: 24–37 (May 30); and *Mao ji*, 9: 179 (April 23), 278–79 (June 27). On the prospects for the U.S. economy and U.S. economic aid to China, see *Mao bujuan*, 8: 29–30; and Gelder, *The Chinese Communists*, 46.

84. ZYWJ, 13: 89–90 (Military Affairs Committee directive, June 15, 1945), 91–92 (CC directive, June 16, 1945), 95–96 (CC directive, June 24, 1945), 107 (Mao directive, July 22, 1945); KRMZ, 3: 807–808 (CC directive of June 17, 1945).

85. *Jiefang ribao*, June 14, 1945, in ZYWJ, 13: 88.

6. The Trials of Adversity, 1945–1951

1. Central Committee [hereafter CC] directive, July 15, 1945, Military Affairs Committee directive, July 22, 1945, and Mao directive, July 22, 1945, all in *Zhonggong zhongyang wenjian xuanji* [A selection of CCP Central Committee documents], comp. Zhongyang dang'anguan (14 vols.; Beijing: Zhonggong zhongyang dangxiao, 1982–87; "inner party circulation") [hereafter ZYWJ], 13: 103–108; Mao's extensive revisions to a New China News Agency commentary, July 22, 1945, in *Mao Zedong xinwen gongzuo wenxuan* [A selection of Mao Zedong works on journalism], comp. Zhonggong zhongyang wenxian yanjiushi and Xinhua tongxunshe (Beijing: Xinhua, 1983), 339–44.

2. CC directive of August 10, 1945, CC decision (drafted by Mao) of August 11, 1945, CC directive of September 2, 1945, and CC Propaganda Department notice of September 29, 1945, all in ZYWJ, 13: 115, 123–25, 141, 155–56; CC notice, October 1, 1945, in *Zhonggong zhongyang jiefang zhanzheng shiqi tongyi zhanxian wenjian xuanbian* [A selection of documents on the CCP Central Committee's united front during the period of liberation struggle], comp. Zhongyang tongzhanbu and Zhongyang dang'anguan (Beijing: Dang'an, 1988; "internal circulation") [hereafter JFSQ], 17.

3. Military Affairs Committee directives of September 28 and 29, 1945, and CC directives of October 9 and 15, 1945, all in ZYWJ, 13: 151–54, 162, 171–72; Wu Xiuquan, *Wode licheng* [My course] (Beijing: Jiefangjun, 1984), 169–70.

4. *Mao Zedong ji* [Collected writings of Mao Zedong], ed. Takeuchi Minoru (10 vols.; Tokyo: Hokubosha, 1971–72; Hong Kong reprint, 1975) [hereafter *Mao ji*], 9: 291–93. See also *Mao ji*, 9:295–301; *Mao Zedong xinwen gongzuo*, 342–44 (for Mao's additions to newspaper report); and ZYWJ, 13: 99–100 (slogans for eighth anniversary of the anti-Japanese war).

5. CC directive, October 6, 1945, in ZYWJ, 13: 161; New China News Agency commentary, September 30, 1945, in ZYWJ, 13: 157–58; CC directive, October 29, 1945, in ZYWJ, 13: 187–88; Military Affairs Committee directive, November 1, 1945, in *Dangde wenxian*, 1988, no. 1, p. 46; CC telegram (drafted by Mao) to Zhou Enlai and Wang Ruofei, November 7, 1945, in JFSQ, 28–29; CC to Northeast Bureau, November 28, 1945, in ZYWJ, 13: 218–19.

6. Here is another instance where the gaps in the newly available evidence render tentative any generalizations about CCP-Soviet relations.

7. Mao directive, July 22, 1945, in ZYWJ, 13: 107.

8. ZYWJ, 13: 114. Xiang Qing, *Gongchan guoji he Zhongguo geming guanxi shigao* [Draft history of the relations between the Comintern and the Chinese revolution] (Beijing: Beijing daxue, 1988), 268, contends that the CCP learned of Soviet plans belatedly and that Soviet forces initially made no effort to coordinate with party forces despite overtures by the latter.

9. Shi Zhe with Li Haiwen, *Zai lishi juren shenbian: Shi Zhe huiyilu* [Alongside the giants of history: Shi Zhe's memoir] (Beijing: Zhongyang wenxian, 1991), 308.

10. CC directive, October 12, 1945, in ZYWJ, 13: 165–66. This directive was drafted by Mao according to JFSQ, 19. See also inner-party reports, September 13 and 26, 1945, and CC directive (Mao draft), November 5, 1945, in JFSQ, 13–14, 24–25. Mao suffered from poor health in the late fall and had to step back from daily decisionmaking. Nie Rongzhen, *Nie Rongzhen huiyilu* [The memoirs of Nie Rongzhen] (3 vols.; Beijing: Janshi, 1983, and Jiefangjun, 1984), 671, notes Mao's illness but not its precise nature.

11. This transmitter would remain in operation through the balance of the decade except for a hiatus following the fall of Yanan in March 1947. CC directives, August 26 and 29, 1945, in JFSQ, 7–9; ZYWJ, 13: 138–39; Wu, *Wode licheng*, 167–68.

12. CC to central bureaus, September 19, 1945, in ZYWJ, 13: 147–48; CC telegram to Central China Bureau, September 20, 1945, in *Dangde wenxian*, 1988, no. 1, pp. 42–43; CC directive sent out by the Secretariat, September 21, 1945, in ZYWJ, 13: 149–50.

13. Military Affairs Committee directive of September 28, 1945 (ZYWJ, 13: 151–52); CC directive of October 19, 1945 (ZYWJ, 13: 176–77); Military Affairs Committee directive of November 1, 1945 (*Dangde wenxian*, 1988, no. 1, p. 46).

14. The dramatic reversal of northeast strategy is spelled out in the CC directive, November 20, 1945 (ZYWJ, 13: 207). Wu, *Wode licheng*, 172–73, offers a dramatic version of the encounter when Peng Zhen (head of the Northeast Bureau) argued with the Soviet commander against the CCP abandoning Shenyang. The commander responded angrily that he would drive the CCP forces out of the city with tanks if they did not leave on their own accord. Wu then describes the contentious regional bureau meeting in which Peng collided with his military associate, Lin Biao, over the best strategy to follow in the wake of the Soviet reversal. The dramatic adjustment forced on the Northeast Bureau by the Soviet shift is also evident in Peng Zhen, *Peng Zhen wenxuan (1941–1990 nian)* [The selected works of Peng Zhen (1941–1990)] (Beijing: Renmin, 1991), 103–110, and in Chen Yun, *Chen Yun wenxuan* [The selected works of Chen Yun] (3 vols.; Beijing: Renmin, 1984–86), 1: *(1926–1949)*, 221–24.

15. Northeast Bureau, November 26 and 29, 1945, in ZYWJ, 13: 208–210, 219–23; CC directive, November 28, 1945, in JFSQ, 32.

16. ZYWJ, 13: 151–52, 237–39.

17. For evidence on these morale problems, see *Jiefang ribao* editorial, October 19,

1945, in JFSQ, 290–94; CC directives, October 15 and 20, 1945, in ZYWJ, 13: 171–73, 182–83; and *Nie Rongzhen huiyilu*, 593–95.

18. The fullest statement is the CC directive, October 20, 1945, in ZYWJ, 13: 182–83. See also CC directive (Mao draft), September 2, 1945, in ZYWJ, 13: 140–41; CC directive, August 11, 1945, in ZYWJ, 13: 182–83; CC Propaganda Department notice, September 29, 1945, in ZYWJ, 13: 155–56; CC notice, October 10, 1945, in JFSQ, 17; CC directives, October 6 and 29, 1945, in ZYWJ, 13: 161, 187–88; CC directives, November 5 and 28, 1945, in JFSQ, 27, 32; and Zhu De interview with the foreign press, November 28, 1945, in ZYWJ, 13: 214–17.

19. CC directive to Dong Biwu and Wang Ruofei, December 1, 1945, in JFSQ, 33.

20. CC telegram to Dong Biwu and Wang Ruofei, December 9, 1945, in JFSQ, 34; Lu Dingyi speech, December 9, 1945, in ZYWJ, 13: 229–36; New China News Agency to branch offices, December 15, 1945, in *Xinhuashe wenjian ziliao xuanbian* [A selection of documentary materials on the New China News Agency], comp. Xinhuashe xinwen yanjiubu (4 vols.; n.p.: no publisher listed, n.d. [c. 1981–87]), vol. 1: *1931–1949*, pp. 32–33; CCP "spokesperson," December 17, 1945, in ZYWJ, 13: 242–43; CC directive, December 19, 1945, in ZYWJ, 13: 247–48; CC directive of December 20, 1945, in ZYWJ, 13: 249; CCP proposal for renewal of talks, December 27, 1945, in ZYWJ, 13: 253.

21. CC directives, December 20–21, 1945, January 3, 4, 5, 11, 12, 1946, and Military Affairs Committee directive, January 17, 1946, all in ZYWJ, 13: 249–52, 259–61, 270–71, 272, 301. By the end of January the CCP had gotten more than 200,000 troops into the northeast (according to CC directive, January 26, 1946, in JFSQ, 52–53).

22. ZYWJ, 13: 318–22. For other evidence of discontent with the January agreements, see CC directive to the Chongqing delegation, January 26, 1946, in JFSQ, 52–53; and CC directive to the Northeast Bureau, January 26, 1946, in ZYWJ, 13: 315–17.

23. CC directive to Chongqing delegation, January 21, 1946, in JFSQ, 50–51; CC telegram to the Northeast Bureau, February 12, 1946, in JFSQ, 77–78 (quote); CC directive (drafted by Mao) to Zhou Enlai, April 20, 1946, in JFSQ, 97; CC telegram to the Chongqing delegation, April 30, 1946, in *Dangde wenxian*, 1988, no. 1, p. 53; CC directive, May 15, 1946, in ZYWJ, 13: 400–401.

24. ZYWJ, 13: 396–97.

25. CC directive, January 11, 1946, in ZYWJ, 13: 270–71; CC directive to the Chongqing delegation, January 26, 1946, in JFSQ, 52–53 (quote); CC directive to the Northeast Bureau, January 26, 1946, in ZYWJ, 13: 315–17; CC telegram to the Northeast Bureau, February 12, 1946, in JFSQ, 77–78; CC directive to the Northeast Bureau, February 18, 1946, in JFSQ, 82; CC directive on propaganda, February 25, 1946, in ZYWJ, 13: 331–32; CC directive to the Northeast Bureau, March 24, 1946, in ZYWJ, 13: 356.

26. CC directive, March 15, 1946, CC directive to the Northeast Bureau, March 24, 1946, Military Affairs Committee directive, April 4, 1946, CC directive to the Northeast Bureau and Lin Biao, April 12, 1946, CC directive to Peng Zhen and Lin Biao,

April 19, 1946, CC directive, May 15, 1946, and CC directive to Lin and Peng, May 19, 1946, all in ZYWJ, 13: 344–46, 356, 363–64, 377, 387–88, 401, 404; CC directive (Mao draft) to Chongqing delegation, April 1, 1946, and CC directive to Chongqing delegation, May 28, 1946, both in JFSQ, 94, 105–107; Mao draft of CC telegram, June 1, 1946, in *Mao Zedong junshi wenxuan* [A selection of Mao Zedong works on military affairs], comp. Zhongguo renmin jiefangjun junshi kexueyuan (Beijing: Zhonguo renmin jiefangjun zhanshi, 1981; "internal circulation"; Tokyo reprint, 1985), 280.

27. Mao to Yu Guangsheng (editor-in-chief of *Jiefang ribao*), May 22, 1946, in *Xinhuashe wenjian*, 1: 34; CC directive to the Chongqing delegation, May 28, 1946, in JFSQ, 105–107; Mao public statement of June 22, 1946, and CC directive on propaganda (drafted by Mao according to JFSQ, 110), July 6, 1946, both in ZYWJ, 13: 422–23, 440. Other items in the propaganda campaign: JFSQ, 111–17, 123–24; ZYWJ, 13: 412–17, 426–27, 441–48; *Zhongguo jindai duiwai guanxi shiliao xuanji (1840–1949)* [A selection of historical materials on modern China's foreign relations (1840–1949)], comp. Fudan daxue lishixi Zhongguo jindaishi jiaoyanzu (4 vols.; Shanghai: Shanghai renmin, 1977), vol. 2, pt. 2, pp. 382–87; and *Xinhuashe wenjian*, 1: 65–67. A translation of the July 7, 1946 manifesto is available in U.S. Department of State, *Foreign Relations of the United States* [hereafter FRUS], *1946*, vol. 9 (Washington: U.S. Government Printing Office, 1972), pp. 1310–16.

28. CC directive, March 15, 1946, in ZYWJ, 13: 344–46; CC directives to Chongqing delegation, March 16 and May 28, 1946, in JFSQ, 86–87 (quote), 105–107; CC directive, May 15, 1946, in ZYWJ, 13: 400–401; CC directive, June 19, 1946, in *Dangde wenxian*, 1988, no. 1, pp. 54–55; CC directive, July 2, 1946, in JFSQ, 109. For a relatively optimistic estimate on the overall military situation, see CC telegram to Zhou Enlai, July 5, 1946, in *Dangde wenxian*, 1988, no. 1, p. 56.

29. Mao directive in reply to Li and Huang, July 6, 1946, in JFSQ, 109–110. See also Mao's revision along similar lines of a Northeast Bureau resolution, July 11, 1946, in *Mao junshi wenxuan*, 287–88.

30. Propaganda Department directive, July 21, 1946, CC directive to Zhou Enlai, August 12, 1946, and CC statements, October 18 and November 10, 1946, all in JFSQ, 123 (quote), 125–26, 130–34; Mao interview with A. T. Steele, September 19, 1946, in *Mao ji*, 10: 58; CC statements, August 29, and October 18, 1946, in ZYWJ, 13: 478, 506–508. For *Liberation Daily* commentary for August through October, see *Zhongguo jindai duiwai guanxi*, vol. 2, pt. 2, pp. 325–30, 335, 387–88; and ZYWJ, 13: 482–89, 497.

31. Zhonggong zhongyang wenxian yanjiushi (under the direction of Jin Chongji), *Zhou Enlai zhuan, 1898–1949* [Biography of Zhou Enlai, 1898–1949] (Beijing: Renmin and Zhongyang wenxian, 1989), 662–63; CC directive to Dong Biwu, January 16, 1947, in JFSQ, 143–44; Mao to Chen Jinkun, January 16, 1947, in *Mao Zedong shuxin xuanji* [Selected letters of Mao Zedong], comp. Zhonggong zhongyang wenxian yanjiushi (Beijing: Renmin, 1983), 280. Mirroring the shift in policy is the distinct shift in tone in Zhou's December 13, 1946 speech in Yanan, in *Selected Works of Zhou Enlai*, comp. Editorial Committee on Party Literature of the CCP Central Committee (2

vols.; Beijing: Foreign Languages Press, 1981), 1: 278; and in *Liberation Daily* editorials, in ZYWJ, 13: 522–32.

32. For the ample evidence on Mao's central role in directing the major campaigns of the civil war, see *Mao junshi wenxuan*, pt. 2. Additional material on Mao's central military role appears in the other, more general collections, especially ZYWJ and the Takeuchi Minoru series of Mao's writings.

33. Anna Louise Strong, "A World's Eye View from a Yenan Cave: An Interview with Mao Tze-tung," *Amerasia* 11 (April 1947): 122–26. The English-language version of the interview is the basis for the accurate translation back into Chinese in *Mao ji*, 10: 47–55, and for the heavily edited text in *Selected Works of Mao Tse-tung* (5 vols.; Beijing: Foreign Languages Press, 1961–77), 4: 97–101. The circumstances surrounding Strong's visit is described in Tracy B. Strong and Helene Keyssar, *Right in Her Soul: The Life of Anna Louise Strong* (New York: Random House, 1983), 216–29. The implications of the "paper tiger" theme for domestic propaganda is spelled out in Mao to Lu Dingyi, September 27, 1946, in *Mao shuxin*, 275–76. The theme echoes in CC directive (Mao draft), October 1, 1946, in *Selected Works of Mao Tse-tung*, 4: 117.

34. Mao's brief new year message, in *Mao ji*, 10: 61; Lu Dingyi's lengthy "Interpretation of several basic issues regarding the postwar international situation" of January 2, 1947, in ZYWJ, 13: 555–68. A translation of the *Jiefang ribao* version (January 4–5, 1947) of Lu's piece appears in U.S. Department of State, *United States Relations with China, with Special Reference to the Period 1944–1949* (Washington: U.S. Government Printing Office, 1949), 710–719. For other developments of these themes, see Zhou Enlai to Song Qingling, December 17, 1946, in *Wenxian he yanjiu* (collection for 1983), 65–66; Zhou Enlai's extended critique of American policy provided by the New China News Agency, December 28, 1946, in JFSQ, 134–39; and the *Liberation Daily* comment, January 1, 1947, in ZYWJ, 13: 548.

35. Zhang Min, "Jianguo chuqi zhenfan douzheng gaishu" [A survey of the struggle to suppress counter-revolutionaries in the early years of the PRC], *Dangde wenxian*, 1988, no. 2, pp. 38–40; Junshi kexueyuan junshi lishi yanjiubu, *Zhongguo renmin jiefangjun zhanshi* [A battle history of the People's Liberation Army of China] (3 vols. to date; Beijing: Junshi kexue, 1987–), 3: 395–97; *Nie Rongzhen huiyilu*, 715ff. For two illuminating local studies touching briefly on resistance, see Ezra F. Vogel, *Canton Under Communism: Programs and Politics in a Provincial Capital, 1949–1968* (Cambridge: Harvard University Press, 1969), 61–65; and Elizabeth J. Perry, *Rebels and Revolutionaries in North China, 1845–1945* (Stanford: Stanford University Press, 1980), 258.

36. *Nie Rongzhen huiyilu*, 693–94, and Liu Shaoqi talk to cadre conference, July 1, 1948, in *Dangshi yanjiu*, 1980, no. 3, p. 14 (both on concerns over American military intervention in 1948); directive drafted by Mao and issued with the approval of the Political Bureau, January 8, 1949, and Mao telegram, May 23, 1949, both in *Mao junshi wenxuan*, 328–29, 337–38; Military Affairs Committee, telegram of May 3, 1949, in *Dangde wenxian*, 1989, no. 4, p. 44.

37. *Selected Works of Mao Tse-tung*, 4: 370–73. Mao subjected this important speech

to editing subsequent to its delivery. There is to date no copy of the original available for comparison.

38. JFSQ, 161; ZYWJ, 14: 430. For Chen Duxiu's influential formula stressing a principled approach to diplomatic relations, see his January 1927 invitation to all countries (even imperialists) to recognize the Nationalist government on the basis of respect for independence and equality. *Xiangdao zhoubao*, January 11, 1927, p. 1912.

39. *Selected Works of Mao Tse-tung*, 4: 371.

40. Statement by the People's Liberation Army General Headquarters, April 30, 1949, in *Mao ji*, 10: 278; Military Affairs Committee, telegrams of April 23 and 28, 1949, in ZYWJ, 14:639–40, and *Dangde wenxian*, 1989, no. 4, p. 43 respectively. See also Zhou's statement on the moderate CCP position on dealings with the United States in remarks to non-party leaders, April 17, 1949, in *Selected Works of Zhou Enlai*, 1: 360–62.

41. Huang Hua, "A True Account of John Stuart's Departure from China," *Beijing Review* 34 (October 22–28, 1990): 32–35; FRUS, 1949, vol. 8 (Washington: U.S. Government Printing Office, 1974), 741–42, 745–46, 752–53, 766–67; Yu-ming Shaw, *An American Missionary in China: John Leighton Stuart and Chinese-American Relations* (Cambridge: Harvard University Council on East Asian Studies, 1992), 250–59, which deals with not only the Huang-Stuart but also other CCP-U.S. contacts in this confused period, including an overture from Zhou (almost certainly bogus) and Chen Mingshu's attempt at playing an intermediary role. Chen carried Stuart's concerns to Beijing in June, and reported back in early July that Mao and Zhou felt cooperation between countries with different political lines was possible.

42. Mao's remarks at the Political Consultative Conference, June 15, 1949, in *Mao ji*, 10: 283–85; FRUS, 1949, 8: 769.

43. On the Shenyang case (still thinly documented), see the contemporary Chinese indictment in *Shenyang Meiguo jiandie an* [The American spy case in Shenyang] (Guangzhou: Xinhua, 1950); New China News Agency main office to its northeast branch and *Dongbei ribao*, December 3, 1949, in *Xinhuashe wenjian*, vol. 2: *1949–1953*, p. 32; and Chen Jian, "The Ward Case and the Emergence of Sino-American Confrontation, 1948–1950," *Australian Journal of Chinese Affairs*, no. 30 (July 1993): 149–70, which minimizes evidence supporting CCP charges of U.S. espionage. The Acheson-Mao exchange of barbs in August 1949 is treated in more detail at the end of this chapter. On the continued sparring in early 1950: *Jianguo yilai Mao Zedong wengao* [Mao Zedong manuscripts for the period following the establishment of the country], comp. Zhonggong zhongyang wenxian yanjiushi (Beijing: Zhongyang wenxian, 1987– ; "internal circulation") [hereafter JGYL], 1: 245–48; Hu Qiaomu's public statement, translated in *China Digest* 7 (February 1, 1950): 10–11; and the repeated attacks on Acheson in New China News Agency, *Daily News Release*, March 19–April 2, 1950.

44. On terms for diplomatic recognition: JGYL, 1: 15; and propaganda guidance by the main office of the New China News Agency, October 19, 1949, in *Xinhuashe wenjian*, 2: 18. On the barracks seizure and the Soviet-backed U.N. initiative: JGYL, 1: 235, 241.

45. CC directive, February 7, 1948, in JFSQ , 188–89; CC directive, January 19, 1949, in ZYWJ, 14: 514–18; Mao's address to the second plenum of the seventh Central Committee on March 5, 1949, in *Selected Works of Mao Tse-tung*, 4: 370. On the missionary presence: *Zhongguo gongchandang xinwen gongzuo wenjian huibian* [A collection of documents on CCP journalism], comp. Zhongguo shehui kexueyuan xinwen yanjiusuo (3 vols.; Beijing: Xinhua, 1980; "internal circulation"), 1: 206; and ZYWJ, 14: 515–16.

46. CC directive, November 8, 1948, in JFSQ , 222–26; CC directives, January 19 and 25, 1949, in ZYWJ, 14: 516, 531; CC directive, February 10, and CC regulations, January 18, 1949, both in *Zhongguo gongchandang xinwen gongzuo*, 1: 265–66, 272.

47. Mao statement, March 5, 1949, in *Selected Works of Mao Tse-tung*, 4: 371.

48. CC propaganda guidance, July 5, 1947, in JFSQ , 161; CC directive, January 19, 1949, in ZYWJ, 14: 515; FRUS, 1949, 8: 370, 373, 377–78, 379, 763, and vol. 9 (Washington: U.S. Government Printing Office, 1974), 976–77, 992; Yang Ruichang, "Zongguan Mao Zedong de duiwai jingji jiaowang sixiang" [An overview of Mao Zedong's thinking on foreign economic contact], *Dangde wenxian*, 1991, no. 2, p. 75; Wang Dongxing, *Wang Dongxing riji* [Wang Dongxing's diary] (Beijing: Zhongguo shehui kexue, 1993), 163.

49. Gao Gang sought to become Stalin's man in China, according to Ivan V. Kovalev, interviewed by Sergei N. Goncharov, in "Stalin's Dialogue with Mao Zedong," trans. Craig Seibert, *Journal of Northeast Asian Studies* 10 (Winter 1991–92): 45–76. This account by Stalin's liaison with Mao in 1949 suggests a level of subterfuge, manipulation, and anxiety in high-level CCP-Soviet relations that goes beyond anything suggested by materials from the Chinese side.

50. Bo Yibo, *Ruogan zhongda juece yu shijian de huigu* [Reflections on some major decisions and incidents] (2 vols.; Beijing: Zhonggong zhongyang dangxiao, 1991), 1: 36; *Mao ji*, 10: 183, 185–89; *Mao Zedong ji bujuan* [Supplements to collected writings of Mao Zedong], ed. Takeuchi Minoru (10 vols.; Tokyo: Sososha, 1983–85), 8: 217, 219, 223, 233; Niu Jun, *Cong Yanan zouxiang shijie: Zhongguo gongchandang duiwai guanxi de qiyuan* [Moving from Yanan toward the world: the origins of Chinese Communist foreign relations] (Fuzhou: Fujian renmin, 1992), 272–73; Liu Shaoqi, "On Internationalism and Nationalism," November 1, 1948, in *Collected Works of Liu Shao-ch'i* (3 vols.; Hong Kong: Union Research Institute, 1968–69), 2: 140 (quote).

51. On the specialists sent to the northeast, see Kovalev and Goncharov, "Stalin's Dialogue with Mao Zedong," 46–47. On the Mikoyan mission, see the detailed participant account by Shi Zhe, *Zai lishi juren shenbian*, 372–88.

The questions surrounding the Mikoyan visit nicely illustrate the documentary gap still plaguing our understanding generally of Sino-Soviet relations. Xiang, *Gongchan guoji*, 280, suggests that Mikoyan urged the CCP to stop its military advance at the Yangzi River, so as not to precipitate a crisis that would draw in American forces. Such a stand would have been consistent with Stalin's current preference for a mediated end to the Chinese conflict. An article by Yu Zhan and Zhang Guangyou in *Dangde wenxian*, 1989, no. 1, pp. 56–58, sees no evidence that Stalin tried to block the CCP advance. For Xiang Qing's response, see *Dangde wenxian*, no. 6 (1989), pp. 64–66. Nikita Khrushchev, *Khrushchev Remembers: The Glasnost Tapes*, trans. and ed. Jerrold L. Schecter and Vyacheslav V. Luchkov (Boston: Little, Brown, 1990), 143, contends that Mikoyan also presented Stalin's claims to an economic role in Xinjiang. Nie Rongzhen, who was not privy to the talks, contends that Mikoyan had simply come to appraise the state of the CCP and its military forces. *Nie Rongzhen huiyilu*, 675.

52. Kovalev and Goncharov, "Stalin's Dialogue with Mao Zedong," 63–64.

53. "On the People's Democratic Dictatorship," June 30, 1949, celebrated the twenty-eighth anniversary of the founding of the CCP. The translation here is based on Conrad Brandt et al., *A Documentary History of Chinese Communism* (Cambridge: Harvard University Press, 1952), 453–56, and revised on basis of the original in *Mao ji*, 10: 296–99. The translation in *Selected Works of Mao Tse-tung*, 4: 411–23, diverges somewhat from the original. *Mao shuxin*, 327, reveals the role of Mao's secretary, Hu Qiaomu, in drafting the speech.

54. This and the paragraph that follows rely on Zhu Yuanshi, "Liu Shaoqi yijiusi-jiu nian mimi fangSu" [Liu Shaoqi's secret visit to the Soviet Union in 1949], *Dangde wenxian*, 1991, no. 3, pp. 74–80. Kovalev and Goncharov, "Stalin's Dialogue with Mao Zedong," 53–57, has Gao Gang proposing during the visit handing over the northeast to the USSR, privately denouncing his colleagues, and otherwise sowing dissension. This Russian account also claims that Stalin refused Liu's request for help in taking Taiwan.

55. JGYL, 1: 131, 135. Participant accounts of the Moscow summit treated here and the paragraphs that follow: Shi, *Zai lishi juren shenbian*, 433–72; Wu Xiuquan, *Eight Years in the Ministry of Foreign Affairs, January 1950–October 1958: Memoirs of a Diplomat* (Beijing: New World Press, 1985), 7–27; N. Fedorenko, "The Stalin-Mao Summit in Moscow," *Far Eastern Affairs* (Moscow), 1989, no. 2, pp. 134–48; Kovalev and Goncharov, "Stalin's Dialogue with Mao Zedong," 57, 64, 71–72; and Andrei Gromyko, *Memoirs*, trans. Harold Shukman (New York: Doubleday, 1990), 249–50.

56. This and the following paragraph are based on Mao's telegram from Moscow to the CCP CC, January 2 and 3, 1950, in JGYL, 1: 211–13.

57. Shijie zhishi, comp., *Zhonghua renmin gongheguo duiwai guanxi wenjianji* [A documentary collection on PRC foreign relations] (10 vols.; Beijing: Shijie zhishi, 1957–65), 1: 76 (quote). A translation of the security agreement is available in Grant F. Rhode and Reid E. Whitlock, *Treaties of the People's Republic of China, 1949–1978* (Boulder, Colo.: Westview, 1980), 15b–16. Sergei N. Goncharov, John W. Lewis, and Xue Litai, *Uncertain Partners: Stalin, Mao, and the Korean War* (Stanford: Stanford University Press, 1993), chap. 4, offers a preliminary reconstruction of the summit talks that produced these agreements

58. He Di, " 'The Last Campaign to Unify China': The CCP's Unmaterialized Plan to Liberate Taiwan, 1949–1950," *Chinese Historians* 5 (Spring 1992): 1–16.

59. Kathryn Weathersby, "The Soviet Role in the Early Phase of the Korean War: New Documentary Evidence," *Journal of American-East Asian Relations* 2 (Winter 1993): 430, 441–42.

60. *Nie Rongzhen huiyilu*, 744; Bruce Cumings, *The Origins of the Korean War*, vol. 2: *The Roaring of the Cataract, 1947–1950* (Princeton: Princeton University Press, 1990), 362–63; Chen Jian, "The Sino-Soviet Alliance and China's Entry into the Korean War" (Washington: Woodrow Wilson Center Cold War International History Project occasional paper, n.d. [1992?], 13n, 22–23.

61. Michael Y. M. Kau and John K. Leung, eds., *The Writings of Mao Zedong, 1949–1976* (Armonk, N.Y.: M. E. Sharpe, 1986-), 1: 118; Zhonghua renmin gongheguo waijiaobu and Zhonggong zhongyang wenxian yanjiushi, comps., *Zhou Enlai waijiao wenxuan* [Selected diplomatic writings of Zhou Enlai] (Beijing: Zhongyang wenxian, 1990), 18–19; *Renmin ribao*, June 29, 1950.

62. Chai Chengwen and Zhao Yongtian, *Banmendian tanpan: Chaoxian zhanzheng juan* [The Panmunjom talks: a volume on the Korean War] (Beijing: Jiefangjun, 1989), 34–36; Zhang Xi, "Peng Dehuai shouming shuaishi kangMei yuanChao de qianqian houhou" [The full story of Peng Dehuai's appointment to head the resistance to the United States and the assistance to Korea], *Zhonggong dangshi ziliao*, no. 31 (1989): 118–20; JGYL, 1: 429, 454, 469; Chai Chengwen and Zhao Yongtian, *KangMei yuan- Chao jishi* [A record of resisting America and aiding Korea] (Beijing: Zhonggong dang-shi ziliao, 1987; "internal circulation"), 46–47, 51. On downgrading Taiwan, see Xu Yan, *Jinmen zhi zhan (1949–1959 nian)* [The battle for Jinmen (1949–1959)] (Beijing: Zhongguo guangbo dianshi, 1992), 142–44.

63. Chai and Zhao, *KangMei yuanChao jishi*, 55; Zhang, "Peng Dehuai shou-ming," 123; Xu Yan, *Diyici jiaoliang: KangMei yuanChao zhanzheng de lishi huigu yu fansi* [The first test of strength: a historical review and evaluation of the war to resist America and aid Korea] (Beijing: Zhongguo guangbo dianshi, 1990), 22; Weath-ersby, "The Soviet Role in the Early Phase of the Korean War," 435–36, 452–56. For what purports to be the text of Kim's October 1 appeal for help, see Ye Yumeng, *Chubing Chaoxian: KangMei yuanChao lishi jishi* [Sending troops to Korea: a histori-cal record of resistance to American and assistance to Korea] (Beijing: Beijing shiyue wenyi, 1990), 39–40.

64. Chai and Zhao, *KangMei yuanChao jishi*, 47, 50, 55, 58, 61–62, 64–65, 68, 74, 76, 78, 86; Zhang, "Peng Dehuai shouming," 143; JGYL, 1: 545, 2: 43–44; *Mao junshi wenxuan*, 685; Qi Dexue, *Chaoxian zhanzheng juece neimu* [The inside story of the Korean War decisions] (Shenyang: Liaoning daxue, 1991), 184–85; Du Ping, *Zai zhiyuanjun zongbu* [With the headquarters of the volunteer army] (Beijing: Jiefangjun, 1989), 127, 165, 176–77, 185.

65. Mao's cable to Stalin, October 2, 1950, in JGYL, 1: 539–41.

66. Zhang, "Peng Dehuai shouming," 147–48. Shi Zhe, who accompanied Zhou as translator, has offered a detailed description of the trip that is often not congruent with other sources and thus has to be used with care. See Shi, *Zai lishi juren shenbian*, 495–502. For alternative accounts, see Hong Xuezhi, *KangMei yuanChao zhanzheng huiyi* ["Recollections of the war to resist U.S. aggression and aid Korea"] (Beijing: Jiefangjun wenyi, 1990), 25–27; and Qi, *Chaoxian zhanzheng*, 62–63 (for the recollec-tions of Kang Yimin, another member of Zhou's party). For details on the ensuing

Soviet aid program that included air support in Korea, see Xu, *Diyici jiaoliang*, 30–32; Hong, *KangMei yuanChao*, 184; and Goncharov et al., *Uncertain Partners*, 199–201.

67. Contemporary rumor and later Red Guard indictments claimed the opposition came variously from Gao Gang, Liu Bocheng, Lin Biao, Peng Dehuai, Dong Biwu, and Chen Yun. Later Chinese sources concede inner-party differences in early October but are for the most part circumspect in naming names. Lin Biao was almost certainly a holdout. Zhou Enlai may also have had doubts.

68. Zhang, "Peng Dehuai shouming," 124–27; transcript of the Zhou-Pannikar meeting, October 3, 1950, in *Zhou Enlai waijiao wenxuan*, 25. Zhang's account, which offers the most detailed treatment of the October meetings, is a striking exception to the tendency to gloss over or ignore inner-party discussions and the underlying differences that prompted them.

69. Zhang, "Peng Dehuai shouming," 120–21, 132–42; Peng Dehuai zishu bianjizu, *Peng Dehuai zishu* [Peng Dehuai's own account] (Beijing: Renmin, 1981), 257–58; JGYL, 1: 543–45.

70. Zhang, "Peng Dehuai shouming," 147–52; JGYL, 1: 552–53.

71. Zhang, "Peng Dehuai shouming," 152; JGYL, 1: 556 (quote), 559–61.

72. Zhang, "Peng Dehuai shouming," 157; JGYL, 1: 564, 567–68; *Peng Dehuai zishu*, 258–59; Hong, *KangMei yuanChao*, 23.

73. JGYL, 1: 543.

74. Mao's discussion of the strategic options in his cables to Zhou, October 13 and 14, 1950, in JGYL, 1: 556, 559.

75. Rosemary Foot, "Nuclear Coercion and the Ending of the Korean Conflict," *International Security* 13 (Winter 1988–89): 105–106 (summarizing the long available evidence that the CCP leadership thought nuclear weapons had limited utility against China); Hao Yufan and Zhai Zhihai, "China's Decision to Enter the Korean War: History Revisited," *China Quarterly*, no. 121 (March 1990): *Zhongguo renmin zhiyuan-jun kangMei yuanChao zhanshi*, 105; Du, *Zai zhiyuanjun zongbu*, 19–20; 7; JGYL, 1: 616; Mark A. Ryan, *Chinese Attitudes Toward Nuclear Weapons: China and the United States During the Korean War* (Armonk, N.Y.: M. E. Sharpe, 1989), 107–124.

76. See especially *Mao junshi wenxuan*, 649–86, for Mao's deep involvement between October 21 and December 26, 1950.

77. *Mao junshi wenxuan*, 676–84, 691–92.

78. *Mao junshi wenxuan*, 680–81, 683; JGYL, 1: 719; Chai and Zhao, *KangMei yuanChao jishi*, 69–71, 76.

79. *Nie Rongzhen huiyilu*, 741, 750–51; *Mao junshi wenxuan*, 685–86; Chai and Zhao, *KangMei yuanChao jishi*, 77–78; JGYL, 1: 741–42, 2: 104–105, 151–53; Qi, *Chaoxian zhanzheng*, 116–18, 127–28; Hong, *KangMei yuanChao*, 104–105, 109–12. Qi, *Chaoxian zhanzheng*, 132, credits Zhou Enlai and Li Fuchun with originating the idea of "rotational warfare."

80. *Mao junshi wenxuan*, 351, 672, 685. Again indulging a proclivity for seeing the war statistically, Mao somewhat vaguely noted on April 28, 1951 the advantages of inflicting 15,000–20,000 casualties in the fifth campaign. JGYL, 2: 265.

81. JGYL, 1: 749, 2: 61, 174, 229, for evidence of poor health. Commentary and instructions on dealing with counter-revolutionaries dominate the documentation in JGYL for January through May and in all constitute about one-quarter of the material for 1951. It is possible that Mao's apparent turn from the press of Korean War business is only an artifact of the compilation process.

82. *Mao junshi wenxuan*, 352–53; Chai and Zhao, *KangMei yuanChao jishi*, 86–87; JGYL, 2: 322, 344, 350, 355, 357; *Nie Rongzhen huiyilu*, 741–42. Nie claims to have himself supported moving the confrontation with the United States from the battlefield to the negotiating table. For a summary of Peng's pessimistic appraisal of the military situation in late May 1951, see "Dangdai Zhongguo" congshu bianji weiyuanhui, *KangMei yuanChao zhanzheng* [The war to resist America and aid Korea] (Beijing: Zhongguo shehui kexue, 1990), 142–43. Additional details (needing confirmation) on Sino-Soviet-Korean coordination in this period are supplied by Shi Zhe, *Zai lishi juren shenbian*, 506. For the Soviet-U.S. contacts on May 31 and June 5 handled by the Soviet specialist, George Kennan, and Soviet U.N. ambassador Jacob Malik, see FRUS, 1951, vol. 7, pt. 1 (Washington: U.S. Government Printing Office, 1983), 483–86, 507–511.

83. JGYL, 2: 379–85, 390–92, 405, 409–19, 422, 425; Chai and Zhao, *KangMei yuanChao jishi*, 88–91; Wu, *Eight Years in the Ministry of Foreign Affairs*, 85.

84. *Mao shuxin*, 416. A similar sense of paradox had inspired Zhou, also dipping into the treasury of old wisdom, to observe to a group of Beijing students in July 1950 at the outset of the Korean crisis, "Much distress regenerates a nation." Zhongyang jiaoyu kexue yanjiusuo, comp., *Zhou Enlai jiaoyu wenxuan* [A selection of Zhou Enlai's writings on education] (Beijing: Jiaoyu kexue, 1984), 18.

85. But already by 1952 the overall military burden had dropped to 32 percent of the total budget, and economic construction had risen to an impressive 52 percent. Zhongguo shehui kexueyuan and Zhongyang dang'anguan, comps., *Zhonghua renmin gongheguo jingji dang'an ziliao xuanbian* [Selection of materials from the PRC economic archives] (Beijing: Zhongguo chengshi jingji shehui, 1989–), *1949–1952*, pt. 1: *Zonghejuan* [Summary volume], 872, 891, 903. Total costs and military casualties from Xu Yan, "The Chinese Forces and Their Casualties in the Korean War: Facts and Statistics," trans. Li Xiaobing, *Chinese Historians* 6 (Fall 1993): 56, 58.

86. The class categories linked to Mao here had their origins in Comintern analyses that in turn became staples in CCP orthodoxy. They imposed an artificial division on the bourgeoisie, as Marie-Clair Bergère, *The Golden Age of the Chinese Bourgeoisie, 1911–1937*, trans. Janet Lloyd (Cambridge, Eng.: Cambridge University Press, 1989), suggests. Mao may have been more acute in his emphasis on that class's deep implication in international trade and investment and by extension in international politics.

87. On the continuing importance of the united front even after the decision in favor of all-out civil war, see CC directives for December 1946 and January 1947, in JFSQ, 139–40, 142–46. When urban protesters quickly proved vulnerable to Nationalist repression, the party shifted to a more cautious policy intended to preserve these assets.

88. CC directives (all drafted by Mao), July 6, 1946 (in ZYWJ, 13: 440), February 16, 1948 (in JFSQ, 191–92), March 1, 1948 (in *Selected Works of Mao Tse-tung*, 4:

208–209), May 31, 1948 (in JFSQ, 199–200), and August 2, 1948 (JFSQ, 204–205); Mao report to the CC, December 25, 1947, in *Mao ji*, 10: 107–113. For Mao's earlier comments on intellectuals as a group (not a class) which could at least be partially assimilated into the proletariat as "brainworkers" with party protection, encouragement, and guidance, see *Mao ji*, 1: 133 (December 1925), 3: 18 (March 1929), 3: 56–57 (October 1933), 4: 264 (January 1934), 7: 91–93 (December 1939), and 9: 253–54 (April 1945).

89. See for example Mao's July 1948 estimate, in JFSQ, 203.

90. CC directives from January 1948, November 1948, April 1949 (Mao draft), May 1949 (Mao draft), and June 1949, all in JFSQ, 183, 233–36, 263, 268–69, 270. For the prominent concerns of the second plenum of the seventh Central Committee (March 1949) with the united front and the closely related issue of urban control and economic recovery and development, see Zhonggong zhongyang dangxiao dangshi jiaoyanshi ziliaozu, comp., *Zhongguo gongchandang lici zhongyao huiyiji* [A collection on successive important meetings of the CCP] (2 vols; Shanghai: Renmin, 1982–83; "domestic circulation" for vol. 2), 1: 265–73. For similar concerns at the third plenum (June 1950), see Tang Qun and Li Bing, "Zhongguo gongchandang qijie sanzhong quanhui jieshao" [An introduction to the third plenum of the CCP's seventh Central Committee], *Dangshi yanjiu ziliao* 3 (1982), 661–72.

91. JFSQ, 197–98, 204–209, 240–41, 267. Lin Biao's January 26, 1949, welcoming speech to the first formal gathering ended with the chilling reminder that the CCP was in the midst of destroying "old China," of which the assembled delegates well knew they were a part. JFSQ, 248.

92. Documents on economic policy, January 1949–September 1951, in *Dangde wenxian*, 1988, no. 3, pp. 27–42; Ren Bishi's speech of January 12, 1948, in JFSQ, 175–77; CC instruction, February 4, 1948, in JFSQ, 186; Liu Shaoqi talk to the Political Bureau, September 13, 1948, in *Dangde wenxian*, 1989, no. 5, pp. 10–11; CC directive, January 15, 1949, in JFSQ, 238–39; Liu Shaoqi's inner-party report, July 4, 1949, in *Wenxian he yanjiu* (collection for 1984), 85–89; Mao report, March 5, 1949, in *Selected Works of Mao Tse-tung*, 4: 367–69.

93. On the cultivation of intellectuals: Zhongguo renmin jiefangjun zhengzhi xueyuan dangshi jiaoyanshi, comp., *Zhonggong dangshi cankao ziliao* (Reference materials on the history of the CCP) (n.p. [Beijing?]: no publisher listed, n.d. [preface 1979]), 11: 245–46; Ren Bishi speech of January 12, 1948, in JFSQ, 177–80; and Dong Biwu talk of January 4, 1950, in *Dong Biwu xuanji* [Selected works of Dong Biwu] (Beijing: Renmin, 1985), 273–77.

94. CC directive (drafted by Mao), January 8, 1949, in *Mao junshi wenxuan*, 328–29.

95. *Mao ji*, 10: 302, 304, 306.

96. *Mao ji*, 10: 319. The full series of the commentaries are in *Mao ji*, 10: 317–54. A somewhat edited translation appears in *Selected Works of Mao Tse-tung*, 4: 425–59. A sixth commentary in the series was prepared by the New China News Agency editorial department according to *Selected Works of Mao Tse-tung*, 4: 445. See also *Mao shuxin*, 333–35 (for Mao's note to Huang Yanpei stressing the intended educational nature of

the commentary); and New China News Agency, *Daily News Release,* August 14–31 and September 5, 10–12, 1949 (for the broader attack on the White Paper at this time).

97. *Mao ji,* 10: 329–30.

98. For the public side of this mobilization campaign, see the material in Zhongguo renmin kangMei yuanChao zonghui xuanchuanbu, comp., *Weida de kangMei yuanChao yundong.* [The great resist-America, aid-Korea campaign] (Beijing: Renmin, 1954). For an inside view, see JGYL, vols. 1 and 2; and *Xinhuashe wenjian,* vol. 2.

99. JGYL, 1: 646, 701 (quote). Zhou Enlai, playing his accustomed role as spokesman for united-front policies, offered his own set of patriotic arguments to win this same audience. *Zhou Enlai xuanji* [Selected Works of Zhou Enlai], comp. Zhonggong zhongyang wenxian bianji weiyuanhui (2 vols.; Beijing: Renmin, 1980, 1984), 2: 51, 53.

100. JGYL, 1: 666, 669, 677. Whether the resistance was in fact as intense as party materials suggest invites further investigation in local history sources.

101. *Zhonghua renmin gongheguo jingji dang'an ziliao xuanbian, 1949–1952,* pt. 1: *Zonghejuan,* 165 (quote), 341–43.

102. CC directive in *Dangde wenxian,* no. 2 (1988), pp. 32; CC Propaganda Department directive, October 1950, in *Zhongguo gongchandang xinwen gongzuo,* 2: 22–23; JGYL, 1: 669–70 (Mao telegram of November 17, 1949), 2: 68 (Mao telegram of January 24, 1951).

103. Zhang Min et al., " 'Sannian zhunbei' de diernian" [The second year of the "three-year preparation"], *Dangde wenxian,* no. 2 (1989), pp. 75–77; Zhonggong zhongyang tongyi zhanxian gongzuobu and Zhonggong zhongyang wenxian yanjiushi, comps., *Zhou Enlai tongyi zhanxian wenxuan* [A selection of works by Zhou Enlai on the united front] (Beijing: Renmin, 1984), 166.

104. Mao instruction to United Front Work Department, June 6, 1952, in *Selected Works of Mao Tse-tung,* 5: 77; Bai Zhanqun, "Guanyu 'cong xinminzhu zhuyi dao shehui zhuyi zhuanbian' tifa de yanbian" [Concerning the evolution in the formula for "changing from new democracy to socialism"], *Dangshi yanjiu,* 1982, no. 3, pp. 30–33. For an extended discussion of this shift, see Bo, *Ruogan zhongda juece,* vol. 1, esp. 46–49, 61–62, 213–26. Frederick C. Teiwes, *Politics at Mao's Court: Gao Gang and Party Factionalism in the Early 1950s* (Armonk, N.Y.: M. E. Sharpe, 1990), 54–61, 184–92, shows Mao hastening the pace toward socialism in mid-1953 while leaving ambiguous the fate of new democracy perhaps as a way of calming the contention that class and economic issues had by then stirred up among his courtiers.

7. Personality, Ideology, and Decisionmaking

1. An account by Mao's physician from 1954 down to his patient's death in 1976 suggests earlier bouts with malaria and insomnia. In addition, heavy smoking left Mao susceptible to bronchitis that easily degenerated into pneumonia. This account also confirms the pattern of psychological arousal noted above. Mao tended to respond to a new personal or political challenge by becoming intensely involved and going long

stretches without sleep. Initiatives that backfired or fell short of his expectations pitched him into depression or drove him into personal withdrawal. Li Zhisui with Anne F. Thurston, *The Private Life of Chairman Mao: The Memoirs of Mao's Personal Physician* (New York: Random House, 1994).

2. The observations that follow, based on my own reading of the record, support the broad themes in Frederick C. Teiwes's nicely sketched "Mao and His Lieutenants," *Australian Journal of Chinese Affairs*, no. 19–20 (January–July 1988): 1–80; as well as his new introduction to his *Politics and Purges in China: Rectification and the Decline of Party Norms, 1950–1965* (2nd ed.; Armonk, N.Y.: M. E. Sharpe, 1993).

3. Xiao San, *Mao Zedong tongzhi de qingshaonian shidai* [Comrade Mao Zedong's boyhood and youth] (exp. and rev. ed.; Guangzhou: Xinhua, 1950), 36; *Selected Works of Mao Tse-tung* (5 vols.; Beijing: Renmin, 1961–77), 3: 13, 18; Feng Xianzhi, "Mao Zedong dushu baozhang zazhi" [Mao Zedong's reading of newspapers and magazines], in *Mao Zedong de dushu shenghuo* [Mao Zedong's reading habits], ed. Gong Yuzhi et al. (Beijing: Sanlian, 1986), 238–47; Mao's 1959 remarks on daily reading, in *Mao Zedong xinwen gongzuo wenxuan* [A selection of Mao Zedong works on journalism], comp. Zhonggong zhongyang wenxian yanjiushi and Xinhua tongxunshe (Beijing: Xinhua, 1983), 215.

4. Zhonggong zhongyang wenxian yanjiushi and Zhonggong Hunan shengwei "Mao Zedong zaoqi wengao" bianjizu, comps., *Mao Zedong zaoqi wengao, 1912.6–1920.11* [Mao Zedong manuscripts from the early period, June 1912–November 1920] (Changsha: Hunan, 1990; "internal circulation"), 474; Mao quoted in *Mao Papers: Anthology and Bibliography*, ed. Jerome Ch'en (London: Oxford University Press, 1970), 22.

5. Edgar Snow, *Red Star over China* (New York: Grove Press, 1961), 140; Lin Ke, "Yi Mao Zedong xue yingyu" [Recollections of Mao Zedong's study of English], in *Mao Zedong de dushu shenghuo*, 249–54.

6. *Selected Works of Mao Tse-tung*, 1: 300.

7. Benjamin I. Schwartz, "Thoughts on the Late Mao—Between Redemption and Utter Frustration," in *The Secret Speeches of Chairman Mao: From the Hundred Flowers to the Great Leap Forward*, ed. Roderick MacFarquhar et al. (Cambridge: Harvard University Council on East Asian Studies, 1989), 19–24, offers some discerning comments on Mao's mind in the latter half of the 1950s that may apply to earlier periods more than Schwartz recognizes.

8. Otto Braun, *A Comintern Agent in China, 1932–1939*, trans. Jeanne Moore (Stanford: Stanford University Press, 1982), 55–56, comments—to be sure with some asperity—on how pronouncedly Chinese Mao's references were already in the early 1930s.

9. *Mao Zedong zaoqi wengao*, 70.

10. Lawrence R. Sullivan, "Leadership and Authority in the Chinese Communist Party: Perspectives from the 1950s," *Pacific Affairs* 59 (Winter 1986–87): 605–33.

11. Quote from Li, "Lianzhi zhuyi yu shijie zuzhi" [Federalism and world organization], February 1, 1919, in *Li Dazhao wenji* [Collected works of Li Dazhao], comp. Yuan Qian et al. (2 vols.; Beijing: Renmin, 1984), 1: 621.

12. Yang Ruicheng, "Zongguan Mao Zedong de duiwai jingji jiaowang sixiang" [An overview of Mao Zedong's thinking on foreign economic contact], *Dangde wenxian*, 1991, no. 2, pp.74–75; Liu report to Mao, January 2, 1950, in *Zhonghua renmin gongheguo jingji dang'an ziliao xuanbian* [Selection of materials from the PRC economic archives], comp. Zhongguo shehui kexueyuan and Zhongyang dang'anguan (Beijing: Zhongguo chengshi jingji shehui, 1989–), *1949–1952*, pt. 2: *Jiben jianshe touzi he jianzhu gongye juan* [Volume on infrastructure investment and the construction industry], 87.

13. Li Jie, "Dui Mao Zedong fangzhi heping yanbian sixiang de huigu he sikao" [Reviewing and reflecting on Mao Zedong's thinking about guarding against peaceful evolution], *Dangde wenxian*, 1991, no. 3, pp. 39–43; Deng quoted in Richard Bush, "Deng Xiaoping: China's Old Man in a Hurry," in *China Briefing, 1980*, ed. Robert Oxnam and Bush (Boulder, Colo.: Westview, 1980), 10.

14. *Selected Works of Mao Tse-tung*, 5: 304.

15. *Mao Zedong ji* [Collected writings of Mao Zedong], ed. Takeuchi Minoru (10 vols.; Tokyo: Hokobosha, 1971–72; Hong Kong reprint, 1975) [hereafter *Mao ji*], 5: 102 (1936 quote); Mao interview with Edgar Snow in Bao'an, transcript of Snow diary, July 18, 1936, p. 32, Snow Papers, University Archives, University of Missouri at Kansas City; Steven M. Goldstein, "The Chinese Revolution and the Colonial Areas: The View From Yenan, 1937–1941," *China Quarterly*, no. 75 (September 1978): 603 (Zhang Hanfu), 611 (Zhang Ruxin); Zhongyang tongzhanbu and Zhongyang dang'anguan, comps., *Zhonggong zhongyang kangRi minzu tongyi zhanxian wenjian xuanbian* [A selection of documents on the CCP Central Committee's national anti-Japanese united front] (3 vols.; Beijing: Dang'an, 1984–86; "internal circulation") [hereafter KRMZ], 3: 433.

16. *Mao ji*, 8: 29–31, 42. See also KRMZ, 3: 587–89 (CC directive of December 9, 1941).

17. Goldstein, "The Chinese Revolution," 596 (Liu quote); *Collected Works of Liu Shao-ch'i* (3 vols.; Hong Kong: Union Research Institute, 1968–69), 2: 178–79; Zhongyang tongzhanbu and Zhongyang dang'anguan, comps., *Zhonggong zhongyang jiefang zhanzheng shiqi tongyi zhanxian wenjian xuanbian* [A selection of documents on the CCP Central Committee's united front during the period of liberation struggle] (Beijing: Dang'an, 1988; "internal circulation") [hereafter JFSQ] , 209 (Central Committee in September 1948); *Mao ji*, 10: 115 (December 1947), 183 (September 1948). See also the slogans for July 7, 1945, in *Zhonggong zhongyang wenjian xuanji* [A selection of CCP Central Committee documents], comp. Zhongyang dang'anguan (14 vols.; Beijing: Zhonggong zhongyang dangxiao, 1982–87; "inner party") [hereafter ZYWJ], 13: 99.

18. Lu Dingyi, "Zhongguo geming de shijie yiyi" [The global significance of the Chinese revolution], *Xuexi*, July 1951, in Goldstein, "The Chinese Revolution," 619. For the New China News Agency's concern with reaching out to the oppressed of the East, see Chen Kehan's remarks, December 1950, in *Zhongguo gongchandang xinwen gongzuo wenjian huibian* [A collection of documents on CCP journalism], comp. Zhongguo shehui kexueyuan xinwen yanjiusuo (3 vols.; Beijing: Xinhua, 1980; "internal circulation"), 2: 99.

19. Stuart Schram, *Chairman Mao Talks to the People: Talks and Letters, 1956–1971* (New York: Pantheon, 1975), 170, 180–81, 189; King C. Chen, *China and the Three Worlds: A Foreign Policy Reader* (White Plains, N.Y.: M. E. Sharpe, 1979), 3, 39–44.

20. Both CCP sources and standard histories leave murky the relationship with the Korean communist movement from the 1920s onward. Insights on links to the Vietnamese communists are marginally better. See notably King C. Chen, *Vietnam and China, 1938–1954* (Princeton: Princeton University Press, 1969), 231–32, 237, 261–63; Chen Jian, "China and the First Indochina War, 1950–54," *China Quarterly*, no. 133 (March 1993): 85–110; and Chen Jian, "China's Involvement with the Vietnam War, 1964–69," *China Quarterly* (forthcoming).

21. Shi Zhe with Li Haiwen, *Zai lishi juren shenbian: Shi Zhe huiyilu* [Alongside the giants of history: Shi Zhe's memoir] (Beijing: Zhongyang wenxian, 1991), 381–82 (Mao's 1949 remarks to Mikoyan); Central Committee directive, June 25, 1952, in *Zhongguo gongchandang xinwen gongzuo*, 2: 224–27.

22. The CCP's official policy toward Mongols and Muslims between 1935 and 1940 was decidedly accommodating, but references to self-determination increasingly gave way to comments on the CCP's obligations to guide and educate minority peoples. See KRMZ, 2: 41–44 (December 1935), 150–52 (May 1936), 160 (June 1936), 216–23 (August 1936), 381–84 (February 1937), 3: 4–7 (July 1937), 173–80 (November 1938), 409–418 (April 1940), 436–49 (July 1940); and ZYWJ, 10: 555 (June 1938), 613–14 (October 1938).

23. Mao reportedly chafed over the surrender of China's claims to Outer Mongolia in the Nationalist-Soviet treaty of 1945, and Molotov contends that Mao was still nursing claims to that land in the mid-1950s. Snow, *Red Star over China*, 96n; Mao interview with Snow, transcript of Snow diary, July 15, 1936, p. 9, and July 23, 1936, p. 56, Snow Papers; *Mao ji*, 6: 219–20; June T. Dreyer, *China's Forty Millions: Minority Nationalities and National Integration in the People's Republic of China* (Cambridge: Harvard University Press, 1976), 63–64, 67, 70; Stuart R. Schram, "Decentralization in a Unitary State: Theory and Practice, 1940–1984," in *The Scope of State Power in China*, ed. Schram (London: University of London School of Oriental and African Studies, 1985), 81–83; Vyacheslav M. Molotov, *Molotov Remembers: Inside Kremlin Politics: Conversations with Felix Chuev*, trans. and ed. Albert Resis (Chicago: Ivan R. Dee, 1993), 71.

24. In October 1945 Yanan sent an organizer to rebuild the communist movement on Taiwan, and in 1949 following victory in the civil war the CCP laid claim to the island in unequivocal terms. Frank S. T. Hsiao and Lawrence R. Sullivan, "A Political History of the Taiwanese Communist Party, 1928–1931," *Journal of Asian Studies* 42 (February 1983): 227.

25. JFSQ , 249; Shi Zhe, *Zai lishi juren shenbian*, 380, 384 (Mao comments to Mikoyan); Northwest Bureau directive on propaganda, October 22, 1949, in *Zhongguo gongchandang xinwen gongzuo*, 1: 358; Zhou address at the Political Consultative Conference, September 7, 1949, in *Zhou Enlai tongyi zhanxian wenxuan* [A selection of Zhou Enlai works on the united front], comp. Zhonggong zhongyang tongyi zhanxian

gongzuobu and Zhonggong zhongyang wenxian yanjiushi (Beijing: Renmin, 1984), 139–40. Dreyer, *China's Forty Millions*, 79–87, traces steps the CCP took after World War II to secure control over minority regions.

26. Dreyer, *China's Forty Millions*, 87–91; Melvyn C. Goldstein with Gelek Rimpoche, *A History of Modern Tibet, 1913–1951: The Demise of the Lamaist State* (Berkeley: University of California Press, 1989), chaps. 17–21; *Jianguo yilai Mao Zedong wengao* [Mao Zedong manuscripts for the period following the establishment of the country], comp. Zhonggong zhongyang wenxian yanjiushi (Beijing: Zhongyang wenxian, 1987– ; "internal circulation"), 2: 328–30, 333–35; A. Tom Grunfeld, *The Making of Modern Tibet* (London: Zed, and Armonk, N.Y.: M. E. Sharpe, 1987), chaps. 4–7.

27. Morris Rossabi, *China and Inner Asia: From 1368 to the Present Day* (New York: Pica, 1975), chap. 10.

28. See Benjamin Yang's marvelous reconstruction of interaction among the party leaders in "The Zunyi Conference as One Step in Mao's Rise to Power: A Survey of Historical Studies of the Chinese Communist Party," *China Quarterly*, no. 106 (June 1986): 235–71.

29. These hesitations are strikingly detailed in Zhang Xi, "Peng Dehuai shouming shuaishi kangMei yuanChao de qianqian houhou" [The full story of Peng Dehuai's appointment to head the resistance to the United States and the assistance to Korea], *Zhonggong dangshi ziliao*, no. 31 (1989): 111–59.

30. Wang would remain prominent in foreign policy—as Mao's emissary to Moscow in 1937, as the CCP's chief liaison with Moscow before 1949 and its first ambassador to the Soviet Union after 1949, and as head of the Central Committee's Liaison Department on his return home. ZYWJ, 4: 189–90; Wang Jianying, ed., *Zhongguo gongchandang zuzhishi ziliao huibian: lingdao jiguan yange he chengyuan minglu* [A compilation of materials on CCP organizational history: the evolution of leading organs and a name list of personnel] (Beijing: Hongqi, 1983; "internal circulation"), 162–63, 198, 244, 603, 613.

31. This liaison section (*lianluoke* or *zhaodaike*) was later renamed the communications section (*jiaojike*) and then the communications office (*jiaojichu*). By 1942 the liaison office had a staff of about sixteen. Jin Cheng, appointed as head at the instance of Chen Yun, remained in charge until the office was abolished in January 1950. Li Zhongquan, "Shaan-Gan-Ning bianqu de duiwai huodong" [External activities in the Shaan-Gan-Ning border region], *Lishi dang'an*, 1989, no. 1, pp. 109–113; Jin Cheng, *Yanan jiaojichu huiyilu* [Reminiscences of the Yanan communications office] (Beijing: Zhongguo qingnian, 1986); Central Committee directive, September 26, 1948, in JFSQ, 209.

32. Huang Hua and Gong Peng are but the best known of this group. John Israel and Donald W. Klein, *Rebels and Bureaucrats: China's December 9ers* (Berkeley: University of California Press, 1976), 212–13.

33. On the broader Hong Kong operation between 1938 and 1941, directed by Liao Chengzhi and Pan Hannian under the supervision of Zhou's Southern Bureau, see *Dangshi ziliao tongxun*, no. 6–7 (1988), pp. 51–54.

34. Wu Xiuquan, *Wode licheng* [My course] (Beijing: Jiefangjun, 1984), 132–51.

35. Zhang Xianshan, "Yice fang 'zuo' jiu 'zuo' de changshi" [One attempt to guard against "the left" and correct "the left"], *Dangde wenxian*, 1988, no. 5, p. 45.

8. Constructing a History of CCP Foreign Relations

1. The observations that follow draw in part on Jin Liangyong, "Jianguo yilai jindai Zhongwai guanxishi yanjiu shuping" [A review of post-1949 research on the history of modern Sino-foreign relations], *Jindaishi yanjiu*, no. 3 (1985), pp. 193–214; Wang Xi and Wang Bangxian, "Woguo sanshiwu nianlai de ZhongMei guanxishi yanjiu" [Research on the history of Sino-American relations in our country over the last thirty-five years], *Fudan xuebao*, 1984, no. 5, pp. 73–76; Tao Wenzhao, "ZhongMei guanxishi yanjiu shinian huigu" [Looking back on a decade of research on the history of Sino-American relations], in *Xin de shiye: ZhongMei guanxishi lunwenji* [New fields of vision: a collection of articles on the history of Sino-American relations] (Nanjing: Nanjing daxue, 1991), 282–307; a fairly extensive reading in party history periodicals; and conversations with Chinese colleagues working on the CCP's foreign relations.

2. Yao Xu, "KangMei yuanChao de yingming juece" [The brilliant decision to resist America and aid Korea], *Dangshi yanjiu*, no. 5 (1980), pp. 5–14. A new generation of scholarship heralded by Yao's work did greatly improve on earlier thin and domestically oriented accounts such as Hu Zhongchi, *KangMei yuanChao yundong shihua* [An informal history of the resist-America aid-Korea campaign] (Beijing: Zhonghua qingnian, 1956), which had its own, even more pronounced patriotic premises.

3. These tendencies are evident in Ding Shouhe and Yin Shuyi, *Cong wusi qimeng yundong dao makesi zhuyi de chuanbo* [From May Fourth enlightenment to the propagation of Marxism] (rev. ed.; Beijing: Sanlian, 1979), esp. 88–108; Lu Mingzhuo, "Li Dazhao zai wusi yundong shiqi de fandi sixiang" [Li Dazhao's anti-imperialist thought during the period of the May Fourth movement], in *Jinian wusi yundong liushi zhounian xueshu taolunhui lunwenxuan* [A selection of articles from a scholarly conference in commemoration of the sixtieth anniversary of the May Fourth movement], ed. Zhongguo shehui kexueyuan jindaishi yanjiusuo (Beijing: Zhongguo shehui kexue, 1980), 2: 151–63; and Zhu Jianhua and He Rongdi, "Shilun Li Dazhao de fandi sixiang" [An exploration of Li Dazhao's anti-imperialist thought], in *Li Dazhao yanjiu lunwenji* [A collection of research papers on Li Dazhao], ed. Han Yide and Wang Shudi (2 vols.; Shijiazhuang: Hebei renmin, 1984), 2: 515–29.

4. Pei-yi Wu, *The Confucian's Progress: Autobiographical Writings in Traditional China* (Princeton: Princeton University Press, 1990), offers a suggestive introduction to this genre.

5. The earliest Chinese version appears to be *Waiguo jizhe xibei yinxiangji* [A foreign reporter's impressions of the northwest] (Shanghai: Dingchou bianyishe, 1937). A partial copy is in the Wang Fu Shih collection, University Archives, University of Missouri, Kansas City. Hu Yuzhi translated one of the early versions, perhaps this one. Snow's account was also published under the title *Xixing manji* [Notes on a journey to the west]

and *Mao Zedong zizhuan* [Mao Zedong's autobiography]). For details on the production of the autobiography, see Zhonggong zhongyang wenxian yanjiushi and Xinhua tongxunshe, comps., *Mao Zedong xinwen gongzuo wenxuan* [A selection of Mao Zedong works on journalism] (Beijing: Xinhua, 1983), 37–38; Wu Liping, comp., *Mao Zedong yijiusanliunian tong Sinuo de tanhua* [Mao Zedong's 1936 talk with Snow] (Beijing: Renmin, 1979), 1, 6–9; and Qiu Ke'an, *Sinuo zai Zhongguo* [Snow in China] (Beijing: Sanlian, 1982).

Appearing in 1937 along with the Snow account was the first, perhaps rudimentary collection of Mao's essays. For evidence on the existence of such a collection, see *Mao Zedong ji* [Collected writings of Mao Zedong], ed. Takeuchi Minoru (10 vols.; Tokyo: Hokubosha, 1971–72; Hong Kong reprint, 1975), 5: 232.

6. This and the paragraph that follows draw on Xu Quanxing and Wei Shifeng, chief authors, *Yanan shiqi de Mao Zedong zhexue sixiang yanjiu* [Studies on Mao Zedong's philosophical thought during the Yanan period] (Xian: Shaanxi renmin jiaoyu, 1988), chap. 11 (written by Xu); and Thomas Kampen, "Wang Jiaxiang, Mao Zedong and the 'Triumph of Mao Zedong-Thought' (1935–1945)," *Modern Asian Studies* 23 (October 1989): 716–22.

7. Xiao San's *Mao Zedong tongzhi de qingshaonian shidai* [Comrade Mao Zedong's boyhood and youth] (originally published 1948; rev. and exp. ed., Guangzhou: Xinhua, 1950).

8. Zhang Min et al., " 'Sannian zhunbei' de diernian" [The second year of the "three years of preparation"], *Dangde wenxian*, 1989, no. 2, p. 79; *Mao Zedong xuanji* [Selected works of Mao Zedong] (4 vols.; Beijing: Renmin, 1952–60); Li Rui, *Mao Zedong tongzhi de chuqi geming huodong* [Comrade Mao Zedong's initial revolutionary activities] (Beijing: Zhongguo qingnian, 1957).

9. Quotes from Joint Publications Research Service, *Selections from Chairman Mao*, no. 90 (JPRS no. 49826; February 12, 1970), 66, 80. For guidance through the thicket of this Cultural Revolution material, see Timothy Cheek, "Textually Speaking: An Assessment of Newly Available Mao Texts," in *The Secret Speeches of Chairman Mao: From the Hundred Flowers to the Great Leap Forward*, ed. Roderick MacFarquhar et al. (Cambridge: Harvard University Council on East Asian Studies, 1989), 78–81; and Cheek, "The 'Genius' Mao: A Treasure Trove of 23 Newly Available Volumes of Post-1949 Mao Zedong Texts," *Australian Journal of Chinese Affairs*, no. 19–20 (January–July 1988): 337–44.

10. *Mao Zedong xuanji* [Selected works of Mao Zedong], vol. 5 (Beijing: Renmin, 1977); *Mao Zedong zhuzuo xuandu* [A reader of works by Mao Zedong], comp. Zhonggong zhongyang wenxian bianji weiyuanhui (2 vols.; Beijing: Renmin, 1986). More revealing than the public "resolution on certain historical issues concerning the party since the founding of the PRC" ["Guanyu jianguo yilai dangde ruogan lishi wenti de jueyi"] is the limited circulation treatment of sensitive issues raised by this reappraisal, in Zhonggong zhongyang dangshi yanjiushi "Zhonggong dangshi dashi nianbiao" bianxiezu, *Zhonggong dangshi dashi nianbiao shuoming* [Elucidation of "A chronology of major events in CCP history"] (Beijing: Zhonggong zhongyang dangxiao, 1983; "internal circulation").

11. The comments that follow draw on Paul A. Cohen, *Discovering History in China: American Historical Writing on the Recent Chinese Past* (New York: Columbia University Press, 1984); William T. Rowe, "Approaches to Modern Chinese Social History," in *Reliving the Past: The Worlds of Social History*, ed. Olivier Zunz (Chapel Hill: University of North Carolina Press, 1985), 236–96; my own "Meiguo guanyu Zhongguo duiwai guanxishi yanjiu wenti yu qianjing" [The study of the history of Chinese foreign relations in the United States: problems and prospects], trans. Yuan Ming, *Lishi yanjiu* [Historical studies], 1988, no. 3, pp. 150–56 Philip C. C. Huang, "The Paradigmatic Crisis in Chinese Studies: Paradoxes in Social and Economic History," *Modern China* 17 (July 1991): 299–341; and Judith B. Farquhar and James L. Hevia, "Culture and Postwar American Historiography of China," *positions* 1 (Fall 1993): 486–525. For a helpful evaluation of the literature on imperialism accompanied by suggestions on fruitful modes of inquiry, see Jürgen Osterhammel, "Semi-Colonialism and Informal Empire in Twentieth-Century China: Towards a Framework of Analysis," in *Imperialism and After: Continuities and Discontinuities*, ed. Wolfgang J. Mommsen and Osterhammel (London: Allen and Unwin, 1986), 290–314.

12. See for example Susan Naquin and Evelyn S. Rawski, *Chinese Society in the Eighteenth Century* (New Haven: Yale University Press, 1987), which begins by stressing the importance of relating the actions of the state to "the lives of even ordinary citizens" (xi).

13. Bin Yu, "The Study of Chinese Foreign Policy: Problems and Prospect," *World Politics* 46 (January 1994): 235–61, offers a detailed, critical appraisal of this large body of writing. See also Friedrich W. Wu, "Explanatory Approaches to Chinese Foreign Policy: A Critique of the Western Literature," *Studies in Comparative Communism* 13 (Spring 1980): 41–62; and Samuel S. Kim, "China and the World in Theory and Practice," in *China and the World: Chinese Foreign Relations in the Post-Cold War Era*, ed. Kim (3rd rev. ed.; Boulder, Colo.: Westview, 1994), 3–41. Both Kim, *China and the World*, and Thomas W. Robinson and David Shambaugh, eds., *Chinese Foreign Policy: Theory and Practice* (Oxford, Eng.: Oxford University Press, 1994), offer a sampling of the kinds of work now being done by political scientists. Harry Harding, "The Evolution of American Scholarship on Contemporary China," in *American Studies of Contemporary China*, ed. David Shambaugh (Armonk, N.Y.: M. E. Sharpe, 1993), 14–40, helps put this particular body of political science work in the broader context of the general social science literature on China.

14. Wu's 1980 survey, "Explanatory Approaches," tied progress in the field to better theory and methodology as did Michael Ng-Quinn's "The Analytical Study of Chinese Foreign Policy," *International Studies Quarterly* 27 (June 1983): 203–24. More recently James N. Rosenau, "China in a Bifurcated World: Competing Theoretical Perspectives," in *Chinese Foreign Policy*, eds. Robinson and Shambaugh, 524–51, has offered a somewhat defensive presentation along the same lines. Bin Yu, "The Study of Chinese Foreign Policy," 256–59, is considerably more reserved about the prospects for the theoretical enterprise.

15. For an early, vigorous argument for putting Mao at the center of the policy

process, see Michel Oksenberg, "Policy Making under Mao, 1948–68: An Overview," in *China: Management of a Revolutionary Society*, ed. John M. H. Lindbeck (Seattle: University of Washington Press, 1971), 79–115. Frederick C. Teiwes, "Mao and His Lieutenants," *Australian Journal of Chinese Affairs*, no. 19–20 (January–July 1988): 1–80, and Roderick MacFarquhar, *The Origins of the Cultural Revolution* (New York: Columbia University Press, 1974–), with their stress on personality and sensitivity to sources are good examples of the application of this approach. Both are concerned mainly with domestic politics, but their findings have considerable import for foreign policy.

16. One distinguished China-watcher has proposed careful examination of past forecasting as a way of highlighting possible future interpretive problems as well as identifying past successes. Allen S. Whiting, "Forecasting Chinese Foreign Policy: IR Theory vs. the Fortune Cookie," in *Chinese Foreign Policy*, eds. Robinson and Shambaugh, 506–23. This proposal tellingly omits historical reconstruction of the very events analysts were trying to read. Without a fresh, well documented picture of those events it is hard to imagine measuring with any confidence the accuracy of contemporary readings.

17. This point is developed above in chapters 5 and 6.

18. Zhonghua renmin gongheguo waijiaobu and Zhonggong zhongyang wenxian yanjiushi, comps., *Zhou Enlai waijiao wenxuan* [Selected diplomatic writings of Zhou Enlai] (Beijing: Zhongyang wenxian, 1990), 25–27; comments by Chai Chengwen on Pu Shouchang's role as Zhou's translator on this occasion, in *Renwu*, no. 5 (1992), p. 18. For the understandably perplexed reaction of China-watchers, see U.S. Department of State, *Foreign Relations of the United States*, vol. 7 (Washington: U.S. Government Printing Office, 1976), 906, 912–13.

19. The oft-cited authority is Andrew Nathan, "A Factionalism Model for CCP Politics," *China Quarterly*, no. 53 (January–March 1973): 34–66.

20. A glance at the literature on the CCP will reveal numerous instances of works stressing factional struggle on the basis of highly circumstantial evidence. Derek J. Waller, *The Kiangsi Soviet: Mao and the National Congresses of 1931 and 1934* (Berkeley: University of California Center for Chinese Studies, 1973), sees a clear split between Maoists and Russian Returned Students in the early 1930s, with the latter increasingly dominant over the former in the factional struggles. Richard C. Thornton, *The Comintern and the Chinese Communists, 1928–1931* (Seattle: University of Washington Press, 1969), interprets the Li Lisan period in strong factional terms with leaders of each faction driven by a quest for personal power. James Reardon-Anderson, *Yenan and the Great Powers: The Origins of Chinese Communist Foreign Policy, 1944–1946* (New York: Columbia University Press, 1980), and Steven I. Levine, *Anvil of Victory: The Communist Revolution in Manchuria, 1945–1948* (New York: Columbia University Press, 1987), see factions defining the policy alternatives for the CCP in 1945–1946. Reardon-Anderson argues for a Mao-Zhou bloc favoring negotiations with the Nationalists, while the ultimately victorious military leaders wanted a resort to force. For his part, Levine sees differences in strategy in the northeast base area in factional

terms. Donald S. Zagoria, "Choices in the Postwar World (2): Containment and China," in *Caging the Bear: Containment and the Cold War*, ed. Charles Gati (Indianapolis: Bobbs-Merrill, 1974), 109–27, puts Mao and Zhou at the head of a nationalist group, while Liu emerges as the leader of the internationalists. The tendency to find factions persists in the studies of the post-1949 period. See for example Uri Ra'anan's and Donald Zagoria's treatments of Beijing's response to the Vietnam War in 1965–1966 in *China in Crisis*, vol. 2, ed. Tang Tsou (Chicago: University of Chicago Press, 1968), 23–71 and 237–68, as well as Michael Yahuda's response, "Kremlinology and the Chinese Strategic Debate, 1965–66," *China Quarterly*, no. 149 (January–March 1972): especially 74–75. Yahuda rejects easy factional explanations, while stressing the interaction between "foreign and domestic politics."

21. For a thoughtful critique of this approach, now much in vogue, see Bin Yu, "The Study of Chinese Foreign Policy," 244–56. Warren I. Cohen, "Conversations with Chinese Friends: Zhou Enlai's Associates Reflect on Chinese-American Relations in the 1940s and the Korean War," *Diplomatic History* 11 (Summer 1987): 283–89, suggests that historians are not immune to the lure of the experts with "inside" information.

22. These points are treated more fully by Jürgen Osterhammel, "CCP Foreign Policy as International History: Mapping the Field," and by Odd Arne Westad, "The Foreign Policies of Revolutionary Parties: The CCP in Comparative Perspective," both in *Toward a History of Chinese Communist Foreign Relations, 1920s–1960s: Personalities and Interpretive Approaches*, ed. Michael H. Hunt and Niu Jun (Washington: Asia Program, Woodrow Wilson International Center for Scholars, forthcoming, [1995]).

23. See on some of the recent trends, Lynn Hunt, ed., *The New Cultural History* (Berkeley: University of California Press, 1989); John E. Toews, "Intellectual History after the Linguistic Turn: The Autonomy of Meaning and Irreducibility of Experience," *American Historical Review* 92 (October 1987): 879–907; and Bryan D. Palmer, *Descent into Discourse: The Reification of Language and the Writing of Social History* (Philadelphia: Temple University Press, 1990).

24. Levine, *Anvil of Victory*; John W. Garver's *Chinese-Soviet Relations, 1937–1945: The Diplomacy of Chinese Nationalism* (New York: Oxford University Press, 1988); Odd Arne Westad, *Cold War and Revolution: Soviet-American Rivalry and the Origins of the Chinese Civil War, 1944–1946* (New York: Columbia University Press, 1993).

25. For good examples of this notable interpretive proclivity among Chinese scholars, see Hao Yufan and Guocang Huan, eds., *The Chinese View of the World* (New York: Pantheon, 1989); Hao Yufan and Zhai Zhihai, "China's Decision to Enter the Korean War: History Revisited," *China Quarterly*, no. 121 (March 1990): 94–115; He Di, "The Evolution of the People's Republic of China's Policy toward the Offshore Islands," in *The Great Powers in East Asia, 1953–1960*, ed. Warren I. Cohen and Akira Iriye (New York: Columbia University Press, 1990), 222–45; and Chen Xiaolu, "China's Policy Toward the United States, 1949–1955," Jia Qingguo, "Searching for Peaceful Coexistence and Territorial Integrity," and Wang Jisi, "An Appraisal of U.S. Policy toward China, 1945–1955, and Its Aftermath," all in *Sino-American Relations, 1945–1955: A Joint Reassessment of a Critical Decade*, ed. Harry Harding and Yuan Ming (Wilming-

ton, Del.: Scholarly Resources, 1989), 184–97, 267–86, 289–310. For a discussion of the impact of U.S. international-relations approaches on Chinese scholars, marked by this single, signal success, see Wang Jisi, "International Relations Theory and the Study of Chinese Foreign Policy: A Chinese Perspective," in *Chinese Foreign Policy*, eds. Robinson and Shambaugh, 481–505.

26. For perhaps the best-known example, see Alexander L. George and Richard Smoke, *Deterrence in American Foreign Policy: Theory and Practice* (New York: Columbia University Press, 1974), chap. 7.

27. I have developed this point in more detail in "Beijing and the Korean Crisis, June 1950–June 1951," *Political Science Quarterly* 107 (Fall 1992): 475–78.

28. For a helpful discussion of "the rationality model," see Kenneth Lieberthal and Michel Oksenberg, *Policy Making in China: Leaders, Structures, and Processes* (Princeton: Princeton University Press, 1988), 11–14.

29. W. R. Connor, "Why Were We Surprised?" *American Scholar* 60 (Spring 1991): 175–84. Moshe Lewin, *The Gorbachev Phenomenon: A Historical Interpretation* (rev. ed.; Berkeley: University of California Press, 1991); Lewin, "Russia/USSR in Historical Motion: An Essay in Interpretation," *Russian Review* 50 (July 1991): 249–66; and Stephen F. Cohen, *Rethinking the Soviet Experience: Politics and History since 1917* (New York: Oxford University Press, 1985), are notable efforts at moving Soviet history beyond a thin, simple, and strongly judgmental "totalitarian" model associated with the Cold War. An elaborated, well-grounded alternative appears to await the completion of a new generation of historical research.

30. Paul A. Cohen, "The Post-Mao Reforms in Historical Perspective," *Journal of Asian Studies* 47 (August 1988): 518–40, highlights the dangers of a heavy reliance on an abstract Leninist party model to the neglect of long-term historical patterns.

31. For an effort at teasing out an informal foreign-policy ideology that might be applicable to China, see my own *Ideology and U.S. Foreign Policy* (New Haven: Yale University Press, 1987) and my follow-up essay, "Ideology," in "A Roundtable: Explaining the History of American Foreign Relations," *Journal of American History* 77 (June 1990): 108–115. Clifford Geertz's "Ideology as a Cultural System," in *Ideology and Discontent*, ed. David E. Apter (London: Free Press, 1964), 47–76, is a classic still worth reading.

32. George Lakoff, *Women, Fire, and Dangerous Things: What Categories Reveal about the Mind* (Chicago: University of Chicago Press, 1987), 92–93.

33. For an extended argument for the importance of internal categories and outlooks to the understanding of Chinese values, see Thomas A. Metzger, *Escape from Predicament: Neo-Confucianism and China's Evolving Political Culture* (New York: Columbia University Press, 1977). Andrew J. Nathan makes a contrary case in favor of what he calls "evaluative universalism," those externally based judgments that not only are legitimate but also can stimulate better understanding. Nathan, "The Place of Values in Cross-Cultural Studies: The Example of Democracy and China," in *Ideas Across Cultures: Essays on Chinese Thought in Honor of Benjamin Schwartz*, ed. Paul A. Cohen and Merle Goldman (Cambridge: Harvard University Council on East Asian Studies,

1990), 293–314. For instructive exercises in paying serious attention to language in the Chinese context, see Michael Schoenhals, *Doing Things with Words in Chinese Politics* (Berkeley: University of California Institute of East Asian Studies, 1992), and Frank Dikötter, *The Discourse of Race in Modern China* (London: Hurst, 1992).

34. The approach is thoughtfully discussed in James Farr, "Understanding Conceptual Change Politically," in *Political Innovation and Conceptual Change*, ed. Terrence Ball et al. (Cambridge, Eng.: Cambridge University Press, 1989), 24–49, and is applied in Daniel T. Rodgers, *Contested Truths: Keywords in American Politics Since Independence* (New York: Basic Books, 1987); and in Raymond Williams, *Keywords: A Vocabulary of Culture and Society* (New York: Oxford University Press, 1976).

Index

Date Due

DEC - 9 00			